When the Japanese empire ended, it did not necessarily go away. Throughout East Asia, its legacy lingers on. This volume presents fresh and exciting new work, much of it published in English for the first time. It helps us understand how the demise of empire left its mark on the beginning of the Cold War in Asia, and continues to shape political relations in the region to this day.

**Sebastian Conrad**, *Freie Universität Berlin, author of*
What Is Global History? *(Princeton University Press 2016)*

This ambitious volume brings together the latest in Japanese and Western scholarship on the turbulent years following the end of Japan's empire in East Asia. It examines the uneven physical retreat of the Japanese empire, which disappeared abruptly in some places within days of the surrender and yet persisted much longer in other places. More than that, it grapples with mind-sets, with the changes that were forced by the surrender and those that stubbornly resisted pressure to change. It is a rewarding expedition into geographies of the mind in postwar East Asia.

**Robert Cribb**, *Professor of Asian History,*
*Australian National University*

# The Dismantling of Japan's Empire in East Asia

The end of Japan's empire appeared to happen very suddenly and cleanly – but, as this book shows, it was in fact very messy, with a long period of establishing or re-establishing the postwar order. Moreover, as the authors argue, empires have afterlives, which, in the case of Japan's empire, is not much studied. This book considers the details of deimperialization, including the repatriation of Japanese personnel, the redrawing of boundaries, issues to do with prisoners of war and war criminals and new arrangements for democratic political institutions, for media and for the regulation of trade. It also discusses the continuing impact of empire on the countries ruled or occupied by Japan, where, as a result of Japanese management and administration, both formal and informal, patterns of behavior and attitudes were established that continued subsequently. This was true in Japan itself, where returning imperial personnel had to be absorbed and adjustments made to imperial thinking, and in present-day East Asia, where the shadow of Japan's empire still lingers. This legacy of unresolved issues concerning the correct relationship of Japan, an important, energetic, outgoing nation and a potential regional "hub," with the rest of the region which was not comfortably settled in this era, remains a fulcrum of regional dispute.

**Barak Kushner** teaches Japanese history at the University of Cambridge and is the author of *Men to Devils, Devils to Men: Japanese War Crimes and Chinese Justice* (winner of the American Historical Association's 2016 John K. Fairbank Prize).

**Sherzod Muminov** is a Research Associate in the Faculty of Asian and Middle Eastern Studies at the University of Cambridge, UK.

# Routledge Studies in the Modern History of Asia

*For a full list of titles in this series, please visit www.routledge.com/Routledge-Studies-in-the-Modern-History-of-Asia/book-series/MODHISTASIA*

# The Dismantling of Japan's Empire in East Asia

Deimperialization, postwar legitimation and imperial afterlife

**Edited by Barak Kushner
and Sherzod Muminov**

 Routledge
Taylor & Francis Group

LONDON AND NEW YORK

First published 2017
by Routledge
2 Park Square, Milton Park, Abingdon, Oxon OX14 4RN

and by Routledge
711 Third Avenue, New York, NY 10017

First issued in paperback 2018

*Routledge is an imprint of the Taylor & Francis Group, an informa business*

*British Library Cataloguing in Publication Data*
A catalogue record for this book is available from the British Library

*Library of Congress Cataloging in Publication Data*
A catalog record for this book has been requested

ISBN 13: 978-1-138-50013-6 (pbk)
ISBN 13: 978-1-138-18764-1 (hbk)

Typeset in Times New Roman
by Apex CoVantage, LLC

# Contents

# Figures

# Contributors

**Araragi Shinzō** is Professor in the Faculty of Global Studies, Sophia University, and specializes in the sociology of human migration. He has written and edited three books in Japanese: *Human Migration after the Empire: The Crossroads of Globalization and Postcolonialism* [帝国以後の人の移動—ポストコロニアリズムとグローバリズムの交錯点] (2013); *Migration and Repatriation: The Rise and Fall of the Japanese Empire* [日本帝国をめぐる人口移動の国際社会学] (2008); and *Historical Sociological Study on Japanese Agricultural Corp in "Manchukuo"* [満州移民の歴史社会学] (1994), which was awarded the Japanese Association for Rural Studies Prize in 1997.

**Michael Baskett** is Chair of the Department of Film and Media Studies at the University of Kansas, where he teaches courses in film and media history, Japanese and East Asian film, and transnational film. He is the author of *Attractive Empire: Transnational Film Culture in Imperial Japan* (2008) and serves as the Film/DVD Editor for the journal, *The Moving Image*. He is currently completing a book-length manuscript on Japanese Cold War Film and Media in Cold War Asia. Recent publications include "Japanese Film as Seen from Cold War America: The Johnston Plan" [冷戦期アメリカから見た日本映画—ジョンストンプランの役割] in Iwamoto Kenji (Ed.), *Nihon eiga no kaigai shinshutsu* [日本映画の海外進出] (2015); "Japan's 1960s Spy Boom: Bond Meets Imperial Nostalgia," in Michele Brittany (Ed.), *Spy-Fi & Superspies: Analyzing the Cultural Response to the James Bond Phenomenon* (2014).

**Erik Esselstrom** is Associate Professor of East Asian history at the University of Vermont in the United States. He is the author of *Crossing Empire's Edge: Foreign Ministry Police and Japanese Expansionism in Northeast Asia* (2009), and his current research explores Japanese perceptions of Chinese society during the 1950s and 1960s as reflected in popular print and visual media. He has also published articles on Kaji Wataru and other topics.

**Kanda Yutaka** is Associate Professor in Japanese international history at Niigata University, Japan. His first monograph was *Transformation of the Cold War Structure and Japan's Diplomacy toward China: Two Perceptions of Order, 1960–1972* [冷戦構造の変容と日本の対中外交—二つの秩序観1960–1972]

(2012). He has also published articles on Japanese Cold War politics and foreign relations.

**Katō Kiyofumi** is Associate Professor at the National Institute of Japanese Literature, where he conducts research on Japanese modern history. His current research topic concerns Japanese repatriation from East Asia after World War Two. He is the co-author of *The Disintegration of the Japanese Empire and Repatriation/Demobilization* [大日本帝国の崩壊と引揚・復員] (2012); *The Disintegration of the Japanese Empire* [「大日本帝国」崩壊] (2009); and *The History of the South Manchuria Railway Company* [満鉄全史] (2006).

**Kawashima Shin** is Professor of Chinese history in the Graduate School of Arts & Sciences at the University of Tokyo. His first book, *The Formation of Chinese Modern Diplomacy* [中国近代外交の形成] (2004), was awarded the Suntory Academic Prize in 2004. His publications include *Searching for a Modern State: 1894–1925* [近代国家への模索—1894–1925] (2010); *International Politics Surrounding Modern China* [近代中国をめぐる国際政治] (2014); *China Risk* [チャイナ・リスク] (2015). He co-authored *The Road to Global China* [グローバル中国への道程] (2009) and *A Modern History of Sino-Japan Relations* [日中関係史] (2013).

**Sarah Kovner** is a Senior Research Scholar at the Arnold A. Saltzman Institute of War and Peace Studies at Columbia University. She works on modern Japan and its relations with the world in the twentieth century. Her research interests include war and society, gender and sexuality, and international history. Kovner was previously an Associate Professor at the University of Florida and has been a Fellow in International Security Studies at Yale University. Currently she is writing a history of Allied prisoners in the Pacific War. Her first monograph, *Occupying Power: Sex Workers and Servicemen in Postwar Japan* (2012), won the Southeast Conference of the Association of Asian Studies book prize for 2014 and was a 2012 Choice outstanding academic title of the year. Sarah Kovner received her AB from Princeton University and her PhD from Columbia University.

**Barak Kushner** is Reader in modern Japanese history at the University of Cambridge. He has written *Men to Devils, Devils to Men: Japanese War Crimes and Chinese Justice* (2015); *Slurp! A Culinary and Social History of Ramen: Japan's Favorite Noodle Soup* (2012); and *The Thought War: Japanese Imperial Propaganda* (2006). He translated *Media, Propaganda and Politics in 20th-Century Japan* (2015) and also co-edited a volume with former *Asahi Shimbun* editor-in-chief, Funabashi Yoichi, entitled *Examining Japan's Lost Decades* (2015). In March 2013, he launched a five-year European Research Council funded project, "The Dissolution of the Japanese Empire and the Struggle for Legitimacy in Postwar East Asia, 1945–1965."

**Kerstin von Lingen** is a historian and researcher/lecturer at Heidelberg University in the Cluster of Excellence "Asia and Europe in a Global Context." Since

2013, she has led an independent research group, "Transcultural Justice: Legal Flows and the Emergence of International Justice within the East Asian War Crimes Trials, 1946–1954." Her publications include *Kesselring's Last Battle: War Crimes Trials and Cold War Politics, 1945–1960* (2009) and *Allen Dulles, the OSS and Nazi War Criminals: The Dynamics of Selective Prosecution* (2013), as well as the edited volumes *Justice in Times of Turmoil: War Crimes Trials in the Wake of Decolonization* (forthcoming 2016), *Kriegserfahrung und nationale Identität in Europa nach 1945* [War Experience and National Identity in Europe after 1945] (2009); she has co-edited with Klaus Gestwa, *Zwangsarbeit als Kriegsressource in Europa und Asien* [Forced Labor as a Resource of War: European and Asian Perspectives] (2014).

**Sherzod Muminov** is a Research Associate in the European Research Council Project, "The Dissolution of the Japanese Empire and the Struggle for Legitimacy in Postwar East Asia, 1945–1965," at the Department of Asian and Middle Eastern Studies at the University of Cambridge, UK. He recently completed his doctoral dissertation at the same university on the history of the Siberian Internment – the captivity of Japanese former servicemen in Soviet labor camps following the Second World War. His latest publication is "The 'Siberian Internment' and the Transnational History of the Early Cold War Japan, 1945–56," in Pedro Iacobelli et al. (Eds.), *Transnational Japan as History: Empire, Migration, and Social Movements* (2015).

**Park Jung Jin** is Associate Professor in the Department of International and Cultural Studies at Tsuda College, Japan. His research centers on international history in East Asia, North and South Korean politics, Japan–Korea relations and the Korean minority in Japan. He has published multiple works on North Korean diplomacy and the history of Korean repatriation from Japan to North Korea during the Cold War. His works have been published in Japan and Korea. His first monograph, in Japanese, was *The Birth of the Cold War between Japan and North Korea, 1945–1965* [日朝冷戦構造の誕生—1945–1965] (2012).

**Satō Takumi** is Professor in media history at the University of Kyoto. He has written 14 books, including *Modern Media History* [現代メディア史] (1998; Chinese edition 2004); *The Age of "KING": Public Sphere of the National Mass Magazine* [『キング』の時代—国民大衆雑誌の公共性] (2002), awarded the 2003 Suntory Prize for Social Sciences and Humanities; *Information Control: Information Officer Kurazō Suzuki and the Educational Total War State* [言論統制—情報官・鈴木庫三と教育の国防国家] (2004), awarded the 2005 Yoshida Shigeru Prize; *Public Opinion and Popular Sentiments: Genealogy of Japanese Popular Will* [輿論と世論—日本的民意の系譜学] (2008; Chinese edition 2013); and *The Media History of "Tosho": PR Strategy of Japanese Intellectualism* [『図書』のメディア史—「教養主義」の広報戦略] (2015).

**Franziska Seraphim** is Associate Professor of Japanese history at Boston College. Originally from Germany, she earned her PhD in Japanese history at Columbia University. She is the author of *War Memory and Social Politics in*

*Japan, 1945–2005* (2006) and numerous articles on historical memory, visual culture, and comparative history. Most recently, she produced "A 'Penologic Program' for Japanese and German War Criminals after World War II," in Joanne Cho, Lee Roberts, and Christian Spang [Eds.] *Transnational Encounters and Comparisons between Germany and Japan, 1860s–2000s* (2016).

**Shirato Ken'ichirō** is Assistant Professor in the Faculty of Humanities and Social Sciences at the University of Tsukuba. His research interests include media studies and the transnational cultural politics of empire. He has published numerous works on cultural policies of the Japanese Empire and the history of the Manchurian Telegraph and Telephone Company. His works include "The Idea of Radio in Manchukuo" [満洲国のラジオ観], *Media History Studies* [メディア史研究], 38 (September 2015); "The Aftermath of World War II in the Bansei Base for Special Attack Forces" [万世特攻基地の戦後], in *The Birth of "Chiran": How the Memory of Special Attack Forces Was Created*, ed. Fukuma Yoshiaki and Yamaguchi Makoto [知覧の誕生－特攻の記憶はいかに創られてきたのか] (2015); and "The Multicultural Broadcasting Policy of the Manchurian Telegraph and Telephone Company" [満洲電信電話株式会社の多言語放送政策], *Journal of Mass Communication Studies* [マス・コミュニケーション研究], 82 (January 2013), which was awarded the 2014 prize for one of the best articles in the *Journal of Mass Communication Studies*.

**Sandra Wilson** is a historian of modern Japan. She is Professor and Academic Chair of History and a Fellow of the Asia Research Centre at Murdoch University. She is the author of *The Manchurian Crisis and Japanese Society, 1931–33* (2002) and co-author with Robert Cribb, Beatrice Trefalt, and Dean Aszkielowicz of *Japanese War Criminals: The Politics of Justice after the Second World War* (New York: Columbia University Press, 2017). Her current research project, with Robert Cribb, analyzes the causes of Japanese military violence in the Pacific, 1941–1945.

**Urs Matthias Zachmann** is Professor of Japanese–Chinese Relations at the University of Edinburgh. His fields of research are the history of international relations in East Asia, the intellectual and cultural history of Japan, and law and legal history in East Asia. Among his publications are *China and Japan in the Late Meiji Period: China Policy and the Japanese Discourse on National Identity, 1895–1904* (2009/2011) and *Völkerrechtsdenken und Außenpolitik in Japan, 1919–1960* [The Discourse on International Law and Foreign Policy in Japan, 1919–1960] (2013). He is currently completing a book manuscript on the history of international law in Japan, 1854–1960.

# Introduction

## The unevenness of the end of empire

*Barak Kushner*

Beginning in the late 1980s, Western historians started to delve into the methods and policies that drove Japan's empire-building efforts in East Asia, but few examined what occurred after the empire fell. Even as the subject of Cold War studies has expanded and historians in Europe and America have shifted to examining the end of empire and the history of decolonization, there has been little advancement on this issue concerning Japanese history until recently.[1] This volume aims to offer a first step in reconceiving how political and legal authority were reshuffled and re-established after the fall of Japanese imperial rule throughout East Asia. Scholarship in Europe about parallel transformations offers some insight, but we cannot fail to observe that the causes of war and its denouement have absorbed our attention, with less focus given to how wars end and what happens after empires disintegrate.[2] The new and original research presented here centers on the collapse and aftermath – or afterlife – of empire. What happened at the ground level to the administrative staff, military officers and underlings of empire, those who tried and are still trying to find contingency, to create and make sense of narratives for how and why the Japanese empire foundered? The possibility for such research has increased even more over the last decade with newly available archives throughout East Asia and with the more open and internationalized state of historical research in Japan, which now has a much greater influence on scholarship abroad than in the past. Greater opportunities for research collaboration and sharing across languages, national divides and national perspectives provide researchers with pertinent new materials on which to build new historical frontiers.

This transnational and collaborative research was mainly made possible due to a five-year European Research Council (ERC)-funded project, "The Dissolution of the Japanese Empire and the Struggle for Legitimacy in Postwar East Asia." The research team that I gathered together to investigate this history and our various workshops and international conferences over the last few years reveal that the empire did not end as cleanly as is often perceived in domestic national histories of Japan, which until recently tended to ignore the legacy of empire outside Japan's occupied main islands.[3] It is necessary to bring empire back to discussions of postwar East Asian identity and to fold it into a history for the region as a whole with Japan at the center. This orientation will allow for more in-depth analyses of the history of Japan *within* East Asia, as well as offering insights into the relationships between Japan *and* East Asia. One of my central propositions is that the issue of empire remains part of the fabric of identity across the region and continues to haunt postwar East Asian political relationships: hence the need for Japan to find and rebuild its own legitimacy after its defeat. To discuss these ideas, I invited more than twenty scholars from Japan, Europe, and the United States to gather at Cambridge University over several days in the autumn of 2014. The resulting chapters are the fruit of that conference and the intense interaction over those days and over the successive months of rewriting and editing. Moreover, I am also pleased to have the addition of several chapters from scholars (Araragi Shinzō and Satō Takumi) who were unable to attend the original meeting. They graciously allowed the team to rework some of their key research, which is appearing now in English for the first time but which already greatly influences their respective fields in Japan.

One of the key ideas that sets this book apart from other studies is that we were committed during the conference to gaining as much interaction across languages as possible and to providing a voice to Japanese academic opinion leaders. To gain the wider participation of trend-setting Japanese scholars, we held our conference in two languages (English and Japanese) without translation, asking everyone to deliver their presentations in the language they felt more comfortable with and likewise for the discussions. Such a transnational endeavor is not easy, to be sure, and required us to keep focused on the task whether we spoke in English or in Japanese. I feel we achieved a breakthrough in providing a venue outside of Japan where Japanese scholars were not put at a linguistic disadvantage and those of us who are not Japanese were compelled not to rely solely on our native tongues. The resulting engagement and this edited book were ultimately born from this rich collaboration and exchange of different and sometimes opposing points of view concerning the situation in post-imperial East Asia. I aver that this research sits at the exciting juncture of hosting original scholarship across a variety of themes and serves as an extension of my larger research plan concerning the end of the Japanese empire and the pursuit of legitimacy.[4] At the same time, the research here represents a step forward toward identifying the core elements of where the process of decolonization in East Asia became entangled in the circumstances of Japanese deimperialization within the contours of the former empire.

In the seventy years since the end of World War II, we still have scant scholarship that investigates the way in which the Japanese empire dissolved and the significance of this event for the region as a whole. In Japan and elsewhere, the war is not forgotten. However, the history of Japan's empire is obscured. How precisely this happened and what details have been overlaid with the sediment of time, or buried by human agency, is one of the central themes of my research team's current efforts. How did Japan get separated from its former colonies and thus become a country whose history as a former imperial leader has been ignored during the postwar? What have scholars missed in thinking about the variety of issues that arise in tandem with the end of empire: the idea of "justice" and the adjudication of war crimes, the struggle over new boundaries, the shift from empire to state and the administrative gymnastics that requires, the language and equipment that media used to describe the process, and so on. Given the lack of uniformity among the various Japanese imperial experiences – so much varied depending on geography and time in Japan's vast yet short-lived empire – historians need to investigate further so that they can compare with the manner in which European historians treat disruption after the fall of the Nazi empire.[5] There is a conspicuous gap to fill in Japanese history in order to consider Japan at the center of this imperial dislocation in East Asia. What was the history of the regional order and state transformations after Japan surrendered? What is specific to Japan in this story? Given the importance of Japan in the shifts that took place in the postwar order in East Asia, we cannot overstate its role. With the more recent rise of China and the relative neglect for so many decades in academic and journalist circles in Europe and East Asia of the impact that the downfall of the Japanese empire had on a good half of the world, we need to once more emphasize that history should concentrate on defeat as well as on victory.

Ironically, we are not even clear about when World War II ended in East Asia, which only demonstrates the pressing relevance of the topics presented in this volume when thinking about the end of empire. Victory in Europe Day (May 8) is a well established date, but Victory in Japan Day remains an historical anachronism. It is September 2 for the Allies, the day of the signing of the document of surrender on the USS *Missouri* in Tokyo Bay, but August 15 for the Japanese, when a pre-recorded message given by Emperor Hirohito broadcast the fact of the surrender to his imperial subjects, who heard his voice for the first time in their lives.[6] Mainland China celebrates the event on September 3, and it is September 9 for Koreans, while for Taiwan, the end of empire is October 25.[7] But do these dates actually connote when empire ends or when colonies or occupied lands are freed and authority resurrected? How the Japanese remember this process, how they dealt with the changes, and how those changes and the reactions to them fed the subsequent memory and development of historical narratives demands to be explored.[8] The Japanese empire was short-lived, but it was geographically expansive. We need to address this set of circumstances, and measure what historical importance the empire left in lands where it no longer rules. Does the brevity of empire mean that we can ignore the legacy of Japan's imperial machinations, or do we need to wrestle with this fact as well? Moreover, who were or are the Japanese? Does the designation "Japanese" apply only to those who lived on the main islands of the archipelago? During the colonial era, Taiwanese and Koreans were, within certain measures, also treated as Japanese citizens, but the laws that regulated them in different parts of the empire were different. If ethnic Japanese lived in the colonies, they were also afforded different privileges. In effect, as the legal and social circumstances of those who lived, worked, and settled all across the diverse occupied areas, how were they treated as the empire crumbled – what happened to them? What about other former colonial subjects such as in Southeast Asia or Manchukuo? What did the loss of these lands mean for the region and Japan economically, culturally, politically, and psychologically?

This research provides the blueprint for a new Cold War history narrative within a larger contextual framework that will also demonstrate how slippery true transnational history is. While exploring the issue of how Japan's empire dissolved, our conference also aimed to generate a deeper dialogue between Japanese historians and those who analyze Japanese studies in the West. What does the end of empire look like from these two distinct vantage points? In calling into question this era and looking for commonalities, the participants in this endeavor continually ran into a number of conundrums. For example, what does the breakdown of empire mean in terms of process, what does the actual term itself signify, and what were the conditions under which it occurred? Who were the colonizers, and who were those who were colonized? What about collaboration, both during the imperial era and afterward? How do we integrate and synthesize the myriad of different and frequently conflicting narratives in this complex and international mélange? If our historical examination is a process, is it a backward-working process? How did we periodize the postwar era? When precisely does empire end, or does it lead to an "imperial hangover," in the words of diplomatic historian Ian Nish, a legacy that never completely disappears but lingers indefinitely?[9] Or do we assume our narrative is forward-looking? When does the postwar begin alongside the end of empire, for surely the two evolved in tandem for quite a long time given that Emperor Hirohito did not pass away until 1989?

There is no single unifying definition of empire or indeed of post-imperial in the context of Japan, which may be why the time span and indeed the subjects themselves are so elusive. Much ink has been spilled writing about the elements that went into forming Japan's empire, but now energy needs to be turned toward thinking about how it dissolved and how this dissolution affected the region and the rest of the world. At times, imperial areas transformed into completely different arenas that retained the same power structures as before, and at times they created entirely new ruling administrations. These histories feed the idea of continuity, or the "legacy," of empire. We are still dealing with that post-1945 legacy in so many ways in East Asia, for example, in Sino-Japanese relations: the Senkaku Islands disputes; in Taiwan and Korea, issues related to reconciliation or compensation for those labeled as "comfort women"; and all over the former empire, restitution for war crimes, and so on. Within Japan, conservative media debates about the veracity of the war crimes trials, veterans' pension payments, to name just a few, continually gain popular attention as topics of concern.[10]

The manner in which the term "empire" was used in a specific sense in Japan, beginning in 1931 and ending in 1945, differs from the more Europe-focused understanding in the West. The gap between the definitions entails examining two more important themes: the ways in which Japan coped with imperial loss, including the actual physical dismemberment of its land holdings, but also the psychological shifts and the ways in which Japanese and non-Japanese, both within Japan and at the peripheries, responded to no longer belonging to a greater imperial entity and returning to being a "lowly" nation-state only. Japan was an expanding administrative entity until 1945: at the moment of surrender, it suddenly found itself much smaller. Empires by nature exploit resources but also draw on them – there are dividends as well as costs. The loss of empire entailed the forfeiture of a former cosmopolitan world, but it also meant that the new state no longer bore the same financial burden. Scholars have done much theorizing about why empires form but less to understand the end of empire and its place in the world. What does sovereignty for a former empire mean when it has returned to being merely a state and loses its imperial appendages? For Japan and for much of East Asia in the immediate postwar, the consequences of Japan's sudden loss of empire, a sudden amputation of colonial holdings, and the defeat of its imperial ideology require analysis.

It is often stated that the empire in Japan ended without a full resolution of the damage caused by the war. What are the details of that period and what is significant when we consider war and empire in East Asia? After August 1945, many of the countries on the peripheries of Japan's empire split apart, for example Korea, Vietnam, and China, while Japan, the imperial instigator, paradoxically remained whole (with the noted exception of Okinawa, which the Americans took over as a stopgap measure to forestall any chance of imperial remilitarization and re-imperialization). Scholars are now ready to discuss the fall of the Japanese empire and how such an event reshaped East Asia in ways that we did not understand before the "end" of the Cold War.

Lately, scholars in Japan and the West have also begun to identify ways in which the "empire comes home": how the various nations and inhabitants dealt with the conclusion of the war. What were the consequences for Japan having to absorb the former pieces of its empire – war criminals, war repatriates, administrators, demobilized soldiers, and others – into a much geographically smaller Japanese nation after the imperial downfall? Equally importantly, what about the tremendous structural and equipment losses, not only of weapons but of factories, personal wealth, industrial sites, and the like? Military historians have done a good job of looking at one side of the coin of demobilization, but that is only one aspect of the larger historical narrative of imperial failure. In 1945, Japan was an island nation once again reduced to a limited number of islands and had to absorb its massive imperial population and infrastructures, which had a profound effect on containing former imperial ambitions but also required finding new outlets. Japan's inhabitants were used to empire; the idea and actuality of it were ideologically satisfying and formed part of their self-image and existence, and now they were forced to repatriate to Japan. These memories and behavior do not just disappear. They form a postimperial mindset that affects our contemporary world.

In English, historians such as Richard Frank have examined the process of the end of Japan (though more through the lens of the United States).[11] Lori Watt and Mariko Tamanoi have focused on the process of repatriation in a striking yet somewhat more winnowed context, while Herbert Bix wrote about the larger role of the emperor, and John Dower examined the occupation within Japan.[12] The research of these scholars is groundbreaking, but the impact of the downfall of empire on the region with Japan at the center, while a theme in their various works, was not central to their findings. While Japan was defeated militarily, thus leading to its inevitable postwar demilitarization, this experience has not translated into a social recognition that Japan had lost its colonies or even its empire. Japanese intellectuals and scholars have disregarded how much wartime and postwar political and social environments continued after the surrender. The empire was over, but the political and social structures that supported postcolonial societies and postwar Japan remained residual forces much longer. To date, research that actually examines the structure and destruction of what happened throughout the empire after the end and the impact it had on the post-1945 shape and hue of East Asia remains scarce.

The period under consideration was marked by the imperial surrender in 1945, Japan's reinstitution of sovereignty in 1952, and Japan's later entry into the UN in 1956. At the same time, the era witnessed many shifts in areas that had formerly been under Japanese hegemony – the outbreak of the Korean War during 1950–1953, the French "loss "of Indochina in 1954, the Afro-Asia Bandung Conference in 1955, and the explosion of armed conflict in Vietnam from 1945 to 1975. All of these massive transformations and conflicts reflected elements of the lasting impact of Japan's wartime and postwar legacy in the region.

The history of the Cold War in East Asia arguably began with the end of Japan's empire, and this moment remains indelibly linked to that history. This era is also heavily laden with the baggage of Allied and Axis wartime propaganda and the rhetorical legacies that carried over into Japan's occupation and postwar history, when Japan regained its independence. The longue durée of the postwar, the numerous venues across East Asia for Japanese war crimes trials, and the fact that war criminals, Japanese POWs, and others were being repatriated back to Japan up through the 1960s brewed conflicting opinions concerning how to assess the end of Japan's empire and the war in Asia. Here, we can see the naked form of postwar peace in East Asia taking shape over decades, and the analyses offered by the chapters in this book provide a much more textured and closer-to-the-ground estimation of the history than mere diplomatic overviews. As a consequence, I argue that August 15, 1945 is less significant as a marker for the end of the war, and this volume offers readers a chance to reconsider our assessment of when the postwar begins for Japan and the contours of its significance. By including specialists from disparate fields – history, politics, economy, military, migration, media, and film studies – in collaboration with regional specialists, we hope to move away from a U.S.-centered approach to postwar Japanese history and to elucidate how Japan's imperial history is related to East Asian history and the Cold War. The goal is to develop a more sophisticated and inclusive model for interpretation, one that is less teleological or primarily focused on Western scholarship and sources.

This volume is not meant to be exhaustive but rather sets out to prime the field toward thinking about the end of empire in Japan and how its disintegration led to the start of the Cold War in East Asia. We have chosen to divide the period in question into four thematic subsections, which also generally follow a chronological order. Section One, *The new postwar order: meaning and significance*, examines several key transformations that took place after Japan's surrender in August 1945. In Chapter 1, Katō Kiyofumi deciphers the changing hierarchy of the international postwar order in "The decline of the Japanese empire and the transformation of the regional order in East Asia." He provides a larger overview of the last moments of empire and the manner in which it imploded but highlights the fissures that would later cause grave problems in liberated areas. In Chapter 2,

"Deimperialization" in early postwar Japan: Adjusting and transforming the institutions of empire," Kawashima Shin details the perplexing issue of how empires unravel and make the shift back to being states. Kawashima examines what that process entails not only in terms of social psychology but also the legal ins and outs of how those institutions are rebuilt, eradicated, and managed. In Chapter 3, "Imperial loss and Japan's search for postwar legitimacy," Barak Kushner examines how the Japanese responded to the Potsdam Declaration's call to hold war crimes trials and scrutinizes the ways in which Japanese responses reflected conflicting ideologies about the postwar significance of what the empire had meant for Japan. In Chapter 4, "The collapse of the Japanese empire and the great migrations: Repatriation, assimilation, and remaining behind," Araragi Shinzō takes on the enormous topic of the immediate postwar migrations that ensued both within East Asia and also from Southeast to Northeast Asia and considers what they reveal about the nature of Japan's empire. Repatriation and deportation often went hand in hand with both political expediency and wartime imperial notions about racial hierarchies and Japan's place within modern East Asia. It was a mindset, even after defeat, that was hard to eradicate.

Section Two, *War criminals, POWs, and the imperial breakdown*, begins with Sandra Wilson's examination of the public support of Japanese war criminals. In Chapter 5, "The shifting politics of guilt: The campaign for the release of Japanese war criminals," Sandra Wilson shows us that the trials remained a potent political issue long after the verdicts were handed down and that moves to promote clemency were as much popularly led as they were politically motivated. Sarah Kovner's Chapter 6, "Allied POWs in Korea: Life and death during the Pacific War," provides fascinating details on how prisoner of war camps were run within the empire but also outside of Japan and on experiences that are exceedingly difficult to generalize. In Korea, for example, POW camps were initial theaters of propaganda, and the detainees were often able to survive the war in much greater safety than elsewhere in the empire. In Chapter 7, Franziska Seraphim demonstrates the need to consider the war crimes trials and prison systems on a geographical level in "Carceral geographies of Japan's vanishing empire: War criminals' prisons in Asia." She looks at the physical buildings and locations of both trials and incarceration as postwar reminders of empire and their impact on Japanese society. Sherzod Muminov examines the background and indeed the events of the still relatively unknown story of the 600,000 Japanese "detainees" in the Soviet Union, in Chapter 8, "Prejudice, punishment, and propaganda: Postimperial Japan and the Soviet versions of history and justice in East Asia, 1945–1956." He probes Soviet motives and memory of pursuing the Japanese after the end of war and links their lack of repatriation to the goals that other Allies had within East Asia, in contrast to those of the United States.

Section Three, *Diplomacy, law, and the end of empire* analyzes the elements that characterized Japan's attempt to deal with its defeat and to progress forward in the postwar period. In Chapter 9, Matthias Zachmann explores how key Japanese legal scholars and jurists met and dealt with defeat in "Sublimating the empire: How Japanese experts of international law translated Greater East Asia into the postwar period." Zachmann emphasizes the continuity of legal thought and belief about Japan's position in East Asia from prewar to the postwar through close readings of legal scholarly writings and practice. Kanda Yutaka's Chapter 10, "The transformation of a Manchukuo imperial bureaucrat to postwar supporter of the Yoshida Doctrine: The case of Shiina Etsusaburō," investigates the ways in which the Yoshida Doctrine, a key pillar of Japanese postwar foreign policy, was seen by succeeding Japanese postwar politicians. More importantly, through the example of a major Japanese bureaucrat/politician, we can see the ways in which imperial thought affected postwar political practice up until the 1960s. In Chapter 11, Park Jung Jin, in "North Korean nation building and Japanese imperialism: People's nation, people's diplomacy, and Japanese technicians," reveals the fascinating story of how the immediate postwar was experienced within the confines of what became North Korea and the striking differences with the use and appropriation of Japanese talent and former imperial assets. Erik Esselstrom in Chapter 12, "Humanitarian hero or communist stooge? The ambivalent Japanese reception of Li Dequan in 1954," sheds light on a key visit to Japan by one of the first Communist Chinese "people's diplomats" in the postwar period and how it was reported in the Japanese media. Esselstrom makes it clear that while the Japanese government remained silent on the matter, popular interest in Li reflected a social and political divide concerning how Japan should relate to mainland China.

Section Four centers on the issues of *Media and the imperial aftermath.* In Chapter 13, Satō Takumi discusses the start of Japan's most important postwar political magazine, *Sekai*, in his "The 'pacifist' magazine *Sekai*: A barometer of postwar thought." Satō explains how this magazine shaped postwar political debates in Japan and the ways in which it also played a crucial role in bringing to the fore August 15 as a day of political remembrance about World War II. In Chapter 14, "Post-imperial broadcasting networks in China and Manchuria," Shirato Ken'ichirō outlines the radio propaganda apparatus that the Japanese built up in Japan's puppet kingdom, Manchukuo, and how these institutions and administrative framework greatly influenced the structure of Japan's postwar domestic media industry, including television programming. Michael Baskett launches into new territory in an exciting look at Cold War film alliances in East Asia, in Chapter 15, "Parting the Bamboo Curtain: Japanese Cold War film exchange with China." Baskett notes that, even with the somewhat derogatory tone of political rhetoric toward the Communist bloc, Japanese film-makers' film reviews and published discourse about Chinese films were surprisingly open and engaging with this artistic side of the People's Republic of China even during the Cold War. However, in Baskett's estimation, the Japanese film industry, film leaders, and reviewers ironically maintained a continued distance from Chinese film, and both camps persisted with long held prewar assumptions that did not dissipate with the end of empire. Finally, instead of offering a conclusion that would merely repeat the highlights of each chapter, I asked a well known German scholar, an expert in European war crimes but one who also investigates legal flows between East Asia and the West, to offer her assessment concerning how the field is beginning to conceive of comparisons and contrasts between the postwar in Europe and East Asia. In considering these issues, Kerstin von Lingen wrote up what I consider an epilogue for scholars of Asia in Chapter 16, "Germany as a role model? Coming to terms with Nazi war deeds, 1945–2015." In her conclusion, von Lingen delivers cogent advice to scholars of East Asia who oftentimes too easily categorize the German case of pursuing war guilt as a simple success when compared with Japan's inattention. Germany has taken many decades to get to where it has arrived, and the many outside pressures and political will that drove it toward such policies need to be understood if we are to gain any lessons for other parts of the world.

## Acknowledgements

I would like to thank the European Research Council for its support with a five-year grant (2013–2018) to conduct the research, workshops, and conferences with funds to draw together an excellent cohort of scholars as part of the project, "The Dissolution of the Japanese Empire and the Struggle for Legitimacy in Postwar East Asia, 1945–1965" (DOJSFL 313382). The grant has been a transformative experience for me as a scholar and teacher and has offered untold opportunities on personal and professional levels that I never dreamed possible. This funding also allowed us to bring in a stream of internationally recognized scholars to offer workshops, to support a series of international conferences, and to provide travel money for us to return to East Asia much more frequently than is normally possible. These years have been indispensable in helping me to push forward my own scholarship, as well as that of the graduate students and postdoctoral researchers on my team and to build new networks. The grant made it possible to bring to Cambridge a full range of historians and specialists not only on Japan but also on Korea, Taiwan, and China, from Europe, America, and East Asia in order to learn, interact, and establish new academic and personal relations. I hope that these exchanges have not been fruitful only for me but for those in my research team and those with whom we have worked over these last years. It has been a pleasure to work with my co-editor, Dr. Sherzod Muminov, for his valuable input and assiduous attention to detail, as well as his ability to work long hours under deadlines, all the while juggling a new job and a young family. And we cannot forget our internal editor, Dr. Lucy North, who helped us bring out the best and clearest writing both from those whose native language is English and for those for whom it is a secondary or even tertiary language. Of course, I need to express my heartfelt appreciation to the members of my research team, current and past, Dr. Lily Chang, Dr. Deokhyo Choi, Dr. Arnaud Doglia, Dr. Andrew Levidis and Aiko Otsuka, for their work on the conference and the volume as well. Jill Cooper, who helped with all the finances, has been indispensable as project administrator, while Mujeeb Khan and Sherzod Muminov ably translated key articles. Dr. Matthew Funaiole did an excellent job on the index.

Cambridge University Faculty of Asian and Middle Eastern Studies librarian Francoise Simmons and Cambridge University Japanese Librarian Koyama Noboru and his successor Dr. Kristin Williams, along with Chinese Librarian

Charles Aylmer, are always there to aid, as have been my colleagues in the FAMES faculty and the Faculty of History. Obviously, my ERC research team and I would also like to extend our appreciation to all the participants at the 2014 conference, "The Breakdown of the Japanese Empire," who gave their time and shared their expertise as well. Peter Sowden, our publisher, was supportive from the start and has proved key to helping us usher this project along.

### *Note on transliteration*

Japanese, Chinese, and Korean names appear in the East Asian order, with family name first. Japanese words are normally printed in italics, except when the word, such as saké, anime, daimyo, samurai, manga, or miso, has entered the English language. Long vowels in Japanese are indicated by a macron, as in *shōyu*, although this rule has not been applied to commonplace names, as in Tokyo, Osaka, and Kyoto.

## Notes

1  Peter Duus, Ramon H. Myers, and Mark R. Peattie, eds., *The Japanese Informal Empire in China, 1895–1937* (Princeton, NJ: Princeton University Press, 1989); and Peter Duus, Ramon H. Myers, and Mark R. Peattie, eds., *The Japanese Wartime Empire, 1931–1945* (Princeton, NJ: Princeton University Press, 1996). At almost the same time (1992–1993), Iwanami Publishers in Japan produced an eight-volume series on Japanese colonialism, *Iwanami kōza kindai nihon to shokuminchi*. (Unless otherwise noted, all Japanese books are published in Tokyo.)
2  A recent Japanese volume offers insight into a little examined European–East Asian post-colonial comparison. See Hosoya Yūichi, ed., *Sengo ajia yōroppa kankeishi: reisen datsushokuminchi chiikishugi* (Keiō juku daigaku shuppankai, 2015).
3  As Kawashima Shin notes in Chapter 2 of this book, changes are afoot in Japan. The field is changing with new scholarship and questions from public intellectuals like Kang Sang-jun in *Ajia kara nihon o tou*, Iwanami bukkuretto no. 336 (Iwanami shoten, 1994), and scholars such as Asano Toyomi, *Sengo nihon no baishō mondai to higashiajia chiiki saihen: seikyūken to rekishi ninshiki mondai no kigen* (Nagoya: Chūkyo daigaku kigyō kenkyūjo, 2013).
4  The five-year ERC project website is www.warcrimesandempire.com.
5  Norbert Frei's *Adenauer's Germany and the Nazi Past: The Politics of Amnesty and Integration* (New York: Columbia University Press, 2002); Henry Rousso, *La dernière catastrophe: L'histoire, le présent, le contemporain* (Paris: Editions Gallimard, 2012); and Kerstin von Lingen's *Allen Dulles, the OSS and Nazi War Criminals: The Dynamics of Selective Prosecution* (Cambridge: Cambridge University Press, 2013).
6  Satō Takumi expounds (in his Chapter 13 of this volume) on the questions of how and when August 15 took on new meaning as the symbol of the end of empire and the beginning of postwar Japan.
7  It is even more fascinating to see how the Chinese Communist Party has appropriated its "victory" over Japan in 2015 when it arguably had very little to do with Japan's surrender. See Sergei Radchenko, "China Lost World War Two," *Foreign Policy*, September 3, 2015.
8  Satō Takumi, *Hachigatsu jūgonichi no shinwa: shūsen kinenbi no mediagaku* (Chikuma shobō, 2005); and Akiko Hashimoto, *The Long Defeat: Cultural Trauma, Memory, and Identity in Japan* (Oxford: Oxford University Press, 2015).

9 Ian Nish, "Regaining Confidence – Japan after the Loss of Empire," *Journal of Contemporary History* vol. 15, issue 1 (January 1980): pp. 181–195.

10 On December 28, 2015, the Korean and Japanese governments, 70 years after the end of World War II, appeared to have reached a sort of consensus concerning resolving political definitions and responsibility regarding comfort women, though public backlash in Korea demonstrates this might be short-lived: "Japan and South Korea Settle Dispute over Wartime 'Comfort Women'," *The New York Times*, December 28, 2015. At the same time, the politics and ensuing legal cases that surround Park Yuha's research on looking beyond Japanese shores for responsibility about comfort women, in her book *Teikoku no ianfu: shokuminchi shihai to kioku no tatakai* (Asahi shimbun shuppankai, 2014), demonstrate that such conclusions are also maybe premature.

11 Richard Frank, *Downfall: The End of the Imperial Japanese Empire* (New York: Random House, 1999).

12 Lori Watt, *When Empire Comes Home: Repatriation and Reintegration in Postwar Japan* (Cambridge, MA: Harvard University Asia Center, 2009); Mariko Asano Tamanoi, *Memory Maps: The State and Manchuria in Postwar Japan* (Honolulu: University of Hawaii Press, 2009); Herbert Bix, *Hirohito and the Making of Modern Japan* (New York: Harper Collins, 2000); John Dower, *Embracing Defeat: Japan in the Wake of World War II* (New York: W.W. Norton & Co., 1999).

# The new postwar order: meaning and significance

# 1 The decline of the Japanese empire and the transformation of the regional order in East Asia

*Katō Kiyofumi*

World War II was fought on a global scale, and yet there were major differences between Asia and Europe in terms of the nature of the war and the events that unfolded. This difference became apparent during the postwar reorganization of the political and military regional order. With the collapse of the Soviet Union in the early 1990s, the expansion of democratic norms brought greater stability, if not somewhat temporary in retrospect, to Eastern Europe. However, the hostilities of the Cold War era remain intact within East Asia even today. This discontinuity can be traced back to the distinct nature of the two sides, or "spheres," of World War II.

Before World War II, the Japanese empire was the main regional power in East Asia. The expansion of the Japanese empire had begun during the 1894–1895 Sino-Japanese War and continued into the early twentieth century as Japan established itself as the regional power with the Russo-Japanese War in 1904–1905 and the annexation of Korea in 1910. Following the Manchurian Incident in 1931, Japan resumed its imperial expansion by extending its territory from East Asia to Southeast Asia before eventually collapsing after its defeat in World War II. During this fifty-year period, the rule of the Japanese empire can be said to have maintained regional order in East Asia to a greater or lesser extent. Japan's influence during its era of colonial rule cannot be ignored, particularly with respect to its long-established colonies, Korea and Taiwan. This Japan-centered regional order came to a close as a result of World War II; however, it was a closure that was brought about through external pressure from the United States and the Soviet Union and not due to internal resistance from the colonized peoples, as was the case for the wars of decolonization of Southeast Asia, such as Vietnam and Indonesia.

At the same time, colonial rule in China, the country that arguably suffered the most from Japanese aggression, was not dismantled by the military efforts of the Allies, and the Japanese occupation continued even after its imperial defeat in 1945. The only colony that was truly "liberated" from Japanese rule by military force was Manchuria, and this process was set in motion by the Soviet Army when Stalin entered the Pacific theater a few days before Emperor Hirohito announced Japan's surrender.

Thus, while the Japanese colonies were "liberated" from colonial rule when Japan lost the war, the way in which they were freed from colonial management differed among regions. This chapter will clarify the means through which Asian countries achieved independence or were subordinated after the dissolution of the Japanese empire, with reference to the intentions and mistakes of both the Soviet Union and the United States. One can compare my analysis with that of Sherzod Muminov in Chapter 8, where he more specifically examines Soviet intentions and Japanese responses toward the end of empire. In addition, I will consider how Japan, as a vanquished nation, was involved in the East Asian regional transformations that began after the war. These issues raise all sorts of questions about the significance that the conclusion of World War II might have had for East Asia.

## The formation of Asia's new postwar order and the Soviet war against Japan

The year 1943, a crucial moment in the shaping of Asia's postwar order, saw the United States and the Allied powers launch a counter-attack against Japan. In Europe, Italy surrendered, and the Cairo Conference, during which it became apparent that the Axis powers were outmaneuvered, took place from November 23 to 26. Held in Egypt, the Conference was attended by the leaders of the United States, the United Kingdom, and the Republic of China (Roosevelt, Churchill, and Chiang Kai-shek), and was followed by a December 1 announcement that the Allies had agreed to continue to fight against Japan until its unconditional surrender. The Allies stated their aim of returning the Pacific Islands as well as the territories that Japan had "stolen" from China, namely Manchuria, Formosa (Taiwan), and the Pescadores, and releasing Korea from Japanese colonial rule. Although the Cairo Declaration was succeeded by the Potsdam Declaration, which set out the framework for the new regional order in East Asia following Japan's surrender, the Cairo Declaration itself was no more than a general pronouncement to the press, and no official diplomatic document signed by the three leaders was drafted at that time. Moreover, the ambiguous treatment of the issue of Korean independence caused serious problems later on.

The leader with the strongest interest in the Cairo Conference was Chiang Kai-shek, who argued loudly for the establishment of an independent sovereign state on the Korean Peninsula. Prior, a traditional regional order centered on China had existed in East Asia, but that order collapsed in the late nineteenth century. This breakdown was prompted by a power struggle between Japan and China over control of the Korean Peninsula, which began after the mid-nineteenth century. After its defeat in the 1895 Sino-Japanese War, China felt threatened by the presence of Japan in the East. When viewed through this historical lens, it is evident that the construction of a bulwark to shield China from the military threat from the East (i.e., Japan), by establishing a pro-Chinese administration on the Korean Peninsula, was critically important from the perspective of Chinese national security.[1]

In fact, when the Sino-Japanese War began in 1937, China gave sanctuary to the Provisional Government of the Republic of Korea and, with the support of the

United States, formed a military unit comprising Koreans who prepared for war against Japan.[2] China was the nation that had a political and military interest in the Korean Peninsula. By contrast, the Korean Peninsula held far less strategic importance both for the United States and the United Kingdom than it did for China. The United States was planning to attack Japan from the Pacific, and so the Korean Peninsula held next to no military value, and this did not change even as the war drew to a close.

At the 1943 Cairo Conference, President Franklin D. Roosevelt approved the plan to liberate Korea from Japanese colonial rule and to establish an independent, self-governing state. He was, however, skeptical about Korea's capacity for self-governance and suggested that Korea should make the transition to independence once the foundations for political and economic development had been established during a period of trusteeship under the Allied forces, which he reckoned would last for twenty to forty years. British Prime Minister Winston Churchill was even more non-committal. During the drafting of the Declaration, he initially suggested that Korean independence should be achieved "at the earliest possible moment," but he revised this to "in due course" in the final draft.[3] Churchill's primary concern was the creation of a second front in Europe, and he was more focused on the subsequent late November 1943 Tehran Conference than on the Cairo Conference. Nonetheless, relations between the United States and China were strong at the time of the Cairo Conference, and Roosevelt was contemplating a decision to re-establish a supply route to China by sending troops overland via Burma. Regardless, Churchill's primary concern was that delaying the Burma Campaign could open up a second front in Europe by diverting the number of U.S. landing ships headed toward Europe.[4] In addition, Churchill feared that Korean independence would affect the growing calls for Indian independence: therefore, he did not wish to discuss the issue of Korea's future in depth. In line with Churchill's passive attitude, Roosevelt, who had initially shown little interest in Korea, contented himself with a compromise that did just enough to save Chiang Kai-shek's reputation, and hence the issue of Korean independence was shelved without reaching a clear solution.

Even though World War II was fought in both Europe and Asia, in the latter the objectives included the additional dimension of the issue of decolonization, since the question of how to resolve the issue of Japan's colonies after the war was unavoidable. At the same time, however, it was unthinkable that an Allied power like Great Britain – the largest colonial empire in the world, which received support in the war from India and its other colonies – would even consider following the mantra of decolonization. Decolonization was likewise unacceptable for France, the second largest colonial power, and the Netherlands, which had colonized Indonesia. The United States was the sole nation, among all the Allied powers, that had agreed, in 1935, upon the independence of Commonwealth of the Philippines after ten years. As such, the Allies agreed to liberate Korea from Japanese colonial rule but shelved the issue of Korean independence. This bifurcated result, in part, led to the division of Korea after the Soviet Union's entry into the war in August 1945.

The fact that the Allies developed their postwar vision for Asia on an ad hoc basis can be easily inferred from the subjects that were discussed at the Potsdam Conference in July 1945. The main subject discussed at this conference was the construction of a new European order after Germany's surrender, or, to be precise, the "Poland problem." Although it was only a matter of time before Japan surrendered, only a small portion of the conference was dedicated to any discussion regarding Japan, and there was no detailed consideration of what the new Asian order would entail following Japan's surrender. More importantly, China, the country that was supposed to play the leading role in this new postwar Asian order, had not been invited to Potsdam.[5] During the Yalta Conference in February 1945, Stalin had agreed to enter the war against Japan, and the United Kingdom and the United States negotiated that the Soviets would be granted privileges in Manchuria (Northeast China) in return for their efforts (namely, they would receive a priority lease on the Changchun Railway, which was to be placed under joint Sino-Soviet management, as well as the ports of Dalian and Port Arthur). In the Cairo Declaration, it was agreed that Manchuria would be returned to China, but the privileges bestowed on the Soviet Union by the Yalta Agreement effectively stripped China of its sovereignty in this region. The Chinese government had not been informed of this secret agreement with the Soviets, primarily due to the fact that relations between China and the United States, which had been favorable at the time of the Cairo Conference, atrophied toward the end of the war.

Another, more direct reason for the decline in relations between China and the United States concerned Operation Ichigō (known as the *Tairiku Datsū Sakusen*, in Japanese), or "Cutting Across the Continent Operation"), the final campaign pursued by the Japanese Imperial Army from April to December 1944. The goals of this offensive strike were (1) to open up a land route from mainland China to the oil-rich region of Southeast Asia (French Indochina) to replace the sea route that had been blocked by the United States military and to destroy air bases in southeast China, from which American bombers were attacking the Japanese main islands and (2) to strip the Chinese government of its will to fight and cause it to break away from the Allied powers. Operation Ichigō was conducted in tandem with the Battle of Leyte Gulf, in the Philippines, for which the Japanese Army mobilized its remaining naval vessels in an attempt to contain the Allied invasion. The Imperial Headquarters implemented the largest operation in military history in a bid to create an opportunity for peace negotiations with the United States by delivering a blow to the U.S. Army and Navy in the battle of Leyte Island.[6]

The China Expeditionary Army, the Japanese Imperial Army stationed in China that executed Operation Ichigō, attempted to keep a tight grip on its expansive territory – in central and southern China – by concentrating its dispersed military units on key cities and railways and to advance southward to the Vietnamese border in a single push. Its mobilization included units stationed in northern China to secure a land route to French Indochina, which was then under Japanese control. However, the Japanese army ran out of supplies during the six-month campaign and was ultimately unable to reach the border of French Indochina. Essentially, Operation Ichigō failed because the Japanese Army ran out of resources. Moreover, Japan's transportation routes to Southeast Asia were severed when it started to lose its hold on the Philippines due to the destruction of the Japanese fleet in the Battle of Leyte Gulf. At this point, the Japan imperial military faced imminent defeat.

These campaigns, however, had an unexpected negative effect on relations between the United States and China. When Chiang Kai-shek attempted to avoid a direct confrontation with the Japanese forces in a bid to preserve his Chinese Nationalist forces, his relationship with the U.S. commander in China, General Joseph Stilwell, grew more problematic in July 1944. While the European and Pacific theaters of World War II were led by Generals Dwight Eisenhower and Douglas MacArthur respectively, Chiang had been named Supreme Commander of the Chinese theater, and he refused to transfer the right of command to the U.S. Army. As the United States formulated its plan to invade the Japanese mainland, it sought to transfer the right of command of the Chinese theater to Stilwell in an attempt to draw back the Japanese Army that was advancing into mainland China and restore the weakened Chinese forces under American command. Chiang Kai-shek vehemently opposed this policy and maintained his position as Supreme Commander by calling for Stilwell's removal from command in October 1944.[7]

On the heels of this incident, relations between China and the United States became paralyzed, and the Americans' disregard for China increased as feelings of distrust rose among both parties. The United States government then turned its attention to the Soviet Union's entrance into the war against Japan in a bid to prevent further American losses during the Japanese resistance, which was expected to intensify during the coming months. By the end of 1944, the United States began to attach more importance to its relations with the Soviet Union than to its relations with China. In addition, as a result of the China Expeditionary Army's campaign, the Imperial Japanese Army in northern China had transferred its resources to central and southern China, leaving large areas of northern China without any significant military presence. These vacated areas were then occupied by the Red Army, as the Communist Party began to expand its influence across the whole of northern China.[8] This was one of the reasons the Chinese Communist Party was able to establish a base in Manchuria faster than the Nationalist Army in the immediate postwar.

## The decline of the Japanese Empire and the liberation of the colonies

The country most affected by the collapse of the Japanese empire was Korea. On August 9, the Soviet Army invaded Manchuria and began advancing into North Korea.[9] Japan's Imperial Headquarters predicted that the Soviet Union would enter the war during the battle for mainland Japan, and, on May 30, it commanded the Kwantung Army (the Japanese military in Manchuria) to relinquish two-thirds of Manchuria and establish two lines of defense along the railways operating between Changchun and Tumen and between Dalian and Changchun, while holding the area north of the 38th parallel on the Korean Peninsula to prepare for a long, drawn-out war in the mountainous region of east Manchuria (Imperial Army Orders No. 1338 and 1339). At this stage, the Kwantung Army was responsible for defending the Korean Peninsula north of the 38th parallel in addition to Manchuria.[10]

In response to Japan's defensive stance, the Soviet Army intercepted the Kwantung Army's retreat from the Korean Peninsula and employed a pincer movement from the north. However, this was a secondary operation aimed at mobilizing lateral support for the Soviets' main campaign in Manchuria: the Soviets had not mustered the political will of occupying the central city of Keijō (present-day Seoul) or the entire Korean Peninsula. Having secured a lease on the Changchun Railway, the major transport artery in the region, and on the ports of Dalian and Port Arthur at the Yalta Conference, the Korean Peninsula was of little political or economic value to the Soviet Union.[11] At the same time, the strategic importance of the Korean Peninsula had always been low for the United States. However, its army had fought against Japan almost single-handedly for almost three and a half years, and this made it difficult for them to agree to the establishment of a Soviet zone throughout the entire Korean Peninsula based on a few days of fighting against Japan.[12]

On August 10, the second day of the Soviet-Japanese War, Washington was informed of Japan's intention to accept the Potsdam Agreement for the first time, and the State-War-Navy Coordinating Committee (SWNCC) was held from the evening of August 10 through to the next morning. During this meeting, plans were made to issue General Order No. 1 for the surrender of Japan. While General Order No. 1 outlined the zones where the Allies would disarm the Japanese forces, the Soviet Union was set to gain full control of the Korean Peninsula. At the time, the United States Army lacked the time and capacity to send troops to Korea. Then, in the space of just thirty minutes, two military officers, who had no expertise with Korean affairs, devised a plan to divide the country approximately in half based on the 38th parallel, leaving the capital of Seoul under American control. This plan was immediately adopted and written into General Order No.1 at the SWNCC.[13] After the SWNCC, Stalin agreed to the plan without hesitation. This fact alone demonstrates the Soviet Union's lack of political direction for the Korean Peninsula. The Korean Peninsula was divided along the 38th parallel because neither overlord, the United States or the USSR, had a clear vision for Korea's future. This general lack of attention would lead to future confusion.

Before the end of the war, some Koreans already assessed that Japan would eventually lose and that Korea would become an independent country. In August 1944, Yo Un-hyung, a distinguished leader of the independence movement, organized a nationwide underground organization to prepare Korea for independence following Japan's imminent defeat.[14] Meanwhile, the president of the Provisional Government of the Republic of Korea, Kim Gu, formed the Korean Liberation Army under the protection of the Nationalist Government of China and prepared to join the war against Japan.[15] The communist activist Pak Hon-yong went into hiding, hoping to reorganize the Korean Communist Party.[16] However, Japan's defeat came unexpectedly early and took them all by surprise.

Kim Gu was the most shocked by Japan's surrender. He was concerned that Korea's autonomy had been neglected in the international political arena because the Korean Liberation Army was unable to join in the war, and Korea itself was not included as an Allied member in the war against Japan. Kim believed that this would have a negative effect on Korea's push for independence.[17] In fact, when Japan launched its attack on the United States, the Provisional Government of the Republic of Korea declared war on Japan. However, the United States and the United Kingdom ignored this appeal, and only the Kuomintang (KMT) recognized it. The main reason for this lack of recognition was that, unlike the Polish government – which had fled to London when Poland was partitioned at the Eastern Front – Korea had already lost its independence thirty years earlier, and the Provisional Government had never been in power.

In this manner, Korean "independence," neglected and postponed by the Allies, eventually arrived from an unexpected quarter. The Government General of Korea, the administrative body of the Japanese colony in Korea, learned about Japan's acceptance of the Potsdam Declaration on August 10. At that time, the Japanese Governor-General was concerned that the Soviet Army, which had already invaded Korea, would occupy the entire Korean Peninsula and establish a new communist government. The Japanese therefore created a plan to secure the safety of the 700,000 Japanese citizens living in Korea by forming an independent government comprising Korean citizens and transferring power to this administrative unit before the Soviet Army could make its advance. The Governor-General liaised with Yo Un-hyung and sought to promote the establishment of an independent government of Korean nationals.[18] Yo agreed to the Japanese Governor-General's proposal, and the two parties reached an agreement to transfer power on August 15. Immediately after the Japanese surrender, Yo formed the Committee for the Preparation of Korean Independence (CPKI), with himself as chairman. When the CPKI was established, the political prisoners of the Provisional Government were released, and the movement to establish an independent government for the whole of Korea gained momentum.

However, disorder intensified when the Soviet Army continued its offensive attack north of the 38th parallel even after Japan's surrender on August 15. The Soviet Union had set its sights on occupying all territory north of the 38th parallel, as agreed upon with the United States. The influence of the CPKI's formation also increased in the north, where a group of Korean nationals had formed an autonomous political organization. The Soviet Union was cautious of the nationalist-heavy CPKI and promoted the formation of another autonomous organization that would contain communist members. It then proceeded to appoint Kim Il-sung, who was under the leadership of the Soviet Red Army from December 1940, as the central figure in its umbrella organization.[19]

As the independence movement gathered momentum south of the 38th parallel, various political groups arose – against Yo Un-hyung's expectations – and threats that eroded public safety escalated when a fierce internal power struggle ensued among the Korean people. The Japanese Government General had failed to anticipate this situation and had already lost the power that was needed to contain those involved. Faced with this situation, the Japanese 17th Area Army, which had surrendered with minimal casualties in the south of the Korean Peninsula, began to play a greater role.[20] Fearing that the CPKI might have been hijacked by communists, who would undermine the peace, the 17th Area Army began maintaining security on behalf of the Japanese Government General on August 20 and swiftly restored public order in Seoul.[21] It then became clear on August 22 that the United States Army would occupy the area south of the 38th parallel. Since the worst-case scenario of a complete Soviet occupation had been avoided, the Japanese Government General of Korea changed its initial plan to transfer power to the CPKI and began to liaise directly with the United States Army. Subsequently, the 24th Corps of the U.S. Tenth Army arrived in Incheon from Okinawa on September 8, and on September 9 an instrument of surrender was handed over to the U.S. Army to mark the unconditional surrender of the Japanese 17th Area Army and the transfer of administrative rights from the Government General of Korea.

We should note that on September 6, before the arrival of the U.S. Army, the CPKI proclaimed the foundation of the "People's Republic of Korea" and unsuccessfully attempted directly to contact the American Army. On September 7, General Douglas MacArthur, the Supreme Commander for the Allied Powers, issued General Order No. 1, which placed the area south of the 38th parallel under the control of the United States Army. Consequently, the immediate independence pursued by the CPKI was completely denied, and the U.S. Army abolished the People's Republic of Korea by military decree on October 10. Moreover, even though Kim Gu, the president of the Provisional Government, returned to Korea from exile in China in November, the United States Army denied his request for a triumphant return as the leader of the Provisional Government, and the Americans treated him as a mere regular returnee. With these postwar policies, the United States ignored the existence of the CPKI and the Provisional Government and instead decided to install their handpicked candidate Syngman Rhee, who was still in exile in the United States at the time. On October 16, Rhee returned to Korea and proceeded to expand his political influence by obtaining the backing of the U.S. Army and the support of right-wing factions.[22] As Yo Un-hyung and Kim Gu lost influence, Rhee strengthened his power base. Nevertheless, Pak Hon-yong opposed Rhee's rise to power, and the rifts intensified the political conflict between the left and right.

Meanwhile, in contrast to the United States' direct rule, the Soviet Army adopted a system of indirect rule based on local people's committees comprised of Korean nationals. Although these committees initially included a balance between nationalists and communists, the communists gradually seized the upper hand. The Korean communists formed separate camps, namely a partisan group, led by Kim Il-sung after his return from the Soviet Union, and a Korean Communist Party camp led by Pak Hon-yong. While the Korean Communist Party camp was initially the more powerful of the two groups, Kim Il-sung – backed by the Soviets – expanded his influence and, on February 8, 1946, established the Provisional People's Committee of North Korea. This group eventually developed into the

Democratic People's Republic of Korea and decided to break away from the Korean Communist Party. Kim Il-sung gained the support of the Soviet Union and successfully managed power in the north, whereas political confusion mounted in the south. The Korean people were particularly shocked to discover that, at the Moscow Conference of Foreign Ministers held in December 1945, the Allied powers had decided to establish an interim government and a trusteeship for up to five years, thereby postponing the reunification of Korea.

In South Korea, a decisive struggle developed between political factions, as the right-wing nationalists opposed the trusteeship rule, whereas the left-wing socialists had come to terms with it. In March 1946, a Soviet–U.S. Joint Commission was held in Seoul but was adjourned *sine die* due to a political disagreement between the United States, which argued that all political parties and organizations should be consulted, and the Soviet Union, which attempted to exclude the right-wing parties and organizations that had opposed the result of the Moscow Conference of Foreign Ministers. When the Commission was abandoned, Syngman Rhee argued for the establishment of a single-party government south of the 38th parallel, and Korea's internal political situation was thrown into further disorder. In response, the U.S. Military Government began to arrest Communist Party members, forcing Pak Hon-yong to seek sanctuary in North Korea. Ultimately, the shelving of the Korean problem by the Allied powers during World War II was one of the reasons for the chaos that occurred after Korea was liberated from Japanese rule. Moreover, the appointment of leaders in exile with limited connections to the homeland (Syngman Rhee and Kim Il-sung) led to the formation of two separate Koreas in 1948 and served in part as a catalyst for the Korean War in 1950. After the economic turmoil caused by the Korean War, Japan entered a period of economic growth triggered by the wartime U.S. military purchases of materiel and began to rearm, as the politics of the region changed and the United States altered its policy on the occupation.

## Ambiguous relations between Japan and China

Japan and China had been engaged in full-scale war since 1937, before the outbreak of World War II in Europe. Over a period of eight years, China's key cities were occupied by the Japanese Army, and China sustained enormous human and material damage in the war.[23] With this in mind, one would have expected China, as a victor, to request stringent compensation and to exact retaliation. As it turned out, however, a strangely cooperative relationship began to develop between Japan and China from August 15 onward. Unlike the Japanese armies in Southeast Asia and the Pacific Islands, which had faced the full force of the Allied troops, the China Expeditionary Army retained a large presence of around one million soldiers and suffered minimal casualties. Dealing with the relatively intact China Expeditionary Army was an important task for Chiang Kai-shek. Although it was necessary to disarm swiftly the Japanese soldiers and repatriate them to the Japanese islands, the Chinese (Nationalist) Army was inferior in military strength and lacked the capacity to complete this task alone. Furthermore, the Nationalists' conflict with the Communist Party had already soured the atmosphere and Chiang's KMT government faced numerous problems in terms of securing social order and restoring the economy.

Japan's defeat was confirmed on August 15, when Emperor Hirohito's announcement of Japan's acceptance of the Potsdam Declaration was broadcast over the radio. At the same time, Chiang Kai-shek delivered a speech and spoke of "rewarding hatred with virtue" and cautioned against taking revenge on the Japanese. His altruistic stance was motivated by the complex circumstances that existed in China at the time. Above all, Chiang was pragmatic and strongly aware of the presence of the China Expeditionary Army and the strong military power it still could muster, even after the surrender broadcast. Meanwhile, the Japanese Imperial Army in China, which had expected to suffer due to the defeat, was surprised by the benevolent treatment afforded by the Chinese; former imperial soldiers began to admire Chiang's character in a reversal of the atmosphere that had prevailed during the war. Subsequently, in order to lend full support to the reconstruction of China under Chiang Kai-shek, the former Imperial Japanese Army formulated the General Plan for Dealing with China Immediately after the Establishment of Peace, which involved a policy of leaving behind Japanese technicians in China, using them to demonstrate Japan's postwar cooperative attitude (these men were known as *ryūyō* in Japanese, or "detained to be employed").[24]

Chiang likewise attached importance to the requisition of Japanese assets and the retention of technicians that were essential for postwar Chinese recovery.[25] During this period, China also experienced great difficulties in its international relations. First, with respect to Manchuria, China was forced to conclude the Sino-Soviet Treaty of Friendship and Alliance (signed on August 14, the day on which Japan accepted the Potsdam Declaration) as a result of the Soviet Union's entry into the war against Japan (August 9) and reluctantly approved the privileges obtained by the Soviets at the Yalta Conference. In addition, due to the terms of the treaty, China effectively approved the independence of the Mongolian People's Republic in a reversal of its previous policy. Furthermore, even after Japan accepted the Potsdam Declaration, the Soviet Army continued its military operations in Manchuria and advanced from Mongolia to Beijing. The Soviet Army also frequently transgressed the border with China in its western regions.[26]

Although the Soviet Union attempted to capitalize on the Japanese defeat by securing its superiority in terms of its military and diplomatic relations with China, at the same time China was also involved in a dispute with the United Kingdom concerning the seizure of Hong Kong. China took on the task of controlling Hong Kong and disarming the Japanese forces that had occupied it during the war. However, fearing that this might lead to the recovery of Hong Kong by the Chinese, the United Kingdom dispatched a warship and completed the handover before the Chinese Army arrived on the island. The actions of the United Kingdom humiliated Chiang Kai-shek, and his resulting resentment was directed at the United States, along with his dissatisfaction with the situation in Manchuria.[27] Although Chiang's dissatisfaction with the United States deepened around this time, the

United States refrained from intervening in China's complex domestic problems. Washington's primary concern at that time was to swiftly repatriate its own forces, and it had no intention of becoming deeply involved in China, a country that was on the brink of civil war.[28] Therefore, the United States did not interfere in international boundary and political control disputes surrounding areas such as Manchuria and Hong Kong. The United States sided with the British and sought to appease China instead.

From the moment of the Japanese surrender, China had faced significant obstacles in the sphere of international relations. As these events unfolded, the former Japanese Imperial Amy and the Chinese Nationalist Government, which were once fierce rivals, quickly converged and an unexpectedly amicable relationship emerged between China and Japan. Cautious of this improved cooperative relationship, the United States argued strongly to end the retention of Japanese in China. Regardless, the KMT continued to retain Japanese officers as the extent of their cooperation increased, ranging from technical assistance with transfers of industrial plants and social infrastructure in zones occupied by the Japanese Army to the supply of military advisers for the Kuomintang Army.[29] As this was going on, the Chinese Communist Army expanded its rule in areas where the Nationalist Government had yet to take control. In these areas, the Chinese Nationalists approved of the Japanese Army's efforts to fight back against the communists.[30] As the cooperative relationship extended to the military sphere, the Japanese Army became involved in the Chinese Civil War, with many Japanese soldiers participating in the war on both the nationalist and communist sides. A special case was that of Shanxi Province, where the Japanese First Army (2,600 soldiers, including civilians) joined ranks with KMT General Yan Xishan, who had formed an independent sphere of influence in the province, and fought against the Chinese Communist Army until 1949. The improved relationship between the former Japanese Imperial Army and the Kuomintang may also have led to the failed prosecution of Japanese Commander-in-Chief Okamura Yasuji for war crimes. The relationship between the two parties continued even after Chiang Kai-shek fled to Taiwan upon losing the Chinese Civil War, when a group of Japanese military advisers known as the *Baituan* (*Paidan* in Japanese and the "White Group" in English) lent their support to the Taiwanese Army (the Kuomintang Army).[31]

As the war ended, nothing changed more than the Japanese public's evaluation of Chiang Kai-shek. Despite being a target of hate up until Japan's defeat, Chiang Kai-shek was now exalted to such a degree that he was considered an outstanding leader after the war. This evaluation continued during his rule after fleeing with remnants of his KMT troops to Taiwan, when the Cold War began in earnest. Chiang became the ideological backbone of Japan's political support of Taiwan as a member of the international liberal camp. However, this favorable view of Chiang also restricted Japan's ability to see beyond its own narrow confines and consider options regarding its policy toward the communist People's Republic of China.[32] More problematic still was the fact that the Japanese people failed to recognize the true significance of Taiwan's liberation from Japanese colonial rule as a result of this Cold War mentality.

Due to the Chinese Nationalist Army's late arrival in Taiwan, Taiwan was returned to China on October 25, more than two months after Japan's defeat. Japan had ruled Taiwan for fifty years, and because Taiwan had modernized under the tutelage of the Japanese empire, its people (those who had lived in Taiwan before the Kuomintang-related immigration wave) had developed a specific set of cultural values and a way of life that were different from those of the mainland Chinese (who migrated there after World War II). When these world views clashed after Taiwan was returned to China, antagonism grew between the two groups, and this developed into the wide-scale political oppression of the Taiwanese following the February 28 Incident in 1947. Subsequently, the conflict between mainland Chinese (*waishengren* in the Chinese language) and the local inhabitants (*benshengren* in Chinese), who now proclaimed their identity as Taiwanese, became institutionalized. This sequence of events marked a historical tragedy for the native Taiwanese, and this relationship was closely related to Japan's colonial rule of the island. The Japanese were relatively unaware of these internal Taiwanese rifts, and, due to the exigencies of the Cold War era, most Japanese attempted to understand Taiwan only by seeing it within a simplistic paradigm that reduced the situation to a conflict between the Communist Party and the Kuomintang. In this way, Japan developed a telescoped view of China and Taiwan in the postwar period, yet the reasons for this can be found in the fact that the Sino-Japanese War itself was not appraised in its entirety because of the speed at which Sino-Japanese relations had improved during the immediate postwar period.

## Conclusion

The decline of the Japanese empire significantly altered the political landscape and international relations of East Asia, and this impact continued to be felt for a long time afterwards, arguably leading to the formation of the People's Republic of China in 1949 and causing the Korean War in 1950. In this sense, World War II in East Asia cannot be understood without considering the developments that led up to the Chinese Civil War and the Korean War. However, in seemingly inverse proportion to the significance of the Japanese empire's decline, the awareness of the situation in East Asia among the Allied powers was limited and their vision for a postwar regional order was ambiguous at best. It can be argued that these knowledge gaps further exacerbated East Asia's postwar climate.

The United States focused exclusively on the war against Japan, and it was inconsistent in its policy toward China. It also failed to develop a vision for East Asia after the fall of the Japanese empire, even though it had some clearly defined goals for Japan proper. The United Kingdom's only concern was restoring its extensive suzerain–colony relationships that had existed before the war. The Soviet Union did not envisage the growth of communism in East Asia but acted only in its own national interests, while China lacked the capacity to participate in the formation of a regional order from the outset.

Against the backdrop of these different Allied interests, it was ultimately the Soviet Union that destroyed the traditional order in East Asia and that had the greatest influence on what was to replace it. Indeed, it was even more influential than the United States in this regard. In the immediate postwar period, links were established between Soviet territories in the Far East and North Korea, Manchuria, Sakhalin, and the Kuril Islands, and a sphere of human and material exchange emerged in Northeast Asia. In short, the East Asian regional order that had developed with the expansion of the Japanese empire at the end of the nineteenth century made way for a postwar Northeast Asian order that centered on the Soviet Union. However, under the Cold War structure, this regional order became insular in nature and in effect narrowed the sphere in which the people of the region could migrate, a sphere that had been very active in East Asia since the turn of the nineteenth century. This order began to crumble with the fall of the Berlin Wall in 1989 but the Korean Peninsula remains divided and the conflict between China and Taiwan is still unresolved.

The impact and consequences of World War II in East Asia were vastly different from the impact and consequences of World War II in Europe. Clarifying the essential differences enables us to reconsider World War II not only from a European perspective but also from a world history perspective that includes Asia.

## Notes

1 "Reflection on Last Week September 1945," in *Chiang Kai-shek Diaries*, Hoover Institution Archives, Stanford University, No. 2006C37.

2 Kim Gu, *Hakuhan isshi: Kim Gu jijoden* (Heibonsha, 1973), pp. 300–302. The Provisional Government of the Republic of Korea was formed when members of the independence movement defected to Shanghai after being suppressed during the March 1, 1919 movement that occurred throughout the Korean Peninsula. After the Second Sino-Japanese War, the defectors moved to Chongqing and were placed under the protection of the Nationalist Government of the Republic of China. (Unless otherwise noted, all Japanese books are published in Tokyo.)

3 U.S. Department of State, Foreign Relations of the United States (FRUS), Diplomatic Papers, *The Conference at Cairo and Tehran*, 1943, pp. 399–404.

4 Winston S. Churchill, *The Second World War, Vol.5: Closing the Ring* (Boston: Houghton Mifflin, 1951), pp. 328–334. Churchill's lack of enthusiasm for the Cairo Conference and low evaluation of China are apparent in his memoirs.

5 See the following source for a detailed discussion of the Potsdam Conference: FRUS, *The Conference of Berlin (The Potsdam Conference)*, 1945, Vol. II, 1960.

6 For a detailed discussion of Operation Ichigō, see The Defense Research and Training Institute, the Defense Agency, *Senshi sōsho ichigō sakusen*, Vols. 1–3 (Asagumo shimbunsha, 1967–1969). Emperor Hirohito expected that the success of this operation would create an opportunity for peace negotiations with the United States.

7 See the following source for a detailed discussion of the conflict between China and the United States regarding the right of command in the Chinese Theater and the removal of General Stilwell: Barbara W. Tuchman, *Stilwell and the American Experience in China, 1911–45* (New York: Russell & Volkening, 1971); J. W. Stilwell, *The Stilwell Papers* (New York: William Sloane Associates, 1948).

8 See the following source for a detailed discussion of the expansion of the Red Army in northern China: The Defense Research and Training Institute, the Defense Agency, *Senshi sōsho hokushi no chiansen* (Asagumo shimbunsha, 1971).

9 See the following source for a detailed discussion on the Governor-General of Korea's response before and after the defeat and his negotiations with the American Army:

Katō Kiyofumi

Yamana Mikio, *Chōsen sōtokufu shūsei no kiroku–shūsen zengo ni okeru chōsen jijō gaiyō* (Yūhō kyōkai, 1956).

10 The Defense Research and Training Institute, the Defense Agency, *Senshi sōsho, kantōgun 2* (Asagumo shimbunsha, 1974), p. 378.

11 The most important task during the Soviet Union's advancement into the Far East was securing the Liaodong Peninsula, whereas the Korean Peninsula offered little strategic or economic benefit. This situation had remained unchanged since the days of the Russian Empire.

12 See the following source for an outstanding account of the United States' views on Korea and the confusion of postwar occupation: Bruce Cumings, *The Origins of the Korean War: Liberation and the Emergence of Separate Regimes, 1945–1947* (Princeton, NJ: Princeton University Press, 1981).

13 Dean Rusk with Richard Rusk and Daniel S. Papp, *As I Saw It* (New York: W.W. Norton, 1990), p. 124; FRUS, 1945, Vol. 6, p. 1039.

14 Yo Un-hyung (1886–1947) went into exile to Shanghai as an independence activist and was a member of the Provisional Government. However, he returned to Korea due to his aversion to power struggles among members of the Provisional Government. He conducted progressive activities under the surveillance of the Governor-General and was held in high repute in Korea.

15 Kim Gu (1876–1949) was a nationalist and participated in the Provisional Government after the March 1st Movement. He became the president of the Provisional Government after Syngman Rhee was impeached over an internal power struggle and organized terrorist bombing attacks against Japan.

16 Pak Hon-yong (1900–1955) was a key member of the Korean Communist Party, which was established in May 1924. He remained undeterred despite being arrested twice and was famous as a leader of the Korean communist movement.

17 Kim, *Hakuhan isshi*, pp. 302–303.

18 Morita Yoshio, *Chōsen shūsen no kiroku: beiso ryōgun no shinchū to nihonjin no hikiage* (Gannando shoten, 1964), pp. 67–72.

19 The history of Kim Il-sung (1912–1994) is somewhat obscure. After the March 1st Movement was suppressed, the Korean Independence Movement group was divided into two camps, the members of the Provisional Government in exile in Shanghai and an anti-Japan partisan camp that engaged in guerilla activities in Manchuria and the border regions. Kim Il-sung belonged to the latter camp and joined the Chinese Communist Party branch of the anti-Japanese organization after the 1931 Manchurian Incident. However, this group gradually weakened while fighting the Japanese, and, in 1940, Kim escaped to the Soviet Union and was assigned to a unit in the Soviet Red Army before he was sent back to North Korea on September 19, following the Japanese surrender.

20 The 17th Area Army was a new army that was formed by the Empire of Japan to prevent the Allied forces from dividing the Korean Peninsula and mainland Japan at the time of the homeland defense war, and it was assigned to the territory south of the 38th and headquartered in Keijō (Seoul). Since the army did not engage in combat, it surrendered without having incurred casualties and retained approximately 230,000 troops.

21 Nagao Shosaku, leader of the Communications Division of the Japanese Korean Army, *Chōsen no jōkyō hōkoku*, The National Institute for Defense Studies Military History Research Center, No. Bunko/Yuzu/175.

22 Syngman Rhee (1875–1965) participated in Korean independence activities from the end of the 19th century and traveled to the United States in 1904, where he studied at Harvard University and Princeton University and continued to press for Korean independence from his base in the United States. Although Rhee was the first "president" of the Provisional Government of the Republic of Korea in Shanghai, he often acted self-righteously and was impeached in 1925 while he lived in exile in America.

23 Over a period of fourteen years – when measured from the Manchurian Incident – China continued to suffer at the hands of the Japanese Army.

24 Inaba Masao, *Okamura Yasuji taishō shiryō, jō* (Hara shobō, 1970), pp. 10–23.

25 September 19 and October 16, 1945, in *Chiang Kai-shek Diaries*, No. 2006C37.

26 For a detailed discussion of Sino-Soviet relations, see Chinese Ministry of Foreign Affairs, ed., *Waijiaobu dangan congshu – jiewulei*, di erce "zhongsu guanxijuan" (Taipei: Chinese Ministry of Foreign Affairs, 2001).

27 August 16, 18, 22, and 26, 1945, in *Chiang Kai-shek Diaries*, No. 2006C37.

28 See the following source for a detailed discussion of U.S.–China relations in the aftermath of the war and subsequent changes: Albert C. Wedemeyer, *Wedemeyer Reports!* (New York: The Devin-Adair Company, 1958). It is important to note that the United States officially changed its policy regarding China in December 1945 to focus on mediating between the Kuomintang and the Chinese Communist Party and actively support the Nationalist Government.

29 By June 24, 1946, the number of army officials and civilians retained by the Nationalist Government were 829 and 36,521, respectively (27,883 of whom were formally retained: 27,107 in Taiwan, 6,955 non-formal, and 1,683 others). Inaba, *Okamura Yasuji taishō shiryō*, p. 77.

30 "Shina hakengun shūsen nikansuru kōshō kiroku tsuzuri," in *Fukuin kankei shiryō shūsei 3*, ed. Hamai Kazufumi (Yumani shobō, 2009).

31 See Barak Kushner, "Ghosts of the Japanese Imperial Army: The 'White Group' (Baituan) and Early Post-War Sino-Japanese Relations," *Past and Present*, vol. 218, suppl. 8 (*Transnationalism and Contemporary Global History*) (2013): pp. 117–150.

32 The deeply rooted pro-Taiwanese faction of the Japanese Liberal Democratic Party had, as its ideological base, a sense of gratitude for the generous attitude shown by China after Japan's defeat in the war, which was typified by Chiang's speech about "rewarding hatred with virtue." See the following source for a detailed discussion of the logic employed by this particular camp: Kaya Okinori, *Senzen sengo hachijūnen* (Keizai ōraisha, 1976). In addition, see the following source for a discussion on their recovery during the restoration of diplomatic ties between Japan and the People's Republic of China: Fujita Yoshirō, *Kiroku Shiina Etsusaburō gekan* (Shiina Etsusaburō Memorial Publishing Foundation, 1982). See Kanda Yutaka in Chapter 10 of this volume, where he discusses Shiina's role in postwar Japan.

# 2 "Deimperialization" in early postwar Japan

## Adjusting and transforming the institutions of empire

*Kawashima Shin (translated
by Takashima Asako)*

This chapter examines the processes through which the Japanese empire transformed its imperial institutions after its defeat in World War Two into ones that
were consistent with managing a modern nation-state. The issues surrounding what
individuals within the empire experienced while being demilitarized and "deimperialized," if such a term can be used for Japan, as its colonies were unilaterally
confiscated by the Americans and European former colonial powers, are fascinating and important historical tropes. The course of these changes also traces how
Japanese academic discussions in the immediate postwar were both bequeathed to
posterity and repressed in subsequent generations.[1]

According to Yamamuro Shinichi, a leading Japanese historian of the Japanese
empire, the modern empire takes the shape of a "mother country" that maintains
a special set of relationships with all sorts of polities and ethnicities outside of its
home borders, which it then has to manage remotely.[2] Decolonization, after Japan's
defeat, involved two simultaneous processes: "both the renunciation by the nation-
empire (*kokumin teikoku*) of its existence as an empire, and the granting of independence of the former colonies through the acceptance of the mother country's
own new existence as a nation-state. It is through these shifts that the destruction
of the nation-empire is completed."[3] Although the "nation-empire" (or "modern-
empire") seems to be in opposition to the principle of the nation-state, it does in
fact emanate from it. In Japan's post-imperial case, colonies did not revert back to
their previous form of governance; instead, they turned into new nation-states in
their own progressive forms. However, when a colony – a by-product of the nation-
empire – becomes independent, a paradox emerges in that the colony now has to
also transform into a nation-state. Imperial dissolution foisted such immediate
burdens on Japan's former colonies.

Generally speaking, when a territory is "decolonized" and becomes a nation-
state, it gains independence when its former guardian – the nation-empire – collapses,
and it is then recognized by other nation-states as a sovereign state in its own
right. At the same time, the mother country also has to transform into a nation-
state, and it is obliged to reorganize its diplomatic relationships with its former
colonies.[4] These procedures are immensely complex and interrelated and often
require long periods of reform. In this sense, decolonization contains two different

facets. The former might represent decolonization in the narrow sense, the latter in the broad sense. The relationship between the two aspects comes into sharp relief in a term frequently used in Japan (*shokuminchi sekinin*), which translates perhaps best as "a sense of responsibility toward former colonies," in a similar way as seen with Britain's relationship with Hong Kong or perhaps France's with Algeria.

The question of how history treats the relationship between Japan and its former colonies is an important one. As Mitani Taichirō has pointed out, "some historians have examined aspects of colonization, but consideration of the process of decolonization and the particular effects it had for Japan has been rare," as Barak Kushner also pointed out in the introduction to this volume.[5] The Japanese people appear to have rather limply accepted decolonization, that is to say, the separation of Japan's colonies and dependencies from the former empire; according to Mitani, however, this was not a conscious decision. Scholars have tended not to pay enough attention to the attendant problems – which are, as he emphasizes, "different from [the problems of] demilitarization."[6] Because demilitarization and decolonization were treated as essentially the same process in immediate postwar Japan, Mitani writes, "[D]ecolonization was [always seen as] the problem of the other country; it was never considered as something that belonged to the experience of Japan itself."[7] Nevertheless, Japanese researchers have not completely neglected the issue of deimperialization and decolonization. Ikeda Toshio, a scholar of Taiwan studies, for example, has explored the Japanese historical assessment of colonial rule after the uprising against the Chinese National government in Taiwan in 1947, known as the February 28 Incident (or the 2.28 Incident).[8] The incident was a moment when native born ethnic Chinese residents of Taiwan (those who had grown up under Japanese colonial rule) grew distraught over what they perceived as unfair political treatment and economic exploitation and rioted against the newly installed Chinese Nationalist administration:

> There are several reasons why Taiwan studies in Japan never got off the ground, or at least lagged behind after World War Two. One is that Japanese [researchers] have been unable to overcome their [prewar] feelings of superiority over Taiwan. The field of New Taiwan studies could only be formed by taking into account issues surrounding [Japanese] social responsibility [for its colonization of Taiwan]. Take the general evaluation of the February 28 Incident, for example . . . [T]he prevailing view in Japan is that the Taiwanese people preferred the rule of the Japanese Governor-General [during the colonial era] to that of the Chinese Nationalist (KMT) government. Such a view adds an element of ambivalence to the Japanese rule of Taiwan and suggests that Japanese people might be absolved of any blame in their colonization projects. In turn, this meant or encouraged a positive interpretation of Japanese colonialism, when the incident occurred two years after the end of the war, or at least it allowed an ambivalence in Japan to interpret this incident to its own historical advantage.[9]

Few researchers have made conscious attempts to examine the trends in academic discourse concerning the colonial period, but this kind of critical awareness remains something of an exception within Japanese research circles as a whole. The number of studies on the topic of decolonization and on the relations between Japan and its former colonies, Taiwan, Korea, and the puppet state of Manchukuo, remains limited.[10] Recently, however, a few in-depth investigations on the subject have emerged.[11] Among them, Wakabayashi Masahiro's work is probably the most important among investigations into deimperialization. In his highly theoretical analysis, Wakabayashi separates the process of deimperialization into three distinct stages:

Stage 1: Political and military dismantlement and reorganization of the colonies

Stage 2: Establishment of diplomatic relationship between mother country and new countries [former colonies]

Stage 3: Emergence of "negative legacy" problems concerning the colonial rule of former colonies[12]

Japan as a nation has yet to enter the third stage and is thus still plagued by serious gaps in how it comprehends its own national history.

At the same time, the question of how much research has actually been conducted within each of Wakabayashi's stages remains a potent question. A number of studies have looked at experiences in the first stage, for example the work of Irie Keishirō, who was originally a journalist but studied Japan's peace treaties of the same period.[13] However, this interest did not last long. The second stage coincided with the "two Chinas" era in postwar history, particularly after 1972 when Japan withdrew recognition from the Republic of China (ROC, or known more commonly now as Taiwan) and established diplomatic relations with the People's Republic of China (PRC, or mainland China). This political shift gave rise to a significant number of studies concerning postwar Japanese foreign policy toward Asia and related to the Cold War. The work of Miyagi Taizō is particularly salient here because his research about Japan's foreign policies toward East Asia are the latest to employ a full range of declassified public documents from the postwar era.[14] The third stage is the one we find ourselves in today, with a growing number of academic and political studies trying to more objectively shed light on the darker and understudied aspects of the Japanese colony experience in the prewar and wartime eras.[15]

In order to more broadly investigate this legacy of colonialism and the attendant processes of decolonization, this chapter will analyze a selection of systemic issues – legal, administrative, common practices. – These shape and influence how a political territory becomes independent and what is actually entailed in the formation of a new relationship with the mother country. The political and military dismantlement, and reorganization of the colonies as administrative and legal spheres of their own, appear to be simple processes at the higher planes of diplomacy and military engagement. However, at the root level the physical and psychological restructuring of all areas that affect daily life – such as professional certification; medical insurance, pensions, and the like; regulations that oil the wheels of a modern state – were multi-faceted and often times not reorganized in an equal or satisfactory manner. As such, the process of decolonization for the Japanese and former Japanese imperial subjects also reflects their lingering feelings of still being in control of the colonies, in a hierarchical relationship, not dissimilar perhaps to the entangled U.S.–Puerto Rico relationship or the French–Algerian situation in the 1960s.

## Institutional "deimperialization": the three steps from empire to nation-state

The Japanese empire always maintained a plurality of institutions that were legally tied to the geography of place, both on the part of the main islands (like the island of Hokkaido, which had its own administration separate from other parts of Japan) and in its colonies. Some of Japan's colonies were held under a League of Nations mandate issued during World War One (for example, the Marshall Islands), while others came in a variety of other forms, such as the South Manchuria Railway Zone in Manchuria, the Kwantung Leased Territory (which included Lushun (Port Arthur) and Dalian), and Japanese concessions in Tianjin or Hankou since the nineteenth century. At the end of World War Two, a consensus was reached among the Allies that all of these different legally operated territories would gain sovereignty as new nation-states. Immediately after the defeat, following a pattern that had already been long established in Japan, the colossal discord and mistrust that were rife between Japan's Ministry of the Army, Ministry of the Navy, and other central government ministries that were in charge of certain aspects of colonial management, not to mention the offices and departments of governor generals and ministries that were directly connected with colonial rule, began to tussle for control of the postwar operation of this web of administrative systems. What this meant at the base level was that, for example, someone studying to be a doctor in Taiwan who had already obtained the correct state certification there would not be allowed to merely transfer that status to Japan proper after the war but would have to apply for recertification or study in further coursework. The same was true for lawyers and many other professions – if not all professions necessary for the proper functioning of a modern state. In addition, pensions, insurance, and the sundry accoutrements of state protection and/or support were legally distinct within each zone of Japan's empire. No one legal requirement or protection was standard, and so the post-empire became the moment in time to rearrange all of these minute details so that colonies and Japan could operate as separate and independent states on their own.

Another distinctive feature of Japan's empire was the variegated status held by the governing institutions within these territories. The empire was composed of a multitude of imperial subjects and sojourners who all had different rights and obligations – not everyone was equal. In the Army there was a hierarchy among soldiers; for example, the conscription system was created in a way that made the draft mandatory for eligible Japanese males of a certain age but not for Koreans until 1944 and not for Taiwanese until 1945. Imperial military service was essentially compulsory only for ethnic Japanese even though both Taiwanese and Koreans were technically and legally classified as "Japanese" within the empire. These two groups enjoyed "Japanese" rights if they lived abroad, for example in China or Manchukuo, but not completely in the same manner as those who were ethnically "pure" Japanese. Due to the numerous territories and their various legal operating systems, the empire developed many almost Byzantine institutional structures. There were multiple agencies, often duplicating the same administrative work from colony to colony and in their relations with the mother country, where the imperial constitution was applied. These variations had an immense impact not only on daily life in different regions during the colonial era but also on how people were able to make a living, or were deprived of a livelihood, after the fall of the Japanese empire. At the end of the war, all of these layers were forced to flatten into a unified system. Imagine an octopus with the mother country as the main body and the eight arms as colonies or controlled territories. Historically, each arm was directly controlled by the head but also had a variety of obligations to it. The arms had a relationship with one another due to their direct connectedness to the head but remained somewhat separate from one another. But the octopus analogy is also a rich one because octopuses can jettison an arm in time of fright or flight and then that arm wiggles around a little bit longer, putting on a show so that the main body can flee a predator. Like an octopus losing its tentacles, at the end of the Second World War, Japan jettisoned its colonies. Their efforts to grapple with their newfound independence without a leading body – their wiggling – and the efforts of the body, in this case Japan, to figure out how to survive with many fewer arms, complete the aquatic analogy.

The jumble of changes in laws and regulations that affected both the decolonized and the Japanese people struck at the root level of daily existence. For example, the regulations pertaining to licenses for doctors or nurses differed between the mother country (Japan) and the colonies, as did financial regulations regarding savings and stocks, on the basis of discussions in Japan's National Diet. When imperial institutions have to reform to those of a nation-state, there are three possible patterns. In the first, an imperial institution is completely replaced by that of a nation-state agency. In the second, multiple and overlapping institutions in the empire might be merged into new unified institutions within the nation-state – and this might mean some downgrading of licensing, educational skills, or certification as they existed previously, compared to those of Japan. Or the state might institute a requalification exam or new certification process, requiring another examination or a process granting authorization. And, finally, institutions might be completely dismantled, leaving no historical record. By contrast, local hires formally employed by the various governor-generals of Japan, which were the formal administrative arms of colonial government, could find themselves out of work because their expertise was based on an agency that disappeared after the war, whereas Japanese high-level officials of the governor-general's offices might be able to work for the national Japanese government after decolonization without any institutional transformation. In some cases these institutions, which were unique to a specific colony, were also terminated because they were deemed unsuitable to the new nation-state.

One of the most complex issues, and contentious to this day, were the problems surrounding pensions, annuities, and mutual aid associations (*kyōsai kumiai*). These examples correspond to the first pattern of completely replacing colonial institutions with those of a nation-state. Because discussions about how to financially support imperial war veterans aroused some of the fiercest debates in Japan's National Diet at that time, pensions for Japanese repatriates from foreign countries (actually the former colonies or occupied territories), such as Manchukuo, Taiwan, and Korea, were not granted automatically, and this grew into a massive problem for Japan after the end of the war. How to deal with former soldiers' livelihoods and life security was of top priority precisely at this moment when the new nation-state (a recently failed empire) was at its weakest. In September 1949, Asaoka Nobuo, a member of Liberal Party (*Jiyūtō*) and the upper house, spoke about this postcolonial issue in the Diet, though obviously he did not necessarily frame it in those terms:

> I was pleased to learn that the previous committee decided to grant 37,000 yen to fund pensions.[16] However, when I travel through Japan for lectures and discussions, I frequently meet widows repatriated from Taiwan and the Korean peninsula, or elderly people with children who survived the war, who tell me that they feel abandoned by their nation and government.[17]

Five years after the end of war, negotiations were still ongoing about which ministry was actually in charge of Japan's social welfare.[18] This ambiguity was demonstrated in a speech by Yasuda Iwao, administrative vice-minister of health and welfare, on February 25, 1950, at the Committee of Health and Welfare in the Lower House.[19] At the same time, a great number of ministerial-level mutual aid associations were abolished.[20] The Navy's mutual aid society, which was under the aegis of the Ministry of Finance, was dissolved and reshaped into the Cooperative Insurance Association, which was later made into a public service corporation controlled by the Ministry of Health and Welfare. This made it possible to transfer the jurisdiction of all prewar cooperative insurance businesses to the Ministry of Health and Welfare through the Ministry of Finance. This is also why the Ministry of Health and Welfare wrote to the Ministry of Finance and requested more information on budgetary and legal measures at the time. Yasuda gave a roundabout response stating that his ministry would deal with it.[21] His move can be understood as an attempt to coordinate leadership on this issue, based on the assumption that prewar hierarchies and practices were to be maintained.[22] Clearly, the Ministry of Health and Welfare wanted the Ministry of Finance to arrange the delivery of these pensions. In any case, the prewar pension system of the colonies was also applied to returnees in the postwar after certain procedures were in place. The same issues applied to measures for savings and stocks, and there were negotiations to change the competent authorities. However, it should be noted that these systems were available only to those who held Japanese nationality and not to foreign nationals, who actually could have been yesterday's imperial subjects.

The second stage of dealing with crafting a nation-state out of an empire can be seen in the comments of Kuge Katsuji, a bureaucrat in the Ministry of Health and Welfare, when he spoke about the postwar problem concerning medical personnel qualifications in the upper house in October 1947:

> The medical systems that operated in Korea, Taiwan, Manchuria, mainland China and several southern countries were too different for us to be very concerned about how those who have returned from these countries are treated. . . . Particular medical systems in place in Japan's former overseas territories [*gaichi*], for example Southern Sakhalin, Korea and Taiwan, were different from that of the main islands [*naichi*] until the end of the war. This state of affairs has come about because those who had a license to practice medicine or dentistry on the Japanese mainland rarely practiced in overseas territories, so we put together another system for *gaichi* residents. This system was generally of a lower quality than in Japan proper. In Korea and Taiwan, as the population increased, so did the number of doctors. We tried to improve the quality of medical treatment in tandem with this. Sakhalin, on the other hand, had the same medical system as the *naichi*. However, licenses were given to doctors and dentists there on Sakhalin only for limited areas and duration, provided that they managed their own local practices. These medical systems specific to overseas territories – Manchuria and other places – were reformed as thoroughly as possible at the end of the war. We carefully assessed whether these practitioners were qualified to get a Japanese [*naichi*] license. [ . . . ] In comparison with doctors in mainland Japan, there is no denying that doctors in overseas territories were overall less capable. However, we took special measures to give Japanese licenses to those who did not own a local practice, and we also withdrew the limitation regarding areas and duration of practice in Korea, Taiwan and Manchuria. Now we find that doctors with their own local practices in Sakhalin and doctors and dentists who were in Korea, Taiwan, Manchuria and southern countries without their own practices have been left behind [meaning they have to retrain or face the loss of their professional standing].[23]

Kuge explained that he could not give proper Japanese licenses to doctors and dentists who had received their licenses and had work experience in the former colonies due to their lower professional abilities. Some members of Japan's parliament suggested increasing the scope of national qualifying examinations for medical practitioners, and some voiced objections to the view that doctors in the colonies had lesser skills. Put simply, they tried to liberalize, to a certain degree, the regulations to become a doctor in mainland Japan. In the end, efforts were made to loosen the regulations that pertained to mainland Japan.

For those who belonged to the third stage, repatriated judges, prosecutors, and attorneys, there is scant information and few extant materials. This leaves little room for any historical interpretation, but we do know that these individuals were systematically downgraded by one rung in the institutional hierarchy on their return to the *naichi*, the main islands of Japan.[24] It should be noted that those caught up in these readjustments were not only former colonial subjects in Taiwan and Korea but also people in the occupied territories, such as various parts of China and Southeast Asia, who were de facto ignored. Individuals had to be naturalized – to become Japanese citizens – in order to receive any Japanese government institutional assistance, whether to safeguard their savings in former imperial banks, retain military pensions, or gain access to healthcare benefits for atomic bomb survivors. Postwar family registration laws also did not apply to colonial subjects. In any case, the Japanese government guideline was to sever relations with former subjects who had not become Japanese citizens. In this sense, only those who were truly "Japanese" were eligible when multiple institutions in the empire were replaced with the standardized institutions of the new nation-state.[25]

How were former colonial subjects – Taiwanese and Koreans – treated in Japan after the war? From September 2, 1945 onward, these former colonial subjects came under what can be called transitional jurisdiction (*kizoku ga mitei*). As such, they received treatment different from that of the citizens of the Allied nations, who possessed certain privileges within the rationing system, or even that of the Japanese of the home islands, who had existed under the Imperial Constitution. (In the immediate postwar, occupied Japan was very short on foodstuffs, and so a rationing system was implemented). These ex-colonial nationals of Korea and Taiwan were referred to by a term coined by the American administration (General Headquarters, GHQ), *sangokujin*, or third-country persons. Japanese essentially still looked down on these former colonial subjects, even though their secondary class status had changed with the end of empire and they were still treated relatively poorly in postwar Japan. Araragi Shinzō details some of these problems in Chapter 4 of this volume about the impact of post-imperial migration in East Asia.

The issue about Taiwan's legal status was a matter of controversy. From October 25, 1945, when Taiwan was returned to the Republic of China (ROC), the KMT ruled it as its territory, and its inhabitants became ROC citizens. Two decrees issued in 1946 – the June 22 Measures on Settling the Nationality of Taiwanese Residents Abroad and the July 10 Directives on the Chinese Residents in Japan – spelled out the ways in which the Taiwanese could become ROC nationals. According to the latter directives, the Taiwanese residents in Japan who registered with the Chinese Mission (there was no embassy since technically Japan no longer had sovereignty over its domain during the occupation) were entitled to the same treatment as the ROC citizens. The Japanese authorities, however, defined this procedure merely as "registration"; their position was that the status of the Taiwanese could be determined only by a peace treaty.

The ambiguous status of Taiwanese nationals in Japan is in evidence in an analysis of several legal revisions pertaining to postwar Japan. A good example occurred in a 1949 lower house discussion about the "Cabinet Order on the Acquisition of Property by Foreign Nationals," which aimed to limit the acquisition of wealth by non-Japanese. The Minister of State for Economic and Fiscal Policy Aoki Takayoshi stated:

> I come now to the matter of the acquisition of wealth by foreign nationals, and the Cabinet Order enacted according to the SCAP (Supreme Commander for the Allied Powers) note on January 14. The real issue here lies with the definition of the term "non-Japanese." While it is obvious that all foreigners can be defined as non-Japanese, does this term include the people of Korea, Taiwan and overseas Chinese [Taiwanese who had already registered themselves as citizens of the Republic of China]? According to international law, nationality should be determined upon the conclusion of a peace treaty with Japan. In the meantime, international law dictates that these people be legally treated as Japanese unless they have obtained another nationality or have indicated their intention to do so. In this Cabinet Order, therefore, people who had Japanese nationality at the end of the war, as of September 2, 1945, and who have lived in Japan ever since, are treated as Japanese nationals. In contrast, those who since September 2, 1945 have obtained a foreign nationality, or certificates of alien registration issued by foreign missions approved/accredited by SCAP, are to be seen as foreigners or as having the same status as foreigners. Article 2(1) of this Cabinet Order was conceived with exactly the above in mind – overseas Chinese or those who have obtained alien registration certificates via a Chinese delegation are treated as foreigners. On the other hand, those who do not have such certificates are treated in a similar way to Japanese subjects.[26]

In other words, Taiwanese residents in Japan were divided into two groups: those who had an alien registration certificate and those who did not; their international status, in the meantime, was left to be determined by a peace treaty. Put simply, the legal status of the Taiwanese was to be decided by a future Japan–ROC peace treaty. This was a phenomenon linked to what can be called alternate decolonization. For a Taiwanese in Japan at war's end, there were but two solutions to this problem: choose "registration" to resolve your status or become "Japanese."

## Taiwan: a colony consigned to oblivion

In this section, I return to the discussion of how Japan deimperialized, using Taiwan as a case study. The first phase of change between Japan and Taiwan, which involved the reconstruction of diplomatic relations, took place during the 1950s.[27]

Relations during the period were characterized by a string of agreements, such as the trade agreement drafted in 1950 (and concluded by the GHQ during the American occupation of Japan), the Treaty of Taipei 1952, and the Japan–ROC Trade agreement in 1953, as well as the start in 1955 of the exchange of students on government scholarships. This era also witnessed the KMT policy to Sinicize Taiwan and to spread Chinese language, ideas, and the implantation of Nationalist ideology. However, the eradication of Japanese culture from Taiwan's domestic sphere did not necessarily mean that the KMT did not wish to benefit from Japanese higher education or technological training.

At this point, Taiwan had retreated from the world stage in two senses. First, the revamping of Japanese institutions after the war was aimed to benefit only the full Japanese nationals, while the former colonial subjects were not covered. Second, because the ROC ruled Taiwan and had already passed through the first phase with Japan, Taiwan itself was left out of the picture. In a sense, at first, the Taiwanese went unnoticed in the transformation of Japanese institutions, and, secondly, they were neglected in ROC politics.

Moreover, the aboriginal Taiwanese (those who lived in Formosa during the era of colonization and before the arrival of the Chinese Nationalists) were completely forgotten due to their previous role as subjects of imperial Japan; these native people were not seen to have played a major role in Taiwanese history. This so-called surrogate-decolonization is a crucial feature that has to be taken into consideration in any discussion of deimperialization in Taiwan. In South Korea, the Korean people built a nation-state by themselves to remake diplomatic relations with Japan, as described by Katō Kiyofumi in Chapter 1 of this volume and by Park Jung Jin concerning North Korea in Chapter 11. However, the original inhabitants of Taiwanese were not given the authority to build their nation; the ethnic Chinese KMT who fled to the island after the Chinese Nationalist loss on the mainland, not the actual Taiwanese residents, eventually concluded the peace treaty with Japan.

The blame for consigning the topic of Taiwan or Taiwanese nationals to oblivion should not lie squarely with the political and legal establishments in Japan. Taiwan was also neglected in the Japanese press and indeed by the academic community as a whole, so that the issues surrounding the empire and Japanese imperialization did not even become a topic of interest for academic researchers for a considerable length of time until about 1971, when mainland China's return to international politics once again highlighted Taiwan's dubious international status. Liberal and progressive intellectuals critical of the Japanese government did not discuss Taiwan because they either supported the socialist politics of the PRC or were generally anti-U.S. The Republic of China in Taiwan stood as a bulwark against the communists, so the Japanese scholars did not consider it worthy of examination. It was not only the Japanese government that seemed to forget the situation of non-Japanese nationals in Japan, who were a direct legacy of Japan's imperialist adventures before the war. Liberals, who criticized the government and advocated peace and disarmament for postwar Japan, also seemed to prefer to leave relations with Japan's former colonies, particularly Taiwan, out of their discussions.

Takeuchi Yoshimi and Maruyama Masao, two greats of the postwar Japan intellectual world, rarely paused for a moment to discuss the Taiwan issue, though readers can see, in Satō Takumi's Chapter 13 of this volume, a more detailed analysis of the impact that the left wing magazine, *Sekai* (The World), wielded in Japan through these thinkers. Japanese conservatives, on the other hand, emphasized "the debt of gratitude owed to Chiang Kai-shek" for the Chinese Nationalists' benevolent treatment of Japanese in postwar mainland China and often talked of Taiwan (ROC) as synonymous with Chiang Kai-shek. This was why liberal intellectuals were hesitant to debate the issue of Taiwan under the ROC.

This is not to say, however, that Japanese researchers completely neglected the issue of Japanese colonial rule. Some useful questions were asked, for example by Ikeda Toshio, who had been a scholar and editor in Taiwan during the colonial era. So, how were Taiwan and Taiwan studies, in fact, discussed in debates in postwar Japan? This issue is intimately related to the debates about decolonization (or lack thereof) within academic research in Japan on the question of empire and indeed the shape of debates surrounding Taiwan as they developed over the last few years. Immediately after the war, a number of researchers reviewed the Japanese rule of Taiwan, recording the final stages of colonial rule.[28] Scholars who repatriated from Taiwan – for example, Iwao Seiichi, Nakamura Takashi (faculty members of Taihoku University, the Japanese name for Taipei Imperial University), Miyamoto Nobuto and Ide Kiwata (in the employ of the Office of the Governor-General of Taiwan) – published papers on the erstwhile colony. Mukoyama Hirō described the history of the Taiwanese Nationalist movement in his works. However, despite such auspicious beginnings, academic discussion on the subject of Taiwan remained limited and fragmentary, and comparatively little was published thereafter.[29]

In 1949, Iwao Seiichi, a scholar of ancient and premodern Taiwanese history, had noticed that researchers were finally starting to pay attention to Taiwan. "Taiwan has been completely ignored in the postwar era and was previously known as the 'closed island' by the Dutch several hundred years ago," Iwao noted, in reference to the island being essentially shut off from outside contact. "However, due to the dramatic expansion of the Communists in mainland China, with the relocation of the Nationalist government to Taiwan, and the growing attention of the US and the UK [to matters Chinese], it seems that Taiwan has once again become the focus of attention."[30] Of course, it was the relocation of the Nationalist government to Taiwan that promoted it to increased academic scrutiny. Five years later, in 1954, historian Nakamura Takashi discussed Taiwanese history since the age of the island's discovery. Evaluating the 50 years of Japanese colonization, Nakamura offered a moderately positive opinion on the Japanese rule of Taiwan. According to Nakamura, when Japan took control of Taiwan:

> Japanese capital was still immature and incapable of completely dominating the market; Japan could not afford to be an imperialist and finance its own capitalism. However, it chose the path of imperialism, developing its ideology along the lines of pragmatic imperialism. Kabayama Sukenori,

Governor-General of Taiwan, held meetings with Qing Chinese Representative Li Jingfang concerning the handover of Taiwan and in June 1895 the Japanese began their administration. For the first few decades Taiwan remained a thorn in Japan's side with anti-imperial guerilla fighting and opposition to Japanese rule. Japan managed to restore public order and ensure peace in the society through a thorough purge of anti-Japanese guerrilla groups (*Dohi*). The spread of epidemic diseases was reduced through improving hygienic facilities, communications grew vastly, industrial development was encouraged. As a result of all these policies, production rates skyrocketed. The Japanese administrators also reformed the education system and advanced an assimilationist "Japan" policy toward the aboriginal Taiwanese population. At least on the surface, Taiwan had literally become what the Portuguese had once labeled it, "Ilha Formosa," or "beautiful island." After only a decade of Japanese rule, the historian and policymaker Takekoshi Yosaburō was already hailing the successes of Japanese colony policy; indeed, the effect of the institutional reforms in the fields of assets, weights and measures, as well as currency policies – all carried out by 1907 – had on the development of Taiwanese capitalism was remarkable. Despite these successes, the Japanese colonial rulers were still faced with a different set of challenges posed by class warfare and national liberation movements, such as the movement aiming at repealing Law No. 63, and the suffrage movement. There were demands for the establishment of indigenous institutions: Taiwan's own parliament (*Shinminkai*), the Taiwanese Cultural Association, the Taiwanese Farmer's Association, labor unions, and there were other instances of armed insubordination. The Japanese government's response to these movements was the policy of assimilation – the *kōminka* ["Japanization"] movement.[31] How should we evaluate fifty years of Japanese rule of Taiwan? A correct and fair evaluation will need more time.[32]

Nakamura used the vocabulary of the Marxist historians in his analysis, and while he showed an understanding that an accurate evaluation of Japan's colonial rule in Taiwan would only be possible with time, Nakamura acknowledged the fruits of this rule. His analysis became a model for research on the Japanese rule of Taiwan thereafter.[33]

Taiwanese area studies in postwar Japan took off with the establishment of the Institute of Developing Economies (IDE), under the Ministry of Economy, Trade and Industry (formerly MITI) in the late 1950s. By this time, Taiwan was stable as an Asian economy, which made it a worthy subject for research. Sasamoto Takeji, who led Japanese research on Taiwan at the IDE in the 1960s, analyzed Taiwanese economics from the standpoint of Japanese colonial rule. According to Sasamoto:

Even after fifty years of Japanese rule, Taiwan managed to develop a "national economy" in the space of a few postwar years. The Taiwanese economy is very unique in that it took shape in a context of enormous economic growth and political and economic predisposition toward Western Europe . . . The economic growth rate [of Taiwan] was outstanding among the countries of Southeast Asia. This growth was achieved through aggressive restructuring plans that built on the high economic development established under Japanese colonial authority.[34]

Sasamoto also noted, however, that "such astounding economic growth would not have been possible without the generous support and guidance from America."[35] He acknowledged that the prewar militarization and Japan's policies of colonizing Taiwan's economy were a problem. But they were not the only issue: "[d]ue to its massive scale and its unproductive nature, the war economy had started to become a burden to economic growth."[36] Sasamoto also drew attention to Taiwan's proclivity to depend economically and politically on the United States and noted that this dependence "could be the source of rigidity in the Taiwanese economy and create limitations in the Taiwanese market."[37] Thus, while he credited the colonial economic policies of the Japanese in Taiwan with providing a foundation that could be built on, Sasamoto also underlined the limits of this perspective.

Academic discussion and evaluation of the Japanese rule of Taiwan and the legacy of Japanese imperialism carried on along these lines until the end of the 1960s. From the 1970s, however, the discussion of Taiwan in magazines and academic journals underwent a complete transformation. This was an outgrowth of the normalization of diplomatic relations between Japan and China in 1972 and due to the fact that the liberal intellectuals and researchers, who had been ignoring Taiwan until then, cast a new glance at the island. Kobayashi Fumio, a researcher in modern and contemporary Chinese studies, pointed out that it was not acceptable to emphasize only the success of the Treaty of Taipei with Chiang Kai-shek, avoiding all the while any debate about Japanese responsibility for colonial rule. This, according to Kobayashi, would undermine Japanese and Chinese solidarity in the long term. According to Kobayashi, "a feature of Japanese colonial policy was forcing people into slavery through despotic subordination and the *kōminka* movement." "Most Japanese, "he added, "seemed to have forgotten these aspects of colonial rule, or at least were reluctant to allow it to become a topic of discussion." Kobayashi surmised that this was due to a feeling of lingering attachment on the part of Japanese leaders toward Taiwan and a tendency to see Taiwan in a completely different light from mainland China. He suspected that this was what lay behind the feeling of a great debt of gratitude to Chiang Kai-shek. Kobayashi also emphasized the importance of the 50 years of Japanese rule of Taiwan for Chinese history.[38] His perspective showed a concern not only with Japan's colonial responsibility but also with the normalization of diplomatic relations between Japan and China and with Taiwan's relations with the People's Republic of China.

Niijima Atsuyoshi, a leading scholar of Chinese studies, similarly insisted on discussing Taiwan as part of China, although in Japan it was believed to be "progressive" to detach Manchuria or Taiwan from China and not to dispute Taiwan's independence.[39] This way of viewing Taiwan as part of China, at the same time with drawing attention to the island, denied Taiwan its own, independent identity. In other words, just as it was neglected as part of the Republic of China in the past, this time Taiwan was being attached to the People's Republic of China and hence denied recognition as an independent country.

Under a subtle shift in the discussion about Taiwan in Japan, a prominent Taiwanese academic who worked at the Asian Economic Research Institute, Tai Kokuki (Tai Kuo-hui), thus responded to Niijima:

> I have thought about the Japanese understanding of Taiwan and Taiwan area studies in Japan as my theme . . . I believe that our side (Taiwanese) had an obligation to reconsider the Japanese rule of Taiwan too. The generations that came before mine did not. However, the Japanese did not do these things either. If we approached the issue properly, from both sides, it could be very productive, I believe . . . The Japanese academic community involved in Asian studies has not come up with any ideas that summarize or reorganize this academic legacy (which might be positive or negative) . . . It is possible to have a conference and scrutinize the ways in which Japanese academic predecessors viewed and studied China and Taiwan.

At first glance, Tai's argument looks in agreement with Niijima's view, but Tai is actually voicing his disagreement with the generally accepted view that "Japanese conservatives have considered Taiwan as their own problem since the early 1950s, whereas Japanese liberals have never considered it."

Japanese "responsibility for the war and colonial question" was also discussed by China specialist Ubukata Naokichi and writer Ozaki Hotsuki. The former claimed that "[a]s a researcher, I felt it might not be right so late after the war to consider war responsibility and the question about Japanese rule . . . However, even when the term 'war responsibility' was widespread in Japan, the responsibility for Japanese rule was rarely discussed."[40] Ozaki argued that the rupture between prewar and postwar created a "pragmatic interest in focusing on the positive sides of Japanese rule over Taiwan and other colonial territories. Thus, after August 15, 1945, it has become meaningless to shed light on alternative aspects, and the whole subject died as an area of research."[41] Ikeda Toshio pointed out that Japanese movies and pop songs were in fashion even after the war in Taiwan, and this created the illusion of Taiwanese nostalgia for Japanese rule. Moreover, this image influenced researchers, and they missed opportunities to reflect and to critically approach their subject. These Japanese views of the Taiwanese were first highlighted in discussions of Taiwanese researchers like Tai Kokuki.

These debates of the early 1970s occurred at the same time with the restoration of diplomatic ties between Japan and China (PRC) and the rupture of relations between Japan and Taiwan. These tectonic political changes pushed some Japanese scholars and journalists to rethink Taiwan as an entity separated from the ROC. However, the discussions were still confused. Academics such as

Kobayashi and Niijima discussed this transformation in relation to the People's Republic of China, and others, including researchers at the IDE, concluded that Japanese decolonization had been "meaningless." These attitudes demonstrated once again the low interest accorded to Taiwan in academic discussions and in the press, even though Iwao, Nakamura, and Sasamoto had penned initial important investigations in the 1950s and 1960s. As Niijima ironically pointed out, many "progressive" liberal intellectuals in the postwar era in Japan were anti-American and were much taken with left-wing thought, including Maoism. However, they seemed happy to turn a blind eye to the ongoing legacy of Japan's past imperialism in Taiwan.

## Conclusion

It is clear that the meaning and historical significance of Taiwan, both within imperial Japan and later for postwar democratic Japan, has gone through several iterations. At first the Japanese felt a responsibility toward former colonies, which meant that in addition to questions of decolonization issues of deimperialization had to be considered. This chapter has focused on the deimperialization of institutions, historians, and researchers as a novel way of analyzing the processes that empires undergo when they transform into states. Second, institutional rearrangements in the course of Japanese deimperialization can be categorized in three patterns in which the complicated Japanese empire modified itself and became a normal nation-state. As I hope to have shown, the status of Taiwanese and Korean nationals was overlooked and neglected in Japan in this process of redesigning postwar administrative arrangements. In postwar Japan, only Japanese people could be regarded as the proper citizens of the "nation" (*kokumin*), in a class that was distinct from former colonial subjects. The former colonial subjects were in effect not Japanese and occupied a grey area in the law that often took many years to reformulate, stretching to periods long after the Japanese empire itself had ceased to exist.

Finally, this institutional neglect of the existence and status of Taiwanese and Korean nationals within Japan was not limited only to legal discourse. Academic interest and research into the history of Japan's colonization of Taiwan and its imperial adventures were consigned to a tacit silence as well, and one could say that for the most part this pattern was mirrored in the social and political realms. Political conservatives in the early postwar valued relations with the ROC too much to want to over-evaluate Taiwan and the Taiwanese people; they preferred to emphasize Japan's "debt of gratitude to Chiang Kai-shek." On the other end of the political spectrum, liberals did not discuss Taiwan out of consideration toward mainland China because the political status of the island and its people was considered an overly sensitive topic. In this way, international politics and diplomacy contributed to the elision of former colonial peoples out of the social, political, legal, and academic discourses in Japan. In the early 1970s, some scholars tried to rank Taiwan lower than China in the context of normalization of diplomatic relations between Japan and China. However, this view also failed to look directly at the true facts about Taiwan and resulted in an overly complex and in the end whitewashed reading of the situation. In this sense, Japanese deimperialization, especially regarding Taiwan, has developed only very slowly and with many twists and turns to arrive where it is today.

## Notes

1 This chapter is a reworking of material from Kawashima Shin, "Sengo shoki nihon no seidoteki 'datsu-shokuminchika' to rekishi ninshiki mondai – taiwan o chūshin ni," in *Shokuminchi sekininron – datsu-shokuminchika no hikakushi*, ed. Nagahara Yōko (Aoki shoten, 2009). (Unless otherwise noted, all Japanese books are published in Tokyo.)

2 Yamamuro Shinnichi, "'Kokumin teikoku' ron no shatei," in *Teikoku no kenkyū – genri/ruikei/kankei*, ed. Yamamoto Yūzō (Nagoya daigaku shuppankai, 2003), p. 89.

3 Ibid., p. 125.

4 Komagome Takeshi, "Nihon no shokuminchi shihai to kindai – orikasanaru bōryoku," *Toreishi-zu* (Bessatsu shisō, 2001), vol. 2: pp. 159–197.

5 Mitani Taichirō, "Maegaki," in *Iwanami kōza kindai nihon to shokuminchi 8: ajia no reisen to datsu-shokuminchika*, ed. Mitani Taichirō (Iwanami shoten, 1993), p. viii.

6 Ibid., p. x.

7 Ibid., pp. vii–viii.

8 The Taiwan provincial administrative office suppressed the movement against the central government with force on February 28, 1947. More than 10,000 people were killed or injured, and this incident became the origin of conflict between *honshō-jin* (native-born Taiwanese, *benshengren* in Chinese) and *gaishō-jin* (someone who moved to Taiwan from the continent after the war, *waishengren* in Chinese).

9 Ikeda Toshio, "Taiwan kenkyū – mondai teiki," *Ajia keizai*, vol. 11, issue 6 (June 1970): p. 75.

10 Kawashima Shin, "Sengo nihon no taiwanshi kenkyū – seijishi/keizaishi o chūshin ni," in *Kokusai gakujutsu kentōkai ronbunshū "nihon no taiwan kenkyū,"* ed. Atō kankei kyōkai (Chūkaminkoku Gaikōbu, 2005).

11 Komagome Takeshi, for example, has raised the question of "incomplete decolonization" and discussed Japanese views of decolonization (deimperialization). Komagome, "Nihon no shokuminchi shihai."

12 Wakabayashi Masahiro, "Shiron: nihon shokumin teikoku 'datsu-shokuminchika' no shosō: sengo nihon – higashi ajia kankeishi e no ichi shikaku," in *Dongya shijiezhong de riben zhengzhi shehui tezheng*, ed. Huang Tzu-chin (Taipei: Center for Asia-Pacific Area Studies, Academia Sinica, 2008).

13 Irie Keishirō, *Nihon kōwa no kenkyū* (Itagaki shoten, 1951).

14 Miyagi Taizō, *Bandon kaigi to nihon no ajia fukki – amerika to ajia no hazama de* (Sōhisha, 2001) and his *Sengo nihon no ajia gaikō* (Minerva shobō, 2015).

15 Ōe Shinobu, Asada Ryōji, Mitani Taichirō, Gotō Ken'ichi, Kobayashi Hideo, Takasaki Sōji, Wakabayashi Masahiro, and Kawamura Minato, eds., *Iwanami kōza kindai nihon to shokuminchi* (Iwanami shoten, 2005); Yamamoto Taketoshi and Kōji Tanaka, eds., *Iwanami kōza "teikoku" nihon no gakuchi* (Iwanami shoten, 2006); Nihon no sensō sekinin shiryō sentā, ed., *Kikan sensō sekinin kenkyū* (Nihon no sensō sekinin shiryō sentā, 1993).

16 Pensions in Japan were abolished in 1946 and restored in 1953. Asaoka is not talking about general pensions but about special pensions for injured soldiers, or seriously ill patients. The amount of 37,000 yen was added to the budget of a "pension for ill patients." The government budget that year was 976 million yen.

17 National Diet of Japan, House of Councilors Special Committee on the Issue of Repatriation of Japanese Nationals Overseas, 5th cong., 3rd session, September 6, 1949.

18  For a history of this in English, see Lee Pennington, *Casualties of History: Wounded Japanese Servicemen and the Second World War* (Ithaca, NY: Cornell University Press, 2015).

19  National Diet of Japan, House of Representatives Committee of Health and Walfare, 7th cong., 5th session, February 15, 1950.

20  The list of agencies that required change or adaptation to the new nation-state framework is endless. To name only a few: the mutual aid associations of the Navy, Army, Ironworks, those for the Governor-General of the Taiwan Railway Staff, the Governor-General of Taiwan Communication Station and Communication Staff, the Governor-General of Taiwan Local Forestry Office, the Governor-General of the Taiwan Monopoly Bureau Clerical Staff, the Taiwan Police, the Governor-General of the Korea Railway Clerical Staff, the Governor-General of the Korea Communication Office Clerical Staffs, the Governor-General of the Korea Monopoly Bureau Clerical Staff, the Korea Police, the Kwantung Agency Communication Station Staff, the Kwantung Agency Police, the Sakhalin Agency Railway and the mutual aid associations of the Sakhalin Agency Post Office Clerical Staff.

21  National Diet of Japan, House of Representatives Committee of Health and Walfare, 7th cong., 5th session, February 15, 1950.

22  Ibid.

23  National Diet of Japan, House of Councilors Special Committee on the Issue of Repatriation of Japanese Nationals Overseas, 1st cong., 9th session, October 14, 1947.

24  The relationship between Japan and Taiwan was replaced with one formed by Japan and the Republic of China. For example, as trade in the empire between Japan and Taiwan transformed into foreign trade, only an international trade port could conduct this business and Taiwan was defined as "abroad" in Japan's postwar Customs Act.

25  However, some policy makers argued that the graduates of medical schools, such as Kōa igakukan or Tōa igakukan, which were established due to a shortage of doctors in Manchuria, should be able to take the national medical examination for repatriates, even if they were not naturalized. This was an exceptional action. The Japanese government recruited doctors in Taiwan for medical care in remote imperial sites and did not necessarily want them to be naturalized.

26  Aoki Takayoshi, Minister of State for Economic and Fiscal Policy, National Diet of Japan, House of Representatives, Committee of Foreign Affairs, 5th cong., 7th session, April 20, 1949.

27  Although traditional studies about the Peace Treaty between Japan and ROC focused only on the discussion about the two-China problem, I believe that the process in which Japan and the ROC ended the war and restored their relationship should be studied as a form of deimperializaion and peace. See Kawashima Shin, Shimizu Rei, Matsuda Yasuhiro, and You Ei Min, *Nittai kankeishi, 1945–2008* (Tokyo daigaku shuppankai, 2009).

28  See Taiwan sōtokufu zanmu seiri jimusho, ed., *Taiwan tōchi shimatsu hōkokusho* (Taiwan sōtokufu zanmu seiri jimusho, 1946). See also, Teikoku senni kabushiki gaisha taiwan jigyōbu, ed., *Hōgen shō 40 nen no kaiko: taiwan seima gaisha o kataru* (Teikoku senni kabushiki gaisha taiwan jigyōbu, 1946).

29  Mukoyama Hirō, "Taiwan minzoku kaihō undōshi 1," *Rekishi hyōron* vol. 4, issue 8 (1950): pp. 59–65; "Taiwan minzoku kaihō undōshi 2," *Rekishi hyōron* vol. 5, issue 1 (1951): pp. 49–54.

30  Iwao Seiichi, "Sekaishi jō no taiwan," *Nihon rekishi* vol. 19, issue 11–15 (September 1949): p. 11.

31  After the Sino-Japanese War in 1937, Japan compelled colonial subjects to visit Shintō shrines and to use the Japanese language and made people change their surnames to a Japanese style.

32  Nakamura Takashi, "Taiwanshi gaiyō (kindai)," *Minzokugaku kenkyū (taiwan kenkyū tokushū)* vol. 18, issue 1, 2 (March 1945): pp. 121–122.

33 A typical case that has Nakamura's framework is Asada Kyoji, *Nihon shokuminchi kenkyū shiron* (Miraisha, 1990).
34 Sasamoto Takeji, "Sengo ni okeru taiwan keizai no hatten," *Ajia keizai* vol. 4, issue 7 (July 1963): pp. 2–14.
35 Ibid., p. 14.
36 Ibid.
37 Ibid.
38 Kobayashi Fumio, "Taiwan mondai/mō hitotsu no shiten – '50 nen shihai' wa ikiteiru," *Sekai* vol. 311 (October 1971): pp. 130–139.
39 Tai Kokuki and Niijima Atsuyoshi, "Shisō hōhō toshite no taiwan," *Shin nihon bungaku* vol. 26, issue 11 (November 1971): pp. 7–8.
40 Ubukata Naokichi, "Taiwan kenkyū – mondai teiki," *Ajia keizai* vol. 11, issue 6 (June 1970): pp. 52–75.
41 As quoted in Ubukata, "Taiwan kenkyū."

# 3 Imperial loss and Japan's search for postwar legitimacy

*Barak Kushner*

Despite all the slogans put out by Japan in World War II about Asian unity and solidarity ("one hundred million hearts beating as one," "eight corners of the world under one roof"), imperial Japan remained at loggerheads with itself. Long-standing divisions and a lack of trust between the people and the nation's leaders had existed since the 1868 Meiji Restoration. The Imperial Army and Navy had also long held each other in contempt, competing for a share of the national budget, pressuring the already hard-pressed populace to accept what each saw as good for the nation. Media companies seemed fickle and volatile: at first, in the early 1930s, they voiced opposition to militarization, then they condoned the Army's efforts by 1937 in China, finally throwing their support behind all-out war even before 1941.[1]

It should thus come as no surprise that in the first few days after officially announcing its surrender on August 15, 1945, Japan remained at odds with itself about the meaning of the war and its defeat.[2] Equally, there was scant agreement about responsibility for the war: the term *sensō sekinin* (war responsibility) seemed vague. Did it mean responsibility for launching the war against China in the 1930s or later against the Western Allies, for continuing the war when it was clearly already bringing the country to ruin, or for losing the war? At times, various post-war Japanese agencies – the Ministry of Foreign Affairs, the Imperial Army and Navy, and others – postured to monopolize control and at times shared authority. However, more often than not, they did not cooperate and chose instead to protect themselves and their ruling cliques from whatever backlash the imperial defeat held in store. To me it is clear that we should not think of the immediate postwar just as an era of transition or continuity but rather see it as an era in which, consciously and unconsciously, the idea of *competitive justice* reigned. Japan was looking to salvage what it had not yet lost and aimed to deflect, to the extent possible, the intrusion of the great powers who seemed so set on returning and once again ruling the world stage. Controlling the postwar conversation about "justice" demonstrated the importance that both the Allies and the Japanese attributed to being able to define the meaning of the war: had it been, as the Japanese claimed, about the "liberation" of Asia or a war of democracy versus fascism as defined by the West? The situation in East Asia saw a collection of crumbling imperial spheres – Japan's and those of former European hegemons – competing for space while two new ones (the USSR and United States) now vied for dominance. China was able to gain a seat at the international table of elites for the first time at the tail end of World War II, but its ascent to world power did not begin really until the start of the twenty-first century.

We now know that there was no one Japanese response to the sudden dissolution of empire and to the war crimes trials that most people knew defeat would bring in its wake. A kaleidoscope of postwar attitudes both reflected and reproduced the hierarchy and duplicity of wartime Japanese society and authority. Fundamentally, we can break down Japan's reactions into five strata: (1) the civilian government, (2) the emperor, (3) the Imperial Army, (4) the Imperial Navy (both the Army and the Navy had their own ministries and demobilization bureaus that pursued separate if not conflicting goals), and (5) the Japanese media. The fact that each group, which managed elements of wartime Japanese society, held competing ideologies concerning how to deal with or respond to the Allied calls for war crimes trials demonstrates the fractured nature of authority and rule both in wartime and in immediate postwar Japan. Each institution wished to mitigate its own losses, lessen the responsibility that it would be seen to hold for the war, and press for continued privileges. In many ways, postwar Japan reflected the same disparate notion of state and authority that had plagued it prewar. In fact, what was apparent in the cacophony of voices surrounding the surrender was how little consensus existed within Japan concerning the issue of responsibility – responsibility for both launching the war and then for losing it.

Exactly who was responsible for the resounding defeat that saw the majority of Japan's urban areas flattened in the last year of the war? The question was an important one because it was linked to the fate and future of the nation.[3] The Japanese government had calibrated that "the war in its entirety destroyed one quarter of the nation's wealth." This does not take into account the loss of Japanese lives, as well as those of non-Japanese who inhabited the empire. Chinese estimates were of twenty million killed and tens of millions left as refugees as a result of Japan's war of aggression. Further, the significance of the defeat depended almost entirely to which subgroup one belonged. The Army might feel able to bask in the self-deluding satisfaction of unshackling East Asian and Southeast Asian countries from the bonds of European colonialism. But at what cost? The Navy took pride in the belief that its sailors had at least conducted themselves better than their cruel and intractable Army brethren, but neither group really managed to come to terms with the destruction that their imperial "liberation" had wrought, either domestically or internationally. The announcement of Japan's defeat came suddenly and shocked many, even elite graduates from the University of Tokyo.[4] The question of responsibility or of even thinking about the end of the war was dumbfounding to most, so psychologically unprepared were they for the possibility. Once over the initial shock, every institution scrambled to retain what influence it could.[5]

Scholarship abounds, in numerous languages, on the lead-up to the end of World War II and Japan's tortured surrender decision-making process. There is noticeably less analysis that accurately deciphers how the country came to respond to international calls for war crimes trials, calls that predated the actual surrender.[6] How

Japan dealt with the Allied push for war crimes adjudication is significant because within this process lies the key for understanding how Japan defined the war and its own imperial behavior. If the nation could remove the stain of war guilt, then wartime propaganda and claims of keeping "Asia for the Asiatics" and removing the shackles of colonialism from Asia could shine that much brighter for the exhausted and impoverished Japanese, brought to their knees by their own war. If war crimes trials proved otherwise, then the war would have been fought in vain and the nation might collapse, give in to its own humiliation, or, worse yet, be taken over by the expanding forces of communism, it was believed. While smoke was still rising from the ashes, Japanese officialdom was busily trying to shore up its positions. The Army and Navy ministries moved with the greatest alacrity, wanting to make sure that the Allied occupation did not take positions that contradicted not only Japan's own interests but the military's as well. That meant defining the terms of what the war had meant, that it had been "inevitable" and necessary to push back against Western colonialism. Such military efforts show that the Japanese civilian government was still not in control of the country because it did not fully manage the immediate postwar. I assess that one major reason that Japan ended up in the position it faces today, so reluctant to engage fully with the legacy of the war, is that divided civilian and military opinions about the war competed with vested interests concerning discussions about war responsibility. These did not appear out of the blue at the end of the war but emerged from deep and long-lasting internal antagonisms from the immediate postwar that never resolved themselves. The wounds remain fresh today.[7] Japan's failure to resolve the issue of war crimes trials is not a 1980s or a twenty-first-century problem. It is a problem that began at the moment of surrender and originated in the highest echelons of leadership.

As Robert Bickers suggests in his groundbreaking work *Empire Made Me*, "Empire is with us, in our waking lives, and in our dreams and nightmares."[8] This is so, no matter how much we may want to mask or deny it. Though Bickers focuses on the United Kingdom, his statement is appropriate for thinking about Japan and East Asian history. He pushes the context of empire further, as we should, writing that in the postwar period, "empire hasn't gone. Its detritus litters once-colonized cities and cantonments, its legacies both tangible – statues, monuments, buildings, roads – and intangible – philosophies, policies, memories."[9] Bickers tells us that we cannot draw an artificial line between home and the colonies. Those of us who are engaged in examining early postwar Japanese history would do well to pay heed to his admonition that empire and the war crimes that occurred in its name remain a potent force.

## Nearing the end

For all of their unpreparedness, Japanese leaders generally knew that war crimes trials would take place because the conclusion of World War II was prefaced by a series of major international Allied conferences that set the stage for such an eventuality. Katō Kiyofumi touches on this in Chapter 1 of this volume. Nothing was necessarily crystal clear, but the Japanese recognized that something was coming; they were just not sure what legal shape it would take. The Japanese had sent an enormous delegation to the Versailles Peace Conference that brought a dissatisfying closure to World War I, and they were fully aware of the subsequent international push to arrest the German Kaiser and the trials at Leipzig.[10] Jackson Maogoto suggests that World War I was a turning point where, for the first time, states tried to "individualiz[e] criminal responsibility for violations of laws of war and for crimes against humanity."[11] Decades later, in the heat of battle in World War II, the Japanese could see the warning signs of impending war crimes trials. The 1943 Moscow Conferences brought together the foreign ministers of the United States, Great Britain, and the Soviet Union to decide the fate of Nazi Germany. They announced, focusing on Nazis in Europe, that those who were:

> responsible for or have taken a consenting part in the above atrocities, massacres and executions will be sent back to the countries in which their abominable deeds were done in order that they may be judged and punished according to the laws of these liberated countries and of free governments which will be erected therein.[12]

At the Cairo Conference that followed in late November 1943, American President Franklin Roosevelt, British Prime Minister Winston Churchill, and Nationalist China leader General Chiang Kai-shek met to concur on the end of World War II in East Asia and to discuss Japanese atrocities.[13] The public announcement was not as detailed as that of the Moscow Conference, but it alluded to penalties against Japan nonetheless: "The Three Great Allies are fighting this war to restrain and punish the aggression of Japan. They covet no gain for themselves and have no thought of territorial expansion."[14] Finally, at the Potsdam Declaration in July 1945, which grew out of a meeting between Churchill, American President Harry Truman (Roosevelt had died in April), and Chiang Kai-shek, negotiations took place on the particulars of the terms of Japan's surrender. At this point the Allies announced that "stern justice shall be meted out to all [Japanese] war criminals" even though the details were far from clear what form this justice would take and along what sort of schedule.[15]

## The beginning of the end

The Japanese imperial government had difficulty formulating a reply to the Potsdam Declaration, initially offering a non-response, *mokusatsu*, as a rebuff. Suzuki Kantarō, prime minister until August 17, was replaced by Higashikuni Naruhiko, a member of the royal family and uncle to Emperor Hirohito. He was in office for just about two months and was then replaced by Shidehara Kijūrō, who remained for just slightly longer.

Prince Mikasa Takahito informed Higashikuni on August 10 that the emperor would accept the Potsdam terms as a way to break the deadlock between the government leaders and imperial military officers, but Higashikuni questioned whether such a move would allow for the protection of the "national polity" (*kokutai*), that all-encompassing term that stood for both the imperial house and national unity.[16] Roger Brown has detailed the drafting of the imperial rescript announcing the emperor's decision, a laborious process that began early on August 10 and continued until the afternoon of August 14 – laborious because the language had to please so many different parties.[17] On August 15, Higashikuni noted in his diary that he was saddened by the broadcast, which had allowed the Japanese for the first time to hear the sacred voice of the emperor. At the same time, Higashikuni noted, "[W]e need to deeply consider the circumstances that brought our country to this defeat." If we do not, he cautioned, then the country was doomed. However, as researchers have noted, there was some ambiguity in the emperor's message about what the loss of the war signified: rather than telling the Japanese people to admit defeat, he called on them to "pave the way for a grand peace for all the generations to come by enduring the unendurable and suffering what is insufferable."[18] Society at the upper levels looked at war responsibility as a means of figuring out how Japan lost and of rebuilding quickly with an eye toward the future. An emphasis was not placed on identifying the significance of the defeat or crimes committed during the war, a specific intention of the Allies.[19]

Higashikuni was not far off the mark in terms of assessing the larger issue of wartime responsibility, and his comments were repeated in early 1946 by the Japanese Communist Party (JCP). Their manifesto on the war crimes issue, published as a short pamphlet entitled "A People's Court to Try War Criminals," is truly fascinating in that it demonstrates the manner in which the discussion of war crimes trials developed almost as soon as the occupation began. "The exploitative and cruel war is over and the Allies are democratizing Japan," the pamphlet joyously announced. However, the JCP told its followers, what awaited them was deprivation, unemployment, sickness, and poverty at never before seen levels. This was the result of a war labeled as "the liberation of the Asian peoples" and the "establishment of the new world order."[20] What the JCP was calling for was a social revolution. Where were the war criminals, and where should they be pursued? Chillingly, what the communists realized and proclaimed before the nation was that war criminals were everywhere – they were "in every factory, every hamlet, every organization, within every managerial group . . . within villages and towns and within schools."[21] Who was going to conduct the trials of these criminals? Was it going to be the Upper House of parliament, those who guarded their special class privileges and "who applauded the budget for the war, who strengthened for the worse the 1938 Peace Preservation Law?" Or should they expect justice to emerge from the lower house of the Diet, from those "who pushed forward the decision to pursue the holy war with a standing ovation?" "It is obvious," the pamphlet concluded, that "these groups do not have one iota of qualification to stand at the forefront of a democratic movement."[22] The pamphlet ended by touching on the issue of war responsibility and the emperor, asking who announced the start of the war? And in whose name were those who opposed the war thrown into prison?

## The official response

Despite all the swirling questions about the issue of war responsibility, by August 31, 1945, the *Asahi Shimbun*'s new editor-in-chief Suzuki Bunshirō was already meeting with the first postwar Prime Minister Higashikuni to discuss the arrival of U.S. soldiers and the imminent landing of many more foreign news correspondents. It was important to have the latter understand what was happening in Japan and to be able to offer an impression, Suzuki suggested to the prime minister. The clear implication was that it would be to Japan's benefit if Japanese reporters were able to establish friendly relations with the foreign news staff. Higashikuni invited the heads of the Japanese newspapers to discuss the future. On the same day, Japanese newspapers published a letter from the prime minister's office to the people asking them to write to his office with their hopes, complaints, and other input. One reason for the loss of trust between government and people, Higashikuni wrote, is that the government did not know the real situation of the people, and thus their grievances grew. The prime minister's office was receiving about eighty to ninety thousand letters a day in response, a number that continued to rise.[23]

On September 4, 1945 the eighty-eighth imperial parliament opened, and Higashikuni delivered a speech detailing just how devastated Japan's armed forces were. The military was displeased that he released such facts because they were still unused to facing reality, although Higashikuni defended the move as necessary for effective regeneration of the country. Minister of State Obata Toshirō objected that such openness could only bring harm to the situation, and he strongly criticized Higashikuni's attitude.[24] On September 10, 1945, and over the next few days, Suzuki Tadakatsu, chief of the Yokohama bureau of the Central Liaison Office (*Shūsen renraku chūō jimukyoku*), established on August 26 and which coordinated communication between the Japanese government and Supreme Commander for the Allied Powers (SCAP), spoke with General MacArthur's right-hand man, Colonel Sidney Mashbir. He was struck that the U.S. occupation forces were moving ahead in preparation for war crimes trials much more quickly than the Japanese had foreseen. Suzuki subsequently contacted the head of the surrender liaison committee, Okazaki Katsuo, and reported the alarming situation. The two agreed that Japan should quickly take action and initiate its own trials, but on September 11 the U.S. occupation leaders had already put out a call to arrest General Tōjō Hideki. A young *Asahi Shimbun* reporter, Hasegawa Yukio, was also there at the same time and achieved a scoop. He burst into the house to catch what he believed might be the last words of the general who had just tried to commit suicide and who said that he "wanted to die with a single shot."[25] Tōjō lived and later faced trial as a Class A war criminal.

In its September 11, 1945, report, "Research on Problems Related to Punishing War Criminals," the Treaty Bureau of the Ministry of Foreign Affairs expressed surprise at the jumble of responsibility and authority within the higher levels of the Japanese government and officialdom. The report ventured into a discussion of war crimes trials and suggested that they would probably not be implemented only against those who abused POWs but also against those who bore political responsibility for the war. Japanese officials were aware of how their leadership structure was different from that of Nazi Germany, and the document lucidly contrasts how Nazis had clearly delineated layers of authority while the Japanese had not, which made the full pursuit of responsibility difficult, to say the least. Structurally, the Japanese civilian government was not designed to allow for individuals to be seen as "responsible" for decisions.[26]

On September 12, 1945, Prime Minister Higashikuni, Foreign Minister Shigemitsu Mamoru, Minister of the Army Shimomura Sadamu, Minister of the Navy Yonai Mitsumasa, Chief of the Army General Staff Umezu Yoshijirō, Chief of the Navy General Staff Admiral Toyoda Soemu, Minister of State Konoe Fumimaro, and Minister of Justice Iwata Chūzō met at the Council for Dealing with the End of the War (established on August 22) to discuss putting together investigation boards to examine Japanese war crimes. The group announced that in accordance with Allied demands and legal jurisprudence Japan would try those who had been listed by the occupiers as criminals or those who had committed war crimes.[27] A postwar Japanese government summary of Japan's early policies toward war crimes trials states that at the meeting on September 12, the group decided that even if the Allies were to put Japanese in the dock, Japan should move first to investigate war crimes and conduct trials of major individuals and of those responsible. This policy was taken as the means to "clarify the merits of the case" (*shirokuro o akiraka ni shite*), the report noted.[28] Japanese officials wanted to take these countermeasures so that the Allies could not conduct adjudications unilaterally. After having made their decision, Kido Kōichi, the Lord Keeper of the Privy Seal, presented the Council's argument to Emperor Hirohito. The emperor responded: "While these individuals have been designated as war criminals by the Allied Nations, from the imperial [my royal] point of view these are loyal subjects, and furthermore include some, I believe, who have achieved great success for the nation. It is very difficult to accept that they will be criminally punished for having fought in my name." Kido brought the imperial utterance back to the Council for Dealing with the End of the War and they redebated it, given the emperor's hesitation. But the group was adamant about what it had decided in the morning and believed that such a decision was appropriate. Then "in their regular clothes," the summary adds, the prime minister, minister of foreign affairs, and minister of justice all went to see the emperor again. (Notes in the report state that normally when visiting the emperor officials wore their morning suits.)[29] Kido and the group received imperial dispensation to push forward on domestic war crimes trials with the rationale that this could guarantee the trials were kept "proper," or "just" (*kōsei*). The summary also cautioned that handing over those who had been named as war crimes suspects unconditionally would "go against the traditional precepts of *bushidō*."[30]

According to some sources, a few trials did indeed take place on the Japanese side; others list only one. Tanaka Hiromi suggests that because these trial records cannot be found either way, they are "phantom trials," *maboroshi saiban*.[31]

However, the draft English text of the cabinet decision, which was never released, survived in Suzuki Tadakatsu's postwar collection of documents.

> The Japanese government is determined to hold, on the basis of the lists and evidences which will be furnished by the Allied Powers, strict judicial trials of war criminals, particularly of those who mistreated prisoners of war and civilian internees and of those who otherwise violated the rules of international law.[32]

The Japanese government and Army pursued and investigated a selection of war crimes but eventually in March 1946 General Headquarters (GHQ) ordered such investigations to be dropped, according to one source.[33] Japan was in the end permitted only to collect evidence for trials, and the only case of someone being brought to trial that can be confirmed was that of General Honma Masaharu who had his pay docked as punishment.[34] By this point, Prime Minister Higashikuni had already released an announcement that the entire nation regretted the war – "*ichioku sō zange*" – a public and collective admission of, if not guilt then at least national contrition, which neatly avoided any mention of individual responsibility and thus conveniently sidestepped the issue of apology. Japan was quick to pretend it had suddenly changed from a month prior, and on September 15 the *Manchester Guardian* reported Higashikuni pleading with America to "forget Pearl Harbor" because "the Japanese people now intend to be entirely peaceful."[35] The final move on September 18, was Higashikuni's press conference with foreign correspondents, held at 1 p.m. in the afternoon with approximately one hundred journalists in attendance. This was an epic moment since Japan had been essentially closed off to foreign media for the better part of a decade. Most of the journalists asked about the Doolittle executions or the mistreatment of allied POWs. One directly asked whether the emperor had war responsibility, and Higashikuni replied emphatically, "Absolutely not."[36]

It is telling that no mention was made in these early discussions, held with a view to countering war crimes trials, of atrocities or issues regarding the abusive and exploitative manner in which Japan's empire was managed. The Japanese were concerned about the causes of the war in general and about the failure of the empire. But then they immediately turned to how to rebuild and the need to strengthen people's relationship with the emperor, to implement new education programs, and to build transport while providing jobs for veterans. Pausing to reflect on the harm that Japan caused at the fringes of the empire did not arise, and it remained a non-existent feature of mainstream Japan's policies toward war crimes trials from those days until the present.[37]

On October 23, 1945, the Council for Dealing with the End of the War laid out more of its policy for proceeding with potential war crimes trials. The pursuit of justice appeared secondary to the aim of mitigating any blemish on the imperial prestige of Japan – seemingly unsullied even with the unconditional surrender. The goal was to minimize to the extent possible damage to both individuals and "the empire" as it was termed in the Japanese plan. In some ways this move mirrored the government and military's goal to protect that vaguely defined "national polity," or *kokutai*. The strategy laid out in the council's report suggested several possible avenues of logic to minimize damage. The primary argument hinged on the claim that on the level of international law, the pursuit of "so-called" war criminals was irrational. Second, officials insisted that the emperor was an entity, separate from the evolution of the war, and that he stood above the imperial constitution. The third element of the report argued that the pressures of the international situation during the 1930s had forced the nation into a corner and that Japan had no choice other than to wage war or face annihilation.[38] John Dower cites another document that he suggests was one of Japan's early postwar strategies for touting its brand of "loser's justice." This was a plan that never saw the light of day; it was entitled "Urgent Imperial Decree to Stabilize the People's Mind and Establish the Independent Popular Morality Necessary to Maintain National Order."[39] As Dower explains, the war was depicted as a "tragic perversion" of the emperor's trust. "Loser's justice, like victor's justice, ultimately would have entailed arguing that Japan had been led into 'aggressive militarism' by a small cabal of irresponsible militaristic leaders."[40] A postwar summary examining the problem with Class A war criminals suggested that examining their culpability could potentially touch on the emperor's role; this being so, three major policies were laid out for any matter dealing with war crimes:

1   Do not touch on anything related to the emperor's responsibility.
2   Protect the nation.
3   Within the framework of the first two points and to the extent possible, defend individuals.[41]

Shidehara Kijūrō took over as prime minister on October 9, 1945, and he wanted to examine precisely what had brought Japan to its knees. Only by building on this knowledge, he explained, could Japan rebuild. On October 30, 1945, a cabinet decision discussed the reasons for defeat and the establishment of an investigation body to examine the issues. On November 20, this body became a government entity charged with that mission.[42] Initially the section was known as the Greater East Asia War Investigation Council (*Daitōa sensō chōsakai*), but in January 1946 it changed its name to the War Investigation Council (*Sensō chōsakai*). Shidehara as prime minister headed the organ, but the Allies were suspicious that this was a group designed to aid the rise of Japan's military again, and the group did not last long before having to disband.[43] Aoki Tokuzō, who was made chief secretary of the council, recalled that the emperor had spoken with Higashikuni about needing to look into the war and its origins so that Japan did not make the same mistake twice. Higashikuni's cabinet had not lasted long enough to take charge of such matters, and it was left to Shidehara to create a commission to accomplish this task.[44] It had been divided into five subsections to examine various sectors of Japanese society, including (1) politics and foreign policy, (2) military matters, (3) finance and economics, (4) thought and culture, and (5) technology. However, on September 30, 1946, the commission disbanded.[45]

On December 1 and 4, 1945, in response to discussions in the upper house concerning the investigation council, Shidehara provided rather vague responses concerning what exactly was meant by *sensō sekinin*, or war responsibility. On December 4, Shidehara stated in the upper house that Japan needed to assess the reasons and truth about the war, determining whether the result of the Pacific War was the outgrowth of militarism. On December 6, he explained that if Japan conducted this investigation on its own, it would be able to find, once the efforts were complete, where the locus of responsibility was and mete out either political or criminal judgements. On December 6, in a budget meeting, Shidehara remarked that he did not accept the Allied basis for choosing who was responsible for the war and that only the Japanese could ascertain who or what had caused their loss. On December 12, Shidehara said in a lower house meeting that the investigation was to make sure that the Japanese understood the reasons behind the war and did not repeat the same mistakes again. Public opinion was already posing difficult questions about war responsibility, he said, and reprimands from the media were growing harsh.[46]

We can sense the push for answers coming from various directions within the civilian leadership. One diplomat, Nakamura Toyoichi, believed it important to think about Japan's strategy toward the war crimes trials early on. Nakamura was the father of Ogata Sadako, the respected Japanese diplomat, academic, and former UN High Commissioner for Refugees. (Sadako married the son of Ogata Taketora, former editor-in-chief of the *Asahi shimbun* and head of Japan's wartime propaganda bureau.) On November 20, 1945, Nakamura proposed a strategy for Japan's response to the war crimes trial process. Part of the strategy would be to gather a group of specialists who would offer up documents and analyses of events to help with the legal defense. Nakamura wanted to set up two committees to examine war crimes issues. The first one was to be headed by the Ministry of Foreign Affairs Vice-Minister and staffed by loaned members from the Army, Navy, and Ministry of Justice, among others, to analyze documents and in turn provide them to prosecutors and defense lawyers. The second committee, the War Criminals Countermeasures Committee (*Sensō hanzainin taisaku iinkai*), was to be smaller and focus more on countermeasures for political issues and trials dealing with atrocities, like a sort of brain trust. It was to be devoid of political affiliation and staffed by civilian intellectuals. Nakamura's proposal was rejected out of hand, in part because the Japanese government wanted a unity of opinion to show its opposition to the Allied pursuit of justice and to demonstrate government unanimity.[47] Eventually, however, this goal was abandoned, and in fact we know that each Japanese civilian and military agency mostly pursued their own policies to save themselves.

Yoshida Shigeru, as Foreign Minister in the Shidehara cabinet (he had already taken over from Shigemitsu Mamoru in mid-September because Shigemitsu was being pursued by GHQ as a Class A war criminal), was not a fan of the government's attempt to unify its stance on war crimes. Yoshida believed that twisting the truth and hiding facts to get individuals absolved was not in Japan's long-term interests (and it seems Yoshida might have won that argument for the government side but could not convince the military). But then the Foreign Office could not sit by and do nothing. So, in a sense, both sides compromised as a way not to directly guide defense lawyers but to assist them. Yoshida, together with University of Tokyo Professor of Law Takayanagi Kenzō, formed the Judicial Affairs Deliberation Office (*Hōmu shinsa-shitsu*). This office was similar in effect to what Nakamura Toyoichi had proposed, and it was established in December 1945, under the aegis of the Foreign Ministry, providing materials to the court. Sone Eki was put in charge, and on December 14 the heads of various ministries were called to the prime minister's residence for a colloquium in which Okazaki Katsuo, who was working directly for the Foreign Minister, informed them that the plan to take a unified stance on Allied war crimes trials was being scrapped and that the emperor bore no war responsibility. In effect, this meant that Japan would follow orders from GHQ when dealing with the war crimes trials but that officials should not think about blaming the emperor.[48] Matthias Zachmann provides more details on how the legal community reacted postwar in his Chapter 9 of this volume.

Higurashi Yoshinobu, a historian of the Tokyo Trial, questions why Yoshida Shigeru was so accommodating of the Allied policies to pursue war crimes trials. Was it, he asks, due to the fact that Yoshida wished simply to adhere to the terms of the surrender treaty? Shimoda Takezō, who was a diplomat and later ambassador to the United States, reports that Yoshida had opined to Ministry of Foreign Affairs (MOFA) officials, when he returned in the immediate postwar period to a high-level post, that this was the first time in Japan's history that the country had been vanquished: it was a defeated nation. Japan was now "on the chopping board like a dead fish," Yoshida told the staff, which essentially meant that Japan was faced with a hopeless situation and needed to buck up and deal with it. Higurashi sees in this statement Yoshida's strategy for rebuilding Japan, using the Allied trials as the means to purge Japanese society of those who had brought it to defeat. Yoshida in fact refused to sign a petition in support of wartime Foreign Minister Tōgō Shigenori because, as Yoshino stated, Tōgō was minister at the start of the Pacific War and should have taken responsibility and stepped down after negotiations with the United States failed.[49] We should not forget that while this stance might have been Japan's policy toward the Class A war criminals and those within the home islands of Japan, the situation elsewhere throughout the former empire varied dramatically according to regional conditions, and the opinions espoused by other leaders were far from similar.

Higurashi admits that while the Japanese government did not issue a unified official directive toward war crimes trials, unofficially each agency or administrative unit did internally. The Ministry of Foreign Affairs did not oppose the indictments publicly but subjected them to analysis and was not at all conciliatory. The office within MOFA that managed war crimes issues was the End of War Liaison Bureau, War Crimes Office, First Section (*Shūren daiichibu no senpan jimushitsu*). It took care of all war criminal administrative matters, including assistance, offering documents, and answering lawyer's questions. There was also an organ called the Domestic and Foreign Legal and Political Study Group (*Naigai hōsei kenkyūkai*), more commonly known as the Hōsei, which was like a prep team for the trials. On the heels of a push from Nakamura and with some support from the financial world, this organization was established. Officially appearing in February 1946, it was a private entity not linked with the government and was established as a way to offer assistance and analysis for war crimes trial defense. It was staffed by the very best of Japan's legal minds, including the University of Tokyo's Takayanagi Kenzō, Takagi Yasaka, Kyoto University's Taoka Ryōichi, Keijō University (Japan's imperial university in Seoul, known as Keijō in the period of Japanese colonial rule) legal scholar Ukai Nobushige, along with a host of others. These men produced high-level legal scholarship on questions of war responsibility.[50]

## Imperial interference

While it is possible that the emperor, in his talks with General Douglas MacArthur, pleaded for general leniency and attempted to take some responsibility for the war upon the throne, the result never bore fruit.[51] Little more than a year later, the emperor took a much more proactive stance. The public clamor to limit the areas placed under judicial scrutiny concerning war responsibility soon led to a large portion of society being forgiven when Emperor Hirohito on November 3, 1946, the day of the announcement of the new constitution, offered a "great amnesty." In fact, the decree ended prison for many, including those convicted of lèse-majesté, thought crimes, and political crimes. At the same time the imperial fiat also granted amnesty to soldiers who had gone AWOL, those who had been convicted in courts martial, those who had not followed orders of a superior officer during the war, and more importantly, members of the Imperial Navy and Army who had committed crimes against POWs or other crimes abroad.[52] The *Asahi shimbun* labeled this scope "unprecedented." The imperial measure contained a clause stipulating that such amnesty was not applicable to those who committed crimes "against the goals of the occupation."[53] In some ways, Hirohito's imperial pronouncement offered an imperial pardon for the very type of war crimes that the Allies were starting to pursue against the Japanese, though it remains unclear whether the edict had any legal impact. Regardless, it certainly set the moral contours for the internal debate on war crimes soon after Japan's surrender. Japanese newspapers wrote of seven types of crimes being pardoned, which led to 330,000 suspects being granted amnesty.[54] The fact that this imperial benevolence extended to improper wartime laws, which had terrorized Japanese liberals, as well as laws that related to war crimes and crimes against non-Japanese, would serve to dull even further Japanese postwar interest in the need to address the legacy of war crimes because in this Great Amnesty the emperor appeared to have dealt with it and essentially delivered the verdicts.

## The imperial military response

This chapter mostly centers on the Japanese civilian responses to the political fracas surrounding the war crimes debacle, but we should not neglect the far more effective military positions. There were essentially four prewar military groups that vied for ascendency at any one time: the individuals staffing two cabinet military posts, the Imperial Japanese Army and Imperial Navy ministers, who were in charge of administrative matters, and those surrounding the Chief of the Imperial Army General Staff (*sanbō sōchō*) and Chief of the Imperial Navy General Staff (*gunreibu*), who dealt with operational and battle strategy matters and were consultative offices directly under the aegis of the emperor. The Navy had already moved on September 10 to establish the Seventh Subcommittee of the Committee to Deliberate about the End of War, a section that would carefully manage and arrange the files of matters dealing with POWs and international law. The Army had responded on September 17 with its own Plan Concerning Summary of Responses to Allied Investigations of Treatment of POWs, which it sent to all of its officers. This plan admitted that previous orders to burn documents left the Army with little evidence to defend its own actions, so that each unit needed to organize and forward all the materials that it could to the Army Ministry. To prove that POWs were not maltreated, the committee actually amassed data about the items served for POW meals to show that they were properly cared for, though the morbidity statistics released thereafter seem to contradict these data.[55] In short, Japanese military officials took the war crimes trials lightly, especially those taking place outside of Japan. Men like Army Lieutenant General Tanaka Hisakazu, charged in China for war crimes, were contemptuous in internal reports about the meaning and value of their trials. Tanaka wrote to military headquarters complaining about Chinese war crimes trial procedures, stating that he could accept the Chinese attempts to charge his underlings with crimes, but they needed to do it lawfully and bear in mind the burden of proof. Tanaka claimed that he was not trying to avoid responsibility, but courts could not sit idly by and rely on Chinese oral testimony or newspaper articles because these materials were too flimsy for the purposes of an indictment.[56] The Navy was even more diligent in its long-term efforts to keep its men out of war crimes trials.

These postwar efforts continued for decades even after the war crimes trials were finished, demonstrating that long-term Japanese postwar military fear about its image did not cease even with defeat.[57] By 1970, the former military groups' efforts to collect trial data – in America, France, the Philippines, Holland, and other countries – had allowed them to prepare a grand narrative unmatched by the Allies' single country-specific accounts, though the material was only piecemeal. Overall, in terms of complete trials, including indictments, evidence, trial transcripts, lawyers' discussions, and judgements, only 14 percent of the war crimes cases were amassed. From 1958 to 1970, teams had gone all around Japan interviewing former war criminals and recorded their experiences in seventy-eight volumes of oral history on the Class BC war crimes trials.[58]

## Media and society

By 1947, attitudes toward the war and responsibility for the debacle, however defined, were changing in Japan to the point that even the Chinese and Americans recognized this. Wang Yunsheng, a Chinese journalist, was invited as part of a newspaper team of ten people to Japan by General Douglas MacArthur from February 27 to March 15, 1947. The Chinese group traveled to several major Japanese urban sites and met with Japanese in the political world, finance, media, and literature. After his return home, Wang wrote up his findings in a book, *Riben banyue* (*Half a Month in Japan*), which was first serialized in the newspaper, *Dagongbao*, from March 22 to April 15, 1947. Wang delivered a series of speeches the following month at Beijing University, Yanjing University, and several other key academic venues about his distaste for U.S. support of Japanese remilitarization. The Chinese were deeply troubled to learn within two years of the end of the war that the Japanese were no longer the enemy that had committed atrocities against them but were now being used as a bulwark against the Soviets and the threat of expanding communism. A rival Chinese newspaper, the *Zhongyang ribao*, claimed that Wang was only "throwing oil on the fire" by appraising the Chinese of the situation. On June 28, 1947, Wang responded with an op-ed in the *Dagongbao*, writing "China should not stand idly by" while all this was going on in Japan.[59]

## Conclusion: after the occupation

Years after the war and the international war crimes tribunals were finished, the War Crimes Office within the Ministry of Justice conducted a set of interviews with military leaders, including former generals Hata Shunroku and Araki Sadao. Araki had been arrested and charged as a Class A war criminal at the Tokyo Trial and sentenced to life imprisonment, but he was released for purported health reasons in 1955.[60] On December 3, 1958, in a conversation with Toyota Kumao, Hara Chūichi, and others, Araki shrugged off his trial as "a drunken charade!"[61] He did not mince his words. He claimed that the biggest problem was the interpretation while he was being questioned during the indictment process. The interpreter was definitely not up to snuff, and his vocabulary apparently so poor that Araki took a dictionary with him to correct him when it was needed.

Japanese efforts to reframe the defeat and deflect the locus of war responsibility are not unique. We might find it useful to start comparing Japanese struggles to come to terms with Japan's role in World War II with American attempts to understand America's own Civil War. This was a war that, as Gary Gallagher notes, almost brought America to its knees but the legacy of which found white Southerners "thoroughly beaten but largely unrepentant."[62] The comparison is not meant to trivialize the horror of Japan's aggressive war in Asia but rather to demonstrate that domestic squabbles about the historical legacy of tumultuous change are not limited to the Japanese archipelago. The follies of the Japanese military and the civilian leadership and the inadequacy of the Japanese political structure brought the Japanese nation to the brink of total destruction. As Eri Hotta shows, however, Japan's war was a greater tragedy in the sense that while "some leaders were misguidedly hopeful . . . *none* were confident of Japan's eventual victory."[63]

In May 2015, American historian David Blight presented the Alistair Cooke Memorial Lecture for BBC Radio 4, in which he examined the legacy of the

American Civil War and connected it to contemporary events in American society. Blight asked how it could be possible that Southern American states celebrate the very leaders who nearly brought about the complete dissolution of the American Republic. One could easily ask the same about Japan. How can a nation vaunt leaders whose goals almost caused the complete and total destruction of Japan, both as a society and as a nation?[64] Japan may have accepted the tragedy that World War II brought to its domestic civilian population because this allowed the country to quickly put the past behind it and get on with reconstruction. Unfortunately, the national amnesia about empire in the narrative, which the war crimes trials uncovered and revealed both to the international community and to Japan itself, demonstrates that this understanding of tragedy was limited and did not include the damage that Japan visited upon the rest of East Asia and the Allies.[65] It is in this propensity to recognize the tragedy visited on one's own nearest and dearest, while denying its wider effects and the linkage to wider geopolitical history, where we see that Japan's policies toward war crimes trials ultimately failed and thus continue to serve as arena for friction with its closest Asian neighbors.

# Notes

1 The Asahi Shimbun Company, *Media, Propaganda and Politics in 20th-Century Japan*, trans. Barak Kushner (London: Bloomsbury Academic, 2015), pp. 62–69, 71–81.
2 See Barak Kushner, "The International Community and Japan's Early Postures toward War Crimes and War Responsibility in the Aftermath of WWII," in *War Crimes Trials in Asia: Collaboration and Complicity in the Aftermath of War*, vol. 2, ed. Kerstin von Lingen (New York: Springer, forthcoming 2016).
3 John Dower, *Japan in War and Peace: Selected Essays* (New York: New Press, 1993), p. 12.
4 Ishizaka Kimishige, "Shūsen zengo no tōdai to wareware ga uketa kyōiku," in *Nanbara Shigeru no kotoba: 8-gatsu 15-nichi, kenpō, gakumon no jiyū*, ed. Tachibana Takashi (Tokyo daigaku shuppankai, 2007), pp. 31–32. (Unless noted otherwise, all Japanese books are published in Tokyo.)
5 Nagai Hitoshi, *Firipin to tainichi senpan saiban: 1945–1953 nen* (Iwanami shoten, 2010), p. 62. See also Kerstin von Lingen, "Setting the Path for the UNWCC: The Representation of European Exile Governments on the London International Assembly and the Commission for Penal Reconstruction and Development, 1941–1944," *Criminal Law Forum* vol. 25, issue 1 (2014): pp. 45–76; Dan Plesch and Shanti Sattler, "Before Nuremberg: Considering the Work of the United Nations War Crimes Commission of 1943–1948," in *Historical Origins of International Criminal Law: Volume 1*, ed. Morten Bergsmo, Wui Ling Cheah, and Ping Yi (Brussels: Torkel Opsahl Academic EPublisher, 2014), pp. 437–473.
6 Tsuyoshi Hasegawa, *Racing the Enemy: Stalin, Truman, and the Surrender of Japan* (Cambridge, MA: Belknap Press of Harvard University Press, 2005); Richard B. Frank, *Downfall: The End of the Imperial Japanese Empire* (New York: Random House, 1999); and Hosaka Masayasu, *"Haisen" to nihonjin* (Chikuma shobō, 2006).
7 See Barak Kushner, *Men to Devils, Devils to Men: Japanese War Crimes and Chinese Justice* (Cambridge, MA: Harvard University Press, 2015), pp. 47–57.
8 Robert A. Bickers, *Empire Made Me: An Englishman Adrift in Shanghai* (London: Allen Lane, 2003), p. 1.
9 Ibid., p. 2.

10 David Crowe, *War Crimes, Genocide, and Justice: A Global History* (New York: Palgrave Macmillan, 2014), pp. 94–101.

11 Jackson Nyamuya Maogoto, *War Crimes and Realpolitik: International Justice from WWI to the 21st Century* (Boulder, CO: Lynne Rienner Publishers, 2004), p. 5.

12 "Joint Four-Nation Declaration," the Moscow Conference, *The Avalon Project, Yale Law School Lillian Goldman Law Library*, http://avalon.law.yale.edu/wwii/moscow. asp, originally in Staff of the Committee and the Department of State, *A Decade of American Foreign Policy: Basic Documents, 1941–1949* (Washington, DC: Government Printing Office, 1950); Keith Sainsbury, *The Turning Point: Roosevelt, Stalin, Churchill, and Chiang-Kai-Shek, 1943: The Moscow, Cairo and Teheran Conferences* (Oxford: Oxford University Press, 1985), pp. 61–109.

13 Wu Sihua, Lu Fangshang, and Lin Yonlue, eds., *Kailuo xuanyan de yiyi yu yingxiang* (Taipei, Taiwan: Center for Humanities Research of National Chengchi University, 2014).

14 "Joint Four-Nation Declaration."

15 "Potsdam Declaration," in "Birth of the Constitution of Japan," the National Diet Library, 2003–2004, http://www.ndl.go.jp/constitution/e/etc/c06.html, originally from the Ministry of Foreign Affairs, "Nihon gaikō nenpyō narabini shuyō bunsho: 1840–1945," vol. 2, 1966.

16 Higashikuni Naruhiko, *Higashikuni nikki: nihon gekidōki no hiroku* (Tokuma shoten, 1968), p. 197.

17 Roger H. Brown, "Desiring to Inaugurate Great Peace: Yasuoka Masahiro, Kokutai Preservation, and Japan's Imperial Rescript of Surrender," *Saitama daigaku kiyō* (kyōyō gakubu), dai 50kan, dai 2gō, 2015, p. 202.

18 Ibid., p. 199.

19 Higashikuni, *Higashikuni nikki*, p. 204.

20 Nihon kyōsantō shuppan-bu, ed., *Jinmin no te de sensō hanzainin o* (Jinminsha, 1946). (Prange collection in National Diet Library, Tokyo), p. 3.

21 Nihon kyōsantō shuppan-bu, *Jinmin no te de*, p. 23.

22 Ibid., p. 24.

23 Higashikuni, *Higashikuni nikki*, pp. 226–227.

24 Ibid., p. 229.

25 Ibid.

26 Tanaka Hiromi, ed., *Bi-shi kyū senpan kaneki shiryōshū*, vol. 3 (Ryokuin shobō, 2012), pp. 33–35.

27 Nagai, *Firipin to tainichi*, p. 68.

28 "Senpan yōgisha no toriatsukai ni kansuru nihon seifu tōsho no sochi," within Senpan jimu shiryō (shōwa 16–20 nen) sono 1, Honkan 4B-023–00, Hei 11 hōmu 06335100 (National Archives of Japan, Tokyo, Japan).

29 Ibid. See also "Senpan mondai ni kansuru moto rikusō Shimomura Sadamu-shi no kōjutsu, Showa 42 nen 1 gatsu," part of Inoue Tadao archives in Yasukuni kaikō bunko (Yasukuni Archives), 393.4 (followed by hiragana sound e); Nagai Hitoshi, "Sensō hanzainin ni kansuru seifu seimeian – Higashikuninomiya naikaku ni yoru kakugi kettei no myakuraku," in "Teikoku" to shokuminchi – "dainihonteikoku" hōkai rokujūnen, ed. Nenpō nihon gendaishi henshū iinkai, *Nenpō nihon gendaishi*, vol. 10 (Gendaishiryō shuppan, 2005), pp. 277–321; and Shibata Shin'ichi, "Nihongawa senpan jishu saiban kōsō no tenmatsu," *Gunjishigaku* vol. 31, issue 1–2 (September 1995): pp. 338–349.

30 "Senpan mondai ni kansuru moto rikusō Shimomura Sadamu-shi no kōjutsu."

31 Tanaka, *Bi-shi kyū senpan kaneki shiryōshū*, vol. 1, p. 331.

32 Suzuki, *Shūsen kara kōwa made*, p. 37. In his personal memoir, Toyoda Kumao says this cabinet decision was never officially released: *Sensō saiban yoroku* (Taiseisha, 1986), p. 51.

33 Tanaka, *Bi-shi kyū senpan kaneki shiryōshū*, vol. 1, p. 330.

34  "Senpan yōgisha no toriatsukai ni kansuru nihon seifu tōsho no sochi."
35  "Japanese Appeal to U.S.," *The Manchester Guardian*, September 15, 1945.
36  Higashikuni, *Higashikuni nikki*, p. 239.
37  Sugita Ichiji, "Sensō shūketsu ni tomonau kongo no taikan to teikoku ni tsuite," September 15, 1945, Chūō – sengo shori – 80, Bōeishō kenkyūsho, shiryō etsuranshitsu (Military Archives, the National Institute for Defense Studies), Tokyo.
38  Senpan jimu shiryō (showa 16–20 nen) sono 1, Honkan 4B-023-00, Hei 11 hōmu 06335100 (National Archives of Japan, Tokyo, Japan).
39  John W. Dower, *Embracing Defeat: Japan in the Wake of World War II* (New York: W.W. Norton & Company, 2000), p. 477.
40  Ibid., p. 480.
41  Inoue Tadao shiryō, "Sensō saiban ni taisuru nihon seifu no kihon taido narabi ni hōshin," 61023, 393.4. This is written on "Daini fukuinkyoku zanmu shoribu" stationery, no pagination (Yasukuni Archives). See also Toyoda, *Sensō saiban yoroku*, pp. 48–62; Higurashi Yoshinobu, *Tōkyō saiban* (Kōdansha, 2008), pp. 147–150.
42  Yoshida Yutaka, *Nihonjin no sensōkan: sengoshi no naka no henyō* (Iwanami shoten, revised edition, 2005), p. 31. Aoki remembers it as the 24th in Shidehara's memoirs. See Shidehara heiwa zaidanhen, ed. *Shidehara Kijūrō* (Shidehara heiwa zaidan, 1955), p. 590.
43  Ibid., p. 589.
44  Ibid., p. 590.
45  Ibid., p. 592.
46  See the five-volume *Sensō chōsakai kankei shiryō*, a set of mostly handwritten documents housed in the Modern Japanese Political History Materials Room (Kensei shiryōshitsu) of the National Diet Library, Kensei shiryōshitsu shūshū bunsho 1244. These details I cite are from volume 1. Tomita Kei'ichirō, "Haisen chokugo no sensō chōsakai ni tsuite – seisaku o kenshō suru kokoromi to sono zasetsu," *Referensu* vol. 63, issue 1 (January 2013): pp. 85–108.
47  Higurashi, *Tokyo saiban*, p. 149.
48  Ibid., pp. 151–152.
49  Ibid., p. 153.
50  Ibid., pp. 154–155.
51  See Fujiwara Akira et al., eds., *Tettei kenshō showa tennō "dokuhakuroku"* (Ōtsuki Shoten, 1991).
52  Full text in *Chokurei dai 511 gō*, in Ōkurashō insatsukyoku, ed., *Kanpō*, gōgai, November 3, 1946, the National Diet Library Digital Collections, http://dl.ndl.go.jp/info:ndljp/pid/2962456?tocOpened=1.
53  The edict is reprinted in full in Ōkurashō, *Kanpō*, gōgai.
54  "Sanjūsanmannin ni onsharei taishatō nana shurui no kōhan'i ni wataru," *Yomiuri shimbun*, November 3, 1946 (morning edition).
55  Ōe Hiroyo and Kaneda Toshimasa, "Kokuritsu kōbunshokan shozō 'sensō hanzai saiban kankei shiryō' no keisei katei to bi-shi kyū sensō saiban kenkyū no kanōsei," *Rekishigaku kenkyū* (April 2015): pp. 19–33.
56  Chūō – shūsen shori – 546, "Dai 23 gunshireikan rikugun chūjō Tanaka Hisakazu-shi ni kansuru chūgoku saiban kiroku, sono 4," Bōeishō kenkyūsho, shiryō etsuranshitsu (Military Archives, the National Institute for Defense Studies), Tokyo.
57  Alessio Patalano, *Post-war Japan as a Sea Power: Imperial Legacy, Wartime Experience and the Making of a Navy* (London: Bloomsbury Academic, 2015).
58  Ōe and Kaneda, "Kokuritsu kōbunshokan shozō," pp. 28–29.
59  Wang Zhichen, *Yidai baoren Wang Yunsheng* (Wuhan: Changjiang wenyi chubanshe, 2004), p. 155. See also Adam Cathcart "Urban Chinese Perspectives on the U.S. Occupation of Japan, 1945–1947," *Studies on Asia Series II* vol. 3, issue 2 (2006): pp. 21–48.
60  "Araki moto taishō karishussho," *Yomiuri shimbun*, June 15, 1955, morning edition.

61  "Hata Shunroku, Araki Sadao chōshusho," Honkan-4B-023-00 Hei 11 hōmu 06420100 (National Archives of Japan, Tokyo, Japan).

62  Gary W. Gallagher, "Introduction," in *The Myth of the Lost Cause and Civil War History*, ed. Gary W. Gallagher and Alan T. Nolan (Bloomington: Indiana University Press, 2000), p. 1.

63  Eri Hotta, *Japan 1941, Countdown to Infamy* (New York: Alfred A. Knopf, 2013), p. 11, italics in original.

64  David Blight delivered the Alistair Cooke Memorial Lecture: Blight, BBC Radio 4, May 5, 2015, http://www.bbc.co.uk/programmes/b05t5jxf.

65  Udagawa Kōta, "Senpan no 'sengo': senpan no sensō sekininkan, sensōkan, sengo shakaikan," *Sensō sekinin kenkyū*, vol. 78 (2012): pp. 22–31.

# 4 The collapse of the Japanese empire and the great migrations

## Repatriation, assimilation, and remaining behind

*Araragi Shinzō (translated by Sherzod Muminov)*

On September 2, 1945, Japan accepted the terms of the Potsdam Declaration and unconditionally surrendered to the Allies. The downfall of the Japanese empire gave rise to a spectacular surge of migration within East Asia. The 3.67 million Japanese servicemen and civilians in military employ (*gunzoku*), deployed to imperial outposts in Asia, were demobilized. At the same time, around 1.6 million Koreans and other non-Japanese residents, including Okinawans living in the Japanese home islands (*naichi*), were sent back to their home regions. In quick succession, Japanese imperial subjects were repatriated from Korea, Taiwan, the South Pacific (*Nan'yō*), the Kwantung Leased Territory, the Japanese puppet kingdom of Manchukuo, Karafuto (Southern Sakhalin), and parts of China, altogether reaching up to 3.21 million people.[1] Of the more than 2.3 million Koreans living in Manchuria, close to 800,000 were transported to the Korean Peninsula or else repatriated of their own accord.[2] The total number of migrants moving in all directions approached 9 million people, equivalent to 9 percent of the total population of the Japanese Empire, estimated at 100 million people at the time. It was one of the largest human migration moments in history.[3]

Parallel with this massive multidirectional flow of human beings, the aftermath of Japan's defeat witnessed two further phenomena: the assimilation of those who chose to stay and the massive change in the lives of those who remained behind due to circumstances beyond their control. These individuals included Koreans living in Manchuria (now northeast China), ethnic Koreans who remained in Japan, Japanese residents forced to remain on the Chinese mainland, Japanese and Korean people stranded on Sakhalin, and indigenous Taiwanese people who were left behind in China. Kawashima Shin discusses issues related to the Taiwan aspects in Chapter 2 of this volume, while Katō Kiyofumi touches on the larger issues of imperial dissolution in Chapter 1, and Park Jung Jin focuses particularly on the case of North Korea in Chapter 11.

When Japan made the dramatic transition from a premodern to modern society in the nineteenth and early twentieth centuries, it underwent a series of tectonic structural changes and social shifts. One of these changes was a demographic transformation that saw Japan evolve from being a society with a high birth–high death ratio to being a high birth–low death rate country. In other words, Japanese

society experienced a demographic surge, and its population increased by 1 percent each year. In 1872 Japan's population stood at 35 million, by 1936 it had
doubled to 70 million, and in 1970 it had tripled to reach 100 million.[4] This was a
true population explosion, observed most dramatically in the farming villages of
the home islands, which saw an unprecedented increase in the number of residents.
This increase in population meant that more and more people turned to urban areas,
foreign countries, or Japan's overseas spheres of influence in search of work and
a livelihood. In the early twentieth century, the financial policies that Meiji Finance
Minister Matsukata Masayoshi had initiated in 1884 triggered the rapid dismantling of the Japanese agricultural working class. As a result, the scope of surplus
population struggling to make ends meet increased rapidly, contributing to an
increase in the number of displaced rural dwellers. An agreement with the Hawai-
ian government became a godsend, allowing farmers struggling with poverty to
make their way to Hawaii as labor migrants and boosting the domestic economy
with the remittances they sent home.

From 1885, at the same time as families in Japan's farming villages started
sending their daughters to urban areas as factory workers, men from agricultural
areas and the urban working class crossed the Pacific Ocean to become low-
wage contract workers in Hawaii and North America. Later, following a 1907
gentleman's agreement to limit the inflow of Japanese migrants into North
America, the stream of Japanese migration turned toward Central and South
America. Thus, in the fifty years leading up to World War II, the total number
of Japanese migrants to North and South America reached 650,000 people and
Japanese communities blossomed. At around the same time, as European colonial empires expanded in earnest to East and Southeast Asia, around 160,000
Japanese migrated to these regions as well, as a labor force, where they often
played the role of intermediaries – a "management-minority" between the European colonizers and the local populations.[5] Transnational labor migration from
Japan occurred within the same context as the coolie trade from China, born out
of a convergence of the demand on the international labor market and the demographic surplus in Japan's farming villages.[6]

## Migration to Japan's colonies and spheres of influence

As evidenced in the Meiji-era slogan of "rich nation, strong army" ( *fukoku kyōhei*),
modern Japan was a "national empire" (*kokumin kokka teikoku*). If we imagine it
as a cart, the nation-state system and the empire were the two wheels on which the
entire apparatus advanced. Once the foundations of the Japanese nation-state were
laid in the late nineteenth century, the first Sino-Japanese War (1894–1895) and
the Russo-Japanese War (1904–1905) provided Japan with opportunities to transform itself into a colonial empire. The formation and expansion of the Japanese
empire not only triggered the migration of Japanese imperial subjects but also
wielded an enormous influence on migration flows in East Asia during the first half
of the twentieth century.

The migration of Japanese to Asia started around the mid-nineteenth century with the development of colonial outpost cities in the European empires, such as Vladivostok, Shanghai, and Qingdao. This was followed by waves of labor migrants to the Philippines and French Indochina. The population movements to colonies and spheres of influence that accompanied the formation of the Japanese empire added a second layer to these earlier migrant communities. Moreover, these relocations, enabled by the empire's expansion, were not limited to the transfer of people from Japanese home islands (*naichi*) to overseas areas (*gaichi*). As Japan replaced Qing China and Tsarist Russia as the leading power in East Asia, large numbers of people from its newfound colonies, especially the Korean Peninsula, were flowing into Japan's large cities and coal mining regions. Yet another type of population transfer occurred between Japan's colonies, as exemplified in the migration of Koreans (who were formal members of the Japanese Empire) to Manchuria. The colonial migration of Japanese to their imperial spheres of influence involved 3.65 million people – almost six times the number of those who had emigrated to North and South America. This number – 3.65 million – accounted for over 15 percent of the total population increase in Japan. These vectors of population movements often intermingled, creating a large-scale and complex migration network throughout the Japanese empire.

The movement of Japanese citizens to Manchuria began after 1906, when the Kwantung Province became Japanese-leased territory and the rights to the South Manchuria Railway Company (SMRC, or *Mantetsu*) were transferred to Japan following the end of the Russo-Japanese War in 1905. However, the flow of Japanese to the mainland reached its height only after the founding in March 1932 of the Japanese puppet kingdom of Manchukuo. In 1906, the number of Japanese residents in the Kwantung Leased Territory and SMRC-controlled areas stood at just 16,613 people; by 1910, it had nearly quadrupled to 61,934, reaching 135,470 people in 1920. This steadily increased to 215,463 Japanese residents by 1930. In 1940, eight years after the establishment of Manchukuo, this number had surged to 1,000,303 people in the Kwantung Leased Territory and Manchukuo combined. By 1944, this total reached 1,662,234 residents. Including servicemen and their families, the total number of Japanese residents in Manchuria was well over 2 million people.

Populating the colonies with ethnic Japanese settlers was not the only way of tying them to the metropole for the long term. One of the characteristic features of colonial rule in the Japanese empire – a latecomer trying to catch up with Western imperial powers such as Great Britain, the United States, France – was its assimilationist policy to "Japanize" the social systems in the colonies. Dictated also by the geographical proximity between the colonies and the metropole, this "Japanization" program was carried out with an aim to raise production standards in the colonies to the level of the home islands. The aim also involved the positive endorsement of Japanese citizens settling in the colonies and spheres of influence. These settlers would serve as the vanguards in the enterprise of transplanting Japanese-style social order and culture to the colonies. Perhaps the best example of these efforts was the migration of 270,000 agricultural settlers to the farming villages of Manchuria as part of a government settlement policy. This move was taken with the goal in mind to eradicate anti-Japanese guerrilla movements, preserve public order, and install Japanese-style rule in the agricultural areas of Manchuria.[7]

Agricultural migration into Manchuria was one of the harbingers of the "total war" that exploded in 1937 – the Asia-Pacific War. After 1937, this was what determined most of the movements of people throughout the Japanese empire. The outbreak of this conflict meant that in the home islands, 7.9 million young males – the core of the nation's workforce – were pulled into the large-scale military conscription system. To counteract this loss of manpower, a mobilization system was created to enroll large parts of the domestic population, starting with women and adolescents, into production. For example, to compensate for the labor loss of the conscripted workforce, young men in their late teens were sent to Manchuria as part of "youth volunteer armies" (*seishō giyūgun*), and workers' units from the home islands or urban areas of Manchukuo were dispatched to alleviate the labor shortages in agricultural settlements. These measures were also extended to Taiwan and Korea, contributing to the increase of labor migration from Korea to Manchukuo. Moreover, as detailed by historians Tonomura Masaru and Sugihara Tōru, over 850,000 so-called forced laborers were sent from Korea and China to Japan's home islands.[8] In an extreme case, from 20,000 to 40,000 women from the home islands, colonies, or occupied areas accompanied the troops to the battlefields as so-called comfort women.[9]

## Imperial collapse and migration

What significantly transformed these patterns of human migration once again in East Asia was Japan's defeat in the Pacific War. Following the war's end, all of Japan's erstwhile empire, with the exception of Taiwan, came under the jurisdiction of either the United States or the Soviet Union. Consequently, the handling (repatriation) of civilians by these occupying powers greatly varied from region to region. While repatriation from Taiwan, controlled by the Chinese Nationalist Government (Kuomintang, KMT), and from the southern part of the Korean Peninsula and the Pacific Islands (*Nan'yō*), occupied by the U.S. Army, proved relatively trouble-free, the task of returning Japanese citizens from the now Soviet-controlled areas – Karafuto (Southern Sakhalin), the occupied sectors of what would become North Korea, and Manchukuo – was beset with difficulties. The migration of non-military elements from Manchukuo and northern Korea back to Japan also produced many casualties. This tragedy was, in part, the result of not only the Soviet Union's absolute disregard for the repatriation of Japanese citizens from Manchukuo but also the civil war between the KMT and the Chinese Communist Party (CCP), as well as the fact that the pace of repatriation was determined by the vicissitudes of Sino-Japanese relations.[10]

In addition, the KMT and CCP had adopted competing policies on the issue of repatriation (deportation) of Koreans from Manchuria.[11] Although, under KMT jurisdiction, the deportation of Koreans had begun immediately after the war's end, the CCP quickly adopted a policy that permitted Koreans to settle as an ethnic minority within China. On the other hand, when it came to the question of ethnic Koreans in the Japanese home islands (*naichi*), both the American occupiers and the Japanese government adopted the general principle that they should be returned to Korea. The transportation of these Koreans had actually started in 1945 but never reached its completion. The reason for this lay in the postwar transformations on the Korean Peninsula: the repatriation of ethnic Koreans was seriously disrupted by the confrontations and strife caused by the ruptures concomitant with the formation of a new state. As a result, around 600,000 ethnic Koreans remained in Japan, forming the community of *Zainichi* Koreans (*zainichi* means "being in Japan"), as Park Jung Jin's aptly describes in Chapter 11. Moreover, the United States' decision to detach and manage Okinawa separately from Japanese rule in Tokyo gave rise to the return of the ethnic category of Ryūkyūans in relation to its indigenous population, and their repatriation was carried out in a yet another way different from that of the Japanese on the main islands.

Importantly, although new borders were drawn, these boundaries did not lead to sudden changes in the realm of people's daily life. For example, the "borders" between northern Korea and the Chinese northeast were defined very loosely until the 1948 founding of the Democratic People's Republic of Korea (DPRK), and people casually crossed the frontier almost on a daily basis.[12] On the other hand, among those repatriated to the south of Korea were those who, trying to avoid the rampant chaos after the liberation of the peninsula from colonialism, managed to slip through the border controls via "secret passages" to rejoin family or relatives in Japan.[13] Moreover, as detailed by Tamura Masato, the indigenous Ainu population of Karafuto chose not to remain in the land of its ancestors and, using their relationship with the Japanese, many joined the repatriation flows to the Japanese home islands.[14] There were those who chose to remain in the lands of their settlement, and they were not limited to the ethnic Koreans in China or in Japan. Starting with the Japanese war orphans who were left behind in China, Japanese also remained in the Philippines and Indonesia. When these "remnant" groups resurfaced in the 1970s and 1990s, they drew significant political attention to lingering imperial legacies.

## Repatriation of Japanese citizens from Manchuria

Although Japan's puppet kingdom of Manchukuo was founded in 1932, 83 percent of its Japanese population, or 1.28 million people including those in the Kwantung Leased Territory, lived in urban areas. Many of these Japanese city dwellers were civil servants, employees of large corporations, or managers of small and medium-sized enterprises. They enjoyed a comfortable urban lifestyle as colonizers. On the other hand, Japan's increasingly ambitious policies toward the Soviet Union and the need to reign in the anti-Manchukuo, anti-Japanese guerillas meant that from 1932, the remaining 17 percent of the Japanese settlers – the 270,000 agricultural pioneers – colonized more and more of the frontier areas in northern and eastern Manchuria.

Especially during these initial periods, pioneers settled in areas that were strong-holds of anti-Japanese guerillas and met with dogged resistance – the Japanese settlers had to contend with more than just land reclamation. Although these settle-ments were part of a government policy from 1937 onward, because Japanese pioneers operated in areas with cultivated land, this form of colonization was often fraught with trouble. The colonists were confronted by fierce opposition even from ordinary Chinese people, who viewed the Japanese as an advance guard of land-grabbing invaders. Although there were some who had achieved "success" in farm-ing by settling during the early era of migration or by occupying areas in the vicinity of cities, as well as some who had established "friendly relations" with the neighboring Chinese and Korean villages, many of the Japanese settlements were isolated from the local population. The settlers of many of these communities struggled to adjust to the change of their environment and the daily challenges of managing a farm. Further, as Japanese ownership of the land expanded, the fragile economic base and shallow generational roots of these migrants in a new land meant that many of the settler communities remained essentially Japanese colonies of stragglers.[15]

As the Pacific War intensified after 1941 and Japan became bogged down in a war on many fronts, conscription from among the ranks of the pioneer settlements in Manchuria escalated, and the number of men in these communities visibly plummeted. On August 8, 1945, when the Soviet Army invaded Manchukuo, the lives of the Japanese, especially those living in the farming villages in the hinter-land, further changed dramatically. From then on, Manchuria was turned into a genuine battlefield. Under the "evacuation order," over 60 percent of the Japanese pioneers left their settler communities and started the trek to major cities, experi-encing hellish journeys along the way. During this mass exodus, many children, the elderly, and the sick were abandoned, people took their own lives, as witnessed in mass suicides, and some were even killed by their own blood relatives. The escape from Manchuria became a "flight of death."[16]

By October 1945, things had settled down. Japanese were accommodated in camps, and in what remained of the pioneer settlements they found the means and resources to eke out a modest existence. However, amidst the lack of food and, needless to say, appropriate clothing in the face of the approaching cold winter and deteriorating hygiene standards, contagious diseases spread very quickly, killing numerous displaced residents. Facing defeat in the inland outposts of the Japanese empire of Manchukuo, the Japanese settler colonists were left defenseless; it was as if the shield of the nation-state, under which they had been safely guarded, was suddenly removed. Deprived of this protection, these settlers were left as individu-als to face the upheavals of Manchurian society after defeat, abandoned in a situ-ation where "'life and death stood side by side."[17]

After the fall of Manchukuo, its territory came under the control of the Soviet Army. Although the Soviets were very enthusiastic about taking to Siberia around 600,000 Japanese Army prisoners of war and subjecting them to forced labor, as analyzed by Sherzod Muminov in Chapter 8 in this volume, the Russians further demonstrated little if any interest in protecting Japanese civilians. The Manchukuo police force was disbanded, but the police force of the reigning power, the Soviet Army, was not sufficient to keep order. In fact, not only did the Soviet Army neglect village-level policing, as an occupying army it also exposed Japanese citizens to such dangers as plunder, violence, and rape.

The organization that eventually took charge of protecting the remaining Japanese citizens was not the fallen kingdom of Manchukuo nor the Japanese embassy, which had stopped functioning. It was rather an organization called the Association of Japanese (*Nihonjinkai*), which operated in all the major cities. The Association not only played an active part in addressing unresolved issues in the lives of the city dwellers but also assisted with problems such as accommodation and support for a great number of refugees who had poured into the cities from frontier regions. Despite such internal efforts, the living standards of the Japanese residents in Manchuria were rapidly deteriorating. The city folk had their property and homes confiscated by the Soviet Army. Former Manchukuo government bureaucrats and civil servants, as well as employees of Japanese enterprises, were impoverished, having lost their jobs after the Soviet invasion. In the years following defeat, around 170,000 Japanese residents in Manchuria lost their lives. The ratio of casualties was especially high among agricultural settlers. Although they comprised not more than one-sixth of the entire Japanese population in Manchuria, almost half of their number died at the end of the war.[18]

Although the repatriation of Japanese former imperial subjects from areas occupied by the U.S. Army – for example, the Southern Pacific Islands – had already begun in October 1945, Japanese who found themselves in postwar Manchuria could see no indication of their repatriation starting at that time. The Japanese government, which favored the policy of Japanese residents staying on and "putting down roots" in Manchuria, was aware of the tragic conditions of its former colonial population. However, Tokyo had no direct diplomatic channels to the Soviet government, and appealing to the USSR through the General Headquarters (GHQ) of the Supreme Commander for Allied Powers (essentially the American military in Japan) had little effect. The repatriation of the Japanese from Manchuria finally got underway on May 6, 1946, only after the withdrawal of the Soviet Army from the region.

Following the retreat of the Soviet Army, a full-scale civil war unfolded in China between the Chinese Communist Party's Eighth Route Army and the KMT's Nationalist Army, with Manchuria as one of the major sites of battle. The U.S. Army and the KMT decided that the Japanese residents should be repatriated in order not to create an unnecessary distraction to the KMT's military operations.[19] However, clashes between the Nationalist and the Communist armies intensified, and by 1948, with the repatriation of the Japanese still incomplete, Manchuria came under the CCP's almost total control. On October 1, 1949, the People's Republic of China was established, and the repatriation of the Japanese still remaining behind was temporarily suspended. During the initial period of repatriation before the suspension, 1.05 million Japanese had returned home – 95 percent of all Japanese residents who had found themselves stranded in Manchuria after the war.[20]

# The "birth" of Japanese residents remaining in China

Even those Japanese who had managed to stay alive where "life and death stood side by side" had lost the means to survive, falling into a state of homelessness and destitution. As the extremely cold weather took hold of the region, their biggest concern became how to pull through the imminent winter. To survive in these conditions, many Japanese became day laborers, peddlers, live-in and domestic servants, workers at coal mines, and the like. Some even resorted to stealing – in other words, they took up all possible opportunities at their disposal to survive. Yet another option was to join a Chinese household and become one of their dependents.[21] In China at the time, a system was in place whereby those who could not afford a dowry could not get married; this had caused an imbalance between genders both in terms of class and sex ratios.[22] For this reason, Japanese women who became refugees had no shortage of marriage offers from Chinese suitors who could not pay a dowry. A large proportion of the women who stayed on in China as "remaining brides" (*zanryū fujin*) seem to have temporarily found shelter with Chinese families in this way. The same applied to Japanese children. In Chinese villages, adopting children was not something out of the ordinary; to the contrary, it was seen as a productive way to extend the family line. As a result, many Japanese children whom death separated from their parents or whose families decided to leave them behind in the charge of Chinese people were adopted into Chinese families.[23]

A second major phase of repatriation started in 1953 through the efforts of citizen's organizations. However, it soon became clear that repatriation would not be as simple as in the first phase immediately following the end of the war. Many of the Japanese women left behind had lived for close to eight years in China, and some had children, which made their repatriation situation complicated. For this reason, the second phase of mass repatriation of Japanese was not as efficient as the first. Following the deterioration of Sino-Japanese relations in the wake of the May 1958 Nagasaki Flag Incident, when a group of Japanese ultranationalists pulled down a Chinese flag hanging outside an exhibition hall, repatriation was suspended completely. The situation evolved with the 1959 promulgation of a Special Law on the Non-Returnees (*Mikikansha ni kansuru sochi hō*) and the "Pronouncement on the War Dead" that followed, when over 13,600 Japanese still living in China were officially pronounced dead by the Japanese government. At this point, these people probably lost their last chance to repatriate, and they were compelled to stay on as residents in China.[24]

However, this is not to say that the Japanese orphans and women who were left behind under such circumstances in China were excluded from their new local communities. Although Manchukuo had been branded a "puppet kingdom" and its residents "Japanese devils," the Japanese who stayed behind were wives and children of Chinese people and were generally assimilated as Chinese citizens.[25] At the same time, separated from their own Japanese society and left isolated in their newfound Chinese homes, many of the women who still held on to their strong Japanese identities had to survive amidst isolation and helplessness. These Japanese residents were criticized as "Manchurian puppets" or "Japanese devils" and were persecuted in the great political struggles that followed the founding of the People's Republic of China (PRC) in 1949 – in the 1957 Anti-Rightist Campaigns, the Great Leap Forward in 1958–1960, and the Cultural Revolution from 1965 to 1975. In particular, feelings of insecurity, despair, and fear for their lives as a result of the castigation they were subjected to during the Cultural Revolution are seen to have driven them, in part, to the decision to return to Japan following the normalization of relations between Japan and China in 1978.

## From Koreans in Manchuria to the Korean minority in China

As previously mentioned, the KMT and CCP policies regarding the issue of the assimilation of Koreans resident in northeast China (former Manchukuo) differed. The KMT government advocated Korean repatriation to the Korean Peninsula. The Chinese Communists, on the other hand, had fought for many years alongside one group of Koreans during the war of resistance against Japan. To gain an advantage in the civil war, the CCP was therefore ready to acknowledge the Koreans' right to settle in China in return for their participation and support.[26] As a result, the northeastern region of Yanbian was designated a Korean Autonomous Area (later Province), where the Korean minority's right to self-rule was recognized and Korean culture would be preserved. The willingness of the CCP to subsume the Korean residents into the ranks of Chinese citizens hastened the process of the Koreans' acquiring permanent residence in China. However, in the political upheavals following the PRC's founding, Korean residents were also subjected to persecution and discrimination. Although their treatment was not as harsh as that meted out to Japanese residents, Koreans could not fully shake off their precarious position as a minority within China.

Emerging from these developments, roughly 1.5 million Korean residents in China settled in Manchuria, and roughly 800,000 returned to the Korean Peninsula. People from the elite class of Korean former Manchukuo bureaucrats and Manchukuo military officers, such as the late president of South Korea Park Chung-hee, could foresee the CCP's rise to prominence in the Chinese northeast. Due to their deep hatred of the groups led by Kim Il-sung and backed by the Soviet Army in northern Korea, these Korean elites migrated into the U.S.-administered southern part of the Korean Peninsula. Conversely, among the anti-Manchukuo, anti-Japanese revolutionary soldiers, there were also many who returned to northern Korea following the liberation of Korea. Despite the redrawing of national borders, the changes did not bring such a sudden radical transformation to the daily lives of the people who lived in the area on the border between Manchuria and Korea. The border was porous, as previously mentioned, and did not stop children, for example, from attending high schools on the other side or people working on one side of the border while living on the other. It was not unusual for people to wake up in China in the morning, spend the day working in Korea, and return to China in the evening. They were living in a sort of transnational zone.[27]

## From imperial subjects to *Zainichi* Koreans

At the same time, of the more than 2 million Korean residents in Japan, almost all of the 700,000 forcibly moved to the Japanese home islands during the war were repatriated to the Korean Peninsula immediately after liberation. However, one part of this community of forced migrants – those who managed to escape their workplace and to build new lives in nearby Korean communities – remained in Japan. Moreover, the major groups of Korean residents who had arrived in Japan for reasons other than forced labor migration made their way back to the Korean Peninsula through official repatriation channels or on independently chartered fishing vessels (people-smuggling boats).

In 1945, although Korea was liberated from Japanese colonialism, it was divided along the 38th parallel into two zones, north and south, managed respectively by the Soviet and American armies. In the north, forces led by Kim Il-sung achieved the political upper hand in a very short time, while confusion plagued the south, where the U.S. Army–backed Syngman Rhee seized hegemony. This division presaged the establishment of the Cold War world order soon after the end of World War II.[28] As can be seen in the outbreak of the Jeju Uprising in 1948 (also known as the April 3 Incident), a rebellion on the Island of Jeju that lasted for just over a year in which tens of thousands lost their lives, the political situation was far from stable. Slightly more than two years later, the Korean War erupted, throwing post-World War II Korean society into further turmoil and leading to the death of over 2 million people.[29]

As a result of the chaos and civil war on the peninsula, many *Zainichi* Koreans simply abandoned the idea of returning to their motherland. Many also made the ironic choice of finding a way to be "smuggled back" to Japan to escape the dangers and hardships caused by the political struggles in Korea, such as the April 3 Incident. In a way quite different to the easily traversed borders between the Chinese northeast and northern Korea, making the journey to Japan from southern Korea was far from easy. The Japanese national borders were rigorously guarded by both the occupation authorities (GHQ) and by Japanese sentries. Around 38,000 Koreans were captured as they secretly tried to re-enter Japan and were forcibly sent back to South Korea. Thus, the nearly six hundred thousand-strong *Zainichi* Korean community of today is formed from a core of a number of different constituents: people who did not elect to return to Korea because they had established lives and livelihoods in Japan, people who for one reason of another had missed the chance to return during the initial phase of repatriation, and people who had returned but had then managed to re-enter Japan illegally.

I should point out here that, strictly speaking, these migrations were not ruled solely by macro events such as the collapse of the Japanese empire, the redrawing of national borders, or the establishment of the postwar order. As with the example of those who were "smuggled back" into Japan, the migrations also arose out of people's individual life choices and the various strategies that they adopted to somehow dodge or slip through the net of strict rules and regulations surrounding these arrangements and institutions.

## Deportation and repatriation in and around Okinawa

Of all the many migratory movements in and around Japan during the early postwar period, migration to and from Okinawa deserves special attention. This is because at the same time as some Okinawans were repatriated, much like Japanese residents, from the "outer colonies" (*gaichi*) as "Japanese," they were also deported as "Ryukyuans" from the Japanese home islands (*naichi*) to Okinawa. In a directive titled "Governmental and Administrative Separation of Certain Outlying Areas from Japan," issued on January 29, 1946, GHQ ordered that islands to the south of the 30th parallel be separated from Japan.[30] The directive also made it clear that the Ryukyu Islands would be the exclusive domain of an American military administration. A few weeks later, a February 17 memorandum on the "Registration of Koreans, Chinese, Ryukyuans and Formosans" ordered the registration of "Ryukyuans" as "foreigners" requesting repatriation from Japan, to be treated in the same manner as Koreans.[31] In May 1946, the U.S. military administration of Okinawa introduced a ban on travel from Japan's main islands to the Ryukyu Islands. With this limitation, even Ryukyuans themselves, not to mention the Japanese, could no longer migrate to the Ryukyu Islands. Only the 170,000 "Ryukyuans" who had been repatriated from overseas colonies or those who were living on the main islands and had already expressed their desire to return to the Ryukyu Islands were permitted to repatriate.

These barriers to migration reflected GHQ's intention to impose American rule of Okinawa as essential and indispensable amidst the changing state of affairs in postwar Asia. Following the decision to administer the Ryukyus separately from Japan, the Supreme Commander for the Allied Powers, General Douglas MacArthur, adopted a policy of discriminative control. In June 1947, MacArthur "liberated" the then Japanese-subordinated Ryukyu Islands from Japan by claiming that "the Ryukyus are not Japan, and the Ryukyuans are not Japanese." The categories of "Ryukyu" and "Ryukyuans" were thus constructed based on the United States' strategy for Asia.[32]

Of course, even before this decision, during the official repatriation from South Sea Islands that started in October 1945, the treatment of the "Ryukyuans," who constituted the majority of Japanese residents there, had been different from that of Japanese citizens from the main islands. While Japanese citizens from the main islands were to be all repatriated, those who were registered and had lived in Okinawa for over ten years were, as "Ryukyuans," given the right to choose between settling at their overseas location or being repatriated to Okinawa. In the initial period many of the Okinawa natives, who had by then become accustomed to life in the southern islands, expressed a willingness to settle there. However, as many of them received information about the destruction caused by the Battle for Okinawa in the spring of 1945, the number of those wishing to remain in the southern islands drastically decreased. Many decided to return to Okinawa, at least temporarily, to make sure their relatives were safe. In the end, all of the Okinawans returned to their islands.[33] These distinct categories created for "Ryukyu" and "the Ryukyuans" became the rationale for the American administration of Okinawa and for ruling it separately from the Japanese main islands until 1972, when it was returned to Japan. Over the years, it is clear that Okinawa occupied a primary role as the "cornerstone of the Pacific" in the U.S. military's Asia strategy.

## Human migration in postwar Japanese society and social cohesion

Japanese society in the immediate aftermath of the war was exhausted by long years of total conflict, while production capabilities were severely depleted by the military devastation. Above all, Japan also found itself in dire economic straits, hit hard by the loss of its colonies. The financially and physically diminished nation was forced to accept and accommodate an army of repatriates and demobilized soldiers equaling close to a tenth of its population. Moreover, the country continued to suffer almost from the moment of surrender due to a lack of foodstuffs, even as the economic hardship and social anxiety grew day by day. In such circumstances, while the repatriates were received as "compatriots" (*dōhō*), they were not, in fact, readily assimilated into postwar Japanese society.[34]

Although many repatriates had barely escaped alive from Japan's overseas territories, the public in the home islands had little understanding of these tragic experiences at war's end. Many of the repatriates' family members or relatives, not to mention larger Japanese society, confined the returnees to the position of outcasts, viewing them as "good-for-nothings" or as little more than a "nuisance." The relatives and family members who had sent off these same people to Manchuria with fanfare and cheers during the era of agricultural migration, turned their backs on the repatriates, shutting them out of their homes, ashamed to be seen with them. Wider Japanese society also rejected the returnees, stigmatizing them as pawns of imperialism and collaborators of and participants in colonialism. Although organizations were set up in various localities to provide emergency relief for the repatriate settlers, many settlers lived in isolated areas, excluded from neighboring villages and hamlets and often completely overlooked by Japanese society. While they did not face any danger of plunder or threats to their lives, many of the repatriates had never anticipated the sorts of difficulties they did confront after returning to their motherland. They never expected that they would live in extreme poverty as unwanted nuisances and a burden on their native country.

These hardships, the humiliation of being a repatriate in their own land, caused returnees to once again look abroad. One part of the country's youth looked once again toward emigrating to Central and South America; others set out to North America to study. Of course, along with accelerating their desire to migrate away from Japan, the trauma of the painful experiences postwar repatriates had endured while repatriating also served as a brake that discouraged emigration. This was especially true for those who had returned to Japan from Manchuria or Korea at war's end. Having experienced tragedy and already subjected to severe difficulties in leaving the periphery of the empire and returning "home," these repatriates were determined "never to leave their own land again." In a sense, the experience of having been a repatriate made for an extremely conflicted state of mind, simultaneously promoting and impeding the desire to emigrate abroad.[35]

However, this sense of alienation slowly faded during the Korean War and the windfalls brought by the enormous amount of "special procurements" requested by the American military for Japanese industry to produce. As the era of high-speed economic growth took off in the late 1950s and early 1960s, a social security system was put in place. Amidst this ultimately soaring economic growth, Japanese society's memories of the war quickly grew distant. For the repatriates, who had their hands full just trying to survive, there was little time to remember the past. In any case, they had not been excluded from citizenship, and they were in principle able to enjoy the affluence brought by economic growth as equal members of the nation (though many would argue that Koreans in Japan did not share those same advantages in the early postwar years). This high-speed economic growth contributed greatly to the restabilization of the social order in Japan.[36]

In 1972, as people's lives in Japan entered a more settled phase, and the new generation was preparing to take over the reins of society from the previous generation, diplomatic relations between Japan and China were normalized, and the "stranded war children" left in China resurfaced as a topic in the media. Immediately after diplomatic relations were restored between Japan and China, the repatriation of the war orphans began. In 1981, with war orphan visits to Japan to meet family members, calls for their return to Japan reached a climax. Close-up images of tearful embraces between children and former parents created a television sensation, and these reunions became true media events that blanketed newspapers and other news outlets. These meetings and the subsequent news maelstrom led to a resurgence of memories about the war within Japanese society. This was especially true for the repatriates, whose recollections of living in the former colonies sprang back to life once again. Part of the reason for this revival lay in the fact that the repatriates' memories of colonialism and repatriation had been buried so deeply in their psyche. Their experiences and the memory of such events never really received sympathy or understanding within larger Japanese society and had never been assigned a proper place in Japanese history. This gap led to feelings of alienation that never dissipated as the years passed but rather continued to smolder in the hearts of the repatriates.[37]

## Assimilation and exclusion of the
## *Zainichi* Korean residents

The large number of Japanese from the four Japanese home islands who lived in far-flung overseas colonies was one of the characteristic features of colonial rule in the Japanese empire. Another was the relentless promotion of assimilation policies, as symbolized by the *kōminka* ("Japanization") policies in various colonies. Despite blatant discrimination based on ethnicity, similarities between the peoples of the Empire, rather than their differences, were often emphasized, albeit nominally. Best symbolized by the "Japan–Korea single ancestry theory" (*Nissen dōsoron*), these connections served as a basis for the justification of colonial rule.[38] The ultimate goal was to reform the inhabitants of colonies and transform the colonial populations into Japanese imperial subjects for the purpose of complete assimilation. With the advent of total war, these policies eventually took the shape of forced assimilation policies such as requiring that Koreans adopt Japanese names.

Following defeat in 1945, as imperial Japan shrank its territory to only that of its home islands, the homogeneity and unity of the Japanese people served to legitimize the new nation-state and to bind society together.[39] Kawashima Shin analyzes some of the complexity and pitfalls within this transformation in Chapter 2. This process meant that in postwar Japan, any heterogeneous existence was to be excluded from Japanese society and the most representative example were the Koreans, who were of a different ethnic origin. The 600,000 Korean residents who had remained in Japan after the war became subject to the Alien Registration Ordinance established in 1947. Further, in 1952, with the promulgation of the San Francisco Peace Treaty, these Korean residents were fully divested of Japanese citizenship. Moreover, although the GHQ, whose primary goal was the peaceful occupation of Japan, classified the Koreans as a people liberated from Japanese imperial rule, the Americans viewed Korean residents in Japan as elements that would render the country unstable. As was clearly seen in the so-called Hanshin Education Struggle in 1948, when Korean families in Kobe and Osaka demonstrated against the Japanese government's order to send their children to Japanese schools, the GHQ did not shy away from suppressing Korean minority struggles.

After the signing of the San Francisco Peace Treaty and the establishment of a stable political structure in Japan, political attitudes in Japan started to harden along Cold War political alliances, and the Japanese government took a hostile attitude toward the *Zainichi* Korean community. At the core of this community was the General Association of Korean Residents in Japan (*Chongryon*), which maintained close relations with the Democratic People's Republic of Korea (DPRK, or North Korea).[40] Park Jung Jin, in Chapter 11 in this volume, analyzes in greater detail Chongryon's role in the people's diplomacy established between Japan and the DPRK. While actually legal residents in Japan, the first generation of *Zainichi* Koreans could not let go of the idea that they were still awaiting repatriation to their fatherland; they were beset by "the desire to return." These Koreans considered themselves "expatriates" of the DPRK, or South Korea, and for them Japanese society was simply a temporary abode. They were, in fact, the epitome of "permanent sojourners." For many of these Koreans, who maintained a strong consciousness as expatriates abroad, repatriation to North Korea emerged as a logical and proper choice. During the exodus to North Korea that began in 1959 and continued for almost two decades, around 90,000 *Zainichi* Koreans departed Japan for their historic fatherland.[41]

A key factor in this emigration was the fact that the Japanese government was positively disposed to this mass repatriation.[42] Both the Japanese government and Japanese society at the time held the view that Korean residents should return to Korea. In 1952, a system of military pensions was re-established in Japan, and in the latter half of the 1950s, the national health insurance system, the pension system, and other basic services were introduced. These, however, were circumscribed by the citizenship clause, and Korean residents were excluded from these services, as they were not technically citizens of Japan. Amidst this social exclusion within Japanese society, many of the *Zainichi* Korean residents themselves kept alive the "expatriate" consciousness.

The turning point came in the second half of the 1960s. Following the signing of the Treaty on Basic Relations between Japan and the Republic of Korea in 1965, both parties embarked on a set of measures to improve the conditions of the South Korean citizens among the *Zainichi* Koreans. Rather than viewing it as a place of temporary residence, *Zainichi* Koreans developed deeper ties with Japanese society as their children – second-generation Koreans born in Japan – grew up. However, many of the second-generation *Zainichi* Koreans who graduated from Japanese high schools and universities during the era of rapid economic growth faced persistent discrimination in the job market and in their search for marriage partners. While Japanese citizens naturally enjoyed the opportunities and economic prosperity that came with robust economic growth, Korean residents, who were seen as separate from the Japanese people (*kokumin*), were completely kept out of the loop.[43] Needless to say, Koreans were hardly welcomed into Japanese society even before the war and had suffered inferior working conditions and received discriminatory payment even as imperial subjects. Still, Korean residents on the Japanese home islands had been granted some rights and were, at least for a time, subsumed into Japan's imperial structure, albeit as "second-class citizens." But after the war, especially following the signing of the San Francisco Peace Treaty, Koreans in Japan were more than before fundamentally excluded from society both socially and legally than before, and they truly became foreigners in the eyes of the state.

Occasionally a series of anti-discrimination movements unfolded in Japan, as seen in the example of the so-called Case of Hitachi Employment Discrimination in 1970, when the Hitachi company canceled an employment offer to an applicant after it was discovered that he was a *Zainichi* Korean.[44] Challenges to abolish discrimination were facilitated by the emergence of innovative local and municipal leadership and by the struggle for the citizenship rights of *Zainichi* Koreans, which served to build bridges between their communities and larger Japanese society. At the root of all these transformations was the Korean residents' rising consciousness that they wanted to live permanently in Japanese society with their heads held high, as one generation took the place of another and second- and third-generation Koreans accepted their Korean heritage.[45] Accordingly, through the efforts of teachers, children, and social activists, a more united consciousness of being Korean and Japanese developed in each locality. These developments were given additional momentum as an awareness of international human rights, based on "the principle of equality of foreign and domestic citizens," more thoroughly permeated Japanese society. This was evidenced in the ratification of the International Bill of Human Rights in 1979 and of the Convention Relating to the Status of Refugees in 1981. Starting from the 1990s, amidst the rapid increase in the number of foreigners coming to live and work in and gain citizenship in Japan, as well as the assistance that was extended from many corners of the globe in the wake of the Great Hanshin Earthquake in 1995, the idea of harmonious co-existence among different peoples based on multiculturalism started to take hold and to alter postwar Japanese society.

In this way, the 1970s saw experiments in local communities and innovative methods of self-government, leading to the acceptance of the *Zainichi* Koreans as ideas about citizenship grew in solidarity with the Japanese. These attempts marked a break within Japanese society from the era of colonial mentality and a desire to live together in harmony with the Korean residents. These and other examples of returnees and immigrants who have come to Japan in sizeable numbers having been raised in alien cultures – returnees from China, for example, or refugees from Indonesia hoping to make a life in Japan – have triggered important transformations in postwar Japanese society.

## Conclusion

The massive human movements in East Asia in the first half of the twentieth century can be categorized in at least four different groupings. They were movements necessitated by rearrangements and realignments that occurred in the global system during the second half of the nineteenth century; movements of people toward new frontiers whether overseas or within the same country triggered by population increases or great social change; migrations that accompanied the transformation of Russia and Japan into colonial empires; and, finally, movements brought about by the impact of total war during the Japanese empire's Asia Pacific War. Among these, the migrations caused by Japan's plunge into imperialism and the ensuing war gave rise to enormous countercurrents of repatriation once the Japanese empire experienced defeat. Furthermore, the returning flows of people and their settlement in new locales after the empire's collapse were not defined simply by people moving en masse across "new borders" or choosing to stay where they were. Of great importance were the processes of social integration in the postwar societies and the question of how these people were subsumed into – or excluded from – their respective communities. This history goes well beyond the immediate postwar period and is invariably connected to the Cold War when various returnee groups once again reappeared in Japanese society. The human migration caused by Japanese imperialism and its total war have left an enduring legacy of physical pain and psychological wounds in many countries in ways that continued for decades after the end of the war, and we must now seek to analyze those circumstances and the aftermath.

## Notes

1  "Demobilization" denotes the return of servicemen from battlefronts, whereas "repatriation" signifies the return of civilians from overseas colonies to the home islands. Although there is a difference between the two, "repatriation" sometimes refers to the homecoming of all 6.6 million Japanese citizens at war's end, servicemen and civilians alike. See Wakatsuki Yasuo, *Sengo hikiage no kiroku* (Jiji tsūshinsha, 1995).
2  Tanaka Ryūichi, "Chōsenjin no manshūijyū," in *Nihon teikoku o meguru jinkō idō no kokusai shakaigaku*, ed. Araragi Shinzō (Fuji shuppan, 2008), p. 185. (Unless otherwise noted, all Japanese books are published in Tokyo.)
3  Araragi Shinzō, "Josetsu 1," in *Teikoku igo no hito no idō: posutokoroniarizumu to gurōbarizumu no kōsakuten*, ed. Araragi Shinzō (Bensei shuppan, 2013), p. 20.
4  Kuroda Toshio, *Nihon jinkō no tenkan kōzō* (Kokin shoin, 1979).
5  Okabe Makio, *Umi o watatta nihonjin* (Yamakawa shuppansha, 2002).
6  Sunil S. Amrith, *Migration and Diaspora in Modern Asia* (New York: Cambridge University Press, 2011); Iijima Mariko, "Twice Migration of Japanese Immigrants to Hawai'i: Processes, Motives and Continuity of Domestic and International Migrations," *Journal of American & Canadian Studies* Issue 28 (2010), p. 29.
7  The Study Group for Research into the History of Migration into Manchuria, ed., *Nihon teikokushugi ka no manshū imin* (Ryūkei Shosha, 1976).
8  Tonomura Masaru, *Chōsenjin kyōsei renkō* (Iwanami shoten, 2012); Sugihara Tōru, *Chūgokujin kyōsei renkō* (Iwanami shoten, 2002).
9  Song Youn-ok, "Nihongun 'ianfu'," in *Hito no idō jiten: nihon kara ajia e, ajia kara nihon e*, ed. Yoshiwara Kazuo, Araragi Shinzō, Iyotani Toshio, and Yoshikazu Shiobara (Maruzen shuppan, 2013), pp. 58–59.
10  Katō Kiyofumi, *"Dainihon teikoku" hōkai: higashi ajia no 1945 nen* (Chūō kōronsha, 2009).
11  Tanaka Ryūichi, "Zaichūgoku chōsenjin no kikan: chūgoku kokumintō no sōkan seisaku o chūshin ni," in Araragi, *Teikoku igo*, pp. 73–93.
12  Hanai Miwa, "Teikoku hōkaigo no chūgoku tōhoku o meguru chōsenjin no idō to teijū," in Araragi, *Teikoku igo*, pp. 108–111.
13  Fukumoto Taku, "'Mikkō' ni miru zainichi chōsenjin no posuto-shokuminchisei," in *Teikoku hōkai to hito no saiidō: hikiage, sōkan, soshite zanryū*, ed. Araragi Shinzō (Bensei shuppan, 2011), pp. 477–483.
14  Tamura Masato, "Karafuto ainu no 'hikiage'," in Araragi, *Nihon teikoku o meguru*, p. 210.
15  Araragi Shinzō, *"Manshū imin" no rekishi shakaigaku* (Kōrosha, 1994).
16  Ibid.
17  Ibid. In the roughly six months spent in refugee camps from the August 1945 "flight," one in three Japanese settlers lost their lives.
18  Ibid.
19  Katō Kiyofumi, *Dainihon teikoku.*
20  Katō Yōko, "Haisha no kikan: chūgoku kara no fukuin/hikiage mondai no tenkai," *Kokusai seiji* vol. 109 (1995): pp, 110–125.
21  Araragi, *Manshū imin.*
22  Kaji Itaru, "'Chūgoku zanryū hōjin' no keisei to ukeire ni suite: senbetsu aruiwa senbatsu to iu shiten kara," in *Kokusai imin no shindōkō to gaikokujin seisaku no kadai*, ed. Kajita Takamichi (Ministry of Justice of Japan, 2001), p. 276.

23 This is the Japanese version of the events; needless to say, the views on the Chinese side were different. For example, Asano Shin'ichi and Yan Tong's work superbly documents the humanism of the Chinese foster parents who adopted the children of the enemy – "the little Japanese devils" – in the face of antagonism and social pressure in postwar China: Asano and Yan, *Ikoku no fubo: chūgoku zanryū koji o sodateta yōfubo no gunzō* (Iwanami shoten, 2006).
24 Araragi Shinzō, "Chūgoku 'zanryū' nihonjin no kioku no katari: katari no henka to 'katari no jiba' o megutte," in *Manshū: kioku to rekishi*, ed. Yamamoto Yūzō (Kyoto: Kyōto daigaku gakujutsu shuppankai, 2007), p. 220.
25 Araragi, "Josetsu 1."
26 Tanaka, "Zaichūgoku chōsenjin."
27 Hanai, "Teikoku hōkaigo."
28 Katō Kiyofumi, *Dainihon teikoku.*
29 Fukumoto, "'Mikkō' ni miru."
30 General Headquarters (GHQ), Supreme Commander for the Allied Powers (SCAP), "Memorandum for Imperial Japanese Government" (SCAPIN-677), January 29, 1946; http://www.mofa.go.jp/mofaj/area/takeshima/pdfs/g_taisengo01.pdf.
31 GHQ SCAP, "Registration of Koreans, Chinese, Ryukyuans and Formosans," (SCAPIN-746), February 17, 1946, https://rnavi.ndl.go.jp/kensei/tmp/SCA_1.pdf.
32 Nakano Yoshio and Arasaki Moriteru, *Okinawa sengoshi* (Iwanami shoten, 1976), pp. 14–15.
33 Imaizumi Yumiko, "Nan'yō shotō hikiagesha no dantai keisei to sono katsudō: nihon no haisen chokugo o chūshin toshite," *Shiryō henshūshitsu kiyō* vol. 30 (2005).
34 For a study in English of the repatriation and reintegration of overseas Japanese residents into the postwar society, see Lori Watt, *When Empire Comes Home: Repatriation and Reintegration in Postwar Japan* (Cambridge, MA: Harvard University Asia Center, 2009).
35 Araragi, *Teikoku igo.*
36 Araragi, *Teikoku hōkai.*
37 Yamamoto Chieko, "Kitachōsen kara no hikiage taiken," in Araragi, *Teikoku igo*, pp. 193–200.
38 The "*nissen dōsoron*" theory held that the Japanese and the Koreans descended from the same ancestors and can be traced to the seventeenth-century Confucian scholar Arai Hakuseki (1657–1725). In the twentieth century, the theory was used to justify the annexation of Korea. See Oguma Eiji, *Tan'itsu minzoku shinwa no kigen: "Nihonjin" no jigazō no keifu* (Shin'yōsha, 1995).
39 Oguma, *Tan'itsu minzoku.*
40 Tonomura Masaru, "Posuto shokuminchishugi to zainichi chōsenjin," in *Imin kenkyū to tabunka kyōsei*, ed. The Japanese Association for Migration Studies (Ochanomizu shobō, 2011), pp. 188–195.
41 Tessa Morris-Suzuki, *Exodus to North Korea: Shadows from Japan's Cold War* (Lanham, MD: Rowman & Littlefield, 2006).
42 Ibid.
43 Kim Jeong-won, "Zainichi chōsenjin no sengo to watashi," in Araragi, *Teikoku igo*, pp. 459–475.
44 John Lie, *Multiethnic Japan* (Cambridge, MA: Harvard University Press, 2009), p. 108.
45 Tonomura, "Posuto shokuminchishugi."

# War criminals, POWs, and the imperial breakdown

# 5 The shifting politics of guilt

## The campaign for the release of Japanese war criminals

*Sandra Wilson*

After the Second World War, the victorious Allies brought nearly 5,700 Japanese suspects to trial for war crimes, in two different categories of proceedings.[1] Twenty-eight military and political leaders were presented to the International Military Tribunal for the Far East (IMTFE) in Tokyo, in the equivalent of the Nuremberg trials in which senior Nazis were prosecuted between 1946 and 1948. The Japanese were charged with crimes relating to the planning, initiating, or waging of aggressive war. Using the principle of command responsibility, all except two defendants were also charged with conventional war crimes, which mostly concerned murder and ill-treatment of Allied prisoners of war and local civilians in areas occupied by the Japanese military.[2] Between 1945 and 1951, thousands of Japanese military personnel were also prosecuted in military courts for conventional war crimes under the separate national legislation passed by governments of seven countries – Australia, Nationalist China, France, the Netherlands, the United Kingdom, and the United States – plus the newly independent Philippines. The prosecutions took place in fifty-three locations throughout Southeast Asia, the Pacific, China, and in Darwin and Yokohama. The great majority of defendants were convicted. About a thousand people were condemned to death (though not all death sentences were carried out); others were sentenced to life imprisonment or other jail terms.[3] Those convicted were generally executed or imprisoned in the territory in which they had been tried. The Soviet Union and the People's Republic of China also prosecuted Japanese military personnel whom they designated as war criminals, though these trials took place outside the system created by the other wartime Allies, as also analyzed by Sherzod Muminov in Chapter 8.

Even after the end of the Allied Occupation of Japan in April 1952 and the restoration of Japan's sovereignty, the prosecuting powers retained control of war criminals' sentences. For governments that had ratified the San Francisco Peace Treaty, Article 11 decreed that only the prosecuting government could authorize parole or any form of clemency, in the case of the national tribunals, and a majority of the prosecuting governments had to agree when dealing with IMTFE defendants. Under the terms of the Treaty, the Japanese government could only "recommend" to the relevant foreign governments that sentences should be varied.[4]

From the late 1940s onward and especially after the end of the Allied Occupation, large numbers of Japanese people lobbied vigorously for the repatriation of convicted war criminals held overseas, for an end to trials, for cessation of the death penalty, and, eventually, for clemency to be shown to those serving prison terms. Ordinary people throughout Japan signed petitions, attended rallies, harassed politicians, and turned up in large tour buses at Sugamo Prison in Tokyo, where war criminals were incarcerated, to visit the prisoners. War criminals became a volatile and emotive issue in Japanese domestic politics, and the public campaign became impossible to ignore. Lobbying on behalf of war criminals put strong pressure on the Japanese government to act on behalf of the prisoners, and in turn the Japanese government applied pressure on the foreign governments that retained the power to mitigate sentences of convicted war criminals.

The domestic and international implications of the public campaign were thus closely intertwined. As in Germany, reflection on the current and future situation of war criminals and of the circumstances of their convictions provided an early platform for reformulations of the meanings of the war and of war guilt, and supporters of war criminals were emboldened to demand action from their government. Kerstin von Lingen touches more fully on this topic in her Chapter 16 in this volume. At the same time, Japanese domestic politics, like German politics, intersected sharply with the rise of the Cold War in the international arena. The place of both countries in the postwar order changed rapidly from the late 1940s onward, as the United States and its Allies increasingly accepted their former enemies as partners. Western governments became convinced that they needed Japanese support, and they wanted to deter Japan from leaning instead toward the Soviet Union or, later, toward Communist China. The new importance of Japan regionally and internationally convinced Western governments that they should give serious consideration to Japanese requests for clemency: requests that in turn had been stimulated by the public campaign in Japan. By the end of 1953, all surviving war criminals convicted by the Western Allies and still held overseas had been repatriated to Japan to serve out the remainder of their sentences. At this point, prisoners were still detained in the Soviet Union, and the People's Republic of China held a large number of suspects who had not yet been tried. By the end of 1958, all convicted war criminals held by the former Western Allies had been released, even if their sentences had not expired. Japanese prisoners had also been returned by the Soviet Union and Communist China, to be released on arrival in Japan. In this chapter I investigate the role of the public campaign in Japan on behalf of convicted war criminals in the processes leading to repatriation and release, asking specifically what accounted for the upsurge in support for clemency in this period, and what the impact of the campaign was on the fate of the prisoners.

## Early stages of the campaign

In the immediate postwar period, war criminals had few public supporters in Japan. The Japanese press initially paid little attention to them once they had been convicted, and public opinion toward them seems to have been largely indifferent and sometimes negative.[5] According to later press reports, the families of war criminals had suffered social discrimination in the early years: they were refused employment, for example, and did not fare well in marriage negotiations. Some local authorities apparently denied permission for the construction of graves for executed war criminals.[6]

The Japanese government, which remained in place throughout the Allied Occupation of 1945–1952, was also largely indifferent at first to what happened to former military personnel convicted as war criminals. The exception was officials in the First and Second Demobilization Bureaus, who were former members of the Army and Navy General Staff respectively, now operating as civilian bureaucrats.[7] During the drafting of the San Francisco Peace Treaty from 1949 onward, the Japanese government raised no objections to proposed provisions on war criminals, though it negotiated and argued over other matters, including reparations, fishing rights, renunciation of territory, shipbuilding, possible rearmament, and post-Occupation security arrangements.[8] Foreign Ministry officials, who acknowledged Japan's obligation under the Potsdam Declaration to accept the judgements of the war crimes trials, recorded that they had "no particular reason to object" to Article 11 of the San Francisco Peace Treaty.[9]

Public attitudes to war criminals, by contrast, were showing the first signs of change. The campaign on behalf of war criminals began in the late 1940s, though it kept a fairly low profile at first, given that most of the population appeared to be still indifferent or hostile to those who had been convicted. During the Occupation, support for war criminals was mostly channeled through prefectural-level Associations of the Families of the Missing (*Nihon rusu kazoku kai*), an organization of families of the thousands of soldiers and civilians who had not returned from overseas, especially from the Soviet Union and China, after August 1945. The Associations also worked to end the death penalty for convicted war criminals, encourage repatriation for those still held overseas, produce petitions for clemency and support for the families of war criminals, and asked for aid for these activities from the government's Demobilization Bureaus.[10] Government officials who were concerned about war criminals, like those in the Demobilization Bureaus, were reluctant to show their hand for fear of offending foreign governments before a peace treaty had been signed. Instead, they supported non-government groups, urging them to incite public opinion in Japan on war criminals and to make the case that their sentences should be reduced on humanitarian and religious grounds – that prisoners were incarcerated in foreign lands far from their homes and families, that forgiveness and mercy were warranted now that Japan had turned its back on war – rather than on political or diplomatic grounds.[11]

In 1951, advocates for war criminals began to take a much higher profile. Their heightened visibility was intimately connected to the volatile social and political conditions prevailing in Japan at the time and to more favorable press images of war criminals. Political and social conditions were changing very rapidly. For a start, leading military figures were returning to public life and were taking responsible and respected positions. In October 1951, the ban on former military officers holding public office was lifted in a large number of cases, in what is known as the "depurge" of 122,000 career military personnel who had originally been "purged"; 117,000 had been released from purge restrictions by April 1952.[12] Former senior members of both armed services became conspicuously active in politics and in civil society at the local, prefectural, and national levels.[13] Press commentary cautiously noted that senior military officers, who were generally considered responsible for the war, had returned to normal life and to public office, while war criminals convicted in national tribunals, said to be mostly junior personnel following the orders of their superiors, were still incarcerated.[14] Prisoners themselves, according to one report, considered that the crimes prosecuted in the national courts, as distinct from those prosecuted at the IMTFE, were on a par with the offences committed by those who had been purged; it was therefore wrong, in this view, that MacArthur had shown benevolence to the purged but not to war criminals, and Sugamo inmates were not happy about the lifting of the purge.[15]

In August–September 1951 the contents of the San Francisco Peace Treaty were made public, though the treaty did not come into effect for another seven months or so. War criminals themselves were deeply disappointed with Article 11 because many of them had expected that they would be released or at least that their sentences would be substantially reduced when peace was concluded. Thanks to press stories recording their comments – anonymously, given that identifying them might have endangered their prospects of release – their disappointment became more widely known. Though the press still displayed ambivalence, such stories promoted an image of convicted war criminals as men who had already paid a considerable price for their crimes and were now at the mercy of inscrutable foreign governments. As an unidentified prisoner wrote, "We were simply holding out for the peace treaty, and so were our families, only to find we are as badly off as ever now that it has come."[16] Despite the disappointment, many prisoners, along with some government officials, seem to have assumed there would still be some kind of general clemency when the treaty actually came into force in April 1952. When that did not happen, there was even greater anger and frustration.[17]

The end of the Allied Occupation in April 1952 was a turning point for the public campaign on behalf of war criminals. Press controls imposed by the Americans disappeared, allowing for a much greater range of public comment on and representation of the prisoners. To take the example of the cinema, in November 1945, the Occupation had issued a list of "problematic" cinematic content. Films with military themes were not allowed, "except when militarism [was] shown to be evil."[18] Similar regulations existed for print media. It would have been very difficult to express open sympathy for war criminals between 1945 and 1952 or to portray them in a positive light. In 1952 and 1953, on the other hand, at least five popular movies were made portraying the prisoners favorably. A steady stream of press articles demanded sympathy for the plight of the war criminals convicted in national tribunals, who were presented as ordinary soldiers who had been condemned for doing their job and thus were now paying a price that was too high.[19]

## War criminals and the Japanese press

The Japanese press itself was a major factor in war criminals' rise to prominence as a political and social issue. Mass culture was expanding rapidly in the early 1950s. The cinema was moving into its "second golden age," with movies providing "Japan's primary source of entertainment" until about 1960.[20] Weekly news magazines began to proliferate. In one 1952 survey of 6,700 households throughout Japan, 56 percent said they had bought a magazine in the last month, at a time when poverty was widespread; in the cities, the proportion was 63 percent.[21] The press naturally had an appetite for human interest stories, as did film-makers, and they needed a lot of such stories because the press was expanding so rapidly. Journalists and film-makers sought out and interviewed convicted war criminals, inviting them to tell their stories, or based their works on published collections of war criminals' writings.[22] The resulting articles naturally ended up presenting the war criminals' version of events, whereas in earlier years the voices of the prisoners had rarely been heard. The demand for copy, in a context where Occupation censorship was no longer an issue, was ultimately responsible for the wide circulation of certain stock theses: that war crimes trial verdicts were unfair, that defendants had been mistakenly identified, that they had only been following orders, that punishments were disproportionate to offences, and that relatively junior officers had been made to suffer in place of their superiors. The dominant trend in the press was to report on war criminals as they supposedly were after the war – ordinary men, missing their homes and families, and needed by those families – rather than to describe or reflect on what they had done during the war. The press was thus crucial in the moral reconfiguration of the war criminal in popular Japanese culture.

By 1952, the only convicted Japanese war criminals still in prison overseas were held by Australia on Manus Island in Australian New Guinea and by the Philippines in Muntinlupa Prison outside Manila (Figure 5.1). Those on Manus remained out of reach of the press, and little information about them leaked out. The war criminals in Manila, on the other hand, became celebrities in Japan. Mainstream consciousness in Japan of the prisoners incarcerated in the Philippines had evidently not been high: journalists from Tokyo discovered the prisoners virtually by accident in early 1952, when they accompanied official Japanese delegations sent to Manila to discuss war reparations payments. Once they became aware that war criminals were imprisoned in Muntinlupa, journalists from the major Japanese newspapers started to report on them; war criminals quickly became a more attractive topic than reparations.[23] Their situation was much easier to understand than the technicalities of reparations, and they offered immediate material for human interest stories. The fate of war criminals could readily be positioned as a non-political issue belonging to the private realm: reporting concentrated on the suffering of the prisoners' families, the homesickness of those imprisoned in Manila, the anxiety of life on death row, and the untiring efforts of people working to get prisoners released. The 100 or so Japanese prisoners in Manila became an emotive focus of press coverage of war criminals, and the imposing white walls of the jail

*Figure 5.1* Sketch of Muntinlupa Prison, Manila, *Sugamo shimbun*, May 1953

Source: Reprinted in Chaen Yoshio (ed.), *BCkyū senpan Firipin saiban shiryō*, Fuji shuppan, 1987, p. 158.

in Manila became one of the most distinctive symbols of the prisoners' plight, along with the gates of Sugamo Prison, with their English-language signs in the middle of Tokyo.

It was not difficult for journalists to write about war criminals because the prisoners could be made to fit neatly into standard tropes familiar from wartime. Newspaper reports, journal articles, and films about war criminals were often heavily sentimental. Many examples appeared in the press of a classic type of story, known as the "beautiful story," or *bidan*. Such stories replicated themes from wartime Japanese propaganda and presumably had immediate resonance for that reason. The portraits in journalistic articles and in readers' responses reflect wartime stereotypes of fighting men and of their patriotic, grieving mothers and wives. Soldiers were said to have been convicted because they "burned with patriotism" in carrying out their superiors' orders or in furthering national aims.[24] They now felt, it was suggested, that they were taking responsibility for Japan's defeat on behalf of the Japanese people, just as previously they had fought a war on behalf of the Japanese people.[25] The portrayal of this selfless soldier of 1952 or 1953 or later is not so very different from that of the selfless propaganda soldier who had gone to war between 1937 and 1945. Meanwhile, those who suffered most from their incarceration and absence from home were apparently their grieving mothers. Whereas the ubiquitous propaganda mother in wartime had stoically sent her son to war, in the early 1950s, she was equally stoic in awaiting his return from prison.

Supposedly factual accounts by Japanese journalists focused on such prototypical figures, while feature films presented the same kind of characters in avowedly fictional settings. A 1952 press article described a mother weeping by the radio as she heard her son's voice for the first time in ten years, on a radio program that transmitted messages from prisoners in Manila.[26] In a story of a devoted wife based on an actual case, Ichinose Chiyuri, a young woman in poor health, finally receives news that her husband Ichinose Haruo, a former naval doctor, is alive and incarcerated in Manila (see Figure 5.2). She springs from her bed and rushes off to Tokyo

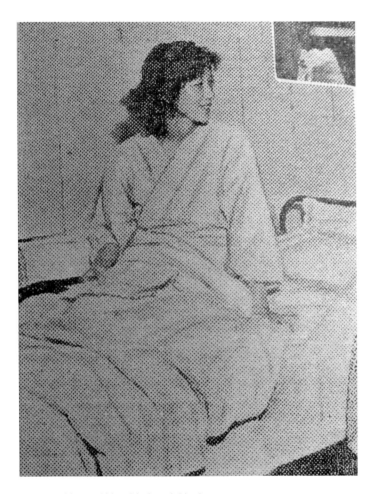

*Figure 5.2* Mrs Ichinose Chiyuri in her sickbed

Source: Ashida Teruichi, "Ima hitotabi no . . . jūnenme, mabuta no otto kaeru Ichinose fujin,'" *Shūkan asahi*, August 2, 1953, p. 9.

where she ceaselessly petitions the authorities on his behalf, until she collapses and is admitted to hospital. Many people come to her aid, and fortunately she survives until her husband's safe return.[27]

The popular film *Sugamo Mother*, produced in 1952, begins with the mother waiting patiently at the dock for the ship that will finally bring her son home from the war. She has already lost her other three sons to the fighting. Unfortunately, her surviving son is arrested as a suspected war criminal on his first night of freedom at home, even before he can taste the meal his mother has gone to great lengths to prepare for him. The long-suffering mother is reduced to dire poverty and illness in the absence of his support and because of her efforts to visit him in prison. At the end of the film, he is allowed out temporarily to attend her deathbed, and she dies happy because she thinks he has been permanently released. In other press reports, readers learned about key people who worked on behalf of the war criminals. The thirty-year-old bureaucrat Ueda Shinkichi was presented as a tireless ally working from Tokyo on behalf of Japanese prisoners in Manila. He apparently swore that he would not marry until the last prisoner had returned to Japan.[28] Numerous stories were written about "the saint of Muntinlupa," the Buddhist chaplain Kagao Shūnin, who ministered to the Japanese prisoners in Manila from 1949 to 1953.[29] The combined effect of such "beautiful stories" was to suggest that loyalty, faithfulness, sincerity, hard work, and true religion were on the side of the convicted war criminals.

Press reports on war criminals did not ignore the question of their crimes. A distinction was sometimes drawn between war criminals convicted at the IMTFE and those convicted in national courts. The press paid much less attention to the former, and public opinion about them appears to have been ambivalent. Some newspapers took up the cause of the prominent figures convicted in the IMTFE, but many people appear to have believed they had got what they deserved: these men had started the war and had plunged the Japanese people into great hardship.[30] In the Diet in July 1953, Naruse Banji, of the left faction of the Socialist Party, expressed "endless sympathy" for the "Class B and C" war criminals, that is, those convicted in national tribunals, but asserted the need to acknowledge the war guilt of the "Class A" criminals, meaning those convicted in the Tokyo trial.[31] When the Diet debated an amendment to the Pension Law in August 1954, designed to allow families of executed war criminals and those who had died in prison to receive the same level of financial support as the families of other deceased soldiers, those who opposed the measure in the Lower House were divided on whether relatives of the men convicted in national tribunals should benefit, but not on the question of the IMTFE: opponents of the proposal thought it wrong to support those found guilty at the Tokyo Trial.[32]

War criminals convicted in the national proceedings appeared to be more easily exonerated or forgiven. Press accounts, statements by activists, and fictional portrayals generally adopted one or more of three strategies: they suggested that the war criminals were not fundamentally guilty; or that they were guilty but had made sufficient recompense; or that they were guilty and had repented. A range of reasons supported the idea that the war criminals convicted in national courts were not really guilty or were not very guilty. Press accounts and statements by activists often asserted that individual war criminals were the victims of mistaken identity, though there is little external evidence for this claim. A 1952 press article focused on a particular group of prisoners in Manila who had been convicted because their unit had committed atrocities against Filipinos, but these specific individuals had had nothing to do with the atrocity, according to the article. One former soldier declared he had slept through the whole thing.[33] Another man was said to have been convicted for a separate offence solely, according to his mother, on the evidence that "a tall Japanese wearing glasses" from his unit had killed a Filipino.[34] In a survey of the 731 inmates of Sugamo Prison in October 1952, eighty claimed to be the victims of mistaken identity, 114 claimed to have been arrested simply because they were Japanese, and 206 said they were victims of some kind of false testimony.[35] Such reports reached the public domain and achieved wide currency because there were so many organs of the press looking for and trading on human interest stories. Works of fiction presented similar cases.

A common defense of convicted criminals, which had also been frequently used during the trials, was that those convicted in national proceedings were lower-ranking soldiers who had merely followed the orders of their superiors and who should therefore be considered innocent or less guilty than senior officers. In reality, superior orders had been tacitly or explicitly recognized as a partial defense in the war crimes trials and during the investigations that had preceded the trials. As a result, comparatively few of the most junior military personnel had been convicted or given long sentences.[36] Popular accounts in Japan, however, did not recognize this reality. Public commentary often claimed that superior officers, responsible for giving the orders that had resulted in war crimes charges, had fled before they could be captured by the Allies or had given false testimony, leaving their subordinates to take the blame.[37] In Kobayashi Masaki's 1953 film *The Thick-Walled Room*, two of the main characters had been victims of more senior officers.

In other cases, press reports asserted that very minor offences, like "slapping" prisoners, had attracted unreasonably heavy penalties. Sometimes this argument was used to draw readers' and viewers' attention to the undeniably selective basis of war crimes trials. All soldiers acted in such a way in wartime, it was claimed, but only the Japanese side, and only some Japanese at that, had been held accountable; therefore, punishment was selective in that it was applied only to the Japanese and not the Allies, and, further, those who were convicted had simply been unlucky to be caught. Some public commentary presented an early version of the argument that trials had constituted "victors' justice," stating explicitly that war crimes had been politically constructed by the victors or that actions considered unremarkable in Japanese culture were singled out by the Allies for condemnation. Thus, in one press account, convicted war criminals maintained that attitudes to the slapping of prisoners of war differed from country to country. In just the same way, polygamy is legal in some countries and illegal in others. As slapping prisoners was "routine" in the Japanese military, it should not have been criminalized for Japanese suspects. More seriously, Sugamo inmates argued that actions that in Japan would have won the Order of the Golden Kite, an imperial award for military valor and leadership, were treated by the Allies as war crimes.[38] The question of exactly which wartime actions could be justified on the basis of military necessity was a real one that recurred throughout the trials, and their aftermath was never satisfactorily resolved.[39] It is unlikely, however, that actions that might have won the Order of the Golden Kite had actually been treated as war crimes, since the Golden Kite was awarded for bravery and leadership in battle, and actions taken in battle were outside the formal definition of war crimes.

Other prisoners claimed to have been blamed for things that were beyond their control or beyond anyone's control. Typically, such cases related to the provision of insufficient food and medical treatment to prisoners of war.[40] Many defendants had indeed been convicted on such charges, and authorities dealing with both the trials and with applications for clemency in later years increasingly acknowledged that food and medicine had been in short supply in wartime, making it difficult for Japanese military personnel to provide adequately for prisoners of war.[41]

The press, political figures, and prisoners themselves admitted that many war criminals were guilty of the crimes for which they had been convicted. According to a 1953 press account, Japanese officials reinvestigating cases in order to make recommendations for release or sentence reduction reported that while one-third of the prisoners completely denied the facts of their alleged crimes, two-thirds admitted their guilt.[42] But many people felt the prisoners had paid sufficient recompense by this time. The Chairman of the Welfare Committee of the Lower House of the Diet, Ōishi Buichi, commented in April 1952 that the prisoners on death row in Muntinlupa might have committed terrible crimes, but spending seven years in jail was enough.[43] As another conservative politician remarked, the lenient peace treaty demonstrated that Japan had been forgiven as a nation; it was now time to forgive the war criminals too.[44] Moreover, public commentary often asserted that prisoners who really had done terrible things had used their time in prison to reflect on their actions and had sincerely repented.[45] In the film *The Thick-Walled Room*, only one of the main characters appeared willingly to have participated in the mistreatment of the captured enemy, in this case in China. He was so haunted by the memory that he hanged himself in his cell.

Not everyone in Japan was happy about the high public profile of the prisoners. The issue of how to interpret war crimes and of the degree of war criminals' guilt remained fraught; aside from politicians, few public figures were prepared to take their side, and some worried that they were being made into heroes, which presumably would turn Japanese society away from peace and democracy.[46] Continued

reports of hardship suffered by paroled and pardoned prisoners, in finding employment, for example, suggest that positive press coverage did not necessarily reflect
wider public attitudes: despite the widespread campaign in support of war criminals, evidently people were still suspicious of them, for whatever reason, once they
were released.[47] In January 1953, officials of the Second Demobilization Bureau,
that is, former members of the Naval General Staff, were convinced that substantial negative feeling about war criminals remained, even though public sympathy
had increased markedly since the end of the Occupation. Families of executed war
criminals and those who died in prison, for example, still did not receive public
support in the form of pensions.[48] Demobilization Bureau officials, who had been
sympathetic to war criminals all along, now rededicated themselves to wide-ranging
efforts to encourage both public sympathy and government action, advocating the
manipulation of mass media, of organizations in civil society, and of prefectural
assemblies; stimulation of the petition campaign; and attempts to influence Diet
members. In their view, the essential task was to deepen public consciousness that
war criminals and their families were victims of the war, just as much as others
were.[49]

## Public advocacy

Organizations specifically representing the interests of war criminals emerged
openly after the departure of the Occupation forces in 1952. Four days before
the peace treaty took effect, the official support group, the Association to
Support the War-Convicted (*Sensō jukeisha sewakai*), was formed with over
six hundred members, under the guidance of former Vice-Admiral Hara
Chūichi, who had been convicted by the Americans on Guam and had served
six years in Sugamo. Formally inaugurated on May 10, the Association
became a powerful civilian organization. It was headed by the prominent
businessman and politician Fujiwara Ginjirō, who had been "purged" from
public office during the Occupation. Among its members were many leading
figures from politics, business, and the media, as well as senior military officers, some of whom, like Hara, had been convicted as war criminals and
sentenced to short stints in prison. Executive directors included several men
who had been arrested as potential defendants in the IMTFE but never charged,
among them Kishi Nobusuke and Shōriki Matsutarō. The Association called
for pardons, sentence reductions, the return of prisoners still held overseas,
and relief for all prisoners and their families. By the end of 1952, branches of
the Association or similar organizations had been established in thirty-two of
Japan's forty-seven prefectures (see Figure 5.3). Together with the new
national association, they began to exert strong pressure on the Foreign and
Justice Ministries to bring about releases of and assistance to convicted war
criminals.[50] As did West Germans in the same period, the Japanese public took
up the cause of war criminals.[51] During 1952 alone, more than 10 million
people, it was claimed, signed petitions for the repatriation to Japan of

*Figure 5.3* Poster from Mie Prefecture advertising the petition campaign aimed at repatriation and release of war criminals, dated June 2, 1952

Source: National Archives of Japan, 4B 23–6300, Zenkoku jukeisha sewakai, Ai no undō ni kansuru
tsuzuri (Hōmu chosaka).

convicted war criminals still held overseas and for sentence reduction for all prisoners.[52] In two examples, a Sugamo Prison publication declared that 1.05 million of Gifu Prefecture's population of 1.5 million, that is, 70 percent, had signed petitions on behalf of war criminals and that the All Japan Flower-Arranging Federation (*Zen nihon kadō*) had collected a million signatures in just three days.[53]

Other organizations continued to act diligently on behalf of war criminals. The Japan Federation of Lawyers (*Nihon bengoshikai*) and religious groups were especially vigorous.[54] Not surprisingly, right-wing groups and individuals were also very active. The prominent rightist Sasakawa Ryōichi, who had been jailed as a potential IMTFE defendant but was never tried, was said to have taken hundreds of politicians to visit Sugamo. He told the press that, in many cases, the wrong person had been executed for war crimes because of mistaken identity and insisted that all efforts must be made to free the remaining prisoners as soon as possible.[55] Ultranationalist associations like the *Kenseikai* (Japan Sound Youth Association) and the *Junkoku seinentai* (National Martyrs Youth Corps) conducted petition campaigns, appealed to foreign embassies, and organized rallies.[56] The imprisoned war criminals themselves, or at least those in Sugamo, also worked energetically for their own release and to get their compatriots repatriated from the Philippines and Manus. Their efforts were made more and more openly and aggressively, until they were directly appealing to the Diet, prefectural governments, and other public bodies for release.[57]

Two months after Japan regained its sovereignty, the Diet started passing resolutions calling for the repatriation of convicted war criminals still held overseas by the Philippines and Australia and urging the government to negotiate for parole for those held in Japan.[58] Advocacy of leniency for war criminals became politically useful to politicians. Opposition parties used the apparent lack of progress on leniency to criticize the government of Yoshida Shigeru, and politicians cultivated direct connections with the prisoners. Conservatives and socialists agreed that war criminals convicted in the national tribunals should not be held personally accountable for war crimes; only the Communist Party opposed clemency.[59] In 1952 and 1953, luxury cars lined up at the gates of Sugamo Prison, as politicians representing constituencies throughout Japan competed to make speeches of consolation and encouragement to the prisoners, especially before national elections (see Figure 5.4). "It's exactly as though this were a zoo,"' inmates were reported to have commented in August 1953.[60] Though the fate of war criminals depended on the decisions of foreign countries, the main target of the public campaign was Japan's own government, as people all over the country attempted to persuade the authorities they had to do something first to bring back the remaining prisoners from overseas jails and then to get them freed.

The Japanese campaign for the repatriation and early release of war criminals thrived and became impossible to ignore. Despite any doubts about the real

*Figure 5.4* Sketch of Sugamo Prison, Tokyo, *Sugamo shimbun*, May 1953

Source: Reprinted in Chaen Yoshio (ed.), *BCkyū senpan Firipin saiban shiryō*, Fuji shuppan, 1987, p. 157.

extent of public sympathy, by early 1953 press articles were claiming with increasing confidence that the public wanted to see the prisoners released or at least paroled.[61] When the convicted war criminals from Manila arrived in Yoko-hama in July 1953 (to serve out their sentences in Sugamo, in the case of those originally sentenced to death, or to be released immediately, in all other cases), they were met at the dock by thousands of relatives, well-wishers, officials, and journalists. According to the press, the crowd was bigger than the one that had gathered to say farewell to the Crown Prince on March 31, when he left on his first foreign trip.[62] In July 1954, a Welfare Ministry official claimed that more than 30 million people had signed petitions for clemency.[63] In a very short space of time, war criminals and their supporters had won a large measure of public sympathy and had persuaded their own government to take up their cause. War criminals were to remain in prison for some years yet. Nevertheless, the public campaign in the early 1950s helped to change the terms in which discussion about them took place, within the public arena, in politics, and in diplomatic negotiations.

After the peace treaty took effect, the Japanese government embarked on a long series of representations to foreign governments for clemency for those who had been convicted. The Japanese campaign became a powerful force. Neither the Japanese authorities nor those of the Allied countries holding war criminals could ignore it. A great many petitions seeking the release of particular prisoners were sent directly to foreign embassies and governments by individual Japanese as well as by prefectural bodies, women's associations, and other groups. Embassies of all the governments holding Japanese war criminals were inundated with petitions, and Western diplomats complained that they could not cope with the workload. Embassy officials wrote to their home governments, sometimes in urgent terms, asking them to do something about war criminals because they were under such pressure in Tokyo. The U.S. Embassy in Tokyo reported in October 1952 that "[i]n addition to the petitions and letters, the Embassy receives at least four delegations a week from various parts of Japan who plead for the release of the 424 war criminals held by the United States."[64] (See Figure 5.5.)

*Figure 5.5* Petitions stacked outside the Foreign Ministry, Tokyo

Source: Nationaal Archief, The Hague, Buitenlandse Zaken/Code-Archief 45–54 (1945–1954), 2.05.117 inv. nr.: 7707.

## Conclusion

The politics of war crimes had turned quickly. By the time the peace treaty was signed, international circumstances had already changed dramatically, and the position of convicted war criminals had changed as well. For the Allies, adherence to the law and the pursuit of strict justice were no longer the foremost considerations in dealing with Japanese or German war criminals. By the early 1950s at the latest, most of the Allied authorities had lost interest in continuing to punish Japanese soldiers because they had other and more urgent concerns, because the Cold War seemed to require the cultivation of Japan as a new ally rather than an old enemy, and because they wanted to resume economic ties with Japan.[65] It rapidly became clear that the failure to release war criminals was an impediment to the closer political and economic relationship with Japan that the Western powers now either actively wanted or realized was inevitable. Meanwhile, in Japan, people were less and less willing to accept that only Japanese soldiers had committed reprehensible actions during the war, that ordinary soldiers should be punished for what Japan had done, and that it was reasonable to require Japanese cooperation in the new international arrangements of the postwar world while continuing to incarcerate war criminals.

The United States and its Allies had avoided the temptation of exacting a punitive peace, had declined to use the peace treaty as an opportunity to blame Japan for the war, had allowed and encouraged Japanese rearmament, and had largely sidestepped the matter of war reparations. The U.S. government had also signed a separate defense agreement with Japan at the same time as the peace treaty. In such an environment, the failure to release war criminals stuck out as an anomalous reminder of the past war, at a time when the Western powers were gearing up for the escalating Cold War instead. The task was now to work out how to dispose of the problem of Japanese war criminals without appearing simply to be giving in to Japanese pressure or to be repudiating the verdicts of the military tribunals and without offending domestic opinion in the prosecuting countries, especially former soldiers. The increasing assertiveness with which views sympathetic to war criminals were put from the Japanese side was one of the factors making it more and more difficult for foreign governments to maintain the stance on war criminals that had appeared so fitting in 1945. The campaign in Japan played a significant part in persuading the Japanese and foreign governments that it was now necessary to move on from the war and turn to new concerns. The urgent need for assistance from Japan in the Cold War tipped the balance, and by the end of 1958 the last few of the convicted Japanese war criminals were freed unconditionally.

## Notes

1   This chapter draws substantially on Sandra Wilson, Robert Cribb, Beatrice Trefalt, and Dean Aszkielowicz, *Japanese War Criminals: The Politics of Justice after the Second World War* (New York: Columbia University Press, 2017), Chapter 7.

2  On the IMTFE, see Yuma Totani, *The Tokyo War Crimes Trials: The Pursuit of Justice in World War II* (Cambridge, MA: Harvard University Press, 2008); Neil Boister and Robert Cryer, *The Tokyo International Military Tribunal: A Reappraisal* (Oxford: Oxford University Press, 2008); Tim Maga, *Judgment at Tokyo: The Japanese War Crimes Trials* (Lexington: University Press of Kentucky, 2000); Richard Minear, *Victor's Justice: The Tokyo War Crimes Trials* (Princeton, NJ: Princeton University Press, 1971); Awaya Kentarō, *Tōkyō saiban ron* (Ōtsuki shoten, 1989); Higurashi Yoshinobu, *Tōkyō saiban no kokusai kankei: kokusai seiji ni okeru kenryoku to kihan* (Bokutakusha, 2002); Higurashi Yoshinobu, *Tōkyō saiban (Kōdansha gendai shinsho 1924)* (Kōdansha, 2008); Ushimura Kei and Higurashi Yoshinobu, *Tōkyō saiban o tadashiku yomu* (Bungei shunjū, 2008). (Unless otherwise noted, all Japanese books are published in Tokyo.)

3  The standard work in English is Phillip Piccigallo, *The Japanese on Trial: Allied War Crimes Operations in the Far East* (Austin: University of Texas, 1979).

4  "Article 11, Treaty of Peace with Japan," in John M. Maki, ed., *Conflict and Tension in the Far East: Key Documents, 1894–1960* (Seattle: University of Washington Press, 1961), pp. 136–137.

5  Higurashi, *Tōkyō saiban*, p. 350.

6  "Sugamo no naigai: senpan wa nani o kangaeteiruka," *Shūkan asahi*, February 24, 1952, p. 10; "Zoku. Sugamo no naigai: senpan wa dō naru ka," *Shūkan asahi*, cover story, August 16, 1953, p. 6.

7  In December 1945, the First Demobilization Ministry and Second Demobilization Ministry were created. In a series of administrative changes, the separate ministries were downgraded into a single Demobilization Agency and then into two bureaus. In December 1948, a combined Demobilization Bureau was created and placed within the Ministry of Welfare. See Lori Watt, *When Empire Comes Home: Repatriation and Reintegration in Postwar Japan* (Cambridge, MA: Harvard University Asia Center, 2009), p. 67.

8  "War criminals and the Japanese peace treaty, record of Lord Henderson's verbal response to Lord Hankey during Hankey's visit to Henderson on 25 July 1951 to discuss Article 11," UK National Archives, FO 371/92699; Masahiro Yamamoto, "Japan's 'unsettling' past: Article 11 of San Francisco Peace Treaty and Its Ramifications," *Journal of US–China Public Administration* vol. 7, issue 5 (May 2010): pp. 6–7. For negotiations over rearmament and security, see Michael M. Yoshitsu, *Japan and the San Francisco Peace Settlement* (New York: Columbia University Press, 1982), pp. 39–66.

9  Higurashi, *Tōkyō saiban*, pp. 344–345; "1951 nen 6 gatsu Arison kōtaishi kaikan kara 1951 nen 7 gatsu 13 nichi heiwa jōyaku an kōhyō ni itaru made no keika chōsho," record by Treaty Bureau Director Nishimura, July 20, 1951, in *Nihon gaikō monjo: heiwa jōyaku no teiketsu ni kansuru chōsho, Vol. 3*, ed. Gaimushō (Gaimushō, 2003), p. 605.

10  Higurashi, *Tōkyō saiban*, pp. 350–351; On the Associations of the Families of the Missing, see Beatrice Trefalt, "A Peace Worth Having: Delayed Repatriations and Domestic Debate over the San Francisco Peace Treaty," *Japanese Studies* vol. 27, issue 2 (September 2007): pp. 173–187, here p. 173, 176–177.

11  "Senpansha engo dantai renraku kyōgi giji gaiyō," March 22, 1949, National Archives of Japan (hereafter NAJ), Justice Ministry, 4B-23-5855, *Sensō saiban zatsu sankō shiryō*, [3–4]; "Hagen Comments on Japanese War Criminals," September 5, [1952], in same file.

12  Ivan Morris, *Nationalism and the Right Wing in Japan: A Study of Post-War Trends* (London: Oxford University Press, 1960), p. 212.

13  Sandra Wilson, "War, Soldier and Nation in 1950s Japan," *International Journal of Asian Studies* vol. 5, issue 2 (July 2008): pp. 187–218, here pp. 194–196.

14  Maruyama Masao, quoted in "Zoku. Sugamo no naigai," p. 11. See also pp. 5, 8.

15  "Sugamo no naigai," p. 9.

16  Ibid.

17  Utsumi Aiko, *Sugamo purizun: senpantachi no heiwa undō* (Yoshikawa kōbunkan, 2004), p. 125, and, for example, "Shōwa nijū nana nendo gyōmu yōshi," February 1952, p. 5, NAJ, Justice Ministry, 4B-23-5836, Nifuku kyōdō kenkyū no mono.

18  Quoted in Hiroshi Kitamura, *Screening Enlightenment: Hollywood and the Cultural Reconstruction of Defeated Japan* (Ithaca, NY: Cornell University Press, 2010), pp. 35–36.

19  The five films were *Sugamo no haha* (Sugamo Mother), dir. Adachi Nobuo, 1952; *Araki no naka no haha* (Mother in the Storm), dir. Saiki Kiyoshi, 1952; *Montenrupa no yo wa fukete* (It's Getting Late in Muntinlupa), dir. Aoyagi Nobuo, 1952; *Haha wa sakebinaku* (A Mother Calls Tearfully), dir. Sasaki Keisuke, 1952; *Kabe atsuki heya* (The Thick-Walled Room), dir. Kobayashi Masaki, 1953. *The Thick-Walled Room* was not released until 1956, evidently from wariness about how the Americans would react, even after the end of the Occupation. On *Sugamo Mother* and *The Thick-Walled Room*, see Sandra Wilson, "Film and Soldier: Japanese War Movies in the 1950s," *Journal of Contemporary History* vol. 48, issue 3 (2013): pp. 537–555, here pp. 549–551.

20  Aaron Gerow, "Japanese Film and Television," in *Routledge Handbook of Japanese Culture and Society*, ed. Victoria Lyon-Bestor, Theodore C. Bestor, and Akiko Yamagata (Abingdon: Routledge, 2011), p. 219.

21  "Zasshi wa dō yomareteiruka: zasshi shūkan ni yosete," *Shūkan asahi*, June 8, 1952, p. 14.

22  See, for example, Iizuka Kōji [Katō Kazuo] ed., *Are kara shichi nen: gakuto senpan no gokuchū kara no tegami* (Kōbunsha, 1953).

23  Tsuji Yutaka, "Senpan shikeishū wa inoru: 'nihon yo shizuka ni, heiwa de are,'" *Shūkan asahi*, February 24, 1952, pp. 12–15; Tsuji Yutaka, "Montenrupa kara no 108 nin," *Shūkan asahi*, cover story, August 2, 1953, p. 4; Sharon Williams Chamberlain, "Justice and Reconciliation: Postwar Philippine Trials of Japanese War Criminals in History and Memory," unpublished PhD dissertation, George Washington University, 2010, pp. 172–175.

24  Readers' letters, *Shūkan asahi*, March 9, 1952, p. 56.

25  "Sugamo no naigai," p. 9.

26  "'Montenrupa no haha': higan kanatta 'koe' no taimen," *Shūkan asahi*, March 2, 1952, pp. 36–37.

27  Ashida Teruichi, "Ima hitotabi no . . . jūnenme, mabuta no otto kaeru Ichinose fujin," *Shūkan asahi*, August 2, 1953, pp. 8–9. On Ichinose Haruo, see Dorothy Minchin-Comm and Dorothy Nelson-Oster, *An Ordered Life: The Andrew N. Nelson Story* (n.p.: Trafford Publishing, 2010), pp. 105, 138.

28  Tsuji, "Montenrupa kara no 108 nin," p. 6. On Ueki, see Chamberlain, "Justice and Reconciliation," pp. 136–137, 171–172.

29  Tsuji, "Montenrupa kara no 108 nin," p. 6; "Kagao Shūnin," *Shūkan asahi*, July 26, 1953, p. 30. On Kagao, see Chamberlain, "Justice and Reconciliation," pp. 131, 169–171; Beatrice Trefalt, "Hostages to International Relations? The Repatriation of Japanese War Criminals from the Philippines," *Japanese Studies* vol. 31, issue 2 (September 2011): pp. 191–209, here pp. 197–200.

30  Fukuhara Rintarō, quoted in "Zoku. Sugamo no naigai," p. 10; Hatakeyama Ichirō, "Senpan keishisha no izoku nimo onkyū o: dai hankyō o yonda onkyūhō no kaisei," cover story, *Toki no hōrei* vol. 144 (August 1954), p. 9; Higurashi, *Tōkyō saiban*, p. 360.

31  Higurashi, *Tōkyō saiban*, p. 360.

32  Hatakeyama, "Senpan keishisha no izoku nimo onkyū o," p. 9.

33  Tsuji, "Senpan shikeishū wa inoru," p. 14.

34  "Montenrupa no haha." See also the group interview of prisoners in Usui Yoshimi (chair), "Sugamo bi-shi-kyū senpan no seikatsu to iken: aru hi no shūdan menkai kara," *Chūō kōron* vol. 779 (September 1953), p. 160.

35  "Zoku. Sugamo no naigai," p. 6.

36  Wilson et al., *Japanese War Criminals*.
37  See, for example, Usui, "Sugamo bi-shi-kyū senpan," pp. 160–161, 164–165.
38  "Sugamo no naigai," pp. 9–10.
39  See A. Gledhill, "Some Aspects of the Operation of International and Military Law in Burma, 1941–1945," *Modern Law Review* vol. 12, issue 2 (April 1949): pp. 191–204.
40  Usui, "Sugamo bi-shi-kyū senpan," pp. 160–161.
41  Wilson et al., *Japanese War Criminals*.
42  "Zoku. Sugamo no naigai," p. 6.
43  Ōishi Buichi, "Futatsu no iken," *Shūkan asahi*, April 13, 1952, p. 10.
44  Tajima Kōbun, quoted in "Zoku. Sugamo no naigai," p. 8.
45  Usui, "Sugamo bi-shi-kyū senpan," p. 160.
46  For example, Fukushima Rintarō, quoted in "Zoku. Sugamo no naigai," p. 10; Hatakeyama, "Senpan keishisha no izoku ni mo onkyū o," p. 9.
47  "Sugamo no naigai," p. 10.
48  "Shōwa nijū hachi nendo hōchō kankei gyōmu yōshi," January 1953, p. 7, NAJ, 4B-23-5836.
49  Ibid.; "Shōwa nijū nana nendo gyōmu yōshi," February 1952, pp. 5–6, NAJ, 4B-23-5836.
50  Higurashi, *Tōkyō saiban*, pp. 351–352; Utsumi, *Sugamo purizun*, pp. 147–148; "Issen man en no bokin: sensō jukeisha sewakai sekkyokuteki katsudō e," *Yomiuri shimbun*, June 11, 1952, morning edition, p. 3; Katō Tetsutarō, "Watashitachi wa saigunbi no hikikae kippu de wa nai: senpan shakuhō undō no imi ni tsuite," (first published October 1952), in Katō Tetsutarō, *Watashi wa kai ni naritai: aru bi-shi kyū senpan no sakebi* (Shunjusha, 1994), pp. 75–76. See also "Senpan boshi: kishisan ni shakuhō chinjō," *Yomiuri shimbun*, June 15, 1957, evening edition, p. 5.
51  On Germany see Frank M. Buscher, *The U.S. War Crimes Trial Program in Germany, 1946–1955* (New York: Greenwood Press, 1989), pp. 71–72, 136; Kerstin von Lingen, *Kesselring's Last Battle*, trans. Alexandra Klemm (Lawrence, KS: University Press of Kansas, 2009), pp. 173–178; Norbert Frei, *Adenauer's Germany and the Nazi Past*, trans. Joel Golb (New York: Columbia University Press, 2002), p. 175.
52  Utsumi, *Sugamo purizun*, p. 147.
53  Figures from *Shūhō*, quoted in Utsumi, *Sugamo purizun*, p. 147.
54  Higurashi, *Tōkyō saiban*, p. 352; "Kesshoku no yoi 'sugamo senpan': bengodan sho-kaiken. Omoi wa gaichi no dōhō e," *Yomiuri shimbun*, April 12, 1952, morning edition, p. 3; "Senpan shakuhō no rōhō aitsugu," *Yomiuri shimbun*, June 2, 1953, morning edition, p. 7; Sanada Hideo, "Hikari sashikomu senpan no mado: kari shussho, ichishussho no shikaku, yōken kanwa," *Toki no hōrei* vol. 88 (February 1953), p. 33; "Zoku. Sugamo no naigai," pp. 7–8.
55  Higurashi, *Tōkyō saiban*, p. 352.
56  Ibid. On Nihon kenseikai and Junkoku seinentai, see Morris, *Nationalism*, pp. 314–315, 323–338.
57  "Sugamo no gokuchū kara senpan shakuhō undō: kakuku ni kyōryoku o yōsei – dokuritsugo hetta karishakuhō ni fuman no koe," *Yomiuri shimbun*, July 8, 1953, morning edition, p. 6. See also Sandra Wilson, "Prisoners in Sugamo and Their Campaign for Release, 1952–1953," *Japanese Studies* vol. 31, issue 2 (September 2011): pp. 171–190.
58  Utsumi, *Sugamo Purizun*, p. 119; Higurashi, *Tōkyō saiban*, pp. 354–355.
59  "Zoku. Sugamo no naigai," pp. 7–9.
60  Ibid., p. 7.
61  For example, Sanada, "Hikari sashikomu senpan no mado," p. 34.
62  "Zoku. Sugamo no naigai," p. 4.
63  Toyoda Kumao, letter with no addressee, July 1954, NAJ, 4B-23-5855.

64 American Embassy, Tokyo to Department of State, Washington, Memo, "War Criminals," October 2, 1952, National Archives and Records Administration, College Park,
MD, RG59, 250-39-29-6, Box 3020.
65 See, for example, "[United States] *Aide Mémoire*," handed to British Ambassador
in Washington and contained in Official Secretary, Office of the High Commissioner
for New Zealand, London, to the [New Zealand] Secretary of External Affairs,
"Japanese Peace Treaty," March 21, 1951, in *Documents on New Zealand External
Relations, Volume III: The ANZUS Pact and the Treaty of Peace with Japan*, ed.
Robin Kay (Wellington: Historical Publications Branch, Department of Internal
Affairs, 1985), p. 830.

# 6  Allied POWs in Korea

## Life and death during the Pacific War

*Sarah Kovner*

In April 1945, Lieutenant Colonel Jack Schwartz, a medical officer from Fort Worth, Texas, arrived in Jinsen, Korea, as a prisoner of war. Schwartz had been captured in the Philippines during the Battle of Bataan three years earlier. He had treated survivors of the Bataan Death March and endured wretched conditions in several camps and prison hospitals. A ship that was to transport him from Manila was bombed and sank. Hundreds of POWs died aboard a second "hellship," as the POWs called the vessels that carried them across the Pacific. Finally, a third ship delivered him to Japan. After a comparatively comfortable two-day journey via ship and train, Schwarz and his comrades arrived at their final destination in Korea. They were immediately impressed by the good conditions. "We were placed in a large, well-constructed frame barrack building and were there fed better than at any of our previous camps," Schwartz later wrote. "The Japanese camp officials, on the whole, were more friendly than any we had previously encountered."[1]

The relatively benign conditions of POW camps in Korea surprised Schwartz, and even now they can seem anomalous compared with common accounts of the POW experience. Bestselling biographies, Booker Prize–winning novels, and popular historical works in the United States and Europe commonly portray Japanese POW camps as uniformly awful, with guards regularly humiliating and abusing captives.[2] Authentic historical accounts exist, but they typically focus on the most notorious episodes. The vast majority of historians in Japan have focused on politics and command responsibility rather than the conditions of particular camps.[3] Some, like Utsumi Aiko, challenge nationalist mythmaking. Utsumi's recent work has focused on Korean guards and the ways in which they too were victims. For Utsumi, the inadequacies of the POW system are explained by institutional flaws in the management of POWs, Tokyo's changing attitudes toward international society, and Japan's relative poverty compared to the United States and Europe.[4]

In South Korea, few scholars have studied POW camps. An exception is the Commission on Verification and Support for the Victims of Forced Mobilization under Japanese Colonialism in Korea, which seeks to win recognition and compensation. Korean historian Cho Gun analyzes the Korean guards through the frame of colonialism in Korea and concludes – like Utsumi Aiko – that the guards suffered too, both at the hands of their Japanese officers and war crimes prosecutors.[5] This more subtle argument is an important response to the depiction by popular Western histories.[6] However, it also tends to make Allied POWs themselves mere bystanders in this history.

There are many reasons to recapture the full complexity of POW camps in Korea – a place of particular geopolitical significance as a colony, an occupied country, and a Cold War hot zone. Almost unique among the hundreds of POW camps, POW camps in Korea at Jinsen (Inchon), Keijō (Seoul), and Kōnan (Hŭngnam) were established and organized in 1942 on the direct orders of senior Japanese officials, who typically took little interest in the fate of Allied POWs. They were originally established as propaganda camps, which makes them uniquely valuable sites for exploring how imperial Japan wished to be seen as discharging its responsibilities toward POWs. To show the difference that made – even after they no longer held any propaganda function – it is first necessary to recreate the experience of prisoners, guards, and people in the surrounding community, including the itineraries that brought them together and the varied fates they met at the end of the war. This chapter will also point to the larger implications, both for how we understand the POW experience and also for how that experience can help us understand Korea's place within Japan's wartime empire.

Camps in Korea afford the historian a wealth of primary source materials, which makes it possible to study the guards, the POWs, and the men, women, and children on the periphery of the camps within the same analytic frame.[7] Jinsen offers the only camp commanders' log to survive the destruction of documents at the end of the war. This log allows us to evaluate another primary source: the inspection reports of the International Committee of the Red Cross (ICRC). We can corroborate them with contemporary diaries and camp publications from British and Australian prisoners, as well as news reports and guards' trial records from the U.S. National Archives, and government documents from the British Archives and the Australian War Memorial.

Historians are, however, some way off from identifying individual Korean men, women, and children living outside the camp fence. The end of Japanese rule, partition, civil war, and international intervention erased much of the historical record. But we can begin to bring together some traces in Japanese official documents and Allied war diaries and visual records. Although soldiers' diaries must be used with caution, their words and sketches provide valuable contemporary evidence on Korean men and women.[8] And since POWs like Schwartz came to Jinsen after experiencing very different conditions in other camps, as well as in the ships that transported them from one place to another throughout Japan's expanding empire, their accounts help us make direct comparisons and begin to answer some key questions. To what extent did systematic top-down policy shape conditions on the ground? Did local dynamics, including the attitude of the surrounding community, also shape prisoner treatment? And considering the varied experience this paper will describe, why did guards, especially Korean ones, gain a reputation for such cruelty?

## Planning – or not planning – for POWs

Japanese commanders themselves were surprised and unprepared for the large numbers of Allied servicemen who surrendered at the beginning of the Pacific War. By February 1942, with the fall of Singapore, the Japanese held prisoner more than 135,000 British Imperial troops. While many were held in Changi Prison, Japanese commanders would soon separate some of the high-ranking prisoners and send them to Korea. The idea was to use them to demonstrate Japan's imperial might to Korean colonial subjects.

A Prisoner of War Information Bureau, an extra section of the Department of the Army, had been set up the previous December. Its purpose was to gather information about POWs and transmit it to enemy governments through the ICRC in Geneva and the Protecting Powers for enemy countries.[9] It was not until March 1942 that the Army Ministry began to plan for POWs in earnest. The Army minister set up the Prisoner of War Management Office to deal with the mass of new prisoners from Southeast Asia. This office had responsibility for POW administration and control of camps. Confusingly, the staff of the POW Management Office were also staff of the POW Information Bureau, meaning that individual staff were affiliated with both offices, although they were ostensibly separate organizations.

The same month that the Prisoner of War Management Office was established, General Itagaki Seishirō, a former Army minister and Chief of Staff of the Chōsen Army in Korea, told the Army Ministry that the Governor-General and Army wanted to bring a thousand British and a thousand American prisoners to Korea. They wanted to establish a "strong faith in victory" among Koreans and "stamp out the respect and admiration" among Korean people for Britain and America."[10] On March 23, Itagaki sent more concrete plans, laying out locations and policies. Camps would be located at Keijō, at the former Iwamura Silk Reeling Mill, and at Jinsen, in a former military barracks. The purpose of these camps was to make "Koreans realize positively the true might of our empire as well as to contribute to psychological propaganda work."[11]

The camps also served to create positive impressions for an international audience. Japan had signed the 1929 Geneva Convention on the treatment of POWs but did not ratify it. Nevertheless, Tokyo pledged to conform to the Convention *mutatis mutandis*, a legal term indicating "with the provisions of the existing laws and regulations of the country and with the requirements of the actual situation as it develops."[12] The ICRC would inspect the camps regularly, and its findings were communicated to governments and published in mass media around the world. Japanese journalists would also report on these conditions, taking photographs and filming newsreels for a domestic audience. These photographs were reproduced in the Western media. Allied POWs thus played roles not just in the internal Japanese struggle to maintain control of the colonies but also in the larger international arena.[13] The photographs and newsreels were meant to show Washington and London as well as the ICRC that Japan was not abusing Allied prisoners.[14]

Colonel Noguchi Yuzuru, a graduate of the Japanese Military Academy and lifelong Army man, was in command of the Korean camps. Like many commanders, Noguchi had retired from the Army before his service as a commandant. Being a guard was not a high-prestige posting, and Japanese guards often were older or wounded men. Noguchi initially trained the Korean guards who fanned out across the Japanese empire.[15] Ultimately, a total of 3,016 deployed, mostly to Singapore, Thailand, and Java. A much smaller number of Korean guards remained in the peninsula, perhaps because the Japanese perceived a political risk of having Koreans posted in their own country, a concern that proved prescient.[16]

The Japanese summoned the people of Pusan to come see the first Allied POWs when they arrived from Singapore aboard the ship *Fukkai-maru*. Most of these first POWs hailed from Britain and Australia, but a disproportionate number of the higher-ranking officers were British.[17] Only one of the Australians was a field officer. There would also be senior Malayan and Netherlands East Indies government officials and technicians. The rest of the prisoners were mostly the surviving members of the 2th Battalion Loyal Lancashire Regiment and the Yorkshire-based 122 Field Regiment, Royal Artillery. Japanese journalists watched and snapped photos of the crowded deck. Images of white, high-ranking prisoners would have been impressive to Japanese men and women. The men disembarked and then, as the Japanese military looked on, began a five-mile march through the Pusan streets.

The arrival of 998 prisoners had such an effect that an alleged 120,000 Koreans and 57,000 Japanese lined the roads from Pusan to Seoul to Jinsen. The Koreans sneered at British officers, according to a confidential report to Kimura by Lieutenant General Ihara Junichirō, Chief of Staff of the Korean Army. "[They] confessed their happiness at being subjects of the Empire and expressed their resolve to carry though the Greater East Asian War." One man reportedly said: "When I saw young Korean soldiers, members of the Imperial Army, guarding the prisoners, I shed tears of joy. I was so moved by the sight that I almost felt like shouting to those who weren't aware of the fact: Look! Peninsular youths are guarding the British soldiers!"[18] Ihara concluded, "As a whole, it seems the idea was very successful." But even in Ihara's report, there were signs of trouble. The Korean Christians were harder to convince, he said, since they were not able to "drive out completely their admiration for foreign ideas, due to the fact that their leaders were Europeans or Americans."[19] But they were apparently "moved by the idea that they must establish a Japanese Christianity."[20]

The prisoners themselves knew that they were on display. Interviewed by the Japanese press after a miserable voyage, they slept in a school where hundreds of children gazed at them as at "lions in a zoo."[21] Like Schwartz, the aforementioned American officer, many POWs found the worst part of their captivity was not detention in the camp, but the deprivation suffered en route. After their six-week sea transit, a number of men collapsed during the march through Pusan. After losing some of their number to hospitalization, the men quickly boarded a train and made their way northeast. On their arrival at Keijō, the main camp, Noguchi delivered a stern speech to the prisoners.[22] He warned that "we will punish you if you act against our regulations. For instance, the non-fulfillment of regulations, disobedience, resistance and escape (even an attempt to do so) are understood as manifestations of hostility." Neither would Noguchi tolerate complaints about housing, clothing, or work, noting that prisoners would inevitably experience changes in their lives.[23] But prisoners gradually came to realize that Noguchi's bark was worse than his bite. Lieutenant Colonel Michael Elrington of the Second Loyal regiment – the senior commanding officer of the Keijō camp – knew Noguchi from the 1937 Shanghai Incident, when the Loyals patrolled the Shanghai Bund, and arranged a ceasefire between the Japanese and the Chinese. Noguchi had a habit of disappearing when there was trouble in camp and reportedly used to invite Elrington over for the occasional chat over green tea.[24]

Noguchi could easily disappear because he was responsible for all of the camps in Korea. Keijō initially held 433 British and Australian prisoners, who lived in the former Japanese Iwamura silk-reeling mill, a four-story brick building surrounded by a wooden fence. Up to 60 men slept in each room on beds on tatami mats. They could wash in a separate hut with running water and a wooden trough and bathe in a large Japanese bath where up to five men could fit.[25] The 482 Jinsen prisoners lived in military barracks heated by Russian-style brick stoves.[26] One Lancashire Loyal recalled the prison dormitories as about 80 feet long by 35 feet, divided into sections, with a central passageway. Each prisoner was given a personal space of about 6 feet by 2.5 feet to keep his personal items, including eating utensils and bedding; they also slept on tatami.[27] Jinsen had running water, and like Keijō, prisoners had two baths per week. Two smaller bathtubs were provided for prisoners with skin diseases. The camp had one toilet for every thirteen prisoners.[28] Though obviously spartan, these well constructed camps, with heating and sanitary facilities, compared favorably to other camps, especially in Southeast Asia.

## Life in the camps

The camps were not tightly sealed to the outside, and the prisoners soon realized this. Even so, only a few escape attempts were ever recorded. The most promising route was to Russia, some 200 miles away even from Kōnan. But few of the prisoners spoke Korean, and none could pass for Korean nationals.[29] On the other hand, porous borders permitted interaction with Koreans, mostly women, children, and elderly men. Prisoners bought black market food and newspapers from Koreans. On the way to work details or over the walls, men observed Koreans at work and at play. One drew Korean women doing laundry in a pond and also depicted the "cordial send-off" the villagers gave them on their way to work.[30]

While the facilities at Keijō and Jinsen were adequate and even somewhat open to the surrounding community, the men lacked adequate clothes for Korea's severe winters. They had arrived with tropical-weight gear. As Australian prisoner Captain Guy Round, who had served with the Indian Army, observed, "In January and February at 30 below zero, you see the bullocks with icicles from their bodies."[31] The Koreans were even worse off: Private Harry Kingsley sketched Korean laborers sticking their arms into water to gather lily roots from frozen fields at an estimated 14 degrees below zero.[32] POW diaries include many comments, both good and bad, on the weather conditions, reflecting the tedium of captivity, as did the many references to food. According to the Geneva Conventions, prisoners were supposed to be fed the same as servicemen. Many POWs also compared their diet to what Koreans ate. As Gerald Rosenberg, a private from the 85th Australian Light Aid Detachment, put it, "We cannot complain about the tucker as a whole even though at times it is very light. For we can see that the civilians outside are getting less than us." Dick Swarbrick, a private from the Loyals, observed, "This diet although very poor by Occidental standards was I must admit superior at least in quantity to what the average Korean got. And it was as good as what a Jap soldier got at least if my own observations were anything to go by."[33] Rations from the Japanese Army were supplemented by black market activity, Red Cross boxes, as well as apples and other charity from the Koreans on the borders of the camp. Prisoners also produced food through farming and animal husbandry, though it is unclear how much of it they were able to keep for themselves. At Keijō they had a garden of 5,000 square meters, growing potatoes and vegetables, and they also raised rabbits and hogs.[34] By 1945, they had four hogs and 160 rabbits.

On the way to the farm, they would often see Koreans, sometimes in worse circumstances than their own. This was one of the ironies of the camps: the prisoners often felt fortunate after witnessing what Koreans endured. Alan Toze, a British soldier, described one episode:

> On arrival at [the] [f]arm a heartrending and shameful scene took place: lying in the road was a bundle of rags, which, when kicked by a native boss, proved to be a female of stunted structure and certain age, with blackened hands and a woebegone and tear streaked visage. She resisted all efforts by Jap soldiers etc. to eject her and escaping from them, shuffled to us and fell into our ranks looking pleadingly at us and wailing "America, America." She was then kicked and then as she passed me reached out a grimy paw and plucked my sleeve. I felt rotten but could do nothing about it.[35]

In one remarkable incident he found that Koreans were so desperate to escape their poverty that they attempted to break into the camp. In June 1943, "100 [K]oreans threw a riot outside the camp gates, tried to get in: the guard was turned out with fixed bayonets, took 1/2 hour to disperse them. One presumes poor devils are starving."[36] But this was the only such incident. Much more common are reports of receiving food from Koreans. In 1942, Alex Johnstone reported, "I scored an apple from a kid today."[37] A few days late, "Cec[il] brought me back half an apple and my little Jap guard friend (or should I say Korean) gave me a packet of cigs."[38]

The POWs' diet was also irregularly supplemented from time to time by Red Cross packages. Japanese records indicate that by February 1943 Jinsen had received 250 comfort boxes with canned beef, sugar, cocoa, and salt.[39] Of course, we do not know what prisoners received.[40] Japanese camp management used the packages to supplement the salary of commissioned officers, themselves inadequately fed.[41] Under the guise of "sampling," camp staff also ate and trafficked in relief goods. Although prohibited by international law, this practice was not forbidden until November 1944, when packages started to be addressed to prisoners personally.[42] Even so, occasional and incomplete package deliveries were better than the total embargo that prevailed elsewhere. And there were other contributions besides food that bolstered morale. The Neutral Committee of the World Alliance of the YMCA provided books and musical instruments.[43] The Swiss legation also provided a guitar, a mandolin, and a violin.[44] Jinsen's library grew from 130 volumes in 1943 to 482 in 1945, though 125 were Bibles.[45] The other books were mainly novels, but the library also contained a hymnal, a how-to guide to pottery, a biography of Brahms, and, crucially, a compendium of card games.[46] Prisoners could also read the propaganda organ *Nippon Times*. Australian Corporal Alex Johnstone of the 2/15th Field Regiment, originally attached to the Audit Office, Command Pay Staff of the AIF in Malaya, created elaborate recipe books.

Card games like poker, pontoon, and bridge occupied the prisoners for long hours, even though guards sometimes confiscated the playing cards. Gambling was strictly forbidden, but it went on nonetheless.[47] POWs also played sports. At Jinsen, men organized a baseball league, where the Red Sox faced teams named after the hard realities of camp life – Banjo (*benjo*) Squatters, Yasmui (*yasumi*) Giants, Tatami Pressers. Camp bookies set the odds.[48] Perhaps because prisoners had other activities to choose from, by 1945 few attended weekly church services any longer at Keijō, and Jinsen had no chaplain.[49]

What we usually hear about in accounts of POW camps is back-breaking work. But in Korea, camp commanders struggled to find labor for the Allied soldiers. They were paid for their work but could spend their savings only at the cafeteria, where there often was not much to buy.[50] Near Keijō, there were few large-scale civil engineering projects like the great railway or coal mines that absorbed prisoner labor elsewhere. Eventually, POWs in Korea farmed, cared for livestock, built roads, and repaired harbors and airfields.[51] Others worked as miners or stevedores. For commissioned officers, work would be voluntary and unpaid.[52] They chose to do so nonetheless. But it appears there was less pressure put on the men to work than in other POW camps throughout Japan's empire.[53]

At Keijō, prisoners worked at an Army warehouse forwarding supplies to the Chōsen Army (*Chōsen gunsō rikugun sōko*) or loading and packing raw materials. Some prisoners worked within the camp making Army uniforms or at the carpentry workshop.[54] Imperial Army management also hired out prisoners, loading and unloading railway trucks at Ryusan, small civil engineering jobs, and "one very pleasant job" of "building a racecourse for a wealthy Japanese civilian who provided us with good food and was very gentle and manly towards us."[55] In September

1943, Kōnan was opened to supply workers for a carbide factory owned by Nippon Chisso.[56] Some prisoners were grateful to be transferred, even though it was 190 miles from the Manchurian border, and they endured a harsher climate. The food appears to have been better, with daily rice, vegetables, and fish, at least in the fall and winter. But other prisoners worked at scorching furnaces making dangerous chemicals.[57]

Allied military prisoners were a source of great interest for Koreans as they worked. And POWs appear to have looked right back. Since many Korean men had dispersed through the empire, to attend schools, to fight in the Japanese Imperial Army, or to provide labor, many women were working in Korea. Alex Johnstone reported that dozens of spectators watched prisoners doing excavating work for a new track at Jinsen railway. "Kids by the hundred stood on the railway embankment and threw cigarettes, apples and turnips down, but the guards stopped them." It was not just prisoners who worked, though: "On one side of the railway embankment were working Korean women and on the other us."[58] Sometimes prisoners needed the help: the "loaded skip was too heavy to lift, so young Korean woman dropped her bundle lifted handle on to my shoulder for me!"[59] As Rosenberg observed, "The native power is for the main part women and girls – poorly clad and badly shod. Some women work with a child on the back, one working behind and one in the pouch – very humane conditions I don't think."[60]

While prisoners sympathized with Koreans, they often resented one another. A constant shuffling between camps and worksites undermined unit cohesion. There was already significant tension from the outset between officers and enlisted men. Initially, a large proportion of prisoners who had arrived from Singapore were senior officers. The Japanese permitted them to wear insignia designating rank. According to Dick Swarbrick, a British POW from 1942–1943, the officers had lost their men's trust following the surrender at Singapore. Officers were able to regain respect by standing up to the Japanese and using their own money to buy supplies for the others.[61] But POW representatives – that is, officers – complained continually to the ICRC that morale was suffering because, living in close quarters with enlisted men, officers were not receiving the deference they deserved.[62]

## Punishment and resistance in the camps

POWs might have complained even more, but this risked physical punishment. The main source for knowing about this violence is prisoners' diaries and trial records and the testimony of the guards and commanders. At the postwar trials, testimony noted that Japanese officers were trained in a system in which face-slapping was common. With no penalty for slapping prisoners, witnesses concluded that it was little surprise that the practice would become common, as also noted in Sandra Wilson's Chapter 5 in this volume. But the trial records are not an unbiased source. And even from the testimony of the Yokohama trial – a trial in which prisoners were encouraged to testify against guards – it seems that abuse was not systematic but rather the sometimes random acts of particular guards.

While Korean guards have earned a reputation for violence, first-person testimonies from camps within Korea present a more complex picture. British prisoner Toze wrote, "Korean guards away from their own country seem to have earned dreadful rep[utation], ours may have been superior."[63] Round recalled the compassion of "The Christian," who obtained medicine and other items for prisoners with little concern for himself. Yet some, such as "The Pig," had a dreadful reputation and "delighted in striking us on the flimsiest of pretexts."[64] While many cases seem to show a particular guard's predilection for violence, in others it was punishment for particular infractions. This was not infrequent in the Japanese Imperial Army. Infractions included trafficking in or possessing personal items, arguing with guards, and black market exchanges – either attempts to buy goods or trade cigarettes. In September 1943, for instance, British Private Matthew Thompson was accused of stealing an apple. Thompson was made to stand at attention and struck with a heavy roll of paper. Captain Terada Takeo, adjutant at Keijō, slapped him in the face.[65] Noguchi lectured Thomson and sentenced him to eight days of solitary confinement.[66]

The most serious infraction was an escape attempt. After an officer and a non-commissioned officer attempted to escape Jinsen while on work patrol, they were quickly recaptured and sentenced to eight years and six months of jail at Seidaimon Civil Prison.[67] There is some evidence that Japanese misconduct was kept from Noguchi. What Noguchi liked least was anything that presented the camps negatively to the outside world or to the ICRC. Men who preserved evidence of Japanese misconduct fared poorly, like British Private David P. Lomasney. For instance, he brought an empty Red Cross can of beef into camp as evidence that the Japanese were eating Red Cross supplies. He was taken to military HQ, questioned, beaten, and told to sign a confession.[68] In summer 1943, after being unjustly accused of stealing toothbrushes, Australian Private Arthur Clark was struck with fists and beaten by Captain Terada. Tatsumi Ushihara, a civilian interpreter and UCLA graduate, beat him with a cane after Clark wrote a letter to his wife telling her that he could survive without the Red Cross parcels.[69]

Suspected sedition brought even harsher treatment. In July 1943, Lieutenant R.B. Pigott, a British POW, was confined for alleged circulation of anti-Japanese propaganda. Piggott passed a letter to an elderly Korean whom he knew that contained figures of American aircraft production, shipping, tanks, and manpower, along with an estimate of Japanese forces. It was signed "Freedom."[70] While Round described this as a "trivial matter," it is not difficult to see how the Japanese authorities might have viewed this as a problem.[71] Guards took Piggott to a Ryusan MP (Military Police) camp, where "third degree methods" were used to get a statement that implicated others in the camp. Prisoners coped with the abuse through humor, creating nicknames for their tormentors, such as "The Kicker," or more ironic ones like "Smiler" or "Peaches and Cream."

But even taking these incidents into account, POWs in Korea were treated less harshly than their counterparts in places like Burma and the Philippines. One way we know this is by evaluating the prisoners who arrived from those other theaters, such as Schwartz's group from the Philippines. On February 1, 1945, Noguchi's executive officer, Lieutenant Isobe, inspected the contingent after it arrived in Moji, the main port of Kyushu, on their way to Korea. He described the Americans as filthy and emaciated. Altogether the passage from Manila to Moji had taken seven weeks, and of 1,619 American POWs who originally shipped out, only 556 made it. Of those, 300 more subsequently died.[72]

Isobe judged that immediate transport to Korea was impossible and instead put the men in the charge of the Western Army. Fifty-three of the 193 died in the next three months due to improper medical facilities and a poor diet.[73] On April 26, Schwartz's party finally arrived in Korea and joined a group of twenty enlisted men – all that remained of the original Commonwealth contingent. They were then sent to Jinsen, where they were surprised by their treatment.[74] At this point Jinsen was no longer a propaganda camp, which reflected a larger policy shift to stop highlighting the good treatment of POWs. As the war ministry stressed in December 1943, news on prisoners would be censored so that domestic reports would avoid anything that gave the impression that prisoners were "too well or too cruelly treated." But one American officer, Lieutenant Colonel Arthur Shreve, identified another possible reason for their good treatment. As he wrote in his diary in April 1945: "The trip, for one exception, has been so comfortable and the food has been so good that I am sure that the Japanese have come to the realization that they are losing the war."[75]

Even so, the Americans were struck by the "sadism" of one man, the camp doctor, Mizuguchi Yasutoshi. As Schwartz, a doctor himself, later recalled: "Two officers died while we were in this camp, both of amoebic dysentery, and I made many requests before their death for amoebecides, but was always refused."[76] Even though American Red Cross supplies were available in the camp, Mizuguchi would not distribute them. As the guards' defense counsel Waldo P. Johnson argued in his 1947 defense of Mizuguchi, King had suffered greatly in the Philippines and on the voyage to Japan and to Korea. He was seriously ill upon arrival, and his death "could hardly be said to have been contributed to or accelerated by Mizuguchi."[77] But it is clear that American Red Cross supplies were in the camp and were not used to aid King. Mizuguchi disappeared from the camp in July 1945. Shortly after, the Japanese turned over to prisoners a considerable amount of dressings, drugs, quinine, vitamins, and plasma.

In August, it soon became clear to the POWs at Kōnan that the end was near. On August 9, Gerald Rosenberg heard that Russia had entered the war and was on the march through Manchuria. Air alarms doubled and tripled in number, and the camp population tried to pack camp stores and shift rations to safe positions. On August 12, a Korean guard told Rosenberg that a commander by the name of Otaki had ordered that if the Russians took the camp before a general armistice, the POWs would be shot. In Jinsen when the blackout ended and riots broke out outside the camp, prisoners started to get excited. The next day, the commandant told the Anglo-American prisoner representative that a ceasefire had been declared. On the 19th, the savings of the POWs from their labor were paid out in full. On the 21st, they were allowed to read the *Keijō nippō*, and on the 24th, to listen to the radio.

The Commander-in-Chief of Army Forces in the Pacific (AFPAC) sought to locate and free all Allied POWs and captives. They first sent tactical units, or "liaison teams and recovery teams," to deliver food, clothing, medical supplies, and other necessary equipment for the use of released prisoners of war and civilian internees.[78] Since Captain George Stengel, the commanding officer of the POW liaison team, would not arrive until September 6, American B-29s made three parachute drops of clothing and food.[79] In a cruel irony, the heavy pallets caused multiple deaths and injuries. At Keijō, a Korean woman was hit and died. At Jinsen, the damage was still worse. A prisoner's leg was broken, one Korean was killed, and eight Japanese were injured. On September 9, Lieutenant General John R. Hodge, commander of the XXIV unit of the U.S. 10th Army – and future military governor of South Korea – landed with his troops to receive the Japanese surrender. They soon liberated the 393 Allied prisoners at Jinsen. U.S. forces also liberated about 130 men from Keijō, mostly British and Australians taken prisoner at Singapore.[80]

Meanwhile, in August some prisoners found themselves in the capital celebrating Korea's independence. Koreans initially welcomed American troops, but the jubilation dimmed when Hodge announced that Governor-General Abe Nobuyuki would be kept in office.[81] The correspondent for the London *Times* noted that as a crowd of about five hundred Koreans waved flags, Japanese troops fired on them, killing two and wounding ten others. Guy Round later recalled singing "Auld Lang Syne" as Korean independence leaders sang "Aegukka."[82] Repatriation would soon begin for Allied POWs, now United Nations Prisoners of War, and for civilian internees. Matters were more complicated for everyone else – for example, stateless persons, such as White Russians and German Jews, Italians, Vichy French, Turks, and Germans, and the Koreans who would soon be subject to U.S. military occupation.[83]

At Kōnan, prisoners had to wait until September, when Soviet troops finally freed them. Kōnan was now in the Soviet zone, and Korean men and women were kept outside the gates.[84] One B-29 flew overhead with the intention of dropping supplies, but some of the packages hit a building occupied by Red Army troops, narrowly missing a colonel. This brought an order that any planes flying over the camp should be made to land. On the 20th, Soviet planes intercepted the next B-29, but the pilot judged the designated field too small for a safe landing. The Soviets followed the American plane and fired, forcing the B-29 to crash. But the incident ended peacefully. Korean fishermen picked up the Americans, and a repair crew arrived from Guam. On September 21, the American POWs finally left for Kanko. Russian officers accompanied them and kept the Koreans and Japanese away.

## Aftermath

On or about October 9, 1945, eight members of the Japanese Army were arrested for Acts Committed against the Allied Prisoners. They included Colonel Noguchi, Lieutenant Colonel Okazaki – the commander of Jinsen – and his counterpart at

Keijō, Captain Gotō. Other prisoners included Captain Terada, adjutant at Keijō, Lieutenant Moritomi, paymaster, Corporal Ushihara, a "notorious" interpreter, and the prison doctor Mizuguchi. Three days later, seven more of "lower notoriety" were arrested, for a total of fifteen. The men were held in a stockade in the vicinity of Inchon. On May 14, 1946, they were shipped to Japan for trial. No evidence of guilt was found concerning the other guards, and they were found eligible to be processed and evacuated to Japan with other personnel.[85]

From June to September 1947, twelve Japanese men were tried in a single Yokohama trial for crimes allegedly committed at camps in Korea.[86] The trial of "Yuzuru Noguchi et al." was a group trial for the commanders. Noguchi and Oka-zaki were charged with their failure to "perform specific command functions," while subordinates, including Terada Takeo, Ushihara Tatsumi, Mizuguchi Yasu-toshi, and Uchida Gorō were charged for specific acts against POWs. A review of the records shows that the trial is striking in its reliance on dubious rules of evidence. The men were judged together by a court with "medical conclusions by lay witnesses, hearsay evidence, evidence other than the best."[87] There was a question of jurisdiction, when a U.S.-run court judged Japanese soldiers alleged to have harmed British or Australian prisoners. Only two of the five initial members of the judges' panel remained through the whole trial. And the trial itself took several shortcuts.

In Noguchi's defense, his counsel pointed out that the administration of the Keijō and Jinsen camps was superior to all others: acts of mistreatment were fewer, the percentage of illnesses lower, and deaths more rare. This evidence was not contradicted by the prosecution.[88] Noguchi and Okazaki were tried based on the principle of command responsibility: that they were criminally liable for acts perpetrated by their subordinates "if they knew or had reason to know that their subordinates were committing such crimes, and did not take all necessary or reasonable measures in their power to prevent their commission."[89] Noguchi was sentenced to 22 years in prison, Okazaki received twenty years, and Mizuguchi was condemned to death by hanging.[90] Clearly, the judges were not convinced that Keijō and Jinsen were model camps. And yet the fatality rates were indeed low: just 2.7% of Commonwealth troops died, for instance. We can compare this to camps in Kawasaki and Hakodate, Japan, where almost a quarter of POWs lost their lives.[91] Moreover, the majority of these deaths took place shortly after POWs arrived because of the harsh conditions of transport. Much of the same is true of the Americans.

How do we explain why so many POWs were able to sit out the war in relative safety? Even the official United States military history of the postwar military presence in Korea concluded that "the Japanese need not be blamed too severely for such minor abuses as face-slapping." Quoting Lieutenant Colonel Elrington, it agreed that "'the fault lies with the system rather than the individual. Soldiers in the Japanese Army normally fared little better at the hands of their superiors. Japan can easily feed twelve soldiers on the daily food cost of one American Private.'"[92] Six years after the war had ended, Major W. J. Holohan commented: "[I]t is only those unfortunate people who have suffered the rigor and the utter helplessness and hopelessness of life in a POW camp [who] can realize the situation and our camp was a model."

While many historians highlight unit cohesion as a key factor in determining who survived captivity, pluck and esprit de corps do not seem to be a major factor, at least in this case. The population of prisoners in Korea was transient, with significant tension between officers and the enlisted. It was common practice for officers to enjoy privileged status in POW camps, whether in terms of work, correspondence, or access to black market goods. But the unique circumstances at Jinsen bred resentment. After all, when officers made up a large proportion of the camp population, otherwise customary demands for special treatment – or at least immunity from physical punishment – may have come across as special pleading. Rather than representing the POWs as a group, the large number of officers may have appeared to represent themselves above all.

But whether they were officers or enlisted, upon arrival in Korea, prisoners had adequate facilities and relatively good sanitation. They received army rations supplemented by occasional packages and food they managed to grow or raise, along with gifts from Korean civilians. The work was not, for most, particularly grueling. Even men working at the nitrogen factory at Kōnan ate fish, vegetables, and rice. And as much as they suffered from the cold, POWs from temperate climates fared even worse when exposed to tropical disease. And many of the prisoners in Korea enjoyed periods of leisure and at least sporadic correspondence with loved ones. Moreover, with important exceptions, the guards whom the prisoners encountered do not appear to have been particularly brutal.

Perhaps none of this should surprise us, since the Japanese Army designed Jinsen and Keijō as show camps. But they lost that purpose by 1943. If, as Elrington and Holohan found, the camp was unusually well run, it was in part due to its management. And yet, even in what was intended to be a model camp, one in which the commanders officially proscribed violence, prisoners could be subject to abuse. A sadist such as Mizuguchi appeared to have free rein. Along with the confiscation of care packages, the Mizuguchi case shows how, even when supplies were ample, prisoners might still suffer. This raises questions as to whether Japan's straitened circumstances – a frequently cited factor – is an adequate explanation for the deprivation of prisoners. After all, Korean civilians who may have endured even harsher wartime conditions often went out of their way to aid POWs.

Viewed in a larger context, what is most unusual about the camps in Korea is how, if only for a time, senior military and political leaders seriously considered the proper treatment of Allied prisoners. Ironically, it was not merely to conform to international laws of war but to provide a model for Japan's colonial subjects. And although conditions deteriorated in some respects, they never reached the level where other camps began. Instead, the initial design appears to have created a set of practices and precedents that continued to shape relations between guards and prisoners long after Jinsen ceased being a propaganda camp and most of the original prisoners had moved on.

Of course, physical punishment was also part of the culture in POW camps in Korea, whether or not commanders prohibited the practice, and a character like Mizuguchi could push matters quite far. But the surprising degree of autonomy officers enjoyed also meant that others could act to protect prisoners' welfare, such as when Isobe rejected the idea of immediately subjecting survivors from the Philippines to another ocean passage.

To recapture the full complexity of the POW experience, it is clear that we need many more detailed studies that analyze both how policy was made and how it played out in the home islands, in Japan's other colonies, and those established closer to the war front (and further from the oversight of central authorities). But the history of the POW camps in Korea indicates that when senior Japanese leadership took an interest in the fate of Allied POWs, policy was not one of deliberate cruelty. This raises the question of whether POW camps might have been different – and better – in the rest of Japan's wartime empire if senior officials had created policies and practices with more general applicability.

## Notes

1 "Check List for Col. Schwartz," April 9, 1946, RG 331, Box 920, United States National Archives (USNA), College Park, Maryland, online on Mansell.com (an extensive online research collection of primary documents compiled by Roger Mansell).

2 Laura Hillenbrand's runaway bestseller *Unbroken: A World War II Story of Survival, Resilience, and Redemption* (New York: Random House, 2010) is a striking example. There was also a 2014 film based on the story. See Richard Flanagan's *The Narrow Road to the Deep North* (London: Chatto and Windus, 2014).

3 Hata Ikuhiko, *Nihon horyo: hakusonkō kara shiberia yokuryū made* (Hara Shobō, 1998); Adachi Sumio, *Unprepared Regrettable Events: A Brief History of Japanese Practices on Treatment of Allied War Victims during the Second World War* (Yokosuka: National Defense Academy, 1982), pp. 257–332; Ichimata Masao, "Senpan saiban kenkyū yōron (2): taiheiyō sensō teisen shori kansuru kokusaihō sōsatsu," *Kokusaihō gaikō zasshi* vol. 66, issue 2 (1967): pp. 28–61.

4 See especially Utsumi Aiko, *Nihongun no horyo seisaku* and *Kimu wa naze sabakareta no ka: chōsenjin bi-shi-kyū senpan no kiseki* (Asahi shimbun shuppan, 2008), Utsumi's study of the 148 Korean guards convicted as Class BC war criminals by the Allied Forces. In 2002, Utsumi and Fukubayashi Toru created a bilingual online tool for researchers to work cooperatively and share data, the POW Research Network, http://www.powresearch.jp/en/. The organization works as a clearinghouse for former POWs and their families visiting Japan and a central source of research published in Japanese, especially by the organization's members. Utsumi herself is both historian and activist. (Unless otherwise noted, all Japanese books are published in Tokyo.)

5 Cho Gun, "Ilje kangjum malgi joseonjudunilbongunui joseonin porogamsiwon dongwongwa yenhapgun porosuyongso unyoung," *Hangukgeunhyeondaesahakhoe* vol. 67 (Winter 2013): pp. 451–485.

6 Utsumi, *Kimu wa naze.*

7 Although this chapter does not deal explicitly with issues of collaboration and national identity, they are crucial and will be dealt with in later work. See Barak Kushner, "Pawns of Empire: Postwar Taiwan, Japan and the Dilemma of War Crimes," *Japanese Studies* vol. 30, issue 1 (May 2010): pp. 111–133, here pp. 114–115.

8 For more on the problematic nature of soldiers' diaries, see Aaron William Moore, *Writing War: Soldiers Record the Japanese Empire* (Cambridge, MA: Harvard University Press, 2013).

9 Switzerland was the "Protecting Power" for the United States, Great Britain, and some twenty other belligerents in World War II, with the responsibility to represent the Allies in Japan. Sweden looked after Japanese and Japanese-Americans in Hawaii, and Spain had responsibility for the *Issei* and *Nisei* in the continental United States; Switzerland for the United States and Britain, and Spain and Sweden for Japan. See Sarah Kovner, "A War of Words: Allied Captivity and Swiss Neutrality in the Pacific, 1941–1945," *Diplomatic History*, forthcoming.

10 "Riku-a-mitsu-ju no. 1910," Secret Telegram 2–28, From Chief of Staff, Korean Army, to Vice Minister of War, March 1, 1942 [received March 4 1942], in *The Tokyo War Crimes Trial, Proceedings of the Tribunal* (herafter *TWCT*), vol. 6, ed. R. John Pritchard and Sonia Magbanua Zaide (New York: Garland Publishing, 1981), pp. 14512–14513. Also see Utsumi Aiko, *Furyo toriatsukai ni kansuru shogaikoku kara no kōgishū* (Fuji shuppan, 1989), pp. 14–15; Utsumi Aiko and Nagai Hitoshi, *Tōkyō saiban shiryō: furyo jōhōkyoku kankei bunsho* (Gendai shiryō shuppan, 1989), pp. 32–33.

11 "Report regarding Plans for the Internment of POWs in Korea," From Commander in Chief of the Korean Army, Seishiro Itagaki" to Minister of War, Hideki Tojo," March 23, 1942. *TWCT*, vol. 6, pp. 14, 514–515, 516; "A-mitsu no. 1910 – Part II," received by Army Secretariat April 23, 1942, *TWCT*, vol. 6, pp. 14, 517.

12 Quoted in Utsumi Aiko, "The Japanese Army and Its Prisoners, Relevant Documents and Bureaucratic Institutions," Australia-Japan Research Project, Australian War Memorial, http://ajrp.awm.gov.au.

13 A selection of these photos can be found at the Imperial War Museum (IWM), London, UK. See also Fran de Groen and Helen Masterman-Smith, "2002 History Conference – Remembering 1942, Prisoners on parade: Japan Party 'B,'" Australian War Memorial, http://www.awm.gov.au/events/conference/2002.

14 "Allied POWs" in this chapter applies only to Euro-American Allied prisoners. The Japanese did not place Chinese POWs or other Asians in the same category. In one camp in India, Indians and British were even held in separate areas. See Report No. 16, "The Story of an Indian POW (Non-INA) who manned guns for the Japanese," File 379, Parts 3, pp. 1–250, 4 INA Papers, Private Archives, INA Archives, National Archives of India, New Delhi, India.

15 Utsumi, *Kimu wa naze*, pp. 67–78, esp. p. 74.

16 The Commission on Verification and Support for the Victims of Forced Mobilization under Japanese Colonialism in Korea; Cho Gun, "Ilje kangjum," 2013.

17 "Camp division. Jinsen. Corée," Archives du Service des Camps, Rapports Originaux CICR, vol. 783–786, 790–799, 807–811, Depouillement des camps par matiere, Japon (Corée, Taiwan), ICRC Archives, Geneva, Switzerland.

18 Chief of Staff of the Korean Army Ihara Junichiro to Vice-Army Minister Kimura Hyotaro, August 13, 1942 [Received by Army Secretariat August 19], "Reactions among the General Public Following Internment of British Prisoners of War," in *TWCT*; Groen, in *TWCT*, vol. 6, pp. 14521–14524. Groen, citing Bergamini (pp. 964–965), also notes this material but draws a different conclusion.

19 "Riku-a-mitsu ju, no. 10133," [Received by Army Secretariat, August 19, 1942], from Ihara to Vice-Army Minister Kimura Hyotaro, Submitted to Army General Staff Headquarters and the War Ministry, "Reactions among the General Public following Internment of British Prisoners of War, in *TWCT*, vol. 6., pp. 14521–14529.

20 Chief of Staff of Korean Army from July 9th, 1942, and chief of 17th Area Army and Korean District Army from Feb 11th to the end of the War. "We never chose a place for the purpose of propaganda to Koreans or putting affront upon prisoners." (In his own testimony 30,161), *TWCT*.

21  Guy Round, "The Road from Singapore," unpublished manuscript, 1943–1947, MS 1370, Australian War Memorial (AWM), Canberra, Australia, p. 191; Herbert Stanley Geldard, "Diary/Notebook," 1942, PR 91/194, AWM.
22  Korea initially had two POW camps, the main camp at Keijō (modern Seoul) and the No. 1 branch camp at Jinsen. A third camp, the No. 1 dispatched camp, was later opened at Kōnan (Hŭngnam), in the heavily industrialized north. There were also a number of internee camps that held missionaries and other civilians.
23  "Instructions given by Col. Y. Noguchi, Superintendent of the Chōsen War Prisoners' Camp," September 1942, Chōsen POW Camp Papers, IWM.
24  To Elrington, Col. Noguchi "seemed to be a mild middle-aged man and anxious for a quiet life": Alan Vernon Toze, "Diary, Documents 1133," IWM.
25  Camp principal Keijo-Chosen, "Depouillements des camps par matieres: Japon, Coree, Formose," Archives du Service des Camps, Rapports originaux CICR, Vol. 783–786 790–799, 807–811, Tel. 207 du 27.12.42 G 8/Pa G 17/Ja., ICRC Archives.
26  "Prisoners in Far East: Camp Conditions," *Advocate* (Burnie, Tasmania), June 24, 1943, p. 2.
27  Dave Swarbrick, "Dick Swarbrick's War," 2nd Battalion Loyal's Regimental, http://www.far-eastern-heroes.org.uk/Richard_Swarbricks_War/html/jinsen_camp_-_korea.htm.
28  Archives du Service des Camps Rapports Originaux CICR VOl 790–799, 807–811, CICR SC 023, Folder RV 23, 1, RR (CICR) 783–795, Rapports: Pestalozzi-Angst-Paravicini, 790 Japon-Manchukuo, novembre 1943-fev.-mars.av. 1944. ICRC Archives.
29  Guy Round describes such an unsuccessful attempt in 1944 by Sgt. Griffiths and Private Broughton: Round, "The Road from Singapore," p. 347.
30  Sgt. S. Strange and A. V. Toze, "In Defense of Singapore: Scenes and personal images before and after the fall of Singapore: A Series of Drawings with brief Notes," plate XVII, Lancashire Infantry Museum, Preston, UK.
31  Guy Round, "I Was a Prisoner in Korea," *Western Mail* (Perth, WA), August 17, 1950, p. 3.
32  Harry Kingsley, "Prisoner of war drawings at Keijo P.O.W. Camp, Korea: 1942 to 1945," IWM, 67038.
33  Swarbrick, "Dick Swarbrick's war"; AWM, MSS 1737, Gerald Rosenberg, September 22, 1943.
34  "Prisoners of War Camp, Chosen, Visited by M. Pestalozzi," November 15, 1943, ICRC Archives.
35  Toze, "Diary," November 23, 1943, Documents 1133, IWM, p. 57.
36  Toze, "Diary," June 27, 1943, Documents 1133, IWM, p. 39.
37  Alex Johnstone, "Diary," November 7, 1942, AWM, PRO 1044, p. 84.
38  Ibid.
39  Depouillements des camps par matieres: Japon, Coree, Formose, Archives du Service des Camps, Rapports originaux CICR, Vol. 783–786, 790–799, 807–811, Tel. 207 du 27.12.42 G 8/Pa G 17/Ja., pp. 429–437, ICRC Archives.
40  Camp Division Jinsen, Archives du Service des Camps, Rapports Originaux CICR, Vol 783–786, 790–799, 807–811, Depouillement des camps par matiere, Japon (Corée, Taiwan), ICRC Archives.
41  Utsumi, *Nihongun no horyo seisaku*, p. 219.
42  In November 1944, another shipment arrived from Rashin via Vladivostok, containing 1,670 wrapped packages, meaning 4 boxes for each prisoner. Utsumi, *Nihongun no horyo seisaku*, p. 221.
43  Depouillements des camps par matieres: Japon, Coree, Formose, Archives du Service des Camps, Rapports originaux CICR, Vol. 783–786, 790–799, 807–811, Tel. 1645 du 15.2.45 G 17/76 ExO G 8/Pa, Fev 45, Rap 1179, February 15, 1945, ICRC Archives.
44  Utsumi, *Nihongun no horyo seisaku*, pp. 212–221; *The Daily News* (Perth, WA: 1882–1950), December 7, 1943.

45 Camp PG Chosen, Detached Camp No. 1, Depouillements des camps par matieres: Japon, Coree, Formose, Archives du Service des Camps, Rapports originaux CICR, Vol. 783–786, 790–799, 807–811, Tel. 1645 du 15.2.45 G 17/76 ExO G 8/Pa Fev 45, Rap 1179, ICRC Archives.

46 Supreme Command for the Allied Powers, Legal section, Administrative Division, Miscellaneous Subject File, Box 1241, USNA, College Park, MD; Utsumi, *Nihongun no horyo seisaku*, pp. 212–221.

47 Swarbrick, "Dick Swarbrick's War."

48 Ibid.

49 Archives du Service des Camps, Rapports Originaux CICR, Vol. 783–786, 790–799, 807–811, Depouillement des camps par matiere, Japon (Corée, Taiwan), ICRC Archives.

50 Camp des camps par matieres: Japon, Corée, Formose, February 15, 1945, Archives du Service des Camps, Rapports Originaux CICR, Vol. 783–786, 790–799, 807–811, Depouillement des camps par matiere. Japon (Corée, Taiwan), ICRC Archives.

51 Camp de Zinsen (Jinsen) (Camp division de Keijo), Archives du Service des Camps, Rapports Originaux CICR, Vol. 783–786, 790–799, 807–811, Depouillement des camps par matiere. Japon (Corée, Taiwan), ICRC Archives.

52 Utsumi, *Nihongun no horyo seisaku*, p. 214.

53 Camp PG Chosen, Detached Camp No. 1, February 15, 1945, Depouillements des camps par matieres: Japon, Coree, Formose, Archives du Service des Camps.Rapports originaux CICR, Vol. 783–786, 790–799, 807–811, Tel. 1645 du 15.2.45 G 17/76 ExO G 8/Pa, ICRC Archives. Others worked as miners or stevedores. For commissioned officers, work would be voluntary and unpaid: Utsumi, *Nihongun no horyo seisaku*, p. 214.

54 Camp PG Chosen, February 15, 1945, Depouillements des camps par matieres: Japon, Coree, Formose, Archives du Service des Camps, Rapports originaux CICR. Vol. 783–786, 790–799, 807–811, Tel. 1645 du 15.2.45 G 17/76 ExO G 8/Pa, ICRC Archives.

55 Toze, "Diary," Documents 1133, IWM.

56 ICRC inspector Angst was sick the day of the scheduled inspection and the Japanese "inspected" it in his absence.

57 United States of America vs. Yuzuru Noguchi, Review of the Staff Judge Advocate, September 13, 1945, as found on found on Forsschungs- und Dokumentationszentrum für Kriegsverbrecherprozesse, p. 57, http://www.uni-marburg.de/icwc.

58 Alex Johnstone, private record, November 4, 1942, PRO 1044, AWM, p. 82; Alex Johnstone, private record, November 6, 1942, PRO 1044, AWM, p. 82.

59 Toze, "Diary," Documents 1133, IWM, p. 28. Toze also made a sketch of "Korean coolies" he observed gathering lily roots from frozen fields.

60 Gerald Rosenberg, MSS 1737, AWM, unpaginated.

61 Swarbrick, "Dick Swarbrick's War."

62 Hygiene in Jinsen camp, Korea, Archives du Service des Camps, Rapports Originaux CICR, Vol 783–786, 790–799, 807–811, Depouillement des camps par matiere, Japon (Corée, Taiwan), ICRC Archives.

63 Toze, "Diary," Documents 1133, IWM, p. 86.

64 Round, "The Road from Singapore," p. 201.

65 United States vs. Noguchi et al., p. 31.

66 Ibid., p. 50.

67 Ibid., September 13, 1948, Yokohama Japan, as found on Forsschungs- und Dokumentationszentrum für Kriegsverbrecherprozesse, http://www.uni-marburg.de/icwc.

68 United States vs. Noguchi et al., p. 58.

69 Ibid., p. 34.

70 Round, "The Road from Singapore," p. 347.

71 Ibid., p. 344.

72 "Check List for Col. Schwartz," April 9, 1946, USNA, NARA, RG 331, Box 920.

73 Ibid.

74 Ibid.

75 Shreve transcribed his diary as evidence for the War Crimes Tribunal in 1948. For the War Crimes Office, Judge Advocate General's Department, Department of the Army, United States of America, "Perpetuation of Testimony of Arthur L. Shreve, Lt Colonel, 011176, Taken at: Baltimore, Maryland, Dated: 16 January 1948, In the Presence of: Jack S. Kelly, Special Agent, 109th CIC Det, Second Army," http://www.mansell.com/pow_resources/camplists/fukuoka/fuk_01_fukuoka/fukuoka_01/Shreve.html.

76 "Check List for Col. Schwartz," April 9, 1946, USNA, NARA, RG 331, Box 920.

77 "Defense Motion for Disapproval of Findings and Modification of Sentence as to Yasu-toshi Mizuguchi," March 25, 1948, p. 18.

78 United States Armed Forces in Korea (USAFIK), *Chuhan migunsa: HUSAFIK* (Sŏul T'ŭkpyŏlsi: Tolbegae, 1988) p. 4, Courtesy of Lori Watt.

79 USAFIK, *Chuhan migunsa*, pp. 51–52.

80 James O'Connor, "U.S. Troops Land in Korea," *The Argus* (Melbourne, Victoria), September 10, 1945, p. 16; N.A. "Conditions in Jap Camps," September 24, 1945, p. 5.

81 Our Own Correspondent, "Americans in Korea," *Times* (London, UK), September 10, 1945, p. 4.

82 Round, "I was a Prisoner in Korea," p. 3.

83 USAFIK, *Chuhan migunsa*, p. 7.

84 "Held by Japan," *The West Australian* (Perth, WA), June 28, 1947, p. 5.

85 USAFIK, *Chuhan migunsa*, pp. 53–54.

86 On war crimes trials: on Class A trials, see Yuma Totani, *The Tokyo War Crimes Trial: The Pursuit of Justice in the Wake of World War II* (Cambridge, MA: Harvard University Asia Center, 2008); on Class BC trials, see Kushner, "Pawns of Empire," and Sandra Wilson, "Koreans in the Trials of Japanese War Crimes Suspects," forthcoming.

87 United States vs. Noguchi et al., p. 62.

88 "Defense Motion for Disapproval of Findings and Modification of Sentences as to Yuzuru Noguchi, Kajuro Okazaki and Goro Uchida," October 7, 1948, p. 16.

89 Ibid., p. 4; see also "Command Responsibility for Failure to Prevent, Repress or Report War Crimes," ICRC Website, https://www.icrc.org/customary-ihl/eng/docs/v1_cha_chapter43_rule153.

90 "Military Commission," Orders No. 303, October 2, 1948, RG 331, Box 1604, USNA, unpaginated.

91 The statistics on fatalities are problematic, since records are incomplete and prisoners were transported throughout the war. Toru Fukubayashi, "POW Camps in Japan Proper," http://www.powresearch.jp/en/archive/camplist/index.html.

92 USAFIK, *Chuhan migunsa*, p. 32.

# 7 Carceral geographies of Japan's vanishing empire

## War criminals' prisons in Asia

*Franziska Seraphim*

> We do not intend that the Japanese shall be enslaved as a race or destroyed as a nation, but *stern justice* shall be meted out to all war criminals, including those who have visited cruelties upon our prisoners.
>
> – Potsdam Declaration, July 26, 1945

> It is my earnest hope, and indeed the hope of all mankind, that from this solemn occasion a better world shall emerge out of the blood and carnage of the past – a world founded upon faith and understanding, a world dedicated to the dignity of man and the fulfillment of his most cherished wish for freedom, tolerance, and *justice*.
>
> – General Douglas MacArthur's Opening Statement at the Japanese Surrender Ceremony on the USS *Missouri*, Tokyo Bay, September 2, 1945[1]

When Japan surrendered to the Allied Powers on September 2, 1945, it unconditionally accepted the new world leaders' conception of a postwar order framed in terms of restoring justice rather than peace. The Allies claimed for themselves the mandate to sit in judgement over the criminal acts of war perpetrated by the defeated Axis while building a just postwar world commensurate with their own now undisputed power status. The implementation of this reorganized world necessitated broad territorial and geopolitical change. In Asia, it meant dismantling the Japanese empire, which at its height incorporated large portions of China, Northeast, and Southeast Asia, and much of the Pacific as well.

Exactly how such geopolitical rescaling related to prosecuting and punishing individual wartime perpetrators, however, was much less obvious. In the face of the mass atrocities committed during the war, academic studies of the war crimes trials necessarily focused on the determination of individual guilt and in some cases the criminality of organizations in the context of international law and its historical development. We have learned much about the nature of the crimes committed, the promises and limitations of the law to achieve justice, the interference of Cold War politics, and the public reception and memory of the trials as part of postwar democratic nation building. In part because of the distinctiveness of the legal cases, the prominence of Western prosecutorial practices, and the multiplicity of contexts, the historiography of the trials has remained extraordinarily piecemeal and lopsided. Much more is known about the prosecution of German than about Japanese war criminals, about the international military tribunals of war leaders in Nuremberg and Tokyo (Class A) than about the many more military courts and commissions judging so-called conventional war crimes and crimes against humanity (Class BC in Asia), and about the time of the trials than about the longer history of incarceration of the convicted and their eventual release. Above all, Japan's *war* rather than its wartime *empire* stood at the forefront of criminal investigations, just as the emerging Cold War assumed primary importance as the relevant political context to the virtual exclusion of concurrent European recolonization and Asian decolonization efforts. Tellingly, the Japanese emperor, whose empire the war was meant to defend, escaped prosecution altogether. From this perspective, it is perhaps unsurprising that the empire appeared to have vanished as if overnight, as Barak Kushner partially discusses in the Introduction.

This chapter offers a corrective by proposing a different angle of inquiry: it probes the connections between the Allied war crimes trial program and the unmaking of Japan's empire after World War II from a *geographical* perspective to discover the temporal-spatial dimensions of what Ruti Teitel called "transitional criminal justice" by the successor states.[2] Whereas other important studies have sought to clarify the nature of Japanese wartime crimes through the Allied legal procedures, most recently in the work of Yuma Totani, the focus here is to rethink the place of punishment for individual war crimes in the longer trajectory of political transition, in which its viability as a just measure to build a more just world shifted considerably over time and space and at the hands of multiple agents.[3] I take as my starting point the physical presence of imprisoned war criminals across Asia, which I argue kept the geographical, legal, and concretely human dimensions of empire in public view (whether on local, national, or international scales) long after the region had begun reconstituting itself along old and new national lines (see Figure 7.1).

Seen through the lens of imprisonment, the war crimes trial program ended only in 1958, when Tokyo's Sugamo Prison closed its doors, or even in 1964, when the People's Republic of China released its last Japanese war crimes prisoners, outlasting Japan's Allied occupation, the Chinese Civil War, the Korean War, as well as witnessing the establishment of independent nation-states in Southeast Asia. This research therefore encompasses a global temporality of enormous geopolitical change while drawing attention to the different local temporalities that characterized the dismantling of the Japanese empire and renegotiation of national legitimacy in different regions. A case in point is the San Francisco Peace Treaty, signed in 1951 and ratified in April 1952, which marked the formal end of Japan's empire but impacted the war crimes trial program highly unevenly. Whereas the Nationalist Chinese regime on Taiwan terminated its program with a general amnesty for all the war criminals it had convicted, followed by a French amnesty, the Treaty did not prompt the United States, Britain, Australia, or the Netherlands to speed up releases. Communist

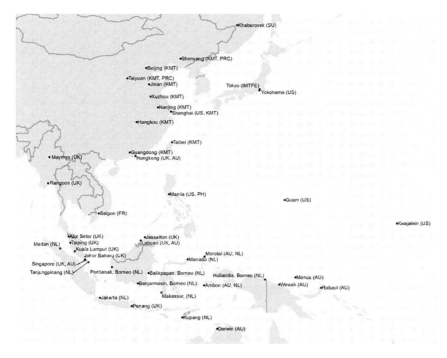

*Figure 7.1* Location of war crimes trials against Japanese in Asia after World War II, 1945–1956

Source: Hōmu daijin kanbō shihō hōsei chōsabu, *Senpan shakuhō shiyō*, Ministry of Justice, February, 1967.

China and the Soviet Union were not even signatories to the Treaty. But the end of the occupation did alter the conditions of imprisonment in Japan when Sugamo Prison came under Japanese management, gradually absorbed repatriated war criminals from everywhere in Asia, and became a focal point of civil activism for the release and systematic governmental efforts to decriminalize and reintegrate war criminals back into Japanese society, as Sandra Wilson illuminates in Chapter 5.

The prison, rather than the courtroom, serves here as a useful site to capture both the challenges that characterized Allied penal practices and the opportunities that this opened up for those privy to them in the ruins of Japan's empire. I build on the work of military historians like Robert Spector and Peter Dennis, who have laid out the extraordinarily complex circumstances in which the Western Allies assumed military control over Japan's far-flung empire after Japan's surrender, as well as targeted case studies that examined the legal reckoning with wartime and early postwar violence as a central part of this power shift in specific local contexts.[4] My focus on geography makes comparisons and connections between place-based experiences of transitional justice to bring to the forefront the physical presence of suspected, convicted, and imprisoned Japanese war criminals as lingering "remnants" of empire in shifting political and social landscapes. It traces the gradual shrinking of Japan's former empire via the shifting places of incarceration of suspected and convicted war criminals. Whereas most war criminals were held near the sites of their trials, which geographically encompassed the full expanse of Japan's occupied territories in Asia (now under the jurisdiction of multiple Allied armies), those still serving sentences by the late 1940s and early 1950s were repatriated to Sugamo Prison in Tokyo, in line with political expediency as the different convicting powers came to see it.

To document this spatial contraction of the empire, I draw upon theoretical insights from a subfield in human geography termed "carceral geography," which critically investigates the "distributional geographies," as well as "geographies of internal and external social and spatial relations" of places of imprisonment.[5] Such an approach draws attention to the diverse, changing, and even contradictory penal practices that the Allies employed toward Japanese war criminals as manifested in the physical places used at different stages of the program, as well as the opportunities to contest Allied justice that this created. Up until now, consideration of the treatment of war criminals has entered historical inquiry outside Japan solely in terms of a Japanese scheme to deny individual responsibility for war crimes, in fact taking at face value the political agenda of nationalist critics of the Allied program in Japan.[6] This misses entirely the practical implementation of legal decisions on the ground with which both the judged and those sitting in judgement had to contend in the midst of the major territorial rescaling in Japan's former empire. Carceral geographers, who see themselves in critical dialogue with the work of Michel Foucault and others, explore "the nature of carceral spaces and experiences within them, the spatial geographies of carceral systems, and the relationship between the carceral and . . . the punitive state."[7] In the present context, this means taking a close look at the location and constitution of the prison spaces used at various stages of the war crimes program and in different places in order to investigate the systemic links between Allied prisons and camps, as well as the mobility of the Japanese prisoners as they navigated the system and the changing nature of the convicting countries' penal policies as they dealt with the breakdown of Japan's empire.

## Territoriality

Central to a geographical perspective is the geohistorical concept of *territoriality.* As Charles Maier postulated in a much discussed essay fifteen years ago, "spatially anchored structures of power" and their conflation with national and ethnic identities was a historical phenomenon that characterized the world from the 1860s to the 1970s, beginning with the intensifying competition among modern empires, in which Japan participated, and cutting right across 1945. In other words, something fundamental did not change but rather stayed intact in the aftermath of World War II: the significance of territoriality as the structural logic of geopolitical and economic as well as social relations. If territoriality is understood, following David Sack's classic study, as "a complex strategy to affect, influence, and control access to people, things, and relationships," then it is only prudent that we take a close look at the ways in which the Allied military conquest, occupation, recolonization, and the forging of new political alliances in the wake of Japan's defeat created new territorial structures, within which legal jurisdiction over the human "remnants" of Japan's empire, most immediately those suspected or convicted of war crimes, was articulated.[8]

Whereas the Japanese islands retained their territorial integrity under the Supreme Commander for the Allied Powers (SCAP), General Douglas MacArthur, the Allies divided Japan's vast empire amongst themselves. In the days and weeks following MacArthur's surrender ceremony on September 2, 1945 in Tokyo Bay, American, Australian, British, Chinese, and Soviet commanders accepted the overall capitulation of Japanese troops in places once representative of Western colonial, Chinese national, or even Japanese imperial power, now turned into the respective hubs of Allied military control. The reuse of space in this way had immense symbolic meaning. Chronologically speaking, regional ceremonies were held first by the commander of the U.S. Army Forces of the Western Pacific, General Wilhelm D. Styler, at the former residence of the U.S. High Commissioner at Camp John Hay, Baguio, in the Philippines, on September 3, marking a triumphant return of American colonial power. The next day, Lord Louis Mountbatten, the British Supreme Commander of the Allied Southeast Asia Command, accepted the formal surrender of Japan's forces in mainland Southeast Asia (Burma, Sumatra, Malaya, French Indochina, and Thailand) onboard a British warship in Singapore. Maritime Southeast Asia (Indonesia), with which Mountbatten had also been charged, saw the Japanese surrender on September 12.

Australia came to preside over formal surrender ceremonies in Rabaul (east of New Guinea), once the headquarters of Japan's South Pacific Command and the center of Japanese power in the Pacific. Chiang Kai-shek's military commanders received the official capitulation of the Japanese in China (excluding Manchuria) at the long-time hotbed of nationalist political ambition, the Central Military Academy in Nanjing, on September 9. In Korea on September 9, American generals presided over the surrender of Japanese troops south of the 38th parallel at the colonial Japanese Government Central Building in Seoul, while the Soviet commander did so for Japanese troops north of the 38th parallel and in Manchuria.[9] The French and Dutch colonial governments arrived from exile only to reclaim their former colonial territories under the military auspices of the British. Both had to contend with major anti-colonial independence movements, the Viet Minh in Indochina and Nationalist forces in Indonesia, who had declared independence shortly after Japan's defeat.[10]

From this sketch of territorial divisions in September 1945, a first picture of the spatial politics of unmaking the Japanese empire begins to emerge. Even if pragmatic considerations determined the venues for surrender ceremonies – and thereafter war crimes trial courtrooms – the selected places carried political and symbolic meaning for local as well as far-away audiences. Places of formal surrender ceremonies (Tokyo, Singapore, Hong Kong, Nanjing), as well as many smaller towns where Japanese commanders raised the white flag (e.g. Rabaul, Morotai, Balikpapan on Borneo, Wewak in New Guinea) became important venues for military courts within the respective territorial jurisdiction that each Allied country's military command claimed at the end of the war. At the same time, the Allies collaborated across territorial jurisdictions for practical as well as for political reasons, namely to collect evidence, conduct trials at or near the site where the crimes had been committed, and to honor alliances. Australia collaborated with the British to hold additional Australian trials in Singapore, Hong Kong, North Borneo, and Morotai, including joint custody over incarcerated war criminals until Australian-convicted criminals were all moved to Australia's naval base on Manus Island. The British, who had territorial jurisdiction not only of their own but also the former French and Dutch colonial territories (today's Vietnam and Indonesia), allowed French colonial courts and Dutch courts martial teams to prosecute Japanese war criminals across the entire archipelago despite misgivings over their European neighbors' ill-conceived and often ruthless colonial endeavors. The United States conducted trials against Japanese and even against Germans in Shanghai, which the Nationalist Chinese, dependent on U.S. aid in their struggle against the Communists, tolerated only reluctantly. In great contrast, Korea, already divided between American and Soviet occupation zones as wartime allies turned into postwar rivals, was the only central part of the former Japanese empire that saw no war crimes trials at all.[11]

On the local level, territoriality, as a framework for social policy, national and ethnic identity, and controlled mobility, informed Allied immediate postwar tasks in at least three overlapping ways: the liberation of prisoners of war, internees, and forced laborers held by the Japanese; the repatriation of roughly 6.5 million Japanese stranded across Japan's far-flung empire, of whom 3 million were civilians; and the apprehension of suspected war criminals. The ability to cope with the practical challenges facing military Allied personnel on the ground and of balancing humanitarian imperatives against judicial needs on a day-to-day basis was commensurate with the level of political control Allied militaries exerted. In the Dutch East Indies alone, the Southeast Asian Command forces liberated and evacuated close to 100,000 Allied POWs, who were eager to return home but often needed to be nursed back to health first and were in high demand as witnesses in war crimes investigations.[12] Screening hundreds of thousands of defeated Japanese armed forces and civilians for war crimes suspects near the site of their capture or, better still, near the site of the crimes was a huge undertaking. Many former imperial soldiers made themselves invisible by joining new local wars, in Burma, Malaya, Indonesia, and China especially. Japanese civilians were desperately needed to run industry and infrastructure, as in Korea and Taiwan.[13]

A fourth task concerned sorting out war criminals from collaborators in all areas of the former empire but nowhere as intensely as in countries trying to establish national legitimacy as postcolonial sovereign states, that is, declaring independence from both the Japanese and Western colonial powers, as in Indonesia, French Indochina, Burma, the Philippines, but also China and Taiwan. Here, the question of territorially based identity, as Charles Maier has it, became particularly vexed. As the Dutch colonial authorities sought to reclaim their positions of authority in immediate postwar Indonesia, hunting down collaborators with the Japanese among indigenous populations assumed priority over securing Japanese war criminals.[14] In the Philippines, war crimes and traitor trials became complexly entangled once the Americans turned such legal reckoning over to the newly independent authorities.[15] Questions of ethnic identity loomed especially large in Chinese Nationalist war crimes trials on Taiwan involving legally Japanese but ethnically Taiwanese Class BC war criminals. Whereas the Western Allies convicted Taiwanese and Korean guards as Japanese war criminals, irrespective of their colonial status during the war, the Chinese Nationalists, eager to "assert their authority over all Chinese," did have to sort out the ethnopolitical identity of the accused to determine legal prosecution and to set them apart from local collaborators.[16] Even though much of the rhetoric was about unmaking the violent order forged in the previous decade, in fact it was not a simple return to a *status qua ante* but one that reflected new hierarchies and power relationships within specific spatial contexts.

A fifth concurrent issue required dealing with local resisters to Allied military rule, that is, not war but postwar "criminals." In Japan, where SCAP faced almost no resistance to its occupation, arrests of Korean "troublemakers" – former colonial people in often underprivileged positions and immediately branded as Communist sympathizers – became conspicuous. Not only did such Koreans share prison space with Japanese war criminals at Sugamo, but the American authorities quite eagerly worked with the Japanese government to "repatriate" Koreans who had remained in Japan after the war, now stripped of their Japanese citizenship.[17] In Indonesia, in contrast, Nationalist violence against Dutch civilians, Eurasians, Chinese, Ambonese, and Menadonese – ethnic groups associated with Dutch colonial rule – was rampant and demonstrated the limited control that British troops were initially able to exert in the Dutch Indies.[18]

The point here is to show how much the breakdown of Japan's empire and the legal reckoning with a violent past was rooted in the geographical rescaling of territoriality. This remapping entailed not just the assumption of military control over a certain area by the victors in war, but more importantly the sorting and reordering of groups of people, whose sense of place and position to one another shifted in the process, voluntarily or involuntarily. Victims and perpetrators were not always easy to separate out simply by national, ethnic, or military group affiliation, and the uncovering of crimes demanded the furnishing of evidence from victims and perpetrators alike. Equally important was the high degree of human mobility that characterized the postwar years as wartime camps were emptied of some and refilled with others, repatriates left and sometimes returned to stand trial near the site of their crimes, and surveillance regimes stretched from local to global (in the form of the International Red Cross, for example). Even though the vectors of territoriality and mobility pointed in different directions after Japan's defeat compared to before, the spatial dynamics as such persisted. In the following sections, I explore the distributional geography of war criminals' prisons across Japan's former empire from two perspectives: the Allies' spatial politics of prison siting with its links to both the European and the Japanese colonial pasts and the Japanese war criminals' visualization of the Allied carceral system as a means to claim a measure of ownership of their experiences both in time and place.

## The spatial politics of imprisonment

Six and a half million Japanese, including many ethnic Koreans and Taiwanese who had been part of the Greater East Asia project as colonial subjects, were stranded across North and Southeast Asia and the Pacific in the summer of 1945, variably and over time classified as Prisoners of War (POW), Surrendered Enemy Personnel (SEP, a British-only designation), War Crimes Suspects, War Criminals, and Cleared War Criminals. Whereas highly ranked officers attending surrender ceremonies were marched straight to high-security prisons, and government leaders ordered to report to Tokyo's Sugamo Prison, the majority of lower-ranked war crimes suspects were arrested bit by bit mainly from among the surrendered and interned, who often found themselves in the very same notorious camps that the Japanese military (and sometimes they personally) had run for Allied POWs and civilian internees during the war and where an estimated third of the crimes on trial had been committed.[19] In Thailand, for example, Japanese SEPs were held at one of the most notorious POW camps they themselves had run during the war while they worked to keep the Siam-Burma Railway going. In Singapore and Jakarta, Japanese were seen all over the city repairing the city's infrastructure as "surrendered personnel."[20]

The pragmatic reuse of existing space for the imprisonment of Japanese, whether surrendered personnel or war criminals, was perhaps not surprising, but it nonetheless carried symbolic if not also personal significance. In many cases, wartime captors and captives "simply" traded places after Japan's surrender. Class BC war criminals apprehended by the U.S. Eighth Army for war crimes against Allied POWs (which made up about 95 percent of all indictments at the Yokohama trials) were first held at Ōmori stockade in Yokohama, one of the largest and most infamous POW camps in wartime Japan, before they were transferred to Sugamo Prison on November 19, 1945. The new custodians marked the transition by cleaning up the "filth" the Japanese had left, "having scrubbed from top to bottom and thoroughly disinfected the place," in effect proudly demonstrating their superiority by offering the Japanese much better conditions of confinement than American POWs had endured.[21] Prison personnel continuities were sometimes even starker. One M. Tamapathy, identified as a Tamil Indian, testified on September 26, 1949, that he had joined the British Prison Service in Singapore in 1926, from 1942 had been employed by the Japanese as a warden in Outram Road (a prison affiliated

*Figure 7.2* Location of main prisons for Japanese convicted war criminals (originally constructed to aid European, American, and Japanese imperialism in Asia)

with Changi Prison), was taken back by the British Military Administration after liberation, and continued working in Outram Road for some weeks before being arrested himself for the murder of a Chinese civilian under the Japanese administration and imprisoned in Outram Road for the next three years as a war criminal.[22] Such reuse of space spoke most loudly to the reversal of power in the unmaking of Japan's imperial reach and perhaps less so to a direct sense of personal guilt (see Figure 7.2).

Japanese suspected of, tried for, or convicted of war crimes shared the same space in the American-run Sugamo Prison in Tokyo, but in Southeast Asia they were more often moved around among rural camps and urban prisons as they transitioned from one status to another. As a Netherlands East Indies delegate explained in a report to the International Red Cross on November 21, 1946, captured Japanese ran through different legal designations, often accompanied by physical relocation: from Surrendered Personnel without POW status (which meant they could be used for labor) to Prisoners of War with all the protections of the Geneva Convention while awaiting or standing trial, to imprisonment in common law jails if convicted (legal status unspecified until the 1949 Geneva Convention, which granted POW status to war criminals), or reversion to Surrendered Personnel if acquitted, in which case they returned to SEP labor camps to await repatriation to Japan.[23] For example, Japanese tried by Dutch courts in Borneo were moved from camps for Surrendered Personnel to stand trial in Balikpapan and Banjarmasin on Borneo and then sent to Cipinang Prison in Jakarta upon conviction. Others moved between different Allied territorial jurisdictions, in part because they were wanted by multiple powers in connection with crimes committed at different locations but also as a consequence of political shifts. War criminals convicted in Australian courts in Singapore and Hong Kong first served time in the British prisons Changi (Singapore) and Stanley (Hong Kong) before being moved to Australian soil on Manus Island to continue their sentences. The often extensive travels of suspected and convicted war criminals in the former empire and the experience of multiple national justice systems made a lasting impression on the prisoners themselves as pawns of the shifting power politics of the time, which is corroborated in the prison diaries and memoirs of famous generals such as Kawamura Saburō and Imamura Hitoshi.[24]

The Allies clearly established a network of prisons and camps for the incarceration of convicted Japanese war criminals that can be analyzed as a "carceral system," whose projected duration was not at all clear at the time. It is well worth recognizing the patterns held in common and contrast among the Allies in the distributional geography of places of punishment. All main prisons used to incarcerate (convicted) war criminals across Asia were of colonial origin and had been built in the preceding half century to discipline and contain local, ethnic resistance to colonial and imperial rule: the British prisons in Singapore, Hong Kong, and Rangoon; the American prison in Muntinlupa, a suburb of Manila; the Dutch prisons in Jakarta (formerly Batavia); but also the Japanese prisons Sugamo in Tokyo and Fushun in Manchuria. Each reflected the colonial history of its specific region: the British colonial government in Singapore operated two prisons, the older Outram Road Prison, built in 1847 by British professionals, and the newer, majestic, state-of-the-art Changi Gaol, opened in 1936 (and demolished in 2000) and considered to be "one of the most modern and best equipped military bases in the world."[25] Upon their victory in February 1942, the Japanese replaced current inmates with an astonishing 45,562 British, Australian, and later Dutch POWs, a number that shrank to 5,399 by June 1943 when most POWs were needed elsewhere. Contrary to the negative image of Changi today, the Japanese actually took over the organizational status quo the British had established, which conformed to the finest reformatory penal regimes of the time with ample educational, work, and leisure facilities, which Allied POWs noted with great admiration. Stanley Prison in Hong Kong was built at the same time, in 1937, but enjoyed a far less favorable reputation both under the British and the Japanese.

Batavia, the capital of the Dutch East Indies, sported three prisons from different eras: the large mid-eighteenth-century Glodok with community cells that accommodated between 8 and 40 inmates; Cipinang which was built around 1915 during the Indonesian National Revival (an anti-colonial movement) and remains to this day a detention place for political dissidents; and the small and more modern prison Struiswijk.[26] In the Philippines, Muntinlupa's colonial roots go back to the Spanish period, when Old Bilibid Prison was built in Manila in 1865, replaced in 1940 by the American-sponsored New Bilibid Prison and moved further out into the suburbs. It was placed under Filipino management, however, and held Japanese nationals before 1942, whereupon the Japanese occupation used it for anti-Japanese indigenous guerillas.[27] After the war, the prison resumed Filipino management and housed Japanese war criminals prosecuted both in U.S. and (after 1948) Filipino courts.

Japan had eagerly participated in the colonial prison-building wave, opening Sugamo Prison in Tokyo in 1895, Fushun Prison in Manchuria in 1936, not to mention prisons in Seoul and elsewhere in the colonies. By the 1930s, Sugamo was used mainly for violators of the Peace Preservation Law, notably prominent Communists and spies (Richard Sorge was executed there in 1944). The complex survived the Allied fire bombings relatively intact and was requisitioned by the occupation forces in the fall of 1945 to house Class A, B, and C war criminals, as well as foreign internees such as the German and Italian diplomatic community and Asian wartime collaborators. After the last Japanese war criminal was released in 1958, Sugamo closed and was eventually replaced by a glitzy shopping center, Sunshine City. Fushun, in former Japanese Manchukuo, held local (Chinese) "insurgents" during the war and about a thousand Japanese war criminals afterwards for reform and re-education under the Communists. The Nationalists in Southeastern China seem to have needed their prisons for local collaborators and insurgents, while Japanese war criminals were housed in Japanese-built munitions and other factory buildings.

The spatial politics of imprisonment take on even more significance in the contrast between the Western Allies, who settled on the reuse of strategically placed established prisons near sites of crimes and trials, and the Soviets, who conducted only one formal trial in Khabarovsk yet dispersed hundreds of thousands of Japanese soldiers across the gulag system of Eurasia.[28] Takasugi Ichirō, the author of one of the most important memoirs of Soviet internment, wrote eloquently about the confusing disconnect between what would have been an appropriate place of his personal punishment, namely where he had engaged in aggression in China, and the Siberian camps in which he found himself.[29] No doubt the Soviet practice of moving the internees around had as much to do with economics as it had with politics, which Sherzod Muminov also analyzes in Chapter 8.

But when Stalin offered to transfer about 1,000 Japanese war criminals to the newly founded Peoples Republic of China (PRC) in 1949, ostensibly to give the PRC an opportunity to earn its place in the international legal system by conducting war crimes trials, Mao and Zhou Enlai opted for the opposite spatial politics.[30] They transported the 935 former officials and military officers of Manchukuo still alive, together with 997 Chinese Manchukuo collaborators and former KMT soldiers to Manchuria, the site of their wartime activities and an undisputed stronghold of the PRC. There they imprisoned them in Fushun, the former Japanese colonial jail, and employed a prison staff of over one hundred persons, all from the Northeast, most of whom had personal experience of victimization by the Japanese in Manchuria.[31] In a remarkable example of social engineering, the PRC managed not only to make the Japanese realize their crimes but the Chinese staff to let go of their personal grudge. Shortly before their public trial and repatriation to Japan, the war criminals were treated to a very public tour through the Chinese heartland to persuade the Chinese population that reconciliation with the former Japanese enemy was not only desirable but possible.[32]

The colonial past and present across 1945 of all the main long-term prisons for Japanese war criminals was a shared characteristic and invoked a persistent geography of empire. In South East Asia Command (SEAC)–controlled Southeast Asia, Changi, Stanley, Cipinang, and other prisons employed an international staff often including British, Australian, and Dutch authorities at the same time or consecutively. The British used Indian guards and wardens, just as the Japanese had once used Koreans and Taiwanese; the Dutch employed Eurasians. The Americans used local Filipinos as guards in Muntinlupa but exclusively Eighth Army personnel in Japan, which created a microcosm of American–Japanese relations as occupier and occupied in Sugamo that John Dower described so vividly in *Embracing Defeat*.[33] Over time, war criminals did end up in well established prisons mostly in large urban areas, and all were eventually transferred to Sugamo Prison in Tokyo, but that had the effect of breaking down the high walls of the prison rather than enforcing them because of family and even political networks available to them in Japan. Everywhere they shared space with other prisoners, whether German internees, Indonesian freedom fighters, Filipino guerillas, or American traitors. All this gave them tools to challenge the penal regimes under which they served their sentences, if not the sentences themselves, and allowed for a surprising degree of agency.

## Visualizing the empire's demise

The Japanese record of the Allied war crimes program, with its many maps, charts, architectural drawings, cartoons, sketches, and paintings, bespeaks an extraordinarily vivid sense of the geographical dimension of postwar transitional justice in the ruins of Japan's empire. There is nothing comparable in Europe, even though experiences of incarceration, including Japanese–American internment camps, Allied POW camps, Nazi concentration camps, and other prison settings, more broadly have produced a huge archive of visual and textual materials. Clearly, incarceration engenders a heightened sense of space, simply because space is restricted, but in this case, the carceral geography of the Allied war crimes program was literally mapped onto the changing territorial geography of Japan's former empire. One case in point was a collection of 150 drawings of the Japanese prison experience in its geographical vastness that a group of convicted war criminals from Hiroshima prefecture put together in 1952 while serving out their sentences in Sugamo after their repatriation from the empire. Entitled *Album of Ordeals* (*Shiren no arubamu*), it began with 34 pages of sketches depicting the various spaces in and around Sugamo Prison followed by 116 pages of illustrations of mainly camp and prison buildings in 16 places across Asia, from primitive island camps for Japanese on trial in Balikpapan on Dutch Borneo to the urban prisons in Singapore, Jakarta, Rangoon, Hong Kong, and Manila.[34] Each drawing, simple in style, was accompanied by explanatory prose or an occasional poem that added cursory information about the uses of the places depicted, past and present, and as much with a sense of ownership as of victimhood.

It was a record of great physical diversity, captured in terms of various spatial arrangements focused on prison buildings, the prison's natural or urban environments, and work assignments. Apart from the tropical settings that marked all these places (palm trees, water buffalo, the ubiquitous Indonesian bungalows), the contrast between the sophistication of the urban colonial prisons with their high walls, which were often depicted from the outside in an iconic way (e.g. Changi's high clock tower, the front gate of Rangoon Central Prison), and the primitiveness of island camps (Morotai, Guam, Saban, Banjarmasin, Mandai), some of which they had to construct themselves, also recalled the empire with its dual imaginary of colonial capitals on the one hand and the "backwardness" of island populations on the other. Continuities with the past were noted as in the Japanese munitions depository that served as a prison in Shanghai, the use of the old Japanese cemetery in Medan on Sumatra as execution ground for war criminals with unmarked graves, or a camp on Morotai having previously housed Australian POWs (see Figure 7.3a). No physical maltreatment was depicted; instead, the "ordeals" alluded to in the

*Figure 7.3a* Medan (Sumatra)

Source: Reprinted in Chaen Yoshio (ed.), *Nihon bi-shi kyū senpan shiryō* (Fuji Shuppan, 1983), p. 117.

*Figure 7.3b* Prokondor (French Indochina)

Source: Reprinted in Chaen Yoshio (ed.), *Nihon bi-shi kyū senpan shiryō* (Fuji Shuppan, 1983), p. 127.[35]

title were conveyed in terms of isolation from humans: the single cells of those on death row and life on prison islands where nobody else lived and no amenities were available. The latter was validated by local lore; even the Vietnamese locals despised the penal colony Prokondor off the coast of French Indochina as an "island of death" and a "hellhole of rotting corpses," and Saban Island off of Sumatra had been "nicknamed the island of demons" (see Figure 7.3b).

In contrast, war criminals' productive engagement inside or outside the prisons as well as leisure activities – more often unsupervised than not – bespoke a sense of active ownership of place. With the agricultural production in and around the four prison buildings near Shanghai "many wanted to make miso and sweets and sell them in the city," an industrial shop in Jakarta, which they claimed had "the best production capacity in all of Java," or relax with varied leisure activities in a cell in Cipinang Prison (see Figures 7.3c–d).

A prominent aspect of the textual explanations revolved around the ethnic mix of people in the prisons, among captors and captives alike. In Changi Gaol,

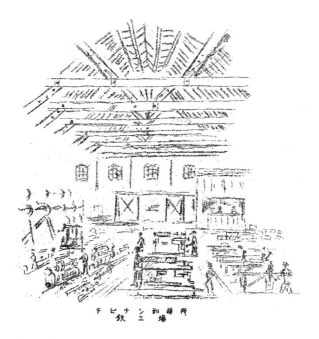

*Figure 7.3c* Cipinang (Jakarta)

Source: Reprinted in Chaen Yoshio (ed.), *Nihon bi-shi kyū senpan shiryō* (Fuji Shuppan, 1983), p. 115.

*Figure 7.3d* Cipinang (Jakarta)

Source: Reprinted in Chaen Yoshio (ed.), *Nihon bi-shi kyū senpan shiryō* (Fuji Shuppan, 1983), p. 111.[36]

administrative and supervisory teams of Australians, Dutch, British, and Indians came and went, in that order. In Stanley Prison, Indian, Chinese, and Portuguese guards worked for the British and showed the Japanese war criminals some kindness. Not only the guards but also the prison population in Stanley were mixed, including Westerners, Indians, Chinese, and Japanese, with the Japanese treated as "Asians" in terms of food and sleeping arrangements. International Red Cross inspection reports corroborate this diversity of ethnicities extensively, as they do Japanese complaints at being treated "like Asians." At the same time, in the *Album*, local Asians were consistently credited with treating the Japanese better than the Europeans in charge, which may reflect the racial affinity propagated during the war. The Indians smuggled in extra food and cigarettes, and the Burmese post-independence were more lenient and humane in their custody of war criminals than the British. Memoirs from New Bilibid in Muntinlupa similarly reported that the Filipinos who took over from the Americans were more accommodating. While Japanese war criminals were grouped according to their specific place in the war crimes trial program – from awaiting trial as suspected offenders to actually standing trial, serving sentences as convicted war criminals or separated out for death roll, and finally being assembled for repatriation – they all seem to have shared space with local Asians as guards, as fellow prisoners, and in the work place.

The carceral network described in the *Album of Ordeals* contrasted markedly with the carceral space of Sugamo Prison in Tokyo, dominated as it was by the daily interactions with the American jailers and the coming and going of local supporters, friends and family, politicians, and other government officials. By the early 1950s, empire had come home in the form of repatriated Japanese war criminals convicted abroad serving out their sentences in Sugamo. If Tokyo was but one of several hubs in Asia where war crimes policy was made, Sugamo Prison ended up as virtually synonymous with the Allied war crimes trial program as a whole. This was not principally because the empire was forgotten but because Sugamo became a microcosm of the lost empire while simultaneously allowing its multiple legacies to be consumed through the everyday interactions with the Americans who managed the prison. SCAP ran Sugamo almost exclusively, with U.S. Eighth Army GIs as guards and administrators, who created a home away from home with all the familiar amenities spiced up with a healthy portion of exoticism. Such experiences led John L. Ginn, a guard there from 1948, to assert years later that "there could have been no place in occupied Japan where an American G.I. would have preferred to serve."[37] Sugamo produced an extraordinarily rich visual commentary on the social interactions between guards and captives as well as among the prisoners, who included Japan's erstwhile leaders, the Class A criminals.

All participants' accounts of Sugamo in the early years of American requisition, from memoirs to interviews with former inmates and American guards, corroborate a harsh climate of enmity as the trials got under way and of punishment through hard labor and exceedingly severe supervisory measures for those who began their sentences.[38] Through much of the year 1947, war criminals transformed the burnt-out landscape surrounding the prison compound into living and recreational facilities for the American overseers while being themselves housed in cold, crammed cells. But by 1949 and especially in 1950, inmates were building a theater, sports courts, goldfish ponds, flower gardens, and the like for their own enjoyment, did farming at a hydroponic farm on the former airfield of Chōfu under minimal supervision, ate meals of their own preparation, ran arts shops, had publications and a school, and organized their own entertainment both inside and outside the prison. By then, the post-trial reviews had been completed, resulting in many sentence reductions and even conversions, SCAP had instituted a "trusty system" as well as "good time credit" system that rewarded good prison conduct, and SCAP's Parole Board had begun its work, conditionally releasing a steady stream of eligible prisoners. When American guards began to leave for Korea, they often took with them gifts and souvenirs made for them by the prisoners, which are now being collected by a New York artist.[39] In sum, what emerged over time in Sugamo was a sense that the Americans stood by the Japanese war criminals, just as the United States sought Japan as its primary ally when the Cold War began to blanket the remnants of Japan's empire.[40] This is brilliantly expressed in a sketch that appeared on the cover of Fujiki Fumio's autobiographical reflections on his time as a war criminal and cartoonist at Sugamo Prison, reproduced in Figure 7.4.

*Figure 7.4* The two figures here are a generic American soldier and a Japanese war criminal (not a POW), an image that speaks loudly to exactly the relationship that developed in Sugamo, and even more broadly between Japan and the United States

Source: Back cover of Fujiki, *Sugamo densetsu.*

## Conclusion

Geopolitics notwithstanding, the messiness of the empire's demise was most vis-
cerally reflected in the multiple and constantly shifting incarceration arrangements
made for Japanese suspected and convicted war criminals across the vast expanse
of the former empire, in the relatively closed social space shared by captors and
captives alike, and in the ways in which the prisons were integrated in their respective locales. It brings home, certainly from Japanese perspectives, an embodied
experience of the Allied program's expanse, which spatially mimicked Japan's
empire, as well as the considerable diversity of the physical manifestations and
everyday social relations that made transitional justice concrete. For even if war
crimes policy was made on paper in London or Washington, it was its execution
in each place, both in the courtroom and in the prison, as well as the inevitable
contradictions that emerged from different local circumstances, that made it real
for both the judged and those who sat in judgement. Conversely, from the Allied
side, it also served as a geopolitical legitimation tool, for which famous prisons
became an important signifier, not only vis-à-vis local audiences but also far-away
domestic publics. When holding Japanese war criminals in local prisons became
a liability for European powers in Southeast Asia in the context of progressing
decolonization movements and civil war, the Allies readily agreed to send them
back to Japan to sit out their sentences while the prisons reverted to local use. For
example, in February 1949, the Chinese Nationalists transferred all 251 convicted
war criminals to Sugamo; in June 1950, France sent all of its 121 convicted war
criminals back to Japan.[41] Today, the years in which they housed Japanese war
criminals is but a negligible interval, hardly worth mentioning given the notoriety
these places acquired in the postwar decades, when they housed famous political
prisoners such as Pramoedya Toer in Cipinang and Aung San Suu Kyi in Rangoon.
Sugamo, in contrast, was bulldozed after the last war criminals had left – but
remained alive in public memory as a signature post of the Allied war crimes trial
program perhaps precisely because it was not used again.

   It is often lamented that Japanese war criminals failed to develop a sense of guilt
but that on the contrary the Japanese public came to consider them scapegoats for
the country as a whole or as victims of Allied vindictiveness. In fact, this was no
different in occupied Germany. Not a single inmate at the U.S.-run Landsberg War
Criminals Prison No. 1 in Bavaria, the counterpart of Sugamo in Germany,
acknowledged personal guilt, as Katharina von Kellenbach's in-depth study of
German war criminals' correspondences revealed, and German politicians at the
highest level went out of their way to effect the release of convicted war criminals.[42] This absence points to the need for a more nuanced understanding of the
war criminals' imprisonment than is usually recognized, that is, of the *nature* of
the carceral space that they inhabited, its *purpose* specifically with respect to war
criminals (as opposed to POWs or Surrendered Personnel), and the *agency* of the
prisoners.[43] All three changed over time in interlinked ways as penal practices
toward enemy war criminals remained up for grabs, in contrast to the substantial
attention paid to the codification of specific crimes and legal tools for prosecution
for the development of international law.

# Notes

1  Emphasis added to both quotes. (Unless otherwise noted, all Japanese titles are published in Tokyo.)
2  Ruti G. Teitel, *Transitional Justice* (New York: Oxford University Press, 2000), esp. Chapter 2.
3  Yuma Totani, *Justice in Asia and the Pacific Region, 1945–1952: Allied War Crimes Prosecutions* (New York: Cambridge University Press, 2015); *The Tokyo War Crimes Trial: The Pursuit of Justice in the Wake of World War II* (Cambridge, MA: Harvard University Asia Center, 2008).
4  Ronald H. Spector, "After Hiroshima: Allied Military Occupations and the Fate of Japan's Empire, 1945–1947," *The Journal of Military History* vol. 69 (October 2005): pp. 1121–1136; by the same author, *In the Ruins of Empire: The Japanese Surrender and the Battle for Postwar Asia* (New York: Random House, 2007); Peter Dennis, "'From War to Peace' Southeast Asia 1945–1946" and other essays in *1945: War and Peace in the Pacific*, ed. Peter Dennis (Canberra: Australian War Memorial, 1999); On China: Barak Kushner, "Pawns of Empire: Postwar Japan, Taiwan, and the Dilemma of War Crimes," *Journal of Japanese Studies* vol. 30, issue 1 (May 2010): pp. 111–133; *Men to Devils, Devil to Men: Japanese War Crimes and Chinese Justice* (Cambridge, MA: Harvard University Press, 2015); on Britain: Hayashi Hirofumi, "British War Crimes Trials of Japanese," *Nature – People – Society: Science and the Humanities* vol. 31 (July 2001), online: www.geocities.jp/hhhirofumi/eng08.htm; Hayashi Hirofumi, *Sabakareta sensō hanzai: igirisu no tainichi senpan saiban* (Iwanami shoten, 1998); On Indonesia: Robert Cribb, "Avoiding Clemency: The Trial and Transfer of Japanese War Criminals in Indonesia, 1946–1949," *Japanese Studies* vol. 31, issue 2 (September 2011): pp. 151–170; On the Philippines: Nagai Hitoshi, *Firipin to tainichi senpan saiban, 1945–1953* (Iwanami shoten, 2010); Beatrice Trefalt, "Hostages to International Relations? The Repatriation of Japanese War Criminals from the Philippines," *Japanese Studies* vol. 31, issue 2 (September 2011): pp. 191–210; On Australia: Dean Aszkielowitz, "Repatriation and the Limits of Resolve: Japanese War Criminals in Australian Custody," *Japanese Studies* vol. 31, issue 2 (September 2011): pp. 211–228.
5  Dominique Moran, *Carceral Geography: Spaces and Practices of Incarceration* (Burlington, VT: Ashgate, 2015). See also Carceral Geography website, http://carceral geography.com/.
6  R. John Pritchard, "The Quality of Mercy: The Right of Appeal and the Gift of Clemency Following British War Crimes Trials in the Far East, 1946–1948," in Dennis, ed., *1945: War and Peace*, pp. 167–198.
7  Erving Goffman, *Asylums: Essays on the Social Situation of Mental Patients and Other Inmates* (Garden City, NJ: Anchor Books, 1961); Michel Foucault, *Discipline and Punish: The Birth of the Prison* (New York: Vintage, 1995); Giorgio Agamben, *State of Exception* (Chicago: University of Chicago Press, 2005); Moran, *Carceral Geography*, p. 2.
8  Robert David Sack, *Human Territoriality* (Cambridge: Cambridge University Press, 1986), p. 216.
9  United States Army Center of Military History, *Reports of General MacArthur: The Campaigns of MacArthur in the Pacific*, vol. 1, Chapter 14, pp. 464–465, http://www.history.army.mil/books/wwii/macarthur%20reports/macarthur%20v1/ch14.htm.
10  Spector, *In the Ruins*, esp. Chapter 11.
11  Spector, "After Hiroshima," p. 1132.
12  Ibid., p. 1130.
13  For an excellent overview of the immense challenges with which the war crimes program had to wrestle, see Robert Cribb, "How Finished Business Became Unfinished: Legal, Moral and Political Dimensions of the Class 'B' and 'C' War Crimes Trials in

Asia and the Pacific," in *The Pacific War: Aftermaths, Remembrance, and Culture*, ed. Christina Twomey and Earnest Koh (Abingdon: Routledge, 2015), pp. 92–109.

14  Cribb, "Avoiding Clemency," pp. 153–154.

15  Konrad Lawson, "Universal Crime, Particular Punishment: Trying the Atrocities of the Japanese Occupation as Treason in the Philippines, 1947–1953," *Comparativ: Zeitschrift für Globalgeschichte und vergleichende Gesellschaftsforschung* vol. 23, issue 3 (2013): pp. 57–77.

16  Among the 5,677 indicted of Class BC war crimes, 173 were Taiwanese and 148 Korean, and twenty-one Taiwanese and twenty-three Koreans were executed. Utsumi Aiko, *Kimu wa naze sabakareta no ka* (Asahi shimbunsha, 2008), p. 7; Kushner, "Pawns of Empire," p. 113.

17  Tessa Morris-Suzuki, "An Act Prejudicial to the Occupation Forces: Migration Controls and Korean Residents in Post-Surrender Japan," *Japanese Studies* vol. 24, issue 1 (May 2004): pp. 5–28.

18  Spector, "After Hiroshima," p. 1130.

19  *Reports of General MacArthur*, vol. 1, Chapter 14, p. 465. According to Japanese Justice Ministry statistics, the overwhelming majority of crimes prosecuted were murder/ill-treatment of civilians (4,389), closely followed by those against POWs and internees (3,581), out of a total of 9,228 crimes (not defendants or cases). See Chaen Yoshio, *Bi-shi kyū senpan. Oranda saiban shiryō, zenkan tsūran* (Fuji shuppan, 1992), pp. 268–269.

20  Spector, *In the Ruins*, p. 85; ICRC prison reports, RG 7, ICRC Archives, Geneva.

21  Margherita Straehler, "Confidential report to the International Red Cross Society," Geneva (8 Feb. 1946) on several visits to Ōmori and Sugamo between September 1945 and February 1946. ICRC Prison Reports, RG 7, "Japanese war criminals," ICRC Archives, Geneva.

22  "Enquiry into certain allegations contained in a Petition by three Japanese recently imprisoned in Singapore for war crimes; held at Supreme Court, Singapore, in Judge's Chambers" (26 September 1949), British Foreign Office Files FO 371, p. 4. I thank Robert Cribb for generously sharing this document with me.

23  "Letter by G.H. Schwartz, N.I.E. Delegate to the International Red Cross Committee of Geneva "Japanese POWs in Batavia Jails" (Batavia, 21 November 1946), RG 7, "Japanese War criminals," file, p. 196, ICRC Archives.

24  Ushimura Kei, *Beyond the "Judgment of Civilization,"* Part III (Tokyo: International House Japan, 2003); "Shiren no arubamu," in Chaen Yoshio, *Nihon bi-shi kyū senpan shiryō* (Fuji shuppan, 1983).

25  Robert Havers, "The Changi POW Camp and the Burma-Thailand Railway," in *Japanese Prisoners of War*, ed. Philip Towle, Margaret Kosuge, and Yoichi Kibata (London: Hambledon and London, 2000), pp. 20–21.

26  "Batavia Jails visited by G.H. Schwartz, Delegate of the International Committee of the Red Cross" (ca. Feb. 1946). Inspection reports of Cipinang by ICRC delegates exist from October 1946, July 1947, and February 1949, RG 7, "Japanese War Criminals," 3rd file, p. 19, also 77, ICRC Archives.

27  Nagai Hitoshi, *Firipin bi-shi kyū senpan saiban* (Kōdansha, 2013), p. 99.

28  This was in spite of a government order by Lavrentii Beria, Stalin's interior minister, on August 16, 1945, specifying that "the Japanese military was not to be transported to Soviet territory but to be held in camps close to where they had surrendered," quoted in Andrew Barshay, *The Gods Left First: The Captivity and Repatriation of Japanese POWs in Northeast Asia, 1945–1956* (Berkeley: University of California Press, 2013), p. 32.

29  Ibid. p. 94.

30  Arai Toshio, *Chūgoku bujun senpan kanrijo shokuin no shōgen: shashinka Arai Toshio no nokoshita shigoto* (Nashinokisha, 2003), p. 14ff. Quoted in Petra Buchholz, *Vom Teufel zum Menschen* (Munich: Iudicium Verlag, 2010), p. 22.

31 Buchholz, *Vom Teufel*, p. 25.

32 Buchholz, *Vom Teufel*, "Introduction." For an account of the trials, see Justin Jacobs, "Preparing the People for Mass Clemency: The 1956 Japanese War Crimes Trials in Shenyang and Taiyuan," *The China Quarterly* vol. 205 (March 2011): pp. 152–172.

33 John W. Dower, *Embracing Defeat: Japan in the Wake of World War II* (New York: Norton, 1999).

34 It was put together by Sugamo inmates Morishige Yoshio and Masaki Fumio of the Sugamo bunkakai in 1952. Reprinted in Chaen, *Nihon bi-shi kyū senpan shiryō*, pp. 66–152.

35 "Arubamu no shiren," p. 46 and p. 56, in Chaen, *Nihon bi-shi kyū senpan shiryō*, p. 117 and p. 127.

36 "Arubamu no shiren," p. 44 and p. 40, in Chaen, *Nihon bi-shi kyū senpan shiryō*, p. 115 and 111.

37 John L. Ginn, *Sugamo Prison, Tokyo: An Account of the Trial and Sentencing of Japanese War Criminals in 1948, by a U.S. Participant* (Jefferson, NC: McFarland & Co, 1992), p. 195.

38 The leading liberal voice on the subject is Utsumi Aiko, *Sugamo purizun: senpantachi no heiwa undō* (Yoshikawa Kōbunkan, 2004).

39 There is a lot of material on life in Sugamo from various perspectives. Chaen Yoshio has reprinted much cultural material in his *Zusetsu sensō saiban Sugamo Purizun jiten* (Nihon tosho sentā, 1994), including the two images appearing here. On the Sugamo Project of the New York artist Bill Barrette, see "JPRI Occasional Paper No. 33," http://www.jpri.org/publications/occasionalpapers/op33.html. Also of interest is "A living legacy of prison life | The Japan Times Online," http://search.japantimes.co.jp/cgi-bin/fl20030622a4.html. For an account of Sugamo by an American guard, see Ginn, *Sugamo Prison, Tokyo*.

40 Chaen, *Zusetsu sensō saiban*; Fujiki Fumio, *Sugamo densetsu: manga de tsuzuru sugamo purizun to GI* (Guddo taimu shuppan, 2012).

41 Chaen Yoshio, "Sugamo nenpyō" in *Zusetsu sensō saiban*, p. 22–23.

42 Katharina von Kellenbach, *The Mark of Cain: Guilt and Denial in the Postwar Lives of Nazi Perpetrators* (Oxford & New York: Oxford University Press, 2013); Norbert Frei, *Adenauer's Germany and the Nazi Past: The Politics of Amnesty and National Integration* (New York: Columbia University Press, 2002).

43 Moran, *Carceral Geography*, p. 22.

# 8 Prejudice, punishment, and propaganda

## Post-imperial Japan and the Soviet versions of history and justice in East Asia, 1945–1956

*Sherzod Muminov*

Among the relationships that have shaped modern East Asia, the nexus between Japan and the Soviet Union has yet to receive the scholarly attention it deserves. One reason for this must surely lie with East Asian historiography as a discipline, described recently as "hopelessly U.S.-centric."[1] Another is that Soviet archives remained off-limits to foreign researchers until the 1990s, posing an obstacle to investigating Moscow's decisions and intentions. In the meantime, Soviet historians produced little more than apologetics for the Communist Party's actions.[2] Even after the archives opened in the early 1990s the USSR's role in defeating the Japanese empire, and in the construction of the postwar, post-imperial order in East Asia remained a marginal topic in English-language historiography.

In this chapter, I take a fresh look at the history of post-imperial East Asia, focusing mainly on the significance of the Soviet Union. I aim to challenge two views that seem to dominate historical discourse on the establishment of post-imperial order in East Asia. The first view disregards the role of the Soviet Union in the defeat of Japan.[3] In response, Soviet experts worked to discredit the "bourgeois views" of the American victory.[4] In Japan, according to historian Sodei Rinjirō, there existed some balance: "[m]ost Japanese, myself included, tend to plac[e] equal weight on the bombs and on the shock of the Soviet Union's declaration of war."[5] Even more controversial has been the issue of Soviet influence in East Asia *after* Japan was defeated. Some historians have claimed that Stalin was cowed by American nuclear supremacy in his dealings with the United States in East Asia in the immediate postwar.[6] Others have discounted the influence of the atomic bomb: "Stalin's keen interest in the bomb does not mean that he was terrified by its awesome power."[7] The Cold War shouting match over who contributed more to the victory in Asia shaped research agendas as well as political attitudes and public opinion; one of the enduring legacies of this information warfare is that the USSR's role in post-imperial East Asia has been limited solely to the Manchurian campaign in August 1945. As I will demonstrate, in comparison to the prewar period, the Soviet influence in East Asia actually increased rather than decreased after World War II.

The second view concerns ideology as a decisive factor in the relations between the two superpowers and in Soviet actions toward post-imperial East

Asia.[8] It is true "the USSR was an ideological state . . . [with] an ideologically driven program for the transformation of world politics."[9] Nevertheless, the Soviet leadership's intentions in East Asia were not always driven by the goal of spreading communism. There were also short-term motives, such as undermining the U.S. gains and fostering positive attitudes toward the USSR. Recent research on Moscow's relations at the time with the Japan Communist Party (JCP), for example, reveals how Stalin aimed to employ Japanese communists not merely to strengthen the international labor movement but as a means to destabilize Japanese society.[10] In short, the history of the Soviet engagement in East Asia after World War II needs to be freed from clichés and expanded beyond the ossified dualities of the Cold War. The rivalry between erstwhile allies – the United States and the USSR – in East Asia, habitually analyzed through the prism of ideology, has to be re-examined.

One episode that illustrates Soviet entanglements in postwar East Asia is the Siberian Internment – the captivity of former Japanese servicemen in Soviet labor camps between 1945 and 1956. The incarceration began following the surrender of the Japanese Kwantung Army to the Soviet troops in northeast Asia in August 1945. Within a matter of days, the Soviet leadership took the unexpected decision to transport half a million Japanese former servicemen to the USSR. Exploited in labor camps and re-educated in the main tenets of communism, the majority of the Japanese were repatriated by the end of 1950, while the last ship carrying Japanese returnees from Siberia crossed the Sea of Japan only in December 1956, following the signing of the 1956 Japanese–Soviet Joint Declaration that restored diplomatic relations. The eleven winters of Siberian captivity became a source of Japanese indignation that augmented the decades of mistrust of the Soviet Union in postwar Japan.[11]

On a juridical level, these events help to trace the transition from joint Allied justice to individuated postwar justice. The fate of the Japanese captives in Soviet custody became one of the first matters of contention in Allied forums between the United States and the USSR; the Japanese government and citizens' groups tirelessly lobbied international organizations to put pressure on the USSR.[12] Later, as the International Military Tribunal for the Far East (IMTFE, or Tokyo Trial) led to more serious disagreements between the American and the Soviet visions of retribution, the debates on Japanese internees in Soviet custody once again moved to center stage. As I show in my discussion of the Soviet trials of the former Kwantung Army leaders and lower-ranking officers, Japanese internees provided important leverage for the USSR in its dealings with the U.S. Occupation Administration in post-imperial Japan. Most importantly, the trials of Japanese "war criminals" in the Soviet camps reflected the USSR's dissatisfaction with the Allied justice of the Tokyo Trial and represented its attempts to impose its versions of history and legitimacy in East Asia.

I start the chapter with an overview of Soviet–Japanese interactions from 1918 to 1941 that are crucial to a full understanding of the prejudice that developed between the two nations. This prejudice, I argue, wielded an influence on Soviet actions at war's end. For two decades before the war, the Soviet Union was, perhaps surprisingly, the underdog in the relationship. Soviet diplomatic documents reflect the apprehension that Japanese incursions into Siberia and Manchuria in the 1920s and 1930s created in Soviet leaders' minds and the effect that they had years later on Stalin's postwar attitude toward Japan. The second part of the chapter focuses on the Siberian Internment itself, a burgeoning topic in English-language history of wartime and postwar Japan.[13] Going beyond the general account of the internment, I look into the Soviet trials of the Japanese former servicemen in Siberia, particularly what can be called the camp trials. Through these trials, I trace the schisms that developed in Allied postwar justice and the Soviet efforts to proclaim and legitimize their own version of justice and order in post-imperial East Asia.

## The struggle for influence in East Asia before World War II

The collapse of the Japanese empire in 1945 removed the USSR's foremost rival, one which had threatened the Soviet state's sparsely populated eastern territories for more than two decades. From the USSR's founding in 1922, as the Bolsheviks grappled with the hostile world after World War I, Japan had lurked dangerously in the region. Russia was left much weakened by the Great War and the Civil War that came on its heels; Japan, on the other hand, had been given a confidence boost: it now felt itself to be a proper player on the international stage. One sign of this confidence was participation in the 1918 Siberian Expedition, when the Japanese Army joined the Western powers in an allied intervention of Soviet Russia that aimed to "re-establish the Eastern Front" following the Bolsheviks' signing of the Brest-Litovsk Treaty in March that year.[14]

The Imperial Japanese Army left Siberia only in 1922, long after the other forces had withdrawn. In the USSR, the scars left by the foreign intervention were kept alive in public memory for decades. Indeed, in 1945, Stalin used the Siberian Intervention as a historical pretext in his unsuccessful request to U.S. President Harry Truman to occupy northern Hokkaido.[15] Nikita Khrushchev evoked the intervention more than forty years after the event, reminding the Americans in a New York speech in September 1959 of the "time you sent your troops to quell the revolution."[16] This grudge against the capitalist interveners, Japan among them, expressed by subsequent leaders, summarized the Soviets' persistent feelings on this episode.

Another decade of strained relations started with the Manchurian Incident in September 1931. "It is natural that these events concern us most seriously," said Soviet Deputy Foreign Minister Lev Karakhan to the Japanese ambassador Hirota Kōki on the day after the Incident because Japan was threatening the Chinese Eastern Railway – the main transport hub providing access to warm-water ports vital to Soviet influence in East Asia.[17] In November 1931, Stalin wrote to Kliment Voroshilov, his defense minister:

> It looks like Japan has decided to occupy not only Manchuria, but also Beijing and adjacent regions . . . Moreover, . . . it is likely that Japan will extend her

hand to our Far East and maybe Mongolia, to tickle her Chinese protégés' vanities, and to compensate for Chinese losses at our expense.[18]

Stalin had ruled out Soviet military involvement in Manchuria in September 1931; he had also dismissed "diplomatic intervention, for this might unite the imperialists; it is more beneficial for us if they quarrel."[19] Nonetheless, Soviet diplomats worked hard to alleviate the Japanese menace. On New Year's Eve, 1931, Foreign Minister Maksim Litvinov received his newly appointed Japanese counterpart Yoshizawa Kenkichi, who was returning to Japan on the Trans-Siberian Railway. "I had the idea to use Yoshizawa," wrote Litvinov in his diary, "in proposing to the Japanese government to start negotiations on a non-aggression pact."[20] Yet almost two years after his meeting with Yoshizawa, Litvinov lamented the fact that the Soviet overtures had fallen on deaf ears. Japan was not only unwilling to negotiate a non-aggression treaty with the Soviets, it was trying to bully the Soviets into selling the Chinese Eastern Railway cheaply. Litvinov claimed that "a threat has arisen not only of a violent takeover of our railway by the Japanese, but also *a direct threat to our borders*."[21] Describing Japanese actions as "the darkest thundercloud hanging over the international political horizon," Litvinov cautioned against the "the risk of waging war with such a powerful, energetic giant" as the USSR. In March 1935, however, the powerful and energetic giant was eventually forced to sell the railway to Japan for a mere 140 million yen having asked initially for the price of 625 million yen.[22]

Paranoia about the Japanese threat spilled over into the Great Terror of 1937–1938, when the state repressive apparatus executed close to a million Soviet citizens. Hiroaki Kuromiya and Andrzej Pepłonski have claimed that Stalin's views about Japan being "the linchpin of an espionage alliance involving Germany, Poland, and Japan" were not unfounded.[23] The few foreigners living in Moscow at the time also felt the atmosphere of mistrust. "[T]his country is highly suspicious as far as foreign residents are concerned," wrote *The New York Times* Moscow correspondent in February 1938.[24] Stalin ordered the round-up thousands of Soviet citizens in the Far Eastern areas, in what *The Washington Post* called "a 'merciless purge' of Japanese spies and Trotskyist conspirators."[25]

The events of the mid-1930s were early portents of the coming storm. In the summer of 1939, a major conflict did erupt with "the most dangerous interwar Japanese–Soviet confrontation of all" on the border of Manchukuo and Mongolia.[26] Known as the Battle of Khalkhin-Gol in the USSR and the Nomonhan Incident in Japan, this conflict, which ended in the Red Army's resounding victory orchestrated by Georgy Zhukov, the future mastermind of the Soviet victory at Stalingrad in 1943, has been described as "shap[ing] World War II."[27] This victory gave the Soviets a much needed reprieve. Stalin's non-aggression pact with Hitler in August 1939 had also led to a "dramatic deterioration in Japan's geostrategic security" vis-à-vis the USSR.[28] In April 1941, on his way back from Berlin, Japanese Foreign Minister Matsuoka Yōsuke stopped over in Moscow and twice met with Joseph Stalin. A decade after Yoshizawa's stopover, Japan's position had reversed; now it sought neutrality with the Soviets. In his April 12 meeting with the Soviet leader, Matsuoka earnestly tried to push through a deal, and after several hours of negotiations, he managed to iron out the disagreements with the Soviets. On April 13, 1941, the USSR and Japan signed the Neutrality Pact.[29] However, the mutual prejudice between the two nations was far from resolved.

## Internment and trials: the Soviet version of postwar order and justice in East Asia

The Second World War turned the tables completely not only in Europe but also in East Asia. On April 5, 1945, as the Soviet troops were approaching Berlin, almost four years after the signing of the Soviet-Japanese Neutrality Pact, Molotov summoned Japanese Ambassador Satō Naotake to the Soviet foreign ministry and informed him that the USSR had decided to renounce the Pact for a second term, beyond April 1946. Nazi Germany was on the brink of capitulation. Unbeknownst to Japan, Stalin was laying the groundwork for entry into the war in the east as agreed secretly in Yalta in February 1945.[30] The Soviet–Japanese pact remained active for another year, which in the final months of the Second World War gave the Japanese hope that the Soviets might act as mediators in surrender talks with the Allies.[31] However, Hirota Kōki, who had so successfully played the waiting game with the Soviets in the 1930s in his ambassadorial role, found that his counterparts were just as good at biding their time. Hirota and Prince Konoe Fumimaro's overtures to the Soviets bore no fruit; on August 8, 1945, Ambassador Satō was once again summoned by Molotov, this time to be informed that "from August 9 the USSR will consider itself in a state of war with Japan."[32] A few hours later, three Soviet armies crossed the Soviet-Manchukuo border from the west, north, and east. The USSR was rushing into the eastern theater of the war, wary that all the spoils would fall to the Americans, who had shocked Japan three days prior with the atomic bombing of Hiroshima.[33]

By the time the second mushroom cloud rose over Nagasaki on August 9, the Red Army divisions were racing at lightning speed through Manchukuo, wreaking havoc and causing panic along the way. The Japanese imperial soldiers entrusted with protecting the community in Manchukuo were completely outgunned and overrun, leaving thousands of Japanese settlers helpless in the face of the onslaught. Already on August 10, according to a memoir by Sejima Ryūzō, a strategist in the Imperial Headquarters, the Kwantung Army command had practically given up on Manchukuo, withdrawing south to "secure Southern Manchuria and Korea."[34] A mere ten days after the Soviets' attack, on August 19, in the small village of Zharikovo in the Soviet Maritime Province, the top brass of the Kwantung Army agreed to the conditions of surrender with the Soviet commanders. The vaunted Japanese Kwantung Army had been humiliated, and Manchukuo, the "jewel in the crown" of the empire, lay trampled under the boot of the Soviet soldier.[35]

The shock of the Soviet invasion was so great that it still lives on in Japanese public memory as a moment of extreme trauma. Thanks largely to heart-rending memoirs of violence against Japanese civilians, the Soviet attack has invariably been portrayed as a stab in the back of the Japanese.[36] On the other side of the border, Soviet historians wasted no time in justifying the Soviet invasion.[37] Their main argument was that the neutrality pact would not have stopped Japan had it decided to invade the USSR, in the same way as it had not prevented Hitler from doing so in June 1941. In fact, the Soviet line went, throughout the war Japan had been actively plotting to attack the USSR; had Nazi Germany succeeded in taking Moscow in late 1941, Japan would undoubtedly have struck from the east.[38] The Soviets' fears had been seemingly vindicated when, two days after the German invasion of the USSR, the Soviet ambassador in Tokyo, Konstantin Smetanin, asked Matsuoka: will Japan observe its neutrality now that Germany had attacked the USSR? In a roundabout way, Matsuoka responded, "The Tripartite Pact is the foundation of Japan's foreign policy." In other words, should the Soviet-Japanese Pact clash with the Tripartite Pact, the former "would have no force."[39] The wartime reports of the Telegraph Agency of the Soviet Union (TASS) show how intently the Soviets followed Japanese public opinion and the official stance of the Japanese government after the German invasion, anxiously expecting an attack from the East.[40] The public pronouncements in favor of the German invasion, as well as the Kwantung Army's August 1941 plans for maneuvers in Manchuria known as *Kantokuen* – "a show of force designed to intimidate the USSR while the Red Army was fighting to survive in the West" – strengthened the Soviet belief that Japan had never stopped planning a USSR invasion.[41]

While it is hard to gauge the impact of such notions on Soviet decisions, propaganda against the Japanese had a formidable effect on the Red Army officers and soldiers taking part in the invasion of Manchuria.[42] And the argument can be made that the grievances against Japan, real and imagined, that had played in people's minds in the Soviet Union over the previous two decades had a direct bearing on the postwar Soviet treatment of the Japanese – servicemen and civilians alike. Soviet attitudes toward Japanese residents in Manchukuo left enduring scars on the Japanese collective memory, and what followed simply augmented the righteous fury against the USSR. On August 23, 1945, Joseph Stalin gave the order to "select up to 500,000 Japanese . . . physically fit to work in the conditions of the Far East and Siberia" and to transport them to the USSR.[43] The bulk of these captives were, following the decree, young men who were to be used as forced labor in rebuilding the war-torn Soviet economy. Among them were Kwantung Army top brass, including its Commander-in-Chief Yamada Otozō, and 191 generals – a total of over 25,000 officers – not to mention lower-ranking officers, members of the *Kempeitai* military police, employees of the South Manchuria Railway, and Manchukuo government bureaucrats.[44]

The question of why the Soviets took such a large number of people captive, in direct contravention of the Potsdam Declaration, remains unanswered even today.[45] It is especially perplexing due to the fact that a week before Stalin's decree,

NKVD Chief Lavrentii Beria and two other top officials had ruled out plans to take the Japanese to the USSR.[46] Indeed, there were few reasons for Stalin to worry about the defeated Japanese Army at war's end. Unlike in the 1930s, Stalin's eastern foe could no longer threaten the Soviet Far East: Japan had suffered massive damage by U.S. aerial attacks, including the atomic bombing of Hiroshima and Nagasaki; its economy lay in tatters; and its future looked bleak. In his victory address on September 3, 1945, Stalin proclaimed as much: Japan was on its knees, "utterly defeated on land and sea."[47] Soviets had retaken southern Sakhalin and acquired the Kurile Islands, which would "no longer serve as means to cut off the USSR from the ocean and as a base for Japanese attacks on our Far East."[48]

Still, Japan remained a source of strategic quandaries for the USSR. David Wolff's suggestion that in 1945 "Japan was central to Iosif Stalin's policy in Northeast Asia" might be stating the obvious, but in reality it hints at a dilemma the Soviet leadership faced at war's end.[49] This preoccupation with Japan was not irrational, and the Siberian Internment was born out of this predicament. It was, as suggested by Andrew Barshay, "the deepest running of . . . channels to exercise influence over . . . occupied Japan."[50] Little can be said beyond speculation, and yet it is clear that the Siberian Internment was inevitably linked in Stalin's mind with the Siberian Intervention (1918–1922) and the Japanese prewar provocations. I argue that the internment was for Stalin a way of stamping his authority on the postwar order in East Asia and challenging U.S. superiority in Japan. On a practical level, the internment was first of all a way of keeping a massive number of officers and soldiers out of Japan and obstructing and delaying the revival of the Japanese Army. More importantly, unlike Germany, Japan had fallen under sole American control in the occupation, as Stalin had failed to secure a foothold on Japan's northern island of Hokkaido.[51] To the USSR, this was potentially more bothersome and dangerous; in the event of the Third World War, talks about which did not sound too fanciful at the time, Japan as a U.S. ally would pose a grave threat to Soviet security. Stalin's insistence on occupying the north of Hokkaido had been borne out of this paranoid calculation. Once that failed, Stalin had to make use of what he had in hand – an army of Japanese former soldiers. They could be used, in the immediate future, as labor in regions suffering from the catastrophic lack of manpower. In the longer term, there would be better uses for the Japanese captives; in addition to their bodies, their minds would be put to good use by the Soviets. True, these decisions were not ready and agreed upon in August 1945, as Stalin was still grappling for ways to retain influence over Japanese affairs, but as the international situation changed, so did the Soviet policies and decisions. Stalin's actions confirm him to be a superbly pragmatic politician who was always employing whatever was at his disposal in achieving Soviet foreign policy goals. The war crimes trials of the Japanese in the Soviet Union, which I analyze later in the chapter, are also highly revealing of the dynamics of Soviet decisions and interests vis-à-vis the United States in East Asia.

An alternative way of looking at the Allied trials by examining prisons is detailed in Franziska Seraphim's Chapter 7 in this volume. Similarly, it is possible to examine Soviet camps, the political institution that in Western and especially in American media and popular imagination epitomized Soviet repressive methods in the mid-twentieth century.[52] The Soviet forced labor apparatus was not only one of the most extensive systems of punishment and control, it was also a pillar of the Soviet economy between 1929 and 1956.[53] Russian historians have shown that the forced labor of foreign captives rarely paid off.[54] Nevertheless, it was vital in a country that had lost 26.6 million of its citizens to the war effort. In addition to 7.42 million Soviet civilians deliberately exterminated by the Nazis, 74 percent of 8.7 million Soviet military casualties were younger than 35 – an important share of the workforce.[55]

In addition to their centrality to the economy, Soviet camps for Axis POWs, over 4 million of whom inhabited the spaces behind barbed-wire across the vast territory of the USSR, had just as important a political and propaganda role to play in the Soviet leadership's attempts to extend its influence in both Eastern Europe and East Asia.[56] The internment – and later trials – of former Kwantung Army servicemen was the USSR's way of imposing its version of justice, separate and independent from the punishment meted out jointly with the Allies, an attempt to show the world that the Soviet Union took its new role as an East Asian superpower extremely seriously.

To trace the evolution of Soviet intentions toward the Japanese prisoners, the Siberian Internment can be divided into two distinct phases: 1945–1949 and 1950–1956. The first phase was that of internment, exploitation, and eventually repatriation of over 600,000 Japanese captives. The majority of these were ordinary soldiers; almost all of them, except around 60,000 who lost their lives on the Siberian plains unable to endure hard labor, malnutrition, and mistreatment in a harsh environment with exceedingly poor living conditions, had returned to Japan by the end of 1950.[57]

The second phase saw the continued imprisonment of officers and any soldiers whom the punitive Soviet authorities deemed to have committed crimes against the Soviet Union. Some 1,578 men who remained in the USSR beyond 1950, with the exception of those who had requested Soviet citizenship, were being investigated or were already convicted by Soviet courts.[58] The transition from the first phase to the second is best reflected in the memoir by Uchimura Gōsuke, a Siberian internee and Japanese intellectual. When told of his arrest three years into internment, Uchimura wondered: "What do you mean by arrest? Were all the years I was interned in the POW camps – when I was confined – not arrest? As POWs, we were detained – we were always under surveillance. Was this not arrest already?"[59] As Uchimura and hundreds of other Japanese internees were to find out, punishment would exist in different degrees for them in the USSR. These degrees corresponded to the changing interests of the Soviet state in relation to Japan, as I demonstrate in the following section.

## Punishment and propaganda: Soviet trials
## of the Japanese internees

As early as 1946, when the International Military Tribunal for the Far East (IMTFE, also known as the Tokyo Trial) commenced, the Soviet Union started using Japanese captives in its camps for propaganda purposes. On June 5, 1946, the Soviet Minister of the Interior Sergei Kruglov presented to Stalin and his deputies the texts of two petitions signed by Japanese POWs. The first, from 782 Japanese former servicemen at Semionovsk camp in the Far Eastern Maritime Province, alleged that "the Japanese aggressive government throughout its existence aimed to capture foreign lands and to enslave other peoples . . . waging a long and unjust war against China and conducting aggressive policy toward the Soviet Union." The signatories asked for its publication "in the newspapers in Japan and the [Soviet propaganda newspaper for Japanese POWs] *Nihon shimbun*." They urged to try "all war criminals, including the Emperor." The second appeal, signed by eleven Japanese former officers at the Rada Camp in western Russia, demanded "a harsh punishment" for four individuals: the erstwhile police bureaucrat and cabinet minister Abe Genki, former prime minister Tōjō Hideki, former Governor-General of Korea and Prime Minister Koiso Kuniaki, and former ambassador to the USSR, Foreign and Prime Minister Hirota Kōki. While the first petition appealed to other Japanese internees in the USSR, the document signed by the Rada internees was addressed directly to the Tokyo Trial. "[Regrettably,] we are far from Tokyo and cannot testify as witnesses to their crimes against the Japanese people," the signatories wrote in the petition, which was clearly doctored by Soviet political officers.[60] As we see later in the chapter, some of the Japanese officers would have the chance to testify against their superiors during the Tokyo Trial.

As communications from former servicemen of the Imperial Japanese Army, these messages could serve as highly effective propaganda measures. In these efforts it is possible to see a Soviet attempt to focus international public opinion on the Tokyo Trial. Clearly, the USSR's leadership hoped for an outcome that would take on board the Soviet version of justice vis-à-vis the Japanese and justify the Soviet invasion of Manchuria. However, the Soviet delegation soon became dissatisfied with many aspects of the Tokyo Trial, most importantly the failure to prosecute Emperor Hirohito and Ishii Shirō, the mastermind of the Japanese bacteriological program and the head of the notorious Unit 731 that conducted experiments on live human subjects near the city of Harbin. The competition over the results of these experiments, traded by Ishii and his accomplices for protection from the Americans, was perhaps the largest factor that derailed Soviet–American cooperation in the trial. While the Soviets had several senior members of the Unit 731 in their own custody – notably former head of the production unit Major General Kawashima Kiyoshi and bacteriologist Major Karasawa Tomio – whether these Japanese captives were as eager to cooperate still remains unknown.[61]

Unhappy with the judgement at Tokyo, the USSR established its own system of adjudication of "war criminals" from among the ranks of foreign captives in its camps. This system was implemented through two types of trials: the Khabarovsk trial and the many camp trials, which were designed to rectify the Allied justice of the IMTFE and to dispense a unilateral Soviet version of justice in postwar East Asia. Despite this common goal, however, there was a major difference between the two courts. The judgement at Khabarovsk of twelve former Kwantung Army officers and "doctors" was conducted to highlight the shortcomings of the Tokyo Trial and to hint at the cover-up by the United States concerning the Japanese biological warfare program. In other words, its main purpose was to protest and amend the Allied, international justice that had been meted out by the victorious powers to the vanquished Japanese at the IMTFE. The camp trials, on the other hand, were the reverse: that is, the Soviet Union took those Japanese whom it deemed guilty of crimes out of the realm of international law and placed them within the mandate of Soviet domestic law.

Within the epistemological frameworks of Cold War historiography, at least in the English language, the Khabarovsk Trial has been denigrated as a kangaroo court. The first U.S. reaction to the news of the trial was indifference and dismissal. Later, the trial was portrayed as another Soviet attempt to camouflage the problem of the Japanese internees in Siberian camps – an issue that was creating considerable dissatisfaction in Japanese society as the Soviet Union refused to provide any information on the Japanese captives in its territory. Taking into account the Soviet show trials of the 1930s, this reaction was perhaps to be expected. William J. Sebald, adviser to the Supreme Commander for Allied Powers General Douglas MacArthur, called the Khabarovsk Trial a "'smoke screen' to divert attention from U.S. demands that they account for Japanese prisoners-of-war."[62] As Cold War rivalry between the one-time allies intensified, it became standard practice to brush off the trial on ideological grounds. While there is no denying the fact that the Khabarovsk Trial was a show tribunal organized for political and ideological purposes, dominant anti-Soviet discourse made it very easy to disregard its importance: for example, that it was the first legal moment when the Japanese human experiments were brought to trial, sentencing twelve top-ranking Japanese officers to imprisonment in the camps.[63] New scholarship is, however, emerging that underlines the trial's significance beyond the traditional Cold War narratives. Valentyna Polunina has analyzed Khabarovsk as resulting from the Soviets' dissatisfaction with the outcome of the Tokyo Trial.[64] Nevertheless the connection between Soviet justice, as seen in the judgement in Khabarovsk and the USSR's objections to the post-imperial order in East Asia, has yet to be comprehensively investigated.

Few people are more important in analyzing the interconnections between the Siberian Internment, the Tokyo Trial, and the unilateral Soviet "justice" toward the Japanese internees than Lieutenant Colonel Sejima Ryūzō. Sejima was a strategist in the Imperial Headquarters who was dispatched to Manchukuo in July 1945, a few weeks before the Soviet invasion, to shore up defenses against the imminent attack. He was captured by the Soviets in August and sent to a POW camp in Khabarovsk. According to Sejima's memoir, in August 1946 he and three other high-ranking Japanese captives, including two Kwantung Army generals, were ordered by the Soviets to go to Tokyo to act as witnesses for the Soviet prosecutors at the Tokyo Trial.[65] On the way, Sejima and his companions had to wait for a month in Vladivostok as the Soviets and the U.S. Occupation Administration sorted out the intricate permissions and checks of the Soviet staff accompanying the witnesses to Tokyo. Sejima wrote in his memoir that he and his companions felt the frigid winds of the coming Cold War confrontation: "[w]e were like frogs in a well with no knowledge of the great sea, but even we could sense the mistrust between the Soviets and the Americans."[66]

Sejima later became a legendary figure, mainly thanks to his exploits as a business leader after repatriating in 1956. From the 1960s, he was soon one of the top managers in the Itoh Corporation, helping it to become one of Japan's largest business conglomerates. By the 1980s, Sejima had the status of a senior statesman in Japan and was revered for his experience, knowledge, and influence. He was friend of and adviser to Prime Minister Nakasone Yasuhiro, a member of several government committees, and chairman of the board of Asia University.[67]

In September 1946, however, Sejima was a prisoner of war. A decade in the Soviet camps lay between him and his final return home. In Tokyo, on a temporary trip home in the custody of the Soviets, he and his fellow witnesses were quartered in a carefully guarded building surrounded by high walls. The Soviets treated their witnesses well, even hiring a tailor who visited to take measurements for their bespoke courtroom suits. Despite this, on September 20, 1946, they woke up to find that General Kusaba Tatsumi had taken his life by poisoning, apparently unable to testify against his former superiors. Perhaps in an attempt to appease the two remaining witnesses, the Soviets arranged meetings with their families; Sejima was allowed two hours with his wife and two children. The Soviet officer in attendance told Sejima's wife to start preparing the house for her husband's return – the Soviets were apparently ready to release him following his favorable attestation.[68] However, when Sejima took the witness stand on October 18, his testimony, read aloud by the USSR's prosecutor Solomon Rosenblit, was hardly what the Soviets had expected. Their main goal was to prove, through Sejima and Matsumura Tomokatsu (former deputy chief of staff of the Kwantung Army), that the Japanese Army had aggressive plans toward the Soviet Union. But in his written statement distributed to the court members and in his responses to the questions from the court, Sejima denied having any knowledge of such aggressive plans. He claimed that he had been involved only in "the military side of the things" and had no knowledge of policy goals. His testimony did nothing to help the Soviets' cause; it ended on the same day, and he was not called on again to testify. In 1992, Ivan Kovalenko – former deputy director of the Soviet Communist Party Central Committee international affairs department and one of the top officials in charge of reeducating the Japanese internees – claimed in an interview with a popular Japanese magazine that Sejima had lied about being coerced into the role of a Soviet witness at the Tokyo Trial. According to Kovalenko, the highest echelons of Soviet power had monitored the selection of witnesses, and Sejima would simply not have been selected had he not agreed to testify against his superiors.[69] One can only speculate what had caused Sejima's U-turn – he does not dwell on his change of mind in his memoir – but clearly it must have contributed to his long internment in Siberia. According to Sejima, the American team at the court requested that the Soviets allow him and Matsumura to stay in Tokyo for interrogations, but the Soviet side flatly denied this request. Sejima and Matsumura were returned to the USSR in November 1946. After that, Sejima was transferred from one camp to another for almost three years and then sentenced to twenty-five years imprisonment in July 1949, charged with "spying against . . . and involvement in hostile activities toward the USSR."

The most important document available to historians on the Soviet decision to start legal proceedings against certain categories of Japanese POWs dates back to August 1949, but Sejima's July 1949 sentence demonstrates that the process had been under way much earlier. The Russian historian Victoria Romanova has claimed that the idea of trying the Unit 731 members in the USSR was first conceived in late 1947–early 1948, although the documents that could substantiate this claim are not yet accessible to historians.[70] On August 3, 1949, a top-secret directive "On the Criminal Responsibility of Japanese POWs and Internees Involved in Hostile Activities against the USSR" singled out categories of Japanese captives to be arrested on charges of "hostile activities against the USSR":

> Japanese POWs who have served in intelligence, counterintelligence and punitive organs of the Japanese Army; the teaching staff and students of espionage schools and units; intelligence agents employed against the USSR; organizers of the military conflicts on Lake Khasan and the Khalkhin-Gol River; the supervisory staff of the fascist Concordia Association [*Kyōwakai*]; and the employees of the "anti-epidemic units" involved in researching bacteriological means and methods of warfare and in planning to use them in the war against the USSR.[71]

The same categories of Japanese had been kept from repatriation over a year prior, following the interior ministry Order No. 00374 on April 12, 1948.[72] In early August 1949, almost five months before the start of the Khabarovsk Trial, the document provided no indication that the employees of the "anti-epidemic units" – the euphemistic name for the bacteriological Unit 731 – would be selected as the main defendants of the Khabarovsk Trial. We can conclude that the decision to conduct "open judicial proceedings against the heads of the Anti-Epidemic Unit 731" was actively worked over starting from August 1949.[73] Records of Politburo meetings show that on October 8, 1949, Stalin approved the draft of the Soviet of Ministers Decree, "On the Organization in Khabarovsk of a Tribunal over Japanese Criminals."[74] Finally the Soviet leadership reached its decision to single out those implicated in the production of bacteriological weapons as the main indictment for the Khabarovsk Trial. The term "open judicial proceedings" (*otkrytyi sudebnyi protsess*) used to describe the trial in the minutes of the Politburo meetings is very important: it demonstrated the

Soviet emphasis on disclosing evidence that they felt was silenced during the Tokyo Trial.

The remaining five categories in the directive "On the Criminal Responsibility" of the Japanese were either to be adjudicated by "camp military tribunals" or transferred to Mao Zedong's newly proclaimed People's Republic of China, who would be expected to exact punishment on them "for grave crimes committed against the Chinese people."[75] Unlike the "open" Khabarovsk Trial, the camp military tribunals were to be closed. On December 20, 1949, Kruglov, Viktor Abakumov (minister of state security), and Grigorii Safonov (chief prosecutor) sent a draft resolution to Stalin and his inner circle, in which they reported that their inter-agency commission had decided to hand over to military courts "2,883 war criminals" from among the 4,547 Japanese internees whose repatriation had been postponed for the purposes of investigation. The remaining 1,664 Japanese, for whom the prosecution found no evidence of "anti-Soviet activities," were to be repatriated.[76] This was the final "sorting" of 1949. From 1950, the second phase of the internment would begin, and all remaining Japanese would be handed down criminal sentences.[77]

If the production of biological weapons with the intention to use them against the Soviet Union was the central indictment at the Khabarovsk Trial, the camp trials were organized around a peculiar set of charges that can be summarized by the larger rubric of "anti-Soviet activities." In the interpretation of the Soviet lawmakers, "anti-Soviet activities" was a broad term rooted in the notorious Article 58 of the 1938 Penal Code of the Russian Soviet Federative Socialist Republic (RSFSR). The article consisted of fourteen clauses that presented the most comprehensive definitions of "counter-revolutionary crimes": from "undermining the security" of the Soviet Union, to spying on behalf of foreign states and counter-revolutionary organizations, and to failing to inform on imminent counter-revolutionary crimes, among others. The prominent Soviet writer Konstantin Simonov referred to Article 58 as "the article under which . . . those involved, or thought to be involved, in Trotskyist or any other leftist opposition" were tried in the years of the Great Purge.[78] But why were foreign citizens – Japanese former officers who had committed their "anti-Soviet crimes" under orders from their superiors and *not* on Soviet territory – tried under an article in the penal code of one of the union republics of the Soviet Union? The absurdity is perhaps best expressed, albeit not explained, through an example of an encounter in a Siberian camp. Takasugi Ichirō, the former internee and author of a 1950 bestselling internment memoir, *In the Shadow of the Northern Lights* (*Kyokkō no kage ni*), vehemently protested when Major Kutnyi, the warden of the camp to which Takasugi had just been transferred, impudently emptied the contents of Takasugi's bag and picked through his belongings. "As a Soviet officer, you should respect international law!" were Takasugi's words to Kutnyi. The Soviet major calmly replied: "International law? There is no such thing in the Soviet Union. We only follow the orders of the minister of internal affairs."[79]

## Conclusion

In the Soviet Union's dealings in East Asia, international law was not always binding for the Soviet leadership. The actions and words of Major Kutnyi, the brazen camp warden just mentioned, were symbolic of the Soviet state's decision to try foreigners according to an article in its own domestic penal code that had no justification in terms of international law. In his reliance on power and prejudice, Major Kutnyi's actions mirrored the way that the leaders of his country behaved – and their power was not questioned. Soviet interests, dictating that the Japanese captives be kept in Soviet hands as a trump card for as long as necessary, ruled supreme.

These interests came on the back of long-held prejudices toward Japan as the USSR's nemesis in East Asia, the enemy that had to be reined in now that the Soviets had emerged victorious from the global conflict. Postwar Soviet propaganda drew inspiration from the decades-long tug of war for power and influence in East Asia. The deep well of Soviet grievances against the overly ambitious Japanese power, dating back to the latter's famous victory in the Russo-Japanese War of 1904–1905, was overflowing in the 1930s. At this time, however, the Soviets were not yet in a position to challenge Japanese power.

The power to do so came with victory over Japan, the victory that provided the Soviets with a carte blanche, as Joseph Stalin saw it at the time, in redrawing the frontiers of influence in East Asia. Yet within days of the Soviet triumph over Japan, the cracks in the Allies' façade were already visible. Sensing this, the USSR pounced on the trophies it held under its control, transporting from the conquered puppet kingdom of Manchukuo both human and inanimate booty: it took prisoner over 600,000 former Japanese soldiers, and it dismantled and appropriated the industrial and other facilities in Manchuria.[80] All of these were to be used in rebuilding the war-torn Soviet economy, but their captors had other designs for the human remnants of the Japanese empire interned in the frigid Siberian camps. The power exercised by the Soviets over the captive Japanese nationals is seen in how Sejima Ryūzō, illegal as his internment in the Soviet Union was according to international law and agreements (Potsdam Declaration and the 1929 Geneva Convention Relative to the Treatment of Prisoners of War), was transported *back* to the USSR from his home country after his testimony proved unfavorable to the Soviets.

In sum, when the Soviet Union lost most of its levers of influence over Japan, it clung to the Siberian internees – the vestiges of Japan's imperial project and now the hostages of the newly emerging empires – as a trump card in its standoff with the United States in East Asia. The Siberian internees endured not only the harsh winters and the inhumane exploitation in camps scattered across the vast territory of the Soviet giant; they also became the first recipients of the unilateral and separate Soviet form of justice. This judgement, meted out in partial protest against the Tokyo Trial to Japanese citizens tried at the Khabarovsk Trial and the many camp trials, reflected Stalin's crushed hopes for a larger role in Japan and for influence that he had eyed but never obtained and for which he tried to compensate with his policies of destabilization and defiance.

## Notes

1 Barak Kushner, *Men to Devils, Devils to Men: Japanese War Crimes and Chinese Justice* (Cambridge, MA: Harvard University Press, 2015), p. 5.
2 See, for example, Robert M. Slusser, "Soviet Far Eastern Policy, 1945–50: Stalin's Goals in Korea," in *The Origins of the Cold War in Asia*, ed. Yōnosuke Nagai and Akira Iriye (New York: Columbia University Press, 1977), pp. 123–146.
3 Rinjirō Sodei provided a good summary of these views, in which a CIA analyst dismissed the Soviet role out of hand. See Sodei, "Hiroshima/Nagasaki as History and Politics," *The Journal of American History* vol. 82, issue 3 (December 1995): pp. 1118–1123, here p. 1119; while Louis Morton took a balanced view on the U.S. and Soviet roles in Japan's defeat, he too believed that all the USSR's entry did was hasten Japan's "unconditional surrender": Louis Morton, "Soviet Intervention in the War with Japan," *Foreign Affairs* vol. 40, issue 4 (July 1962): pp. 653–662.
4 Among many others, L.N. Vnotchenko, *Pobeda na Dal'nem Vostoke* (Moscow: Voenizdat, 1971), Introduction and Chapter 1, pp. 3–28; O.A. Rzheshevskii, "Bourgeois Assessments of the Soviet Victory over Japan," *Soviet Studies in History* vol. 24, issue 3 (1985): pp. 69–79; John J. Stephan, "The USSR and the Defeat of Imperial Japan," *Soviet Studies in History* vol. 24, issue 3 (1985): pp. 3–25; more recently, K.E. Cherevko and A.A. Kirichenko, *Sovetsko-iaponskaia voina (9 avgusta – 2 sentiabria 1945 g.). Rassekrechennye materialy* (Moscow: BIMPA, 2006), esp. pp. 289–293.
5 Sodei, "Hiroshima/Nagasaki," p. 1119.
6 For example, Frank Dikötter, *The Tragedy of Liberation: A History of the Chinese Revolution, 1945–1957* (London: Bloomsbury, 2014), pp. 12–13.
7 Sergey Radchenko, "Did Hiroshima save Japan from Soviet Occupation?," *Foreign Policy*, August 5, 2015, http://foreignpolicy.com/2015/08/05/stalin_japan_hiroshima_occupation_hokkaido/; for an incisive analysis of Stalin's attitude toward nuclear weapons, see David Holloway, *Stalin and the Bomb: The Soviet Union and Atomic Energy, 1939–1956* (New Haven, CT: Yale University Press, 1994).
8 Geoffrey Roberts, *The Soviet Union in World Politics: Coexistence, Revolution and Cold War, 1945–1991* (London: Routledge, 2005), pp. 5–9; Tony Judt, "Why the Cold War Worked," in *Tony Judt: When the Facts Change – Essays 1995–2010*, ed. Jennifer Homans (London: Vintage, 2015), pp. 77–78.
9 Roberts, *The Soviet Union in World Politics*, p. 7.
10 David Wolff, "Japan and Stalin's Policy toward Northeast Asia after World War II," *Journal of Cold War Studies* vol. 15 (2013), pp. 4–29.
11 Sherzod Muminov, "Eleven Winters of Discontent: The Siberian Internment and the Making of the New Japan, 1945–1956," PhD Dissertation, University of Cambridge, September 2015.
12 Through the United Nations Ad Hoc Commission on Prisoners of War (set up in 1946), the Japanese government petitioned both the UN General Assembly and individual governments in attempts to facilitate the repatriation of Japanese citizens from the USSR: United Kingdom National Archives, "UN Ad Hoc Commission on Prisoners of War," FO 371/107018; see also then foreign minister Yoshida Shigeru's 1951 letter to the UN General Assembly, "Foreign Minister's Letter of 14 May 1951 to President of the United Nations General Assembly," Diplomatic Archives of Japan (*Gaikōshiryōkan*), Reel K-0001, pp. 140–173.
13 Andrew E. Barshay, *The Gods Left First: The Captivity and Repatriation of Japanese POWs in Northeast Asia, 1945–1956* (Berkeley: University of California Press, 2013); see also Sherzod Muminov, "The 'Siberian Internment' and the Transnational History

of the Early Cold War Japan, 1945–56," in *Transnational Japan as History: Empire, Migration, and Social Movements*, ed. Pedro Iacobelli, Danton Leary, and Shinnosuke Takahashi (New York: Palgrave Macmillan, 2016), pp. 71–95.

14  Banno Junji, *Nihon kindaishi* (Chikuma shobō, 2012), pp. 315–316; Paul E. Dunscomb, *Japan's Siberian Intervention, 1918–1922: 'A Great Disobedience against the People'* (Lanham, MD: Lexington Books, 2012); Ian Moffat, *The Allied Intervention in Russia, 1918–1920: The Diplomacy of Chaos* (New York: Palgrave Macmillan, 2015), p. 47. (Unless otherwise noted, all Japanese books are published in Tokyo.)

15  "Draft Message from Joseph Stalin to Harry S. Truman," August 17, 1945, Wilson Center Digital Archive, http://digitalarchive.wilsoncenter.org/document/122330.

16  Quoted in William Blum, *Killing Hope: US Military and CIA Interventions since World War II* (London: Zed Books, 2003), p. 8.

17  "Zapis' besedy Zamestitelia Narodnogo Komissara Inostrannykh Del SSSR s Poslom Iaponii v SSSR Khirota," September 19, 1931, in *Dokumenty vneshnei politiki SSSR* (hereafter *DVP*), Vol. 14, ed. P.I Yershov, A.I. Lavrent'iev, B.P. Miroshnichenko, K.N. Svanidze, S.L. Tikhvinskii (Moscow: Politizdat, 1968), Doc. No. 269, p. 529.

18  "I.V. Stalin – K.E. Voroshilovu," November 27, 1931, Russian State Archive of Socio-Political History (RGASPI), fond (f.) 74, opis' (op.) 2, delo (d.) 38, listy (l.) 48–51, in *Sovetskoe rukovodstvo: perepiska, 1928–1941*, ed. A.V. Kvashonkin, L.P. Kosheleva, L.A. Rogovaya, and O.V. Khlevniuk (Moscow: Rosspen, 1999), Doc. No. 91, pp. 161–163.

19  "Telegramma I.V. Stalina L.M. Kaganovichu i V.M. Molotovu," September 23, 1931, in *VKP(b), Komintern i Kitai: dokumenty*, Vol. 4, Part I (Moscow: Rosspen, 2003), Doc. No. 5, pp. 70–71.

20  "Zapis' besedy Narodnogo Komissara Inostrannykh Del SSSR s Ministrom Inostran-nykh Del Iaponii Iosidzava," December 31, 1931, in *DVP*, Vol. 14, Doc. No.401, p. 747.

21  "Vystuplenie Narodnogo Komissara Inostrannykh Del SSSR M.M. Litvinova na IV sessii TsIK SSSR 6-go sozyva," December 29, 1933, in *DVP*, Vol. 16, Appendix No. 2, p. 795 (added emphasis).

22  "Soglashenie mezhdu Soiuzom Sovetskikh Sotsialisticheskikh Respublik I Man'chzhou-Go ob ustupke Man'chzhou-Go prav Soiuza Sovetskikh Sotsialisticheskikh Respublik v otnoshenii Kitaiskoi Vostochnoi zheleznoi dorogi (Severo-Man'chzhurskoi zheleznoi dorogi)," March 23, 1935, in *DVP*, Vol. 18, Doc. No. 134, pp. 204–213.

23  Hiroaki Kuromiya and Andrzej Pepłonski, "Stalin, Espionage and Counterespionage," in *Stalin and Europe: Imitation and Domination, 1928–1953*, ed. Timothy Snyder and Ray Brandon (New York: Oxford University Press, 2014), pp. 73–91, this quote p. 75.

24  "Soviet Increases Its Hunt for Spies: Germany and Japan Head List of Suspected Nations Because War Is Believed Near," *The New York Times*, February 28, 1938, p. 5.

25  "Soviet Purges 'Japan Spies,' In Far East: Stalin Orders Cleanup in Area of Manchukuo Border Disputes," *The Washington Post*, July 28, 1938, p. 5.

26  Alvin D. Coox, *Nomonhan: Japan against Russia, 1939* (Stanford, CA: Stanford University Press, 1994), p. xii.

27  Stuart D. Goldman, *Nomonhan, 1939: The Red Army's Victory That Shaped World War II* (Annapolis, MD: Naval Institute Press, 2012).

28  Roger Moorhouse, *The Devils' Alliance: Hitler's Pact with Stalin. 1939–1941* (London: Vintage, 2016), p. 132.

29  "Pakt o neitralitete mezhdu Soiuzom Sovetskikh Sotsialisticheskikh Respublik i Iaponiei," April 13, 1941, in *DVP*, Vol. 23, Part 2, Doc. No. 773, pp. 565–567.

30  Tsuyoshi Hasegawa, *The End of the Pacific War: Reappraisals* (Stanford, CA: Stanford University Press, 2007), pp. 190–193; Fraser J. Harbutt, *Yalta 1945: Europe and America at the Crossroads* (Cambridge: Cambridge University Press, 2010), pp. 128–129.

31  Tsuyoshi Hasegawa, *Racing the Enemy: Stalin, Truman, and the Surrender of Japan* (Cambridge, MA: Harvard University Press, 2009), Chapter 4, "Decisions for War and Peace," esp. pp. 91–97.

32 "Zapis' besedy narodnogo komissara inostrannykh del SSSR s poslom SShA v SSSR i s poslom Velikobritanii v SSSR, *Prilozhenie:* Zaiavlenie Sovetskogo pravitel'stva," in *Sovetsko-amerikanskie otnosheniia vo vremia Velikoi Otechestvennoi voiny, 1944–1945: dokumenty i materialy* (Moscow: Politizdat, 1984), Vol. 2, Doc. No. 293, pp. 478–479.

33 Hasegawa, *Racing the Enemy.*

34 Sejima Ryūzō, *Sejima Ryūzō kaisōroku: ikusanga* (Sankei shimbun shuppan, 1996), p. 277.

35 The phrase "the jewel in the crown" is from Louise Young, *Japan's Total Empire: Manchuria and the Culture of Wartime Imperialism* (Berkeley: University of California Press, 1999), Chapter 2, pp. 21–52.

36 Among many other works, see Abe Gunji, *Shiberia kyōsei yokuryū no jittai: nisso ryōkoku shiryō kara no kenshō* (Sairyūsha, 2005); Makino Hiromichi, *Senseki ni inoru* (Sankei shimbun shuppan, 2007).

37 N.N. Amel'ko and M.M. Kirian, *Razgrom iaponskogo militarizma vo Vtoroi mirovoi voine* (Moscow: Voenizdat, 1986).

38 Vnotchenko, *Pobeda.*

39 "Iz dnevnika Posla SSSR v Iaponii K.A. Smetanina," June 24, 1941, in *DVP*, Vol. 24, Doc. No. 17, p. 29.

40 State Archive of the Russian Federation (GARF), "The TASS Archive," f. 4459, op. 34, d. 376: "O iaponskoi propagande."

41 As quoted in John J. Stephan, *The Russian Fascists: Tragedy and Farce in Exile, 1925–1945* (New York: Harper & Row, 1978), p. 316.

42 Aleksandr Koshelev, *Ia dralsia s samuraiami: ot Khalkhin-Gola do Port-Artura* (Moscow: Eksmo, 2005).

43 Central Archive of the Ministry of Defence of the Russian Federation (TsAMO RF), f. 66, op. 178499, d. 1, l. 593–598.

44 The numbers of officers are given as of December 1, 1946, when they were at their highest. See "Spravka GUPVI MVD SSSR o nalichii voennoplennykh byvshei iaponskoi armii po sostoianiiu na 1 dekabria 1946 g.," Russian State Military Archive (RGVA), f. 1p, op. 01e, d. 57, l. 9, reprinted in *Iaponskie voennoplennye v SSSR, 1945–1956*, ed. V.A. Gavrilov and E.L. Katasonova (Moscow: Mezhdunarodnyi fond "Demokratiia," 2013), p. 82. The number of generals is taken from S.I. Kuznetsov and S.V. Karasev, "Internirovanie v SSSR vysshego komandnogo sostava Kvantunskoi Armii, Imperatora i pravitel'stva Manchzhou-go (1945 g.)," https://src-h.slav.hokudai.ac.jp/publictn/81/page_0312.pdf.

45 Article 9 of the Potsdam Declaration dictated that "[t]he Japanese military forces, after being completely disarmed, shall be permitted to return to their homes with the opportunity to lead peaceful and productive lives," http://www.ndl.go.jp/constitution/e/etc/c06.html.

46 TsAMO RF, f. 66, op. 178499, d. 3, l. 220–221.

47 "Obrashchenie tov. I.V. Stalina k narodu," *Pravda*, September 3, 1945, p. 1.

48 Ibid.

49 Wolff, "Japan and Stalin's Policy," p. 4.

50 Barshay, *Gods Left First*, p. 22.

51 "Draft message from Stalin to Truman."

52 Susan L. Carruthers, *Cold War Captives: Imprisonment, Escape, and Brainwashing* (Berkeley: University of California Press, 2009); American Federation of Labor, *Slave Labor in Russia: The Case Presented by the American Federation of Labor to the United Nations* (Washington, DC: 1949), http://catalog.hathitrust.org/Record/000324761.

53 Oleg Khlevniuk, "Zony sovetskoi ekonomiki: razdelenie I vzaimodeistvie," in *Istoriia stalinizma: prinuditel'nyi trud v SSSR. Ekonomika, politika, pamiat'*, ed., S.A. Krasil'nikov, O.V. Khlevniuk, and L.I. Borodkin (Moscow: Rosspen, 2013), p. 8.

54 Natalia V. Surzhikova, "Ekonomika sovetskogo plena: administrirovanie, proizvodstvo, potreblenie," in Borodkin et al, *Istoriia stalinizma*, pp. 78–87.
55 All statistics are from G.F. Krivosheev, V.M. Andronikov, P.D. Burikov, V.V. Gurkin, *Velikaia Otechestvennaia bez grifa sekretnosti: Kniga poter'* (Moscow: Veche, 2010), pp. 43–75.
56 Elena Katasonova, *Iaponskie voennoplennye v SSSR: bol'shaia igra velikikh derzhav* (Moscow: Ivran, 2003); Shirai Hisaya, "Hyōsetsu no hi: Saitō Rokurō to shiberia yokuryū / 7: minshu undō – shōri to zasetsu," *Sekai*, December 1994, pp. 294–307.
57 "Soobshchenie TASS ob okonchanii repatriatsii iz Sovetskogo Soiuza iaponskikh voennoplennykh," *Izvestiia*, April 22, 1950.
58 "Dokladnaia zapiska A.Ya. Vyshinskogo, S.N. Kruglova I.V. Stalinu o poriadke repatriatsii . . .," March 5, 1950, GARF, f. 9401, op. 2, d. 269, l. 178–180. Reprinted in *Voennoplennye v SSSR, 1939–1956: dokumenty i materialy*, ed. M. Zagorul'ko (Moscow: Logos, 2000) (Moscow: Logos, 2000), Doc. No. 8.50, pp. 876–877.
59 Uchimura Gōsuke, *Sutārin goku no nihonjin: iki isogu* (Chūō kōron, 1985), p. 13.
60 "Predstavlenie Ministra vnutrennikh del SSSR rukovodstvu strany tekstov obrashcheniia voennoplennykh Seminovskogo lageria MVD Primorskogo kraia k iaponskim voennoplennym i iaponskomu narodu i obrashcheniia voennoplennykh lageria MVD No. 188 k Mezdhunarodnomu voennomu tribunalu," June 5, 1946, GARF, fond (f.) 9401, opis' (op.) 2, delo (d.) 136, list (l.) 429–435. Reprinted in *Iaponskie voennoplennye*, pp. 280–283.
61 "Spravka po delu Iamada Otozoo," GARF, f. 7523, op. 89, d. 4449; V.V. Romanova, "Ot Tokiiskogo suda k Khabarovskomu: iz istorii podgotovki sudebnogo protsessa nad iaponskimi voennymi prestupnikami-bakteriologami," *Istoriia meditsiny* vol. 1, Issue 2 (2015): pp. 72–82.
62 Stephen S. Large, ed., *Shōwa Japan: Political, Economic and Social History, 1926–1989*, Vol. II, 1941–1952 (London: Routledge, 1998), p. 175, n. 1.
63 Boris G. Yudin, "Research on Humans at the Khabarovsk War Crimes Trial," in *Japan's Wartime Medical Atrocities: Comparative Inquiries in Science, History, and Ethics*, ed. Jing Bao Nie, Nanyan Guo, and Mark Selden (London: Routledge, 2013), pp. 59–78.
64 Valentyna Polunina, "The Khabarovsk Trial: The Soviet Riposte to the Tokyo Tribunal," in *Trials for International Crimes in Asia*, ed. Kirsten Sellars (Cambridge: Cambridge University Press), pp. 121–144.
65 The other witnesses were Lieutenant General Kusaba Tatsumi and Major General Matsumura Tomokatsu. Sejima, *Ikusanga*, p. 314.
66 Ibid., p. 315.
67 "Itochu Chief Sejima, Ex-War Strategist, Dead at 95," *The Japan Times*, September 5, 2007, http://www.japantimes.co.jp/news/2007/09/05/national/itochu-chief-sejima-ex-war-strategist-dead-at-95/.
68 Sejima, *Ikusanga*, pp. 317–318.
69 Katō Akira, "Soren tainichi kōsaku saikō sekininsha ga shōgen suru: Sejima Ryūzō – shiberia no shinjitsu," *Bungei shunjū* vol. 70, issue 2 (February 1992), pp. 104–136.
70 Romanova, "Ot Tokiiskogo," p. 78.
71 "Ukazaniia zamestitelia Ministra vnutrennikh del SSSR . . . o privlechenii k ugolovnoi otvetstvennosti voennoplennykh i internirovannykh iapontsev . . .," August 3, 1949, GARF, f. 9401, op. 12, d. 205, tom (t.) 1, chast' (ch.) 2, l. 91–92 ob., in *Iaponskie voennoplennye*, pp. 143–144.
72 "Prikaz MVD SSSR No. 00374 o repatriatsii voennoplennykh iapontsev v 1948 g.," April 12, 1948, GARF, f. 9401, op. 1, d. 855, l. 77–82, reprinted in *Voennoplennye v SSSR*, Doc. No. 8.39, pp. 864–866.
73 RGASPI, f. 17, op. 3, d. 1078.
74 Ibid., punkt (p.) 810.
75 "Dokladnaia zapiska A.Ia. Vyshinskogo, S.N. Kruglova I.V. Stalinu."
76 "Proekt Postanovleniia Soveta Ministrov SSSR, predstavlennyi rukovodstvu strany, ob otpravke na rodinu voennoplennykh i internirovannykh iapontsev, zaderzhannykh ranee

ot repatriatsii," December 20, 1949, GARF, f. 9401, op. 2, d. 236, l. 319. In *Iaponskie voennoplennye*, p. 478.

77 The Japanese citizens who had willingly requested to remain in the USSR and to become Soviet citizens were the exception. A collection of documents in the State Archive of the Russian Federation contains a folder with applications made by such internees. GARF, f. 9526, op. 6, d. 630. See also Kawagoe Shirō, *Roshia kokuseki nihonjin no kiroku: shiberia yokuryū kara sorenpō hōkai made* (Chūō kōronsha, 1994).

78 Konstantin Simonov, "Glazami cheloveka moego pokoleniia: Razmyshleniia o I.V. Staline," in *Stikhotvoreniia i poemy. Povesti raznykh let. Posledniaia rabota* (Moscow: OLMA Press, 2004), p. 447.

79 Takasugi Ichirō, *Kyokkō no kageni: shiberia furyoki* (Iwanami shoten, 1995), p. 186.

80 "O sozdanii komissii po vyvozu trofeinogo oborudovaniia iz Manchzhurii," RGASPI, f. 644, op. 1, edinitsa khraneniia (ed. khr.) 459.

# Diplomacy, law, and the end of empire

# 9 Sublimating the empire

## How Japanese experts of international law translated Greater East Asia into the postwar period

*Urs Matthias Zachmann*

## Introduction

In 1948, the public intellectual and sinologist Takeuchi Yoshimi published an impassioned essay, "What Is Modernity?" in which he compared the case of Japan and China.[1] Takeuchi evaluated what he called Japan's "slave mentality" toward Western civilization negatively as compared with China's resistance against it, and he expressed particular irritation with the apparent success that the "master student" Japan had shown in adopting Western civilization and using it for its own gains. Takeuchi complained:

> [W]hen in Europe a concept becomes discordant (i.e., contradictory) with reality . . ., a movement occurs in which accord is sought by the overcoming of that contradiction, that is to say by the development in place. Hence it is the concept itself that develops. However, when in Japan a concept becomes discordant with reality . . . one abandons former principles and begins searching for others. Concepts are deserted and principles are abandoned. . . . There is no failure of Japanese ideology, for it perpetually succeeds by perpetually failing. It is an infinite repetition, which has been conceived of as progress.[2]

As someone writing just three years after war's end, Takeuchi's frustration is understandable. He was not the only person to protest against, as he saw it, the all too facile transition of Japan from the war period into the postwar period. Ibuse Masuji (for example, in the 1950 story "Yōhai taichō" (translated as "Lieutenant Lookeast") and Ōe Kenzaburō (in the majority of his works), show a similar rueful skepticism concerning the instant democratization of a nation that at least in public had supported the war effort with high-minded rhetoric until the bitter end.[3] But almost overnight, after surrender, former advocates of war began to pepper their conversations with the new watchwords of "peace" and "democracy."[4] The outward trajectory of Japan seemed to confirm Takeuchi's claim that for Japan even the most catastrophic failure is the mother of success. As is well known, already by 1955, Japan's GDP exceeded its prewar level, and the country was preparing for its economic takeoff into high growth in the 1960s. The "reverse course" policy taken by the United States after the rise of the Cold War greatly facilitated Japan's political rehabilitation: the late 1950s saw Japan firmly embedded as the United States' closest ally in East Asia; Japan became a U.S.-sponsored participant of GATT in 1955 and a member state of the United Nations in 1956. Moreover, the legal narrative of the Tokyo War Crimes Tribunal (1946–1948, hereafter IMTFE) had portrayed the Japanese military as the villain of World War Two: the imperial Japanese military had hijacked the Japanese state and seduced and bullied the "common people" into a self-destructive war. The question of war responsibility had been swiftly dealt with, and the "common people" were going to be able to start afresh in their economic-driven pursuit of postwar security.[5]

As plausible and convincing as Takeuchi's complaint about the fickleness and facileness of modern Japanese thought may appear, it is still misleading. Nature does not make jumps in Japan, any more than anywhere else, and the laws of gravity and momentum apply there equally. Ideas follow certain paths and do not easily disappear, but they may change their outward appearance and live to fight another day. The sudden shifts of political tactics and creed that we can see among Japanese intellectuals in the postwar, which were the main target of Takeuchi's vitriol, may have been less a turn of conviction than the result of a radical turn of perspective. The ideas remained fundamentally the same, but their meanings changed with the August 1945 "revolution" as the political context transformed from the Japan-centered Greater East Asian order into a U.S.-centered Cold War order.

Nowhere is this better demonstrated than in the translation, or sublimation, of the ideas that formed the ideological and legal fundamentals of the Greater Co-Prosperity Sphere and the various conceptions of the Japanese postwar order. The Scottish jurist Alan Watson once coined the famous phrase "legal transplants" to describe the process of migrating one legal institute or figure of thought from one culture or legal system into another, along with the changes that may take place in the process.[6] What outward transformations does an idea undergo if it is transplanted from one culture or structure into another? The same question, of course, could be posed in relation to other circumstances that we frequently see in history, that of regime change. The French Revolution, the Meiji Restoration, Japan's "August Revolution" in 1945, and Germany's reunification are but a few potential examples.

This chapter investigates the translation of ideas in the legal concepts that formed the basis of Japan's East Asian International Law (*Tōa kokusaihō*). I argue that the Japanese international lawyers who were tasked with establishing a new legal order during the war mostly retained their positions *after* the war. They "sublimated" their ideas of empire and international order, as it were, and adjusted them to the radically changed political circumstances of the Cold War order in the postwar. Outwardly, they may have seemed opportunistic and were often harshly criticized for being so, but a remarkable continuity of thought informed their positions during the war and into the postwar. The number of international lawyers was small to begin with, and in this chapter I limit myself to discussing three of them – Yokota Kisaburō, Tabata Shigejirō, and Yasui Kaoru – but their positions are nonetheless representative. Politically and ideologically, they were situated in the same spectrum as many figures of the elite that came into power in the postwar years such as Prime Minister Yoshida Shigeru and Foreign Minister Shigemitsu Mamoru. Moreover, as public intellectuals and, in Yokota Kisaburō's case as official legal advisor to the Foreign Ministry, they were able to influence the public and government discourse that shaped Japan's foreign policy in the postwar period. Some of this discourse parallels what Barak Kushner analyzes in Chapter 3 of this volume concerning how the Japanese military, government, and society proposed various means to deal with the international call for war crimes trials.

## The role of international law in modern Japan's foreign policy

To understand the legal transition of wartime Japan into the postwar world, it is necessary to understand the role that international law and legal experts had played in Japan's prewar foreign policy.[7] From the beginning, international law in Japan had an immensely practical and political role. This shaped the engagement of Japanese experts of international law as pragmatic and positivistic, Euro-centric, state-oriented, and apologetic of Japan's foreign policy course.[8] From its reception in Japan in 1853, international law served two goals: first, it assisted in overcoming the so-called unequal treaties between Japan and the Western countries by signaling to those powers Japan's full compliance with the standard of civilization, especially the ability to conduct foreign policy through the use of international law. The second goal was to gain the same position as the Western powers vis-à-vis Japan's neighbors, China and Korea, and to use international law as a diplomatic weapon. In the beginning, therefore, international law was a purely practical matter, and its textbooks were considered more as manuals for good practice in foreign policy. Japanese experts in international law worked for the government, were completely reliant on European interpretations of international law, and had neither the intention nor the power to challenge the European standard or to suggest alternatives.

It is telling that international law as an *academic* discipline in Japan began only after the first unequal treaty with Britain had been rescinded in 1894 and after Japan, through its victory over the Qing Dynasty in China in 1895, had become an aspiring great power itself. In 1895, the first chair of international law was established at Tokyo Imperial University. In 1897, the Japanese Society of International Law (*Nippon kokusaihō gakkai*), the professional organization for international lawyers, which still exists today, was founded, again at first with the expressed aim to better coordinate expertise and government advice for managing the implementation of the unequal treaty with China.

However, outward compliance and a seeming passiveness on the side of Japan's international lawyers and diplomats should not be mistaken as a lack of critique. In fact, the Japanese attitude was characterized by a certain uneasiness and detachment toward international law from early on, especially after the so-called treaty revision (*jōyaku kaisei*) negotiations in the 1880s, Japan's rise to great power status in the 1890s, and the first setbacks (the Tripartite Intervention, the Yokohama Tax House Case) and finally the popular impression that the victory in the Russo-Japanese War had raised Japan only to a status of "pseudo-equality" with Western nations. Japan appeared to many people to face a glass ceiling of racial and cultural bias toward real equality that was impenetrable.[9] This sentiment, combined with a siege mentality regarding its political security, which saw the Japanese believe they were under constant threat from outside forces, led to a victimization complex that shaped Japan's perception of international law in the following decades. This was the case not only within the populace but also among legal experts.[10]

It is true that the 1920s in Japan are often seen as the most cooperative and "internationalist" stage of its modern foreign policy and often associated with its most prominent foreign minister, Shidehara Kijūrō. However, even Shidehara had reservations about the League of Nations and was unshakeable in his conviction that Japan had "special interests" in northeast Asia, particularly Manchuria.[11] Even if Japan joined the "Wilsonian" order of the 1920s *pro forma* by signing multilateral agreements, there was always a mental reservation that these agreements would never interfere with Japan's inherent right to defend its interests in Northeast Asia against potential political disorder or interference. The Kellogg-Briand Pact of 1928, which outlawed war to solve international disputes, was concluded at the same time that Japan made repeated military interventions into China to protect Japanese interests. Japan therefore entered into the agreement with the same reservations as Britain concerning "certain regions" in which it had vital interests, albeit without explicitly declaring these reservations.[12] However, in Japanese domestic discourse, this kind of thinking, which might be termed a "Japanese Monroe Doctrine," was understood as a matter of course. In addition, international lawyers such as Taoka Ryōichi criticized the Kellogg-Briand Pact as naïve and therefore virtually non-effective, for the reason that it sought to "talk away" war but provided few if any specific means to solve political conflicts peacefully.[13] In a sense, the logical foundations for further Japanese expansion on the continent were already in place in the 1920s, and the Manchurian Incident in 1931 that led to the Japanese occupation of Manchuria and initiated Japan's slide into the Asia-Pacific War was but the actualization of the argument.

## The construction of an "East Asian international law"

Only a few international Japanese lawyers raised questions about or voiced opposition to the Manchurian Incident in September 1931. The most famous protest was that of Yokota Kisaburō, a professor of international law at Tokyo Imperial University.[14] In a short article in the university newspaper in October 1931, Yokota declared that it was only natural that the League of Nations would concern itself with Japan's actions, since the military occupation of an entire country in response to the blowing up of 80 centimeters of train tracks near

Mukden (now Shenyang, China) could be hardly called proportional. Yokota received a number of death threats after this publication, and he was harshly criticized in the newspapers. He was instructed by the university dean and his colleagues, as well as by Foreign Minister Shidehara Kijūrō, to lie low and refrain from further "outrageous" remarks. Yokota thereafter remained cautious and circumspect in all his statements till the end of the war. Even so, Yokota's protest served him well in the postwar period, demonstrating his liberal and internationalist integrity.

Another protest, much less well known, came from Yasui Kaoru, a younger colleague of Yokota's and an assistant professor of international law at Tokyo Imperial University. Yasui was a declared Sovietophile, and in a 1933 article he lamented the growing international isolation of Japan as a consequence of the Manchurian Incident, especially Japan's estrangement from the "peace-loving, non-expansionist" Soviet Union.[15] To overcome this isolation Yasui recommended that Japan pursue a strict non-interventionist policy in China and the conclusion of a non-aggression pact with the Soviet Union.

The majority of international lawyers, however, welcomed Japan's interventionist policy on the continent and justified it on the basis of a "Japanese Monroe Doctrine."[16] This eventually became the argumentative nucleus of Japan's New Order in East Asia, the Greater East Asia Co-Prosperity Sphere, and the legal foundation of East Asian International Law. It should be mentioned here that the nature of these arguments was inherently ambivalent. Their primary function was, without doubt, to justify Japan's progressive expansion on the continent and the domination of the Chinese enemy and local elites in the occupied areas. A secondary aim was to co-opt the military elite *at home* and to somehow subject their decisions to a modicum of internal coordination.[17] In a way, the seemingly pan-Asianist declarations of 1938 and 1940 were meant to conjure up not only an "Asian" unity but also a unity of the notoriously fractured internal state of the empire. However, military leaders, if they were diplomatic, resisted these moves by routinely pointing out that these pan-Asianist concepts were much too diffuse and needed clarification, presumably under their direction. More outspoken ultra-nationalists openly resisted every notion of an East Asian community as a "miniature version" of the hateful internationalism of the 1920s and declared its "cosmopolitan" spirit as un-national and incompatible with the emperor-centered polity of Japan (*kokutai*).[18]

The legal structure of East Asian Law (*Tōa kokusaihō*) was similarly ambivalent and unreliable in nature. The process to construct this legal ideology started on December 8, 1941, the day following the attack on Pearl Harbor, when the *Kokusaihō gakkai* (Japanese Society of International Law) formally reconstituted itself as a think tank for the Foreign Ministry with the expressed task to provide the legal foundations for the New Order in East Asia and therefore also a new world order. They subsequently divided themselves into study groups to address particular areas such as the creation of a "Greater East Asian International Law."[19] Every influential international lawyer in Japan was a member of this group, though the more active members were usually found amongst the younger generation.

These included Yasui Kaoru and Tabata Shigejirō, a young international lawyer from Kyoto Imperial University who was, like Yasui, still an assistant professor.

This study group met over the course of two years with members presenting the results of their preparatory research at meetings to lay the framework for East Asian international law. Due to a lack of time, their studies never went beyond these preliminary inquiries, making it hard to estimate from the resulting fragments what the legal framework of the Co-Prosperity Sphere would have looked like as a finished product. However, if the *sources* that these international lawyers took as a model for their new order are of any indicative value, it is possible to put together a rough idea of the very hybrid composition of this "East Asian International Law."[20]

The models and elements consisted of the following:

1   The U.S. Monroe Doctrine. This was the most traditional element of the Co-Prosperity Sphere. A Japanese or Asian Monroe Doctrine had been part of an expansionist, Pan-Asianist discourse ever since the Spanish-American War of 1898 and provided the internal justification for Japan's "sphere of influence" since 1931.
2   Soviet legal thought and especially Evgenii Korovin's concept of a "pluralistic structure of the international legal order." Korovin had developed this concept in his study "International Law in the Transitional Phase."[21] Soviet legal thought provided a logical basis for fracturing the unity of the international legal order and establishing a regional "Asian" order. In particular, Tabata Shigejirō used it in his study of the "Pluralistic Structure of the International Legal Order" (1942–1943).[22] In addition, Yasui Kaoru used the case of the international lawyer Evgeny Pashukanis, who fell victim to Stalin's purges in 1937, to warn against a radical politicization of international legal studies in Japan.[23]
3   Nazi-German legal thought, especially Carl Schmitt's concept of "large spaces" (*Großraum*). Although Schmitt's theses were widely discussed in Japanese academia, Yasui Kaoru's publication, "European Concepts of Large Space International Law," was the most prominent in introducing Schmitt's concepts to wider audiences.[24] By broad consensus, East Asian International Law was explicitly to be a large space law, which would reinforce the barriers of the Monroe Doctrine against intervention of "alien powers" (*raumfremde Mächte*, in the words of Carl Schmitt).

There was a consensus that any legal development was to be gradualist and rational and that the source basis was the historical study of traditional international law. Japanese international lawyers tended to view the idea of East Asian International Law from a conservative perspective. One of the few illustrations of an attempt to develop new concepts on the basis of historical investigation was Tabata Shigejirō's study on "Changing Theories of State Equality," published in 1944.[25] On the basis of European classical law, especially Grotius, Tabata developed the new concept of a "relative equality" of states within the Co-Prosperity

Sphere, depending on their relative "ability" to contribute to the community. This concept was, of course, ambivalent. On the surface it justified Japan's position as the leading nation (*shudō-koku*); on the other hand, it guaranteed "member states" at least a minimum of sovereignty, without which equality would be nonsensical.

As we can see, the legal structure of the Co-Prosperity Sphere was hybrid and ideologically heterogeneous, which may have been due to the diverse composition of its authors participating in the study group. Nonetheless, the outlines and intentions of the envisioned order are clear enough: namely, to establish an autonomous normative sphere for Japan and to fortify it as strongly as possible against outside intervention. This was the true objective of the Co-Prosperity Sphere, and anyone who favored a more internationalist integration or upholding the traditional "unity of the [global] international order," such as Yokota Kisaburō, was forced into internal exile during the war.

## Sublimating the empire: Japan's transition into the postwar order

The project of setting up an East Asian International Law lasted less than two years. By late 1944, it was abundantly clear to most Japanese international lawyers that eventually Japan would be defeated, and they prepared for a takeover through the U.S.-led "United Nations." After the Dumbarton Oaks Conference (August–October 1944), which led to the first draft of a charter for the United Nations, Japanese international lawyers abandoned their own project and, with the encouragement and material assistance of the Foreign Ministry, were already devoting themselves to the new postwar order. Yokota Kisaburō, for example, was approached by a research institute close to the Foreign Ministry to prepare a preliminary study of the institutional structure of the United Nations, a task he finished in March 1945.[26] Commissioned by the same institute, a similar study was undertaken on the Bretton-Woods-system.[27] Kyoto Imperial University professor Taoka Ryōichi also conducted a study on the United Nations, which he eventually published in 1949. In his preface, Taoka described how he and his colleagues at Kyoto University in 1944 set up a study group for the study of "peace institutions" and that he was asked to investigate these from the perspective of positive law.[28] Tabata Shigejirō, his younger colleague, remembered that he and his colleagues met regularly in this study group, discussed the new order, and read books such as E. H. Carr's *The Conditions of Peace*.[29] Material for these studies and banned books such as Carr's were usually hard to come by, but Japanese international lawyers could always obtain them through the Foreign Ministry.

Finally, if they had been wavering over which ideology to follow during the war, some Japanese international lawyers such as Yasui Kaoru finally settled the issue for their postwar days. In his autobiographic writings, Yasui recalled how he was finally able to decide on his scientific, intellectual, and philosophical standpoint during the last phase of the Pacific War and thereby accomplish a personal "spiritual revolution." This became possible when he reread Lenin's *Materialism and*

*Empirio-criticism* (1909).[30] However, it is doubtful whether this was in fact such a fundamental revolution, as Yasui had been a Marxist all along.

When the so-called August Revolution finally transpired, that is, when the emperor announced Japan's surrender on August 15, 1945, the elite, or at least Japanese international lawyers, were already well prepared for the new postwar order. The international and political situation changed radically, of course. Japan's empire was suddenly "downsized" to its original, pre-1879 state, as Kawashima Shin discusses in Chapter 2, and so it remained, until Okinawa reverted to Japanese administration in 1972. For the first time in its history, Japan was occupied by a foreign power, if even for the relatively short period of 1945 to 1952, at the end of which Japan found itself in a tight military alliance with the United States and firmly under its defense umbrella in the ensuing Cold War. The new security architecture was faintly reminiscent of Japan's anti-Russian alliance with Britain in 1902 but completely unprecedented due to new constitutional restraints such as Article 9 and an exclusive security reliance on one superpower. Considering the radically changed environment, it is not surprising that Japan's international lawyers also considerably shifted their stances and convictions. For this they were bitterly criticized as "chameleons," "traitors," and turncoats.[31] Nonetheless, looking more closely at their opinions, we can observe a distinct underlying continuity and an attempt to fit their old ideas into the new environment.

We know that the legal field from prewar to postwar times remained largely intact in terms of both its professional membership and practices. That is to say, most of the international lawyers previously mentioned kept their positions at university and even wielded more influence in the postwar than before, with the exception of Yasui Kaoru, who was forced to leave Tokyo University. This striking continuity was characteristic of all sectors in the legal field: judges and public prosecutors, for example, were not subject to a purge through the American Occupation authorities' order for the "Removal and Exclusion of Undesirable Personnel from Office."[32] Other evidence of this remarkable continuity was the fact that the first entrance examinations for civil servants allowed candidates to choose between the old or the new constitutional law as a subject, and most candidates chose the former.[33]

One significant break with the past for Japan's international lawyers was in their position vis-à-vis the state. By nature, their profession had been close to power and was routinely called upon to justify the nature of Japan's foreign policy before and during the war. After the defeat, those who had been mildly proactive (if sometimes subversive) moved as public intellectuals in the postwar period into the opposition and protested against the new course of the government. Those who had been relegated to inner exile, like Yokota Kisaburō, now became spokespersons for the new policies. In the postwar period, Yokota not only was a prolific public intellectual but also acted as official advisor to the Foreign Ministry and was eventually appointed president of the Japanese Supreme Court (1960–1966).

The most outspoken internationalist before the war, Yokota, finally saw that his moment had arrived. A most ardent advocate of the League of Nations during the interwar period, he now developed a frenetic publication and lecturing schedule, advocating Wilsonian ideals of international cooperation, peaceful interdependence, and "world government," the reality of which he already saw half realized with the founding of the United Nations. Moreover, he extolled Japan's absolute "renunciation of war" (Article 9) as a model for the whole world to follow. In the meantime, Japan's security would be guaranteed by the United Nations, which already, Yokota argued, possessed an effective system of collective security.[34] Of course, he was also one of the very few international lawyers who, in a flood of publications, supported the establishment of the IMTFE and its decisions (which was logically natural, as Yokota advised the Supreme Commander for the Allied Powers (SCAP) in the preparations and helped to translate the judicial decisions).[35]

With the start of the Korean War in the summer of 1950, Yokota finally had to compromise his idealistic stance. Five months after the outbreak of the war, Yokota published his first statement, which betrays the slightly hysterical tenor of the time:

> This is not a matter which concerns only [South] Korea. Japan, too, can meet the same fate. As long as Japan remains a democratic country, we cannot guarantee that we will be not invaded by a communist country in the same, unexpected way. Therefore, we have to carefully think about Japan's future and especially about its security. . . . Several options are possible, but the guarantee of our security by the United Nations seems the most appropriate.[36]

Even with war on the peninsula, Yokota's trust in the United Nations still seemed intact. However, the reality of the war and the political impasse within the Security Council soon forced him to reconsider. Through his voluminous mass of publications, we can observe how Yokota painfully adjusted his arguments and finally reached a conclusion that remained the core of Japan's security policy during the Cold War: that weapons kept for the purposes of self-defense and "policing" the nation did not contravene Article 9 of the Constitution. Nor did he envisage any objections to the contingency that Japan, within a "peaceful" security framework, might have to provide rear support to any country that would defend it.[37] For this, Yokota was, of course, bitterly criticized by the opposition as a "traitor." However, one could argue that, in a way, Yokota remained true to his internationalist convictions in that he continued to propagate the ideal of the supremacy of international organizations over the sovereignty of states, albeit very much modified and limited to the "free world" and geared toward the prime objective of Japan's security interests.

A similar turn can be observed among the international lawyers who had opposed the government's foreign policy. Tabata Shigejirō played a most prominent role in the so-called *Anpo* controversy, in which portions of the Japanese population rioted against the extension and reformulation of Japan's security alliance with the United States in 1960, though arguably more against Prime Minister Kishi Nobusuke's heavy-handed methods. Moreover, in his position as professor of international law, Tabata arguably became the most influential international lawyer in postwar Japan until the 1990s. Representative of his discipline, Tabata pursued a wholly different position from that of Yokota and consequently stood in opposition to the Japanese government. As part of an influential group of public intellectuals, the Peace Problems Symposium (*Heiwa mondai danwa-kai*), Tabata fervently demanded Japan's neutrality and opposed the partial peace treaty of 1951 (San Francisco Peace Treaty), as well as the security alliance with the United States. He lent his expertise in international law to the Forum and co-drafted the sections of its manifestos that declared Japan's absolute pacifism to the point of even refusing any Japanese contributions to United Nations' peacekeeping missions.[38]

Tabata reflected this turn to the opposition in his academic studies. In 1944, he had published a study on the "Changes in the Theory of State Equality" (*Kokka byōdō riron no tenkan*), in which he expounded the concept of "relative equality." However, as preparation for the new postwar international order under U.S. domination, in the summer of 1944, he switched tack and began a "new" study under a similar title "Changing Concepts of State Equality" (*Kokka byōdō kannen no tenkan*), which he published in 1946, with a preface dated November 1945.[39] In this new study, Tabata distanced himself from the idea of a "relative equality," as it privileged existing power imbalances and great powers, and began to emphasize the second element of state sovereignty, namely the aspect of autonomy, as a shield against unwanted intervention by the great powers. True to his characteristic methodology, Tabata sought to develop this new line of argumentation from an inquiry into the history of state equality and particularly focused on the writings of the Swiss lawyer Emerich de Vattel (1714–1767). Tabata interpreted Vattel's theory of sovereignty as the product of an enlightened (Swiss) civil society that had to defend its development as a modern nation-state against the interventions of absolutist powers, such as France.

> A nation that wanted to establish a state on the basis of Vattel's sovereignty of the people was constantly under the threat of intervention by absolutist great powers. Thus, in order to become a nation state as a result of the gradual evolution of the bourgeoisie, it had no option but to defend itself against these interventions.[40]

To contemporaries, the implied parallel with Japan's situation was transparent, not least because of the choice of Vattel. After all, Switzerland and Sweden were the envied examples of the "permanent neutrality" (*eisei chūritsu*) that Japan so desired. Moreover, in the politicized discourse of the day, the implied parallel of absolutist France pressuring small Switzerland as an analogy for postwar "imperialist" U.S. bullying little Japan was obvious. Tabata quite openly spelled out the presentist agenda of his scholarly pursuits:

> The great powers of Vattel's time of course do not exist any more. However, the emergence of enormous transnational monopoly capital and related great

powers are quite obvious. National sovereignty therefore still has its important function as a weapon of resistance [*teikō no buki*]. In this sense, the following words of [the Soviet international lawyer] Korovin addressed to the Academy of Social Sciences of the Communist Party are remarkable: "Sovereignty is a weapon in the struggle of the progressive-democratic forces against the reactionary-imperialistic ones. Under contemporary conditions sovereignty is destined to act as a legal barrier protecting against imperialistic encroachment and securing the existence of the most advanced social and state forms – socialist and those of a people's democracy; it is a guarantee of the liberation of the oppressed peoples in colonies and dependent territories from the imperialistic yoke."[41]

Tabata here clearly demonstrates the strategic translation of wartime ideas into the postwar period. Although Tabata's – and for that matter, most of his oppositional colleagues' – postwar stance seems pacifist and even idealistic, proclaiming Japan's peaceful neutrality in the face of the evolving Cold War, it is at the same a decidedly *realist* position. As Sakai Tetsuya rightly pointed out, the clichéd dichotomy of "Constitutional idealism" (or pacifism) and "Anpo realism," which has been used to characterize the positions of the early postwar period, are of very limited heuristic value. With closer inspection, these positions begin to blend and at a deeper level show considerable overlap.[42] In the case of Tabata, the ultimate goal of his writings, whether wartime or postwar, was to secure an exclusive geostrategic and normative sphere for Japan and fortify it against foreign intervention. The labels changed from "Co-Prosperity Sphere" to "permanent neutrality"; however, the intention never wavered, merely the size and scope of the protected sphere. Article 9 in a way can be called the ideological and functional successor to Japan's Monroe Doctrine, albeit on a much smaller scale.

This positioning explains the remarkable trans-war continuity of Tabata's thought, but also the distinctive ease with which many Japanese political thinkers seemed to accomplish the transition into the postwar order. Although the global situation changed radically, the political ideas at the center, namely Japan's autonomy, did not waver. This may also explain why, for all the outward tumult during the demonstrations against the U.S.–Japan Security Treaty (*Anpo sōdō*), there may have been a tacit understanding and even complicity between the "idealist" and "realist" factions that helped to smooth the transition into the post-*Anpo* period, when Japanese neutrality became a moot point. After all, unlike Switzerland, Japan *did* conclude a security alliance with the United States in 1960, and whatever possibly could have been done to secure Japan's political autonomy had been accomplished.

Ideas in their pure form are often best seen in radical cases that stand out as bizarre or freak "accidents" in their refusal to accommodate to the changes of time, that is, when intellectuals are out of sync with the revolution of political coordinates and less skillful in their adaption to it. No case demonstrates this better than that of Yasui Kaoru. As mentioned before, Yasui was the only international lawyer who was purged from office in the immediate postwar, and in 1948, he had to leave Tokyo University as an "undesired member of staff."[43] Ironically, Yasui was ousted on the grounds that he had helped to propagate Nazi thought in wartime Japan, although by that time he had firmly declared himself a committed Marxist-Leninist. However, Yasui somewhat caustically commented that, considering the "Red Purge," he might not have survived anyway.[44] Afterward, Yasui became a leading figure in the anti-nuclear movement of the 1950s, although with a decidedly anti-American, pro-Soviet edge. For this, he was honored with the International Lenin Peace Award (1958), the Peace Award of East Germany (1960), and the Friendship and Cooperation Award of Czechoslovakia (1967). However, in a last turn of radicalization, Yasui eventually committed himself to the North Korean ideology of *juche*, and in 1978 he was appointed director of the International Institute of the Juche Idea (*Chuche shisō kenkyūjo*) in Ikebukuro, Tokyo. In his own publications, Yasui expounded his understanding of *juche*.[45] On the surface, it might look like quite some distance from Carl Schmitt's *Großraum* theory in the 1940s to the North Korean *juche* ideology of the 1970s. However, as with the case of Tabata Shigejirō, from the perspective of the idea of autonomy, both concepts were but one logical step apart.

## Conclusion

Article 9 of Japan's postwar constitution functioned as a surprisingly generous receptacle to accommodate prewar concepts of political order and smoothly carry them over under different political and intellectual guises into the postwar order. By 1960, this transition had been completed and a tacit understanding established. Due to the nature of Japan's security status, problems were no longer negotiated in international law but were shifted completely to the level of constitutional law, with Article 9 as a conduit for old ideas on autonomy and a shield against new demands by the United States. Japanese international lawyers remained on the sidelines and limited themselves to critical commentary on these developments, no longer attempting to challenge them from a utopian perspective. The profession of international law lost the public's interest and withdrew into obscurity. However, one wonders whether this "inner exile" was not more or less self-imposed due to the lack of alternatives but also in silent complicity with the official position. After all, there was an underlying common consensus on both sides for achieving as much independence and non-involvement for Japan as was possible under the current security system. This remained so until the early 1990s, when Japan's security environment, again, began to change dramatically.

Returning to Takeuchi Yoshimi's complaint at the beginning of this chapter about the fickleness and superficiality of Japan's engagement with ideas and concepts, one could argue that at least in the field of foreign policy thought (*taigai shisō*) Takeuchi's verdict itself proves somewhat superficial. There was consistency and continuity between the wartime and postwar period, as the core ideas of "empire" were translated across the divide of defeat and sublimated into a new lexicon, a point that Kawashima Shin has also demonstrated, in Chapter 2, with the case of Taiwan remaining absent in mainstream Japanese discourse until very recently. This linearity was at the heart of even the most idealistic discourse in postwar Japan, which therefore had a strong realist dimension. It was probably less the successive alternation of ideas than the very fact of adaptation and compromise of the very *same* ideas that was the main target of Takeuchi's quixotic complaint in the postwar period.

## Notes

1  Takeuchi Yoshimi, "Kindai to wa nani ka – nihon to chūgoku no baai," in *Takeuchi Yoshimi zenshū* vol. 4, pp. 128–171. See the translation in *What Is Modernity? Writings of Takeuchi Yoshimi*, ed. Richard F. Calichman (New York: Columbia University Press, 2005).
2  Calichman, *What Is Modernity*, pp. 65–66.
3  Ibuse Masuji, *Lieutenant Lookeast and Other Stories* (Palo Alto, CA: Kodansha International, 1971).
4  On these new watchwords, see John Dower, "Peace and Democracy in Two Systems: External Policy and Internal Conflict," in *Postwar Japan as History*, ed. Andrew Gordon (Berkeley: University of California Press, 1993), pp. 3–33.
5  Ōnuma Yasuaki, *Tōkyō saiban, sensō sekinin, sengo sekinin* (Tōshindō, 2007), p. 128. (Unless otherwise noted, all Japanese books are published in Tokyo.)
6  Alan Watson, *Legal Transplants: An Approach to Comparative Law* (Charlottesville: University Press of Virginia, 1974).
7  For an overview of the history of international law in Japan, see *inter alia* Urs Matthias Zachmann, "Does Europe Include Japan? – European Normativity in Japanese Attitudes towards International Law, 1854–1945," *Rechtsgeschichte – Legal History* vol. 22 (2014): pp. 228–243; Urs Matthias Zachmann, *Völkerrechtsdenken und Außenpolitik in Japan, 1919–1960* (Baden-Baden: Nomos, 2013); Yanagihara Masaharu, "Japan," in *The Oxford Handbook of the History of International Law*, ed. Bardo Fassbender and Anne Peters (Oxford: Oxford University Press, 2012), pp. 475–499; Akashi Kinji, "Japan–Europe," in Fassbender and Peters, eds, *Oxford Handbook*, pp. 724–743; Sakai Tetsuya, *Kindai nihon no kokusai chitsujo-ron* (Iwanami, 2007); Michael Stolleis and Masaharu Yanagihara, eds., *East Asian and European Perspectives on International Law* (Baden-Baden: Nomos, 2004); Matsui Yoshirō, "The Social Science of International Law: Its Evolution in Japan," *The Japanese Annual of International Law* vol. 45 (2002): pp. 1–33; Ōnuma Yasuaki, "'Japanese International Law' in the Prewar Period – Perspectives on the Teaching and Research of International Law in Prewar Japan," *The Japanese Annual of International Law* vol. 29 (1986): pp. 23–47.
8  Ōnuma, "'Japanese International Law'," p. 41.
9  Yanagihara Masaharu, "Japan's Engagement with and Use of International Law: 1853–1945," in *Universality and Continuity in International Law*, ed. Thilo Marauhn and Heinhard Steiger (Den Haag: Eleven International Pub., 2011), p. 459ff.
10  Cf. Hilary Conroy, "Lessons from Japanese Internationalism," *Monumenta Nipponica* vol. 21, issue 3/4 (1966): pp. 334–345.
11  Cf. Thomas Burkman, *Japan and the League of Nations: Empire and World Order, 1914–1938* (Honolulu: University of Hawai'i Press, 2007), p. 44; Ian Nish, *Japanese Foreign Policy, 1869–1942: Kasumigaseki to Miyakezaka* (London: Routledge and Kegan Paul, 1977), p. 156.
12  Zachmann, *Völkerrechtsdenken und Außenpolitik*, pp. 121–157.
13  Urs Matthias Zachmann, "Taoka Ryōichi's Contribution to International Legal Studies in Pre-war Japan: With Special Reference to Questions of the Law of War," *Japanese Yearbook of International Law* vol. 57 (2014): pp. 144–149.

14 Yokota Kisaburō, *Watakushi no isshō* (Tōkyō shimbun shuppankyoku, 1976), pp. 119–122.
15 Yasui Kaoru, "Waga kokusai kankei no hōkai to sono saiken," *Kokka gakkai zasshi* vol. 47, issue 4 (April 1933): pp. 85–97.
16 See, for example, Tachi Sakutarō, "Jieiken gaisetsu," *Kokusaihō gaikō zasshi* vol. 31, issue 4 (April 1932): pp. 1–26.
17 Cf. Nish, *Japanese Foreign Policy*, p. 303.
18 Sakai Tetsuya, "Sengo gaikōron no keisei," in *Sensō, fukkō, hatten*, ed. Kitaoka Shin'ichi and Mikuriya Takashi (Tōkyō daigaku shuppankai, 2000), p. 125; Arima Manabu, "Dare ni mukatte kataru no ka: 'daitōa sensō' to shin chitsujo no gensetsu," in *'Teikoku' nihon no gakuchi, vol. 1: "Teikoku"hensei no keifu*, ed. Sakai Tetsuya (Iwanami, 2006), p. 269.
19 Cf. Takenaka Yoshihiko, "Kokusaihō-gakusha no 'sengo kōsō' – 'daitōa kokusai-hō' kara 'kokuren shinkō' e," in *Shūsen gaikō to sengo kōsō, kokusai seiji*, ed. Nihon kokusai seiji gakkai (Nihon kokusai seji gakkai, 1995), p. 71f.
20 For more details, see Zachmann, *Völkerrechtsdenken und Außenpolitik*, pp. 22–260; and Zachmann, *International Law in Japan, 1854–1960* (forthcoming).
21 E.A. Korovin, *Mezhdunarodnoe pravo perekhodnogo vremeni* (Moscow: Gosizdat, 1924), Japanese translation: *Kato-ki kokusaihō*, trans. Yonemura Shōichi (Kaizōsha, 1933).
22 Tabata Shigejirō, "Kokusaihō chitsujo no tagenteki kōsei," *Hōgaku ronsō* vol. 47, issue 3 (September 1942): pp. 383–302, vol. 48, issue 2 (January 1943): pp. 349–374, vol. 48, issue 6 (June 1943): pp. 908–934.
23 Yasui Kaoru, "Sobieto kokusaihō riron no tenkai – Pashukanisu no *sobieto kokusaihō gairon* no kentō," *Hōgaku kyōkai zasshi* vol. 55, issue 9 (1937): pp. 1708–1726.
24 Yasui Kaoru, *Ōshū kōiki kokusaihō no kiso rinen* (Yūhikaku, 1942).
25 Tabata Shigejirō, *Kokka byōdō riron no tenkan* (Nihon gaisei kyōkai, 1944).
26 Yokota, *Watakushi no isshō*, pp. 171f. The study was published as *Kokusai rengō no kenkyū* (Ginza shuppansha, 1947).
27 Ōuchi Hyōe, *Sekai shin tsūka seido no kenkyū* (Ginza shuppansha, 1947).
28 Taoka Ryōichi, *Kokusai rengō kenshō no kenkyū* (Yūhikaku, 1949); see also Zachmann, "Taoka Ryoichi's Contribution," pp. 160fn.
29 Tabata Shigejirō, *Kokusai shakai no atarashii nagare no naka de: ichi kokusaihō gakuto no kiseki* (Tōshindō, 1988), p. 60.
30 Yasui Kaoru, *Kokusai hōgaku to benshōhō* (Hōsei daigaku shuppankyoku, 1970), p. 147; *Minshū to heiwa: mirai o tsukuru mono* (Ōtsuki Shoten, 1955), p. 31.
31 This happened to Yokota Kisaburō, even among his students. The central library of Tokyo University houses a copy of Yokota's *Chōsen mondai to nihon no shōrai* (Keisō shobō, 1950), in which a student scribbled his bitter disappointment about Yokota, calling him a "chameleon."
32 Obata Kaoru, "Historical Functions of Monism with Primacy of International Law – A View Based on the Japanese Experience during the Early Period of the Allied Occupation," *The Japanese Annual of International Law* vol. 49 (2006), p. 13.
33 Ibid.
34 For example, Yokota Kisaburō, "Sekai kokka-ron," *Sekai* vol. 9 (September 1946), pp. 17–29; *Sensō no hōki* (Kokuritsu shoin, 1947).
35 Yokota, *Watakushi no isshō*, pp. 201–212. See also, for example, *Sensō hanzai-ron* (Yūhikaku, 1947).
36 Yokota, *Chōsen mondai*, p. 1.
37 Yokota Kisaburō, *Jieiken* (Yūhikaku, 1951), p. 201ff.
38 Tabata, *Kokusai shakai*, p. 165.
39 Tabata Shigejirō, *Kokka byōdō kannen no tenkan* (Osaka: Akita-ya, 1946).
40 Tabata Shigejirō, "Kokka shuken no gendai-teki igi," *Shisō* vol. 312 (June 1950), p. 346.

41 Tabata, "Kokka shuken," p. 349. Tabata quotes Korovin from Mintauts Chakste, "Soviet Concepts of the State, International Law and Sovereignty," *American Journal of International Law* vol. 43, issue 1 (January 1949), p. 31.
42 Sakai, *Kindai nihon*, p. 20.
43 Cf. his account of the dismissal process in Yasui, *Minshū to heiwa*. See also James Orr, "Yasui Kaoru: Citizen-Scholar in War and Peace," *Japan Forum* vol. 12, issue 1 (2000): pp. 1–14.
44 Yasui, *Minshū to heiwa*, p. 26.
45 E.g. Yasui Kaoru, "Chuche shisō no taishitsu to shakaikagaku no ninmu," in Yasui, *Minshū to heiwa*, pp. 115–154; or *Chōsen kakumei to ningen kaihō: chuche shisō no gugen* (Yūzankaku shuppan, 1970).

# 10 The transformation of a Manchukuo imperial bureaucrat to postwar supporter of the Yoshida Doctrine

## The case of Shiina Etsusaburō

*Kanda Yutaka*

Until now, the Liberal Democratic Party (LDP) has been in power in Japan, apart from two brief intervals, ever since it formed out of the Liberal Party and the Japan Democratic Party in 1955.[1] From the start, the LDP was composed of numerous groups, or factions, all basically conservative and all centered around powerful figures. Though the conservative factions underwent minor splits and mergers, they can be grouped into two camps, "mainstream" and "tributaries," the former originating with Yoshida Shigeru, a man who was several times prime minister in the postwar period, and the latter with, among many others, Kishi Nobusuke, a Manchukuo bureaucrat, wartime cabinet member, and postwar prime minister. While the "mainstream" factions promoted the foreign policy of the so-called Yoshida Doctrine, which argued for a limited military but pushed for economic development and security ties with the United States, the tributaries generally supported "autonomous diplomacy" (*jishu gaikō*), specifically through rearmament and amendment of the postwar pacifist constitution. Kishi and his followers, in particular, attached importance to Japan's national interests in a traditional sense (i.e. military power) and were "hawks" with strong anti-communist tendencies and pro-Taiwan lobbying proclivities.[2]

Historians often point to the legacy of the prewar era in the stances and preoccupations of Japan's leaders: Yoshida stressed trade and friendly relations with the United States and European nations after the war and yet retained some elements of an imperialist mindset. Kishi had been a leading reform bureaucrat in Manchukuo before the war, one of a group of men who wanted to transform the country along state-managed lines, and even after the war his policies could be characterized as statist. Kishi pushed for strong government control over industry and the creation of a strong Asian bloc with Japan at the center (often referred to as "Asianism" or *ajiashugi* in Japanese).[3] His attitudes often led to the suspicion among neighboring nations in the postwar period that he and members of his faction had residual imperial designs for the region.[4]

In contrast to the two postwar prime ministers, Yoshida and Kishi, Shiina Etsusaburō is perhaps a relatively minor figure in the larger history of twentieth-century Japan. A leading reform bureaucrat who had worked with Kishi before the war, someone who had promoted Japan's imperialist dream of building the puppet kingdom of Manchukuo on the Chinese continent and promoting totalitarian militarism, Shiina continued to have "Asianist" leanings after the war and committed himself to Kishi's nationalistic agendas. As Japan's economy took off in the 1960s, however, he gradually shifted his position toward an economy-centered policy line. His shift demonstrates the impact caused by the success of Japan's high growth, the so-called economic miracle, on Japanese postwar politics. The recent disclosure in 2012 of a collection of diaries and personal documents of Shiina sheds new light onto the intellectual and political development of this relatively minor figure.[5] Shiina "served Kishi like his shadow" before the war and was the "closest of Kishi's aides after the war"; indeed, he was an influential force in the Kishi faction.[6] On the basis of this new collection of Shiina's papers and other significant findings such as diplomatic documents and published secondary sources, this chapter discusses Shiina's life and investigates the shift that took place in his mindset, particularly from the 1960s onward. The fact that even Shiina, who was at the center of Japanese totalitarian militarism before the war, shifted his position to be a supporter of an economy-centered policy line, or the Yoshida Doctrine, demonstrates the broad changes in Japanese political circles that the economic miracle brought about during the 1960s.

## Influences and role models

Shiina was born Gotō Etsusaburō in 1898 in Iwate Prefecture, in northern Honshu, more than 400 kilometers north of Tokyo. He was adopted into the Shiina family, a common practice in Japan at the time. Gotō Shimpei, his uncle, was a premier statesman and cabinet minister in the Taisho and early Showa eras and was known for his support of the pan-Asianist movement and his achievements in colonial Taiwan and Manchuria. He had a proud reputation as a "pro-Russian" politician and indeed contributed to the establishment of diplomatic relations with the Soviet Union in 1925. Shiina's admiration for his uncle remained absolute throughout his life.[7]

Graduating from Tokyo Imperial University in 1923, Shiina began a career as a bureaucrat in the Ministry of Agriculture and Commerce. Between August 1932 and May 1933, he traveled in an official capacity to Europe and the United States. This was not long after the Japanese Kwantung Army had seized control of several provinces in north China in 1931 and turned them into the puppet state of Manchukuo. Shiina later recalled that during his trip he had to field frequent questions about how Japan could hope to govern such an enormous country. Shiina understood that the questions had an ironic implication that Japan would *not* be able to do such a thing, which made him determined to do everything in his power to help Japan succeed in its project.[8] For him, Japan's success in this new colonial venture was a matter of national prestige, demonstrating Japan's equality to the Western powers. On his return to Japan, Shiina found a kindred spirit in Kishi Nobusuke, who was then also serving in the same ministry and also passionately interested in the development of Manchukuo. Shiina later reported that Kishi considered the issue of

Manchukuo to be the single most important concern for Japan since its establishment as a nation. Kishi told him, "[W]e should tackle it [the government of Manchukuo] with courageous decisions and extraordinary efforts."[9] The time Kishi and Shiina met in the Ministry and started sharing their views on colonial development marked the beginning of an enduring partnership between the two men.

In 1933, Shiina was dispatched to Manchukuo as Chief of the Planning Section in the newly established Manchukuo government Ministry of Industrial Development. He held other important posts until his departure in 1939, among other things overseeing the 1935 Five Year Development Plan for Manchuria, which followed the principles of the first Soviet Five Year Plan. Kishi, who had come to Manchukuo in 1936 as the Director of the Bureau of General Affairs in the same ministry in the Manchukuo government, directed this Soviet-model plan. He had been appointed in response to a request by the Japanese Army, with which he had strong personal connections and who believed in a planned economy; Shiina had also put in a good word for him.[10] Shiina and Kishi were leading figures among a group of people who came to be known as the "reform bureaucrats" (*kakushin kanryō*), used to refer to men who had close connections to the military, who wanted a makeover of industry in Japan and its colonies along statist lines, and who supported creating a self-sufficient Asian bloc with Japan as the ruling power.

On his return to Japan from Manchukuo, Shiina lobbied for the appointment of Kishi as vice minister of Commerce and Industry, a post Kishi attained in 1939.[11] In 1941, with the formation of the Tōjō Cabinet, Kishi rose to the position of minister, and he appointed Shiina as his vice-minister. Together, Kishi and Shiina played a central role in the totalitarian control of the Japanese wartime economy.[12] In 1943, Shiina joined the newly established Ministry of Munitions as Director of the Bureau of General Mobilization, and at the end of the war he had risen to the rank of Vice-Minister of Munitions. He quit the Japanese bureaucracy in October 1945, when the wartime regime was finished.

On September 11, 1945, following Japan's surrender, the Occupation Army issued orders for the arrest of Kishi and other members of the former Japanese government. Kishi was put in Sugamo Prison in Tokyo as a Class A war criminal, though he was never indicted and was released in 1948. Probably because Shiina was less influential than Kishi, Shiina was not even arrested; he personally petitioned General Douglas MacArthur, the Supreme Commander for the Allied Powers (SCAP), for Kishi's release.[13] Shiina's personal records for this period show his concern for his former boss: for example, in his notebook for September 30, 1945, Shiina jotted down: "Clothes for Kishi."[14] On November 5, 1945, Shiina wrote: "Get *mikan* [mandarin oranges] for Kishi." This is followed by, "Sent first harvest of *mikan* to the man in jail."[15] Such records are indications of his devoted care and concern for Kishi's well-being.

## The postwar years

Shiina was elected to the Diet as representative of the Japan Democratic Party, of which Kishi was also a member, in the general elections of February 1955. In November of that year, the Japan Democratic Party and the Liberal Party combined to form the LDP, inaugurating a domination of government by this new party, often referred to as the "1955 system." This reign would last uninterrupted until 1993. After Ishibashi Tanzan quickly stepped down from the prime minister's seat due to illness, Kishi became leader of the LDP and prime minister in February 1957. Shiina was appointed chief cabinet secretary in 1958, surprisingly soon for a Diet member only in his second term. Kishi later wrote that he selected Shiina because he trusted him inherently, which was useful in those politically fraught times.[16] Kishi's desire for Japan to take a leading role in Asia found form in his passion to strengthen Japan's ties with Southeast Asian nations. It also underlay his desire to rework Japan's security relationship with the United States and for Japan to pursue a line of "autonomous diplomacy."[17] Kishi chose Shiina as his cabinet secretary because he viewed him as indispensable in achieving these goals. According to Kishi's memoir, Shiina was "a person who underst[ood] all about me, particularly when (because of the campaign against the U.S.–Japan Security Treaty), it was a busy and tense period and it was in phases when we could not spend a long time having discussions and deciding what to do."[18]

Kishi's proposals in 1957 for revamping the Security Treaty with the United States, in addition to his tactics to introduce a new bill to the Diet giving vast powers to the police, aroused the ire of the unions and fomented mass social unrest. People were reminded of the prewar authoritarian regime with Kishi's use of unilateral force, and mass riots ensued to demonstrate opposition, eventually pushing him out of office. The late 1950s and early 1960s were turbulent times when issues and conflicts surrounding Japan's relationship with the United States seemed to dominate the national mood. In 1960, Ikeda Hayato succeeded Kishi as prime minister. With Ikeda, a preoccupation with economic development was the policy of the day. One of the hallmarks of the Ikeda administration was its ambitious "income-doubling plan," that aimed for a twofold increase in the median income over ten years. Partly to differentiate himself from the autocratic, nationalistic Kishi, Ikeda advocated a politics of patience and reconciliation.

In the early 1960s, Shiina was still concerned with carving out a position for Japan as the leader of Asia. And he seems to have been somewhat convinced of the correctness of prewar political ideals. In a book he wrote in 1963, he explained that during the Meiji era, when Western imperialism threatened sovereign states and regions in Asia and Africa, only Japan had resisted.[19] He went on to describe the 1905 Russo-Japanese War as "the dawn of Asia and Africa" (*Ajia afurika no yoake*) and to assert, "[E]ven now, whether we like it or not, the goal of Japan must be the liberation, independence, co-existence and co-prosperity of the nations of Asia and Africa, because we and they share a common destiny."[20] Such rhetoric is redolent with the language of Japan's prewar imperial ideology. In that sense, Shiina argued, a high evaluation had to be made of Gotō Shimpei, who had demonstrated tremendous ability in the colonial administration of Taiwan and Manchuria as a top official of the Governor-General of Taiwan and the president of the South Manchuria Railway Company. Japanese imperialism had, Shiina argued, protected Asia against Western colonialism, and it had lauded Japan's "glorious imperialism" (*eikō no teikokushugi*) with "Gotō Shimpei as a pioneer of the liberation of Asia."[21] During his time in Manchukuo in the 1930s, Shiina explained, his goal had been to "develop Manchuria's underdeveloped resources and to light a fire in Asia," meaning to help develop the region. "Even after the war ended and all the Japanese forces were wiped out, all sorts of progress carried out under my direction had left their brilliant mark," Shiina wrote.[22] For Shiina, clearly, at this time at least, Japan's expansion into East Asia in the lead-up to the war, including the development of Manchuria, had left a positive legacy that was well worth recouping somehow in the postwar era.

When Ikeda became prime minister in 1960, Shiina was a less than a staunch supporter in private of Ikeda's economy-based policies. In his personal notes Shiina wrote:

> The business community has given up all hopes regarding the Ikeda Cabinet, which is treating the economy as its sole policy. And people in the financial world are furious: they consider that Ikeda's phrase "leave the economy to me" was characteristic of a lone businessman. Politicians should realize that their duties lie elsewhere. . . . [The amendment of] the Police Duties Execution Act has failed. The Restrictions of Demonstration Act has come to nothing. Now, the Prevention of Political Violence Bill is being rejected. Shouldn't these matters be what true politics is concerned with?"

At this point in the early 1960s, Ikeda's preoccupation with the economy was, in Shiina's view, causing the prime minister to neglect other urgent and important issues having to do with police powers and social control, which Shiina at this point regarded as essential. Shiina noted: "[Ikeda] has adopted a low profile in order to divert attention from these [errors of judgement.] [However,] now the public needs politics to be what politics should be. Strong politics (*tsuyoi seiji*) is what people long for."[23] By "strong politics" Shiina meant a policy that could control the state and keep the population secure. Here, Shiina can be seen continuing to support traditional strong-handed politics based on surveillance, supervision, suppression, and control – the politics that Kishi had been following.

## Foreign minister in an era of U.S.–Soviet détente

Even though Shiina was initially critical of Ikeda's policy, in July 1964 he was appointed as foreign minister in the new Ikeda administration, a position he retained even after Satō Eisaku took over as prime minister in November that year. Shiina's original appointment to the post was made largely for factional reasons within the LDP. However, his abilities in diplomacy, especially with regard to the Soviet Union, were undoubtedly a factor. A note in Shiina's memoirs showed that Maeo Shigesaburō, a member of the Ikeda faction, had recommended him (Shiina) as foreign minister. "I [Shiina] had put a word in his [Maeo's] ear that we had to soon start thinking about diplomacy with the Soviet Union. Clearly my word had had staying power."[24] For Shiina, working for improving Soviet-Japanese relations as Foreign Minister was a great chance to follow his role model, Gotō Shimpei, who had been known as a "pro-Russian" leader.

Shiina's interest in relations with the Soviet Union is evidenced in his personal records of this period. He made frequent references to trends in Soviet diplomacy, noting in 1964, for example, that at a conference of the Eastern bloc's Council for Economic Assistance (COMECON), a Soviet representative had emphasized the necessity of "improv[ing] relations between Japan and the Soviet Union, so that the Sea of Japan can be a 'sea of peace'."[25] In August, he noted that he met with Kawai Yoshinari, a former politician and the president of the Komatsu Industries Cooperation, who was interested in strengthening economic relations between Japan and the USSR, and discussed the development of "air routes with the Soviets" and a "Soviet–Japanese Chamber of Commerce and Industry."[26] Shiina played an all-important role in the development of Soviet–Japanese relations during the 1960s. The Soviet Union and Japan had agreed in 1956 to restore official diplomatic relations, but since then and until Shiina became foreign minister, progress had lagged. Shiina was the first postwar foreign minister to visit Moscow in February 1966, although Prime Minister Hatoyama Ichirō had taken an official trip in 1956. Despite the fact that the Northern Territories dispute remained unresolved and the Vietnam War was ongoing, Shiina signed the important Soviet–Japan civil aviation agreement that had been in the offing for the prior eight years and also agreed to extend a trade agreement with the USSR for another five years.

As these examples demonstrate, trade and diplomacy with the Soviet Union seem to have had a special importance for Shiina. In an interview at the end of the 1970s, Shina observed that "at that time [the 1960s], Japan leaned too much toward the United States." At this point he was clearly a supporter of the "autonomous diplomacy" that had been advocated by his mentor Kishi.[27] The abiding influence of his uncle, Gotō Shimpei, who had made significant contributions to prewar diplomacy toward Russia and the Soviet Union, seems also to have been a factor.[28] Shiina's prewar experience of engaging in the Soviet-modeled Five Year Plan in the development of Manchuria was also undoubtedly influential.[29] In other words, an interest in the Soviet Union was ingrained in the very fibers of his being. Shiina's emphasis on Soviet–Japanese relations was also based on his unique perception of the overall international environment. He regarded the structure of the Cold War in which hegemony was shared between two superpowers, the United States and the Soviet Union, as a stable one. He saw ongoing international peace as dependent on ensuring the pacific coexistence of these two superpowers and their respective blocs. In this sense, Japan's overtures to the Soviet Union represented proactive support of the "peaceful coexistence" of superpowers, a policy that would in the end ensure international peace. A personal memo from Shiina at the start of October 1964 reads:

Is the international situation rapidly changing, or fluid? It is fluid. Therefore, I conclude that at base things have not changed. Why? In the East, the Soviet Union and China cannot be reconciled perfectly, but both have a will to make

accords with each other. In the West, the United States and the United King-
dom are as before. France is not so cooperative, but there is no split in the Free
Camp. Therefore, despite some evidence of polarization between East and
West, this is a phenomenon that has certain limits.[30]

In other words, Shiina saw little likelihood of worsening relations between the East
and the West. He observed that both China and the Soviet Union had a willingness
for rapprochement. Here, it has to be said, he was incorrect because, as we now
know, the latter half of the 1960s saw a sharp deterioration in the relations between
these two countries.

While Shiina did not view the likelihood of friction between China and the
Soviet Union as particularly serious, he regarded these countries' foreign policies
as another matter. For him, the so-called peaceful coexistence policy of the Soviet
Union toward the United States was particularly important. In a memo written
when he was foreign minister, we find the following jottings:

Position of Japan

1    The status quo of Taiwan, as agreed in the Japan–U.S. Security Treaty,
     is necessary for maintaining the Japan–U.S. security alliance system.
2    As long as Communist China does not accept this [the status quo of
     Taiwan], . . . Sino-Japanese relations will see no change. We [can only]
     hope for a system of peaceful coexistence [to be established between
     Japan and China].
3    . . .
4    As long as the Soviet Union continues to adopt a peaceful coexistence
     policy [with the West], we will be aligned with them, though we should
     not forget that they are a Socialist nation.[31]

Shiina did not rule out Japan's alignment with the Soviet Union if the latter
adopted a peaceful coexistence policy. For a comfortable relationship with China,
on the other hand, which had not adopted a peaceful coexistence policy, a change
was required. Shiina made no bones about his bitter opposition to Mao's foreign
policy. Neither was Shiina of two minds about his own open-mindedness with
regard to the diplomacy of the Soviet Union.[32] According to a memorandum written in 1962, Shiina regarded China as "less advanced" than the Soviet Union. In
Chinese propaganda, he wrote, "[there is the idea that] the essence of imperialism
is colonization and the desire to conquer different nations, and that it is essential
to fight against this for liberation and independence. Compromise on this will
result in the abandonment of the revolution. The power of the people is superior
to that of nuclear weapons." Such arguments, he wrote, resemble those of the early
period of the Soviet Union, that is to say, the era of Stalin. To Shiina, this proved
that the Chinese Communist revolution was in a less advanced phase than the
Russian one. "This is why," he wrote, "the way that the Soviets think at the present
time is not possible for the Chinese to follow. The Russians way is beyond Chinese

understanding."[33] In his 1964 memorandum, Shiina also noted that "the [way of the] international mainstream is peaceful coexistence, while the [way of the] anti-mainstream is armed revolution."[34]

Shiina's eagerness to improve Soviet–Japanese relations tended to follow the current status of U.S.–Soviet détente. Indeed, as Foreign Minister Shiina explicitly indicated, the goal of Japanese diplomacy was to enable this détente. His intervention in the air routes agreement was out of a desire to help form a "bridge" between the two superpowers. As he wrote in his personal notes:

> What is the next goal of [Japan's] foreign policy?. . . (1) It is to connect the Soviet Union and the United States. To achieve this goal, it is desirable that we make every effort possible to mediate between the Americans and the Soviets in such fields as air routes. We could extend the [Moscow-]Tokyo route to New York.[35]

On July 6, 1966, one year after restoring diplomatic relations with South Korea, Shiina met U.S. State Secretary Dean Rusk in Tokyo and emphasized that he was sympathetic to the U.S. policy of détente with the Soviet Union. Shiina told Rusk that, with the resolution of the Cuban Missile Crisis, he was sure that "Moscow was sincerely interested in peaceful coexistence." Japan would continue to improve its relations with the Soviet Union, he said, and it was his conviction that Japan "should not lose sight of the overall direction of Japan–USSR relations" despite the abiding tension over the issue of the Northern Territories.[36]

Shiina was much less bullish about improving Sino-Japanese relations. It would in any case have been difficult for any Japanese foreign minister to approach China in the mid-1960s, since relations between the United States and China were then at an all-time low: the conflict in Vietnam was escalating, and the Chinese carried out their first nuclear weapons test in 1964. But Shiina's personal perception of China as a threat was a factor. Yoshida and Ikeda were skeptical of China's ability to develop nuclear weapons, but Shiina was confident by 1962 that China would succeed in the near future.[37] As a note in his personal diary in 1962 stated: "Acquisition of nuclear force by Communist China: Nuclear tests will be conducted in one or one-and-a-half years. By around 1970 they will have atomic bombs with a strike range of up to 1,500 kilometers." Secretary Rusk proposed to Ikeda that Japan should double its defense capability, yet Ikeda rejected this. "With this kind of attitude, what hope can there be for Japan's security and diplomatic capability?" he wrote.[38] Shiina clearly took an extremely dim view of Ikeda's apparent lack of understanding of the security threat posed by China.

In January 1964, France and China established official diplomatic relations. France was the second European nation to do so, after Britain in 1950. The Japanese public fully expected their government to follow France, and Ikeda expressed a positive attitude toward the idea of Japan doing so. However, Shiina wrote in his personal notes that the geographical differences between France and Japan made it impossible for Japan to have the same policy toward China.[39] "The behavior of a neighbor affects someone who lives close by on a daily basis," he wrote. "But for people who live at a distance, it is of no import at all."[40] After all, for the Japanese, Europe was far away, but China was right next door.

Nevertheless, Shiina was positive about the relaxation of tensions between the United States and China and improvement of Sino-Japanese relations as a long-term objective. Soon after the meeting with Rusk in July 1966, Shiina wrote in his personal memos:

> Separation of politics and economics,. . . Japan has no other way than this in order to enlighten Communist China. Other than [by using] the special type of people who belong to "friendly companies," [friendly firms designed by Communist China]; all people engaging in the trade of Communist China's necessary commodities are free people. Such frequent contact by free people is the only way to approach Communist China. Japan can receive the benefit of trade and enlighten Communist China at the same time. This was what I tried to persuade Secretary Rusk to accept. Soon after that, President Johnson issued a statement for rapprochement with Communist China. Was this [the result of] my successful persuasion?[41]

In a manner that resonates with Yoshida Shigeru's immediate postwar priorities, Shiina seems to have been keen to persuade American leaders of the value of "enlightening" China through trade. Economics could be separate from politics.[42] Perhaps somewhat naively, Shiina wondered whether a conversation he had with Rusk underlay President Johnson's statement announcing a rapprochement between the United States and China.

## Shiina and the realists

Shiina's views on China and the Soviet Union were in fact surprisingly in tune with those of several international affairs specialists in Japan who are often regarded as being in the "realist" camp. The most prominent of these specialists is the leading politics expert Nagai Yonosuke, who in a 1966 article voiced strong support for the idea of "peaceful coexistence" of the superpowers and insisted that Japan make an effort to create a "northern axis that would connect Moscow and Tokyo and Washington" through proactive diplomacy with the Soviet Union.[43] In the mid-1960s, a re-evaluation of Yoshida's political choices began in Japanese academic circles, which credited Yoshida with the achievement of Japan's economic miracle. Kōsaka Masataka, a professor of Kyoto University and the pioneer of the "realist" school who ushered in great changes in Japanese academia previously dominated by progressive idealists, described Yoshida as a man with "a merchant-like view of politics." Kōsaka was referring to Yoshida's determination to prioritize the economy as a basis of the nation's strength even at the cost of the military, which he saw as only of secondary importance, and to Yoshida's view that the economy was the key to Japan's international status. However, Kōsaka worried that the prioritization of the economy could lead to a "spiritual vacuum" (*seishinteki na shinkū*) in Japan. Yoshida's choice to prioritize the economy at all costs, he argued, was due to the "abnormality of the times."[44] Kōsaka was in effect arguing that the policy of prioritization of the economy over the military should not be continued indefinitely.

When Prime Minister Ikeda took on the mantle of the Yoshida policy of prioritizing the economy, Shiina was discomfited. However, by the mid-1960s, Shiina was changing his mind, faced with evidence of the effectiveness of the policy. A personal memo from this period attests:

> A have-not nation, Japan was greedy and fought a war. As a result, her territories (including her spheres of influence) shrank by more than a half. However, Japan has now been blessed with unprecedented prosperity and is the third industrialized nation in the world.
>
> Question: Should Japan now establish its own military force, in order to continue and defend this prosperity?[45]

After noting the complete failure of Japan's ambitions in the Pacific War, Shiina remarked on Japan's undeniable economic success. He then asked whether Japan should, in view of this success, try to shift its security strategy to autonomous defense. "For Japan to continue this situation of depending completely on the United States forever," continued Shiina in a way that seems to echo Kōsaka, "would not be right." But no realistic alternatives seem to exist. He notes the extremely powerful military capacity of the United States. "And yet this very thing," he mused, "seems to prevent [the United States] from conducting peaceful diplomacy." And it is as if an idea occurs to him: "Japan is the best candidate to do this." And in the next sentence: "The powers of persuasion that Japan possesses have universal currency." In this passage it seems to be dawning on Shiina that Japan can play a role in peace diplomacy that it is impossible for the United States, as a military power, to assume. At the end of this memo, Shiina added:

> There is an argument that Japan should develop a nuclear capacity to withstand Communist Chinese nuclear development. However, great changes are occurring on the world stage. We must wait patiently, and be confident that this era of prioritizing arms will gradually pass.[46]

Although Shiina objected to Japan's military dependence on the United States, he was clearly not a hawk in favor of immediate militarization or of Japan developing its own nuclear weapons capability. Despite dissatisfaction with the U.S.–Japan Security Treaty, he seems here to advocate a wait-and-see approach, with if anything an appreciation of the possibilities that non-militarization might offer. Shiina here sits halfway between the Kishi and the Yoshida lines.

## Securing a position in a multi-polarized world

The end of the 1960s saw the start of world transformations and realignments. In July 1971, after signs of thawing in the relationship between China and the United States, it was suddenly revealed that President Richard Nixon had accepted an invitation to visit the People's Republic of China (PRC). This event is remembered as the "Nixon Shock" in Japan: the Japanese government was informed only shortly before the announcement was made. Nevertheless, Shiina wrote in his notes: "The world stage has completely changed. The struggles among nations have ceased and we have entered an era of peaceful coexistence. . . . Even Communist China had no choice but to adjust to this."[47] Shiina interpreted the change in international situation as due to China's shift, motivated by a desire to exclude the "pro-Soviet faction" inside China. The United States was likewise normalizing relations with China in a bid to restrain the Soviet power. Shiina wrote:

> What lies behind the sudden U.S.–China rapprochement? Some people observe that there remains a strong-rooted pro-Soviet faction inside Communist China and it is thought that there is no other way than . . . U.S.–China cooperation in order to wipe them out. This is probably one significant reason. The United States sees through the power of Communist China, but they cannot trust the Soviet Union. I can see why a grand strategy of rapprochement would be born at this point in time.[48]

How should Japan respond to this triangular game being played between the United States, China, and the Soviet Union? Shiina thought that it should do more than simply follow American policy with regard to China and further promote the already improving relationship between itself and the Soviet Union. As Shiina wrote:

> We must adhere to the U.S.–Japan relationship, and we must proceed with determination according to the prearranged program with regard to our relationship with the Soviet Union. The economic partnership between our two nations, in particular, centering on the oil fields of Tyumen, should be developed with all speed.
>
> Until now, we had a partnership with the United States, with economic cooperation with the Soviet Union in second place. That was until today. From now on, we should stand in the middle, with the United States and China on the one hand, and the Soviet Union on the other . . . and keep friendship with each side. We should maintain a "free hand" and thereby secure a unique position.[49]

   Shiina, attempting to strike a balance between China and the Soviet Union, differed here from Tanaka Kakuei, the prime minister at the time. At this time, Shiina was deputy chief of the LDP. Tanaka's government tended to side with China in the Sino-Soviet tensions and moved rapidly toward normalizing diplomatic relations with China. Tanaka was after all one of Yoshida Shigeru's protégés, and he saw the main threat to Japan as the Soviet Union. An economic relationship with China was all-important for him.[50] However, Shiina had a sense of balance, and he wanted to avoid any excessively close alliance with the United States, China, or the Soviet Union. In this point, Shiina was still closer to Kishi than to Yoshida.[51]

Also, this focus on balance was in fact similar to the posture of Henry Kissinger in the Nixon administration, who advocated a "swing position" between China and the Soviet Union, utilizing their rivalry. Of course, we should also remember that Shiina greatly admired his own uncle, Gotō Shimpei, who, according to Kimura Hiroshi, "observed each and every movement of foreign powers" and formulated a diplomatic policy that accommodated "the changing situation of . . . every moment." Gotō was, as Kimura maintains, "a realist," and he regarded the idea of "balance of power" of utmost importance.[52]

## Japan, China, and Taiwan

Even though Shiina was mainly agnostic toward mainland China, he had personal connections with several Taiwanese leaders, including Chiang Kai-shek, in the 1970s.[53] However, this did not mean that he was against the PRC; nor did he want to see the PRC isolated from the international community. Shiina argued that Japan should be cautious about the PRC's designs on regions in Asia and Africa and any moves to form an anti-Soviet bloc and thus weaken the Japanese position, using the Sino-American rapprochement as leverage. But he was convinced that the integration of China into the international community was vital for long-lasting peace in Asia. And he thought it essential that China be admitted to the United Nations.

> Communist China will participate as a member of the United Nations and gradually wake up to the international reality. This should put an end to conflict and bring about a new harmony. Even though China formerly vilified the United States as its mortal enemy, and the United States is the acknowledged bastion of anti-Communism, everything seems now in place. This is especially the case as recently Communist China seems to have considerably changed. We should take the plunge now. While China eagerly hopes to join in the United Nations, if this comes about, it really might bring peace to Asia.[54]

At the same time, just before the normalization of relations with China in September 1972, which also signaled the end of diplomatic relations with Taiwan, Shiina visited Taiwan as the special envoy of Prime Minister Tanaka Kakuei. In his personal notes, Shiina made some observations that were decidedly pro-Taiwanese. In May 1971, five months before a resolution was moved in the UN for China to be represented by the PRC rather than Taiwan, Shiina strongly asserted that the status of international law of the Republic of China in Taiwan should be maintained. "It is said that the legal denomination of Taiwan has yet to be decided, but in fact it has been in existence. Any deficiencies in the law should be compensated in the form of ratification."[55] As suggested here, he even rejected the theory of Taiwan as a renegade province – a move that was used to deny the claim of the People's Republic of China that Taiwan was a part of its territory, even going so far as to insist that Taiwan be established as a territory of the Republic of China.

In short, Shiina viewed Taiwan not as a part of the PRC, nor even as an area of ambiguous possession, but clearly as Chiang Kai-shek's nation. This was a considerably pro-Taiwan stance.

In September 1972, on the very eve of the normalization of Sino-Japanese diplomatic relations, Shiina still hoped that diplomatic efforts would continue to maintain relations between Taiwan and Japan. On September 8, he wrote in his personal notes: "Economic relations between Japan and Taiwan have progressed from the level of a simple exchange of commodities to high level cooperation. . . . [This relationship] can neither be secured nor maintained without a political dimension. In addition, this [economic cooperation] has a great deal of importance."[56]

With the establishment of Sino-Japanese diplomatic relations, Shiina complained in his personal notes about the haste that had characterized the normalization process, and the lack of caution in handling the Taiwan problem. Right after the ceremony for signing the Japan–PRC joint communique, Ōhira Masayoshi, Tanaka Kakuei's foreign minister, spoke to the press about "the end" of the Peace Treaty with the Republic of China, which resulted in breaking official relations with Taiwan. Shiina wrote in 1974:

> Sino-Japanese normalization was accomplished in a mood of overwhelming acceptance shared by all opposition parties and most of the mass media (newspapers). . . . The fervent mood meant that we were being urged from every quarter just to "go ahead, go ahead." But clouds always follow the sunshine. What were we to do if some calamity happened? Additionally, there had not been sufficient time to examine what everyone knew was the most difficult issue, the Taiwan question. How was Japan going to overcome this question and remove the source of future disaster?[57]

Behind Shiina's preoccupation with Taiwanese–Japanese relations there had to have been a strong consciousness of Gotō Shimpei, Japan's early colonial administrator of Taiwan. However, Shiina later changed his stance, from wanting to show sensitivity to and somehow preserve the status of Taiwan to accepting the fact of the break in diplomatic relations. "Everyone was certainly extremely disappointed that . . . diplomatic relations were cut off [with Taiwan] for the sake of Sino-Japanese normalization. A 'shadow' fell over our two countries' relations," he noted. "Nevertheless, there was a historical backdrop. We had to admit to ourselves that there was no other way."[58] In the end, Shiina was willing to let go of the knotty Taiwan question and leave it as something to resolve in the future.

## Shiina and the realists, again

As we have seen, Shiina was keen to maintain a balance between relations with China and the Soviet Union. He was wary of turning exclusively to China for normalizing diplomatic relations. This approach was shared by leading foreign policy experts, such as Nagai Yonosuke and Kōsaka Masataka. In an article in

*Chūō kōron* (*Central Review*), Nagai argued, "First of all, Japan should approach the Soviet Union. Japan should proceed to signing a peace treaty [with the Soviet Union] as soon as possible, even if this means shelving, or completely abandoning, the issue of the Northern Territories."[59] At the same time, Nagai "strongly oppose[d] pursuing diplomacy only toward the Soviet Union" and insisted that Japan should improve Sino-Japanese relations in parallel. The idea behind this parallel approach was, as Nagai later made clear, to strengthen Japan's bargaining power with regard to both countries.[60] Like Shiina, Nagai was against normalizing relations only with China, which he regarded as overly hasty. "What is particularly difficult to understand," he argued in a book he wrote in 1973, "is why Japan has to rush to normalize relations with China as it is doing now."[61]

The end of the 1970s saw the basic building blocks come into place of what is now referred to as the Yoshida Doctrine, a combination of emphasis on economic growth, limited militarization, and a reliance on Japan–U.S. security ties. Shiina, who died in 1979, was no longer actively contributing to the discussion, but he had already relinquished his one-time adherence to the Kishi line. In a 1972 interview, Shiina gave an openly positive assessment of Ikeda's policy of putting the economy first. Ikeda, Shiina explained, "showed [the public] that when everybody, rich or poor, dresses in the same cloth, tailors will prosper." "The purchasing power of the people creates a prosperous national industry. This is the source of the so-called doubling of income." Ikeda's line of argument, Shiina said, "was correct, and well expressed." And again: "He [Ikeda] completely changed thinking on wealth." Such views suggest a massive transformation from his previous attitudes.

In a 1972 memo, Shiina noted that democracy and socialism both had similar objectives, *fukoku kyōhei* ("rich nation, strong army"), which had been adopted as a national slogan in Japan in the Meiji era. However, Shiina noted, the two components of this slogan are not necessarily dependent on each other. "A 'strong army,'" he mused, "does not necessarily lead to a 'rich nation,' and in fact may even bring about poverty; while a 'rich nation' is born from world peace and technological progress."[62] It seems that here too he considered militarization as more harmful than helpful for national development. Rather than militarization, Japan should be aiming to support peace and progress in technology. This is a marked change from the views Shiina had held both as a reform bureaucrat before the war and as a staunch supporter of Kishi.

In a 1969 speech draft, Shiina wrote that it was thanks to the U.S.–Japan Security Treaty, that "we were able to forget any insecurity and turmoil of state and society, and concentrate on building the economy. And this resulted in the establishment of present-day Japan." The Socialist Party and the Communist Party were "attempting to abolish the Security Treaty, spread social unrest and a sense of danger all over the nation, impede prosperity, and throttle the chances of this rapid economic development," he wrote. "In order to reject these irrational arguments and complete the reconstruction of Japan, we need to do our best to maintain our policy of high economic growth."[63] Shiina had by this time separated himself completely from Kishi's policies, the objectives of which were to end the prioritization of the economy, bring an end to military dependence on the United States, and realize autonomous defense by equipping Japan for war.

## Conclusion

In the 1930s Shiina Etsusaburō was a nationalist and a dedicated servant of the Japanese empire. He was a believer in the reformist ideology that connected totalitarian militarism and Asianism, and he was able to put his political beliefs into practice in the puppet state of Manchukuo. Japan's defeat in the Pacific War did not necessarily change these beliefs. In postwar Japan, working devotedly for his former colleague and boss Kishi, Shiina supported moves to bring an end to military dependence on the United States and to strengthen state control of power. However, during the 1960s, the evidence of the economic miracle influenced his thinking. Shiina grew skeptical of armament as a top priority for the nation and accepted the advantages offered by the U.S.–Japan Security Treaty. At the same time, something of a legacy from his prewar experiences could still be observed, as in, for example, the policy he advocated as foreign minister toward the Soviet Union in the mid-1960s. By the late 1970s, Shiina was an open advocate of the Yoshida Doctrine. From this time on, his policy positions were on the side of the conservative mainstream and the realists who praised Yoshida's economy-centered approach.

Two implications can be drawn from our tracing of Shiina's journey. First, the difference in basic policy between the "conservative mainstream" and the "conservative tributaries" within the LDP was less important in practice than it appeared. The economic miracle alleviated the latter group's obsession with high politics in the 1960s and revealed that the differences had much more to do with factional allegiance than unshakeable beliefs. The fact that even Shiina, who had started out as a cadre of the most hawkish faction of the conservative tributaries ended up supporting the mainstream line, demonstrates the breadth of the acceptance of an economy-centered approach among Japanese politicians and indeed the general populace by the 1960s.

Secondly, Japanese history researchers have focused on the period from the 1930s to the 1950s to debate the continuities and changes between the pre- and postwar periods. However, the 1950s and 1960s are equally revealing. Well into the 1950s, many politicians who had taken a leading role both before and during the war, such as Yoshida and Kishi, were still in positions of authority. It was only in the 1960s that truly postwar leaders, men such as Ikeda and Satō, who had started their political careers after 1945, rose to high positions. In this sense, Shiina's gradual shift from Kishi ideologue to supporter of Ikeda's economic plans in the 1960s is a reflection of the gradual and final erosion of a major prewar set of ideas in postwar Japan.

## Notes

1 These brief intervals were in 1993–1994 and 2009–2012, when the LDP was in opposition.

2 For biographies of Yoshida, see Kōsaka Masataka, *Saishō Yoshida Shigeru* (Chūō kōron, 1968); Inoki Masamichi, *Hyōden Yoshida Shigeru*, vol. 1–3 (Yomiuri shimbun, 1978, 1980, 1981); and John Dower, *Empire and Aftermath: Yoshida Shigeru and the Japanese Experience, 1878–1954* (Cambridge, MA: Harvard University Press, 1979). For Kishi's biography, see Hara Yoshihisa, *Kishi Nobusuke* (Iwanami shoten, 1995). (Unless otherwise noted, all Japanese books are published in Tokyo.)

3 See Hara, *Kishi Nobusuke*.

4 For a recent analysis of Kishi's diplomacy as "Asianism," see Kwon Yongseok, *Kishi seikenki no 'ajia gaikō': 'Taibei jishu' to 'Ajia shugi' no gyakusetsu* (Kokusai shoin, 2008).

5 The Shiina Etsusaburō Papers (*Shiina Etsusaburō kankei monjo*, hereafter SEP) are housed in the Modern Japanese Political History Materials Room (Kensei shiryōshitsu) in the National Diet Library, Tokyo.

6 Hara, *Kishi Nobusuke*, p. 56.

7 See "Shiina Etsusaburō hiroku 2," *Sandē mainichi* vol. 58, issue 48 (1979), pp. 78–81.

8 Nikkei Shimbun, ed., *Watashi no rirekisho*, 41 (Nikkei shimbun, 1970), p. 186.

9 Ibid., p. 187.

10 Hara, *Kishi Nobusuke*, p. 59; Nikkei, *Watashi no rirekisho*, p. 196. Shiina, "Shiina Etsusaburō hiroku 2," pp. 83–84.

11 Nikkei, *Watashi no rirekisho*, p. 200.

12 Ibid., p. 212.

13 Hara, *Kishi Nobusuke*, p. 56.

14 Shiina, "Diary entry, September 30, 1945," 16, SEP.

15 Shiina, "Diary entry, November 5, 1945," 18, SEP.

16 *Kiroku Shiina Etsusaburō* (KSE), vol. 1 (Shiina Etsusaburō tsuitōroku kankōkai, 1982), p. 351.

17 In addition to Kwon, *Kishi seikenki no "ajia gaikō,"* see Sakamoto Kazuya, *Nichibei dōmei no kizuna: ampo jōyaku to sōgōsei no mosaku* (Yūhikaku, 2000).

18 KSE, vol. 1, p. 351.

19 Shiina Etsusaburō, *Dōwa to seiji* (Tōyō seiji keizai kenkyūjo, 1963), p. 58.

20 Ibid.

21 Ibid., pp. 58–59.

22 Ibid., p. 94.

23 Shiina, "Diary entry, 1961," 34, SEP.

24 "Shiina Etsusaburō Hiroku 8," *Sandē mainichi* vol. 58, issue 55 (1979), p. 55.

25 Shiina, date unclear, probably September 22, "Desk Note, 1964," 89, SEP.

26 Shiina, date unclear, August 15, "Diary entry, 1964," 90, SEP.

27 "Shiina Etsusaburō Hiroku 8," p. 55.

28 Andō Toshihiro, "Kawashima ha o keishō, jimintō fuku sōsai ni," September 2, 2012, Nikkei shimbun Website, http://www.nikkei.com/article/DGXNASFK27016_X20C12A8000000/.

29 See Kanda Yutaka, *Reisen kōzō no henyō to nihon no taichū gaikō: futatsu no chitsujokan, 1960–1972* (Iwanami shoten, 2012), pp. 175–179.

30 Shiina, no date, probably 1 October, "Desk Note, 1964," 89, SEP.

31 Shiina, "Nihon no tachiba, gaishō jidai memo," 45, SEP.

32 Yoshida and his protégés, such as Ikeda, regarded the Soviet Union as Japan's main threat, rather than China. See Kanda, *Reisen kōzō*.

33 Shiina, "Diary entry, 1962," 36, SEP.

34 Shiina, no date, probably January 6, "Desk Note, 1964," 89, SEP.

35 Shiina, "Diary entry, 1966," 93, SEP.

36 "Memorandum of Conversation between Shiina Etsusaburo and Dean Rusk," July 6, 1966, Box 2386, Subject-Numeric File 1964–66, National Archives II at College Park, Maryland, USA.

37 Kanda, *Reisen kōzō*, pp. 86, 90–91.

38 Shiina, "Diary entry, 1962," 36, SEP.
39 "Ikeda sōri – Pompidū futsu shushō kaidanroku," April 7, 1964 In *Furansu yōjin hompō hōmon kankei: Joruju Pompidū shushō kankei*, A'406, Diplomatic Archives of the Ministry of Foreign Affairs of Japan. Kanda, *Reisen kōzō*, p. 144.
40 Shiina, no date, probably February 10, "Desk Note, 1964," 89, SEP.
41 Shiina, "Diary entry, 1961," 34, SEP.
42 For Yoshida's policy toward China, see Kanda, *Reisen kōzō*, pp. 10–11.
43 For details, see Kanda, *Reisen kōzō*.
44 Kōsaka, *Saishō Yoshida Shigeru*.
45 Shiina, "Diary entry, 1961," 34, SEP.
46 Ibid.
47 Shiina, "Note, 1971," 100, SEP.
48 Ibid.
49 Ibid.
50 Kanda, *Reisen kōzō*, Chapter 3, section 3; Wakatsuki Hidekazu, *Zenhōi gaikō no jidai: reisen henyōki no nihon to ajia, 1971–80 nen* (Nihon keizai hyōronsha, 2006), Chapter 1, section 3.
51 For Kishi's interest in approaching the Soviet Union at that time, see Kanda, *Reisen kōzō*, p. 338.
52 Kimura Hiroshi, "Kaisetsu," in *Gotō Shimpei to nichiro kankeishi: roshia gawa shin shiryō ni motozuku shin kenkai*, ed. Vassili Molodiakov (Fujiwara shoten, 2009), p. 254. Kimura calls Gotō the "Kissinger of Japan."
53 Hattori Ryūji, *Nitchū kokkō seijōka* (Chūō kōron shinsha, 2011), p. 95.
54 Shiina, "Note, 1971," 100, SEP.
55 No date but probably May 9, "Diary entry, 1971," 99, SEP.
56 Shiina, "Diary, 1970–1974," 104, SEP.
57 Shiina, "Nitchū koku kyōtei seiritsu ni tsuite," 61, SEP.
58 Shiina, "Nitchū seijōka ni kansuru oboegaki," 77, SEP.
59 Kawai Hidekazu, Nagai Yōnosuke, and Matsuo Fumio, "Nikuson hōchū go no seiji chizu," *Chūō kōron* vol. 87, issue 3 (1972), p. 117.
60 Nagai Yōnosuke, "Beichū shanhai komyunike no bunseki: igi to mondaiten," in *Beichū shanhai komyunike no bunseki, amerika kenkyū dai 4 kai gijiroku* (America kenkyūkai, 1972), pp. 27–28.
61 Nagai Yōnosuke, "Nitchū fukkō no 'kyō' to 'jitsu," in *Takyoku sekai no kōzō*, ed. Nagai Yōnosuke (Chūō kōron, 1973), p. 203.
62 Shiina, "Diary, 1970–1974," 104, SEP.
63 Shiina, "Jokun shukugakai de no aisatsu genkō (zenketsu)," 85, SEP. This is thought to have been written at the end of 1969.

# 11 North Korean nation building and Japanese imperialism

## People's nation, people's diplomacy, and Japanese technicians

*Park Jung Jin (translated
by Sherzod Muminov)*

The year 2015 marked seventy years since the end of World War Two. In the decades since its liberation from Japanese rule, the Korean Peninsula has been divided into two nation-states. In both Koreas, attempts have been made to settle the domestic social and political legacies of Japanese colonialism, and this division along historical lines of interpretation concerning those who "collaborated" or were pro-Japanese during this era remains a political tinderbox. In the ideological, cultural, and institutional realms it is clear that the decolonization of the Korean Peninsula remains incomplete. This same year, 2015, also commemorates a half-century of normalization of diplomatic relations between South Korea and Japan. Even so, however, it is not rare for friction to arise between these two nations even today. This occurs, for example, in the way that World War Two is commemorated in Japan or presented in history textbooks, how the meaning of Japan's colonial legacy on the Korean Peninsula is explained, and how the "comfort women" issue is understood. During the Cold War, these unresolved issues were largely shelved for a variety of political and strategic reasons, but they have emerged with renewed vigor in the decades since, along with further disputes about territorial boundaries. Relations between North Korea and Japan remain arguably even more distant, marked by distrust, fear, and outright disdain, and diplomatic relations have yet to be restored. Normalization talks between Japan and North Korea began in 1991, but progress has been slow and twice they have completely collapsed. Seventy years after the war's end, it would not be an exaggeration to say that half of the legacy of Japan's colonial past in the Korean Peninsula continues to haunt the present.

Several controversial issues have been at the base of the hostility in Japanese–North Korean relations and are mostly related to the migration and/or repatriation of residents, Korean and Japanese, in the immediate aftermath of the fall of Japan's empire. The official repatriation of Japanese residents from the northern half of the Korean Peninsula was carried out by December 1946, sixteen months later than the official repatriation of Japanese citizens from South Korea and was partly delayed because the North was initially occupied by the Soviet Union.[1] During this decade-long period of repatriation, hundreds of thousands of Japanese attempted to flee the northern half of the Korean Peninsula and return to Japan. Scholarly debates regarding the "problem of Japanese residents left behind" (*zanryū nihonjin mondai*) are rooted in the period between Japan's defeat in August 1945 and the establishment of North Korea as a nation in 1948. However, once North Korea was officially established, a large number of Japanese were also effectively interned in North Korean territory and could not exit. The fate of Japanese residents who remained in the northern regions of the Korean Peninsula following Japan's defeat in 1945 and the remains of the Japanese who died there continue to be a political source of friction in North Korea–Japan relations. We should also include the repatriation of approximately 93,000 ethnic Korean residents from Japan to North Korea from 1959 to the mid-1980s. In the 1980s, the vexing issues of migration and citizenship rose again when some of the Japanese women who had married Korean men and then gone with them to North Korea after the war (*Nihonjin-zuma*, or "Japanese wives"), and other family members expressed the desire to leave North Korea and return to Japan.[2] The final and perhaps most painful issue is the abduction of Japanese citizens by North Korea both from within Japan and on foreign territory, referred to as *rachi mondai*, the "abduction issue." These Japanese were secretly smuggled to North Korea and employed against their will sometimes as teachers and trainers. Rumors of such abductions had persisted in Japan since the 1970s, but after increasing Japanese media attention in the 1990s, the issue reemerged with explosive force when the abductions were acknowledged by North Korean leader Kim Jong Il in a summit held with the aim of normalizing relations with Japan in 2002.[3]

In this chapter I will focus on the issues that developed concerning the "Japanese left behind" – the problems of the Japanese who resided in North Korea after the war, and more specifically on the fate of Japanese engineers and technicians who remained in North Korea after the establishment of the new nation-state. In recent years, new studies about the repatriation of Japanese citizens from the Korean Peninsula at the time of the establishment of the socialist system in North Korea have emerged, but I will start with an overview of North Korea's establishment as a nation-state.[4] Parallel themes concerning similar developments in South Korea and Taiwan are discussed in Katō Kiyofumi's Chapter 1 and Kawashima Shin's Chapter 2 in this volume. I will then investigate some of the roots of contemporary "historical issues" between Japan and North Korea, the period between the founding of North Korea and the start of the Korean War in the summer of 1950, when efforts at nation building more fully emerged. I also aim to explore North Korea's so-called "people's diplomacy" vis-à-vis Japan during this era, and Japan's response to this diplomacy in the period following the Korean War and during the Cold War. Some striking similarities and divergences will emerge from the points that Erik Esselstrom makes in his discussion in Chapter 12 concerning how China tried to use a similar form of unofficial diplomacy in its tentative steps toward renewing political relations with Japan in the early postwar.

## Decolonization and the construction of "a people's nation" in North Korea

One of the top priorities for those who soon came to identify as North Koreans in the process of decolonizing their territory in the early postwar period concerned how to appropriate and exploit the industrial infrastructure left by imperial Japan. Following the end of the war, the ruling agencies of the Japanese empire were gradually replaced by local self-rule organizations in the form of "people's committees" (*inminiwonwhe*), but this did not obviate the need for technical talent. Approximately 700,000 Japanese citizens remained on the Korean Peninsula at the moment of surrender, with almost a third (240,000) resident in the territory that would later form North Korea. We should remember that prior to the end of the war and the imposition of the 38th parallel as the dividing line between Soviet managed "North Korea" and the American controlled "South," the peninsula was not divided: it was a holistic colonial entity. Only with the defeat of Japan's empire and the start of the competition for power between the United States and the USSR, who vied over shared management of the end of Japan's empire, did Korea get caught up and split. The total value of Japanese assets – individual, corporate, or government-owned – in both sectors of Korea was roughly equal in 1945: US$2.97 billion in northern Korea and US$2.3 billion in southern Korea.[5] One of the reasons for this mass of Japanese investment was the role given to northern Korea by the Japanese colonial rulers as the heavy and chemical industries base for Japan's continental expansion in the 1930s. Katō Kiyofumi also discusses this Soviet interest in this region in Chapter 1, while Sherzod Muminov illuminates Soviet maneuvers and their reasons for moving in and out quickly in Manchuria and the surrounding areas in Chapter 8. Ham Gyon province in particular was developed as a model industrial center of Northeast Asia, where leading Japanese industrial conglomerates (such as Mitsubishi Heavy Industries, Sumitomo Metal Mining, and others) invested funds and brought in highly skilled experts for developing the chemical industry, coal mining, and the manufacturing of such diverse products as steel, cement, and paper.[6] Consequently, as decolonization unraveled in northern Korea after the war, along with the simultaneous establishment of "people's committees," these colonial industrial plants were taken over by "self-management movements," in what was essentially a crude form of nationalization of industry that took place even before North Korea was established as a nation-state.[7]

The occupation of the North Korean territory by the Soviet Army accelerated these transformations. On September 14, 1945, the Soviet Army issued its "Guidelines for the Establishment of a People's Government," summarizing its occupation policy of the peninsula. "On the question of Japanese-owned factories," the document stipulated, "all Japanese agency should be eradicated and the management of factories should be transferred solely to the workers and engineers of North Korea."[8] In reality, however, much of the authority in managing these factories was delegated to people's committees. As a result, power gradually started to concentrate in the hands of the Marxist-oriented Korean political elite, with the people's committees at the center. At the same time, the influence of nationalist rightist groups was gradually eliminated. This was the reverse of the situation in South Korea, where the occupation by the U.S. Army brought an end to people's committees and enabled the rightist groups' ascendance.[9] Thus, not only was the Korean Peninsula split geographically, but also fundamentally different processes of decolonization were occurring north and south of the 38th parallel. Following the stationing of over 125,000 Soviet Army troops in North Korea starting from August 1945, people's committees in each locality established "committees for managing enemy-owned industries," which then energetically started appropriating Japanese-owned factories, enterprises, buildings and other assets.[10] These Soviet Army measures put a stamp of approval on the push toward North Korean self-management that was already under way. However, this in itself did not entail an immediate and complete transfer of authority from the Soviets to the people's committees.

Unlike the U.S. Army in South Korea, the Soviet Army had advanced into the north of the peninsula in the face of resistance from the Japanese Army, for example in Chongjin where armed conflict broke out. Consequently, Japanese assets became the "war spoils" of the Soviet Army, while the Japanese servicemen and civilians were held as prisoners of war in Soviet hands. In late September 1945, when the Soviet occupation began, the Soviet Army initiated the transport of a total of 66,000 Japanese former servicemen to the USSR and Soviet-controlled territories.[11] In addition, the Soviets removed raw materials and equipment that were relatively hard to transport, not to mention munitions and products of heavy and chemical industries, from North Korea to the USSR. The labor force and assets acquired in this way were used in the postwar reconstruction of the Soviet Union, where the economy lay in tatters after the Soviet–German war.[12]

In actuality, a good half of all industrial plants and factories in occupied North Korea was not functioning at the time of Japan's downfall. Many of the factories had been put out of action by the retreating Japanese, following orders from the Imperial Japanese Army. Many of the heavy and chemical industry plants scattered across the northern Korean territory had been involved in the production of munitions for Japan's imperial armed forces, and the Japanese military were ordered to destroy as many of them as they could as they retreated. The Japanese also flooded twenty-five coalmines, put out of order nineteen hydroelectric plants, and left the whole transport infrastructure of the North in a paralyzed state.[13] Disruption to a large number of industrial plants and enterprises in some ways was also inevitable due to the absence of skilled managers and the mass demobilization of Korean personnel to their hometowns in the countryside.[14]

Despite the stipulation in the Soviet occupation guidelines that "all Japanese agency [must] be eradicated," in a manner that was consistent throughout the crumbling Japanese empire, the Soviet occupation needed to allow for contingencies, so the "temporary utilization of Japanese technical skills where necessary" was permitted.[15] Consequently, while most Japanese residents in North Korea were taken to internment camps where they were subjected to forced labor, either in the USSR or in Soviet-occupied territories, Japanese technicians received special treatment. As a result, 2,158 registered Japanese engineers and technicians remained in Pyongyang as of January 20, 1946. Of these, 269 were graduates of high schools or vocational schools, 639 had a middle school education, 629 were skilled laborers, and 627 engaged in public engineering works. In 1946, the total number of Japanese residents in northern Korean territory stood at around 209,000 people, a percentage that was not that far off from what available statistics account for in Taiwan given the difference in population and land mass.[16]

In North Korea, once a sufficient number of Japanese technicians had been registered, the Soviet Army turned its attention away from the mass of the Japanese population, who then took the opportunity to flee. A mass exodus of Japanese residents then began, with the Soviet Army's tacit permission, because when their mission in northern Korea was accomplished, the Soviets suddenly lost interest in Japanese residents as either a political trump card or labor force. In February 1946, a central political organ, the North Korean Temporary People's Committee (NKTPC), was established, with Kim Il-sung as its first chairman. This meant that the Soviets, who were planning to withdraw from northeast Asia by May 1946, had achieved their goal of establishing a pro-USSR government in northern Korea. Not coincidentally, this was precisely the time when the Soviet Union finally conveyed to the General Headquarters of the Supreme Commander for the Allied Powers (SCAP) its intention to officially repatriate all Japanese residents from the north of the peninsula. In late October the Soviet Army approved a protocol announcing the official transfer of all Japanese-owned industrial facilities seized by the Soviets to the NKTPC.[17]

The NKTPC under the leadership of Kim Il-sung regarded these Japanese assets as "priority industries" and ordered their nationalization. This process was part of the NKTPC's wider Anti-Imperialist and Anti-Feudalist Revolution campaign. The term "anti-imperialist" was in fact key to the NKTPC's program, and eradicating the "vestiges of Japanese imperialism" was avowedly its foremost goal.[18] This anti-imperialist rhetoric was surprising considering that the threat of Japanese imperialism had all but disappeared by this time. Particularly interesting was the fact that the first chairman, Kim Il-sung, made "rooting out the pro-Japanese groups" and "cleansing North Korea of the vestiges of the Japanese Empire" the top priority of his anti-imperialist campaign in his "Provisions for the Establishment of the NKTPC."[19] This was in fact a conscious and strategic move on the part of Kim Il-sung, who at the founding of the Democratic People's Republic of Korea (DPRK, or North Korea) on September 9, 1948 had become its first leader and ruled the country until his death in 1994. Along with setting up new government institutions, Kim and his administration sought to rally support for the NKTPC by bringing the "struggle against the vestiges of the Empire" to the forefront of people's minds.

Kim chose this strategy of emphasizing nationalistic emotion rather than class struggle with the conscious aim of achieving a united national front. The origins of the strategy lay in the theory of the "people's nation," a political philosophy that had originated in the Soviet Union and the communist elements of Eastern Europe during the 1930s. The "people's nation" was a form of government that advocated the achievement of socialism without establishing the dictatorship of the prole-tariat; rather, it prioritized the creation of a united people's front that would lay the foundations of the "people's nation." One feature of this model lay in its moderate stance toward capitalism, as well as its flexible class policies. The construction of a people's nation in North Korea was already under way through the people's committees that were established nationwide with support from the Soviet Army. North Korea's leftist forces considered the "people's nation" a transitional system for the post-imperial development of the country.[20]

The task of removing colonial-era collaborators in North Korea was realized largely through land reform. This process started when the right to confiscate land that had been owned by collaborators of the Japanese empire, who were seen as "traitors of the people," was passed into law in March 1946, and it ran in parallel with the nationalization of important industrial enterprises. Under the slogan of "anti-feudalism," land reform primarily targeted the class of feudal landowners. The terms "enemies of the people" and "Japanese stooges" were used with basi-cally the same meaning during the early stages of the reform, but the former term gradually expanded, eventually providing the basis to attack any nationalist and right-wing groups that opposed the path of building a people's nation. Meanwhile the term "Japanese stooges" continued to be used in its original sense to refer to collaborators or people who had been associated with pro-Japanese groups in the past.[21] Many of those so stigmatized were passed over in selection for jobs in the new bureaucracy, resulting in a very inadequately qualified new civil servant class in North Korea. Nonetheless, the "traitors" still had to be subsumed into the body politic if the new nation was to be built.

## The rise and fall of Japanese engineers in North Korea

A typical example of a bureaucrat with a pro-Japanese background who was none-theless reabsorbed back into the body politic and who joined North Korea's new civil service was the electrical engineer Lee Mun-han. Lee, the son of a large landowner, became the DPRK's first minister of industry in February 1946.[22] This recruitment policy of making use of some technically qualified people despite their past association with the colonial regime was also extended to Japanese techni-cians. In August 1946, Chairman Kim Il-sung publicized the Decree on Securing the Services of Technicians.[23] Lee Mun-han followed this with an announcement of detailed regulations to each provincial personnel department to ensure that any Japanese technicians who remained would receive housing, living wages, and daily necessities.[24] As well as being an attempt to stem the exodus of Japanese specialists to South Korea, this announcement served to encourage desperately needed Japanese technicians to stay longer in North Korea and was clearly adopted with an eye to the technicians' desire to return home. Some Japanese technicians considered it safer to wait until the start of the official repatriation process than to attempt a dangerous escape on their own. Heeding the North Korean authorities' encouragement to stay on, they established in October 1946 a "Japanese Division" of the North Korean Union of Industrial and Technical Workers. The Japanese

Division soon started negotiations with the Soviet Army and regional people's committees on the fulfillment of the government promises to the Japanese technicians regarding wages and social benefits.[25]

On November 15, 1946, according to the Japanese Division register, 868 Japanese engineers and 2,095 family members were resident in North Korea. Other Japanese civilians – technicians not affiliated with the military and their families, prisoners serving sentences, housekeepers, other personnel employed by the Soviet Army – numbered over 8,000. All of these people were placed under the jurisdiction of the Japanese Division, which thus formed the core of the Japanese community in North Korea.[26] The North Korean government issued the Japanese community members with citizenship certificates, and, although they did not have voting rights, Japanese technicians were exempt from paying taxes. Their salaries ranged from 3,500 to 5,000 Korean won, which at the time was in the range of (or even higher than) Chairman Kim Il-sung's wage of 4,000 won.[27]

Just over a month later, on December 19, 1946, the "[a]greement concerning repatriation of Japanese prisoners of war and civilians from the USSR and from territories under Soviet control, as well as Korean nationals from Japan to Soviet-occupied North Korea," was signed between the United States and the Soviet Union, and the official repatriation of Japanese residents from Soviet-occupied northern Korea began.[28] In response, the North Korean authorities intensified their efforts to persuade the Japanese technicians to stay and to continue to train North Koreans. A new General Union of Industrial Workers and Technicians was established, and a provision of special monetary support was arranged for the education of the family members of these Japanese specialists. The Japanese technicians' salaries were raised yet again and reached unprecedented amounts. For example, Japanese technicians in Ham Gyon Province received a monthly salary of up to 6,000 won, which was six times the average wage of a Korean laborer in Pyongyang.[29] In a letter of gratitude sent to Kim Il-sung, the Japanese specialists from Pyongyang wrote, "We, the Japanese who are contributing to North Korea's reconstruction as a truly democratic nation . . . express our gratefulness to you."[30] These Japanese technicians played an enormous part in North Korea's reconstruction. Among their significant contributions was the rebuilding of North Korea's largest steel plant, Hwanghae Steelworks, and the Hungnam People's Factory. The achievements of some of the Japanese specialists were acknowledged with the North Korea's prestigious award of the honorary title Hero of Labor, which included a medal in the shape of a golden star.

However, on December 14, 1947, when the North Korean General Union of Industrial Workers and Technicians decided to dissolve the Japanese Division, treatment of outsiders suddenly changed.[31] In early 1948, the Japanese communities in Pyongyang and Hungnam started to come under the close scrutiny of the North Korean authorities. As a result, five Japanese engineers in Pyongyang and one in Hungnam were arrested and sent to the Soviet Union, charged with involvement in "counter-revolutionary activities." This was the result of numerous class-related suppression measures that swept through North Korea in 1947–1948, after the announcement of the launch of the Getting Rid of Landowners campaign. This, in turn, reflected a fast spreading international communist front that emphasized class struggle rather than cooperation in the wake of the Soviet-sponsored 1948 attack of the Communist Information Bureau on the "capitalist conspiracy" allegedly led by then Yugoslav leader Josip Tito. As a result of these externally triggered stimuli, the concepts of "people's nation" and "people's democracy" had to be reinterpreted to emphasize class struggle. Amid these shifts, slogans such as "Down with the Vestiges of Japanese Imperialism" and "Rooting out the Japanese Stooges" made a comeback, and the character of the North Korean nation building experiment underwent a complete transformation.[32]

The change in the political environment caused by the outbreak of the Korean War in June 1950 further deepened the travails of the Japanese technicians in North Korea. The already scarce resources of the young North Korean state were diverted to the war effort, and the issue of the former colonies' demands vis-à-vis Japan was postponed indefinitely, until after the planned reunification. Within North Korea, class struggle reached ominous dimensions. Campaigns such as "Purge the Land from the Dregs of the Japanese Empire" raged on until the very eve of the Korean War. In such circumstances, the Japanese in North Korea turned from "residents" by choice into "internees" by force.[33] For North Korea, the Korean War also offered the means to expand on its vision of the future, founded on anti-imperialist premises, to the whole of the peninsula.

As the war dragged on, the Japanese technicians who were now essentially stuck in North Korea increasingly came under suspicion as spies; many met with severe sentences as punishment for suspected crimes and were sent to internment camps. The North Korean leadership feared that if any Japanese engineers were repatriated, they would provide the U.S. intelligence with secret information about North Korea's industrial and military capabilities. This might not have been an unfounded fear as those Japanese technicians who did make it back to Japan via South Korea were without exception interrogated by the U.S. Military Intelligence (General Staff 2).[34] The concentrated U.S. Air Force attacks on the industrial and military targets in North Korea were carried out based on the extensive reports provided by such repatriated Japanese technicians.

## People's diplomacy: the 1954 Telegram

On July 27, 1953, an armistice concluded between North and South Korea brought the Korean War to a close. On January 6, 1954, the Japanese Red Cross Society sent a telegram to its North Korean counterpart via the International Committee of the Red Cross (ICRC), and this came to be known as the 1954 Telegram.[35] In the missive, Japanese Chairman Shimazu Tadatsugu expressed "the grave concern" of the Japanese Red Cross Society and family associations "over the safety of Japanese citizens remaining in the postwar DPRK" and "an earnest desire that these Japanese be repatriated as soon as possible."[36] According to SCAP's "Statistical Table of Repatriation of Japanese Citizens," which summarized the official repatriation figures, no Japanese citizens were remaining in North Korea at the time of the 1954 Telegram.[37] An investigation carried out by the Association of Impatiently

Waiting Hearts (*Machiwabiru kokoro no kai*), a citizen's group in Japan formed during the Korean War by the family members of Japanese citizens who had stayed in North Korea, however, disputed this result.[38] The Japanese Foreign Ministry compiled its own "Repatriation White Paper" in July 1953 and claimed that "2,408 [Japanese citizens were still] residing in North Korea."[39]

The 1954 Telegram was not necessarily sent only due to the wishes of the Association of Impatiently Waiting Hearts. A look at its contents reveals a promise that if the North Korean government agreed to release the Japanese residents who remained in North Korea, "the Japanese Red Cross Society will support the repatriation of the citizens of your country who are currently residing in Japan and who wish to return to North Korea."[40] It is estimated that at the time of Japan's defeat, more than 2 million ethnic Koreans were resident in Japan, but only 4 percent of them originally came from North Korea.[41] Many of them had returned voluntarily to their homeland in the spring of 1946, and the number of those sent to North Korea from Japan during the official repatriation of the following year was 351 people.[42] This was an insignificant number when we consider that the community of Korean residents in Japan (*Zainichi* Koreans) numbered approximately 600,000. Nevertheless, the offer was to return "Koreans" to North Korea. Behind the Japanese Red Cross Society's 1954 offer to repatriate the *Zainichi* Koreans, in other words, was a subtly expressed intention to expel all Korean residents from Japan.

In 1951, Japan had started normalization talks with South Korea with the United States acting as mediator. At the time, Japan was on hostile terms with North Korea; an alliance with the United States during the Korean War had put Japan on the opposite side of the Cold War divide from the DPRK. Yet the Japanese government's real opponent in the war was not the North Korean government nor the North Korean Army. Rather, it was a *Zainichi* Korean militant group, Guards of the Motherland (*Sokoku bōeitai*), based in Japan. This organization was involved in violent acts aiming to sabotage Japan's rear support for the United States during the Korean War. The Guards of the Motherland was established by the *Zainichi* Koreans' United People's Front (*Minsen*), which operated under instructions from the Japan Communist Party (JCP). In other words, the JCP and the North Korea's Workers' Party had formed a united front during the Korean War within Japan. The *Zainichi* Korean community had traditionally held strong leftist political views, and those Korean residents who organized themselves into *Minsen* groups had never made a secret of their support for North Korea and Kim Il-sung.[43] That the Japanese government considered North Korea as a potential destination for repatriating inconvenient domestic Koreans – many of whom originated from South Korea – was thus a direct outgrowth of the Korean War.

The 1954 Telegram can be seen as an attempt on the part of the Japanese government to settle once and for all the *Zainichi* Korean issue by means of an unofficial move that could avoid or at least skirt official channels.[44] For the Japanese government, the *Zainichi* community was both a threat to Japan's public order and a constant reminder of its failed empire. Many of the *Zainichi* Koreans were recipients of welfare payments and were also seen as a burden on the state's finances.[45]

It is possible that the 1954 Telegram was a feeler put out by the Japanese government to North Korea to test the possibility of repatriating *Zainichi* Koreans as a policy solution. The Japanese government could not seriously consider the mass repatriation of *Zainichi* Koreans at this time, simply because such a move would threaten the nascent relations developing with South Korea and might well be seen as outright opposition to U.S. intentions in the region.

North Korea's first clear response to the 1954 Telegram came more than a year later at the Asia–Africa Conference that opened in Bandung, Indonesia, in April 1955.[46] The Japanese delegation at the conference largely consisted of members of the Japanese Peace Committee, with some representatives from the Japan–Korea Association (*Nitchō kyōkai*), such as Kuruma Takudō and Hatanaka Masaharu. The North Korean delegation informed the Japanese that "the North Korean government is currently preparing to repatriate the Japanese residents."[47] A month after the conference, a ten-member delegation led by Hatanaka Masaharu travelled to Pyongyang by train via China.[48] The message conveyed to the Japanese Delegation by the North Korean side was made public by a radio broadcast from Pyongyang to Japan on May 23. In the transmission, Hatanaka stated: "Currently, there are about 210 Japanese residents in North Korea . . . of them, about 20 to 25 Japanese have expressed their willingness to return to Japan."[49] This positive response to the 1954 Telegram from North Korea marked a fundamental transformation in the nation's policy toward Japan.

On February 25, 1955, North Korea's Foreign Minister Nam Il announced the "Declaration on the DPRK's Relations with Japan." In his remarks, Nam Il made clear that "preparations are under way for concrete discussions with the Japanese government on various issues related to the establishment of diplomatic relations, as well as trade negotiations and cultural relations."[50] The Nam Il Declaration championed the principle of "peaceful coexistence" with Japan and was fundamentally similar to the "Joint Declaration by the USSR and the People's Republic of China (PRC) Concerning Relations with Japan" signed on October 12, 1954 in Beijing. Similar to the Soviet–Chinese Joint Declaration, the Nam Il Declaration aimed at promoting the exchange of human and material resources while attempting to resurrect direct contact between the governments. This effort at people's diplomacy, unlike the official, intergovernmental ties, was based on a premise that the accumulation of informal and apolitical contacts would eventually accrete to the point that official diplomatic relations would build up over time.[51] People's diplomacy with the PRC and the USSR already had created footholds in new pro-Soviet organizations in Japan, such as the Japan–China Friendship Association and the Japan–Soviet Union Association. This was the reason why North Korea took note of the Japan–Korea Association in the first place and chose Hatanaka as its counterpart in establishing dialogue with Japan. As the trustee of the Japan–Korea Association, Hatanaka was credited with leading the Association to the status of a nationwide organization. He was one of the few Japanese who enjoyed a close relationship with Kim Il-sung.

The PRC's experience in negotiating repatriation of Japanese residents provided the North Koreans with a precedent on which to construct their own public diplomacy. The repatriation of the Japanese from China, suspended during the Korean War, was resumed yet again in 1955 (after already having started and stopped in 1953). Unlike the case of Japan's negotiations with the Soviet Union, several non-governmental organizations participated in the Sino-Japanese talks. After the signing in March 1953 of the "Beijing Agreement on the Issues Concerning Japanese Repatriation," groups such as the Red Cross Societies of the two countries, the China–Japan Friendship Association, and the Japan Peace Liaison Committee played an active part in the negotiations. This participation came to be known as the Three NGO (Non-Government Organizations) Format of negotiations.[52] Impressed by this formula, the North Korean government requested Hatanaka to bring on board the Japanese Red Cross Society and the Japan–Korea Association.[53] Drawing a parallel with the Japan–China talks, the negotiations between Japan and North Korea could be said to follow a "Two NGO format."[54] On the one hand, the North Korean side aimed to achieve intergovernmental contacts with Japan using the talks between the Red Cross Societies in the two nations as a quasi diplomatic channel. On the other hand, by strengthening the appeal of the Japan–Korea Association, the North Korean government sought to extend the reach of its people's diplomacy toward Japan.

North Korea's stance on *Zainichi* Korean repatriation from Japan was fully spelled out in a statement from its Foreign Ministry on December 19, 1955. This was well after it made clear its position on the repatriation of Japanese residents in the opposite direction.[55] The statement clarified three categories of *Zainichi* Koreans who would be welcomed to North Korea: (1) ordinary ethnic Korean residents in Japan, (2) those who wished to study in North Korea, and (3) the inmates of the Ōmura Internment Camp in Nagasaki Prefecture, where more than 300 Koreans had been held during the Korean War on charges of illegally entering Japan. The DPRK Foreign Ministry also clarified Pyongyang's position on each of the three categories. First, on the issue of ordinary *Zainichi* Koreans, it was expected that "they should settle in Japan"; permission to return to North Korea would be given "depending on circumstances" and only to those forced to leave Japan. Second, for those hoping to study in North Korea, the government adopted an additional measure known as "Cabinet Decision Number Seven."[56] This decision granted scholarships and other types of financial aid and was unrelated to the repatriation issue.

In reality, the 600,000-strong *Zainichi* diaspora in Japan was another lever in North Korea's people's diplomacy toward Japan, an element that was absent from Soviet–Japanese and Sino-Japanese relations. The intricacy of North Korea's diplomacy, compared to the approaches of its Soviet and Chinese allies, is noteworthy. To draw the *Zainichi* Koreans into its net of people's diplomacy, the North Korean leadership issued a special guidance to the *Zainichi* Korean groups in Japan even before publicizing the Nam Il Declaration. Further, it dismantled the *Minsen* groups and established the *Chongryon* (General Association of Korean Residents in Japan) to coincide with the Hanataka Delegation visit to Pyongyang. Soon after that, the character of *Chongryon*–JCP relations changed from previously unequal cooperation, where the JCP ruled over *Chongryon*, to solidarity. At the time of its foundation, *Chongryon*'s potential role to serve as a "diplomatic representational office in Japan" had been considered a possibility. While projecting messages of solidarity and friendship to the whole of Japanese society through its various activities, *Chongryon* completely bypassed the Japanese government.[57] In sum, *Chongryon* saw the *Zainichi* community as a force that could contribute to North Korea's people's diplomacy *within* Japan, rather than as a group whose repatriation would be in North Korea's interest.

Special attention in the DPRK Foreign Ministry statement was given to the third group, ethnic Koreans detained in the Ōmura internment camp, who were seeking repatriation to North Korea. Soon after the statement was publicized, the North Korean Red Cross sent a special telegram to its Japanese counterpart earnestly requesting "to dispatch to Japan" its representative to try to resolve the matter.[58] But there was actually a strategic reason behind North Korea's interest in the few ethnic Korean detainees requesting repatriation. Soon after the enactment of its immigration law in November 1951, Japan had proclaimed the majority of *Zainichi* Koreans illegal residents and planned to deport them to South Korea after detainment in the Ōmura internment camp. However, the South Korean government vehemently refused to accept the internees from the camp, and the disagreement fed deterioration in relations between the two countries.[59] For North Korea, this was all very convenient: achieving rapprochement with Japan could potentially drive a wedge between Japan and South Korea and lead to the South's further alienation.

## The Pyongyang Communiqué

During the month of January 1956, rallies in support of the rescue of the Korean internees in the Ōmura camp were held across North Korea.[60] These were instigated first by the official intergovernmental talks scheduled between Japan and North Korea in Pyongyang. The Japanese delegation arrived in the North Korean capital on January 27.[61] This was also the first time that Japanese citizens were allowed to travel abroad with Japanese passports following the end of the U.S. Occupation. The Japanese side was referred to both as "the Japanese Delegation" and the "Japanese Red Cross Delegation," which caused controversy, as did the affiliation of one of the delegates, Miyakoshi Kisuke. Throughout the visit, Miyakoshi was observed in close contact with North Korea's top policymakers and Japan hands, such as Nam Il and other top-level diplomats. In reality, Miyakoshi had no connection to the Japanese Red Cross. He was involved in the negotiations with North Korea primarily as the deputy chairman of the Japan–Korea Association.[62] This was a sign that the members of the Japanese delegation had been selected with clear appreciation of North Korea's intentions.

However, because the Japanese side had not officially admitted the inclusion of any members of the Japan–Korea Association in the negotiations, Miyakoshi was obliged to wear a Japan Red Cross badge. North Korea had withdrawn to the Two NGO format in the talks. Until that point, South Korea was demonstrating

vehement opposition; Seoul's protests started when news of the Hatanaka delegation's visit to Pyongyang was publicized. Initiated by South Korean President
Syngman Rhee's April 1955 National Assembly speech that raised alarm about the
North's approaches to Japan, "government-orchestrated" anti-Japanese demonstrations took hold of South Korea and continued until July. On August 18, the South
Korean government imposed an "embargo on travel and trade" with Japan. Even
these measures, however, could not impede the Japan–North Korea negotiations,
which continued for a while. In October, the sides informally agreed on the guidelines for trade relations.[63] Soon after, a first delegation consisting of Japan's Diet
members reached a consensus with their North Korean counterparts at the Supreme
People's Assembly on a treaty of friendship and the resolution of pending problems in bilateral relations.[64] Despite all these advances, the moment when the Japanese side would apply the brakes to exchanges with North Korea loomed just
around the corner.

On October 25, 1955, in a vice-ministerial meeting, the Hatoyama Ichirō
Cabinet decided not to approve trade relations with North Korea. Underlying
this decision was the grave concern that intensive contact with North Korea
"would make relations with South Korea practically impossible."[65] This decision completely cancelled out the achievements made in Japan–North Korean
exchanges and negotiations until that point. In response, North Korea had to
come up with new measures to avoid a complete breakdown. In late October,
the DPRK government conveyed to Hoashi Kei, the head of the delegation of
Japanese parliamentarians visiting Pyongyang at the time, its intention not to
adhere to the Two NGO format from that point onward.[66] Faced with this decision, leaders of the two Japanese NGOs – Red Cross Society's Vice-Chairman
Yoshisuke and the Japan–Korea Association Head of the Board of Trustees
Hatanaka – had to forge their own joint strategy. Later, Vice-Chairman of the
Japan–Korea Association Miyakoshi would resign from his position at the association and join the Red Cross Society as a special delegate for repatriation
negotiations. This marked a switch from the Two NGOs to a "special format"
for negotiations.[67]

Immediately before the members of the Japanese delegation for "special format"
talks were selected, the Asia Department of Japan's Foreign Ministry drew up a
"Plan for Resolving the Problem of Voluntary Repatriation to North Korea."
According to historian Tessa Morris-Suzuki's evaluation, this document represented the Japanese government's first official policy guidelines on "sending
home" *Zainichi* Koreans to North Korea.[68] The document specified that the physical repatriation itself was to be "entrusted to the Japanese Red Cross Society." The
Japanese government, ever persistent in its goal to "hasten the repatriation of Japanese citizens from North Korea and other countries of the Communist Bloc," gave
its official consent to the issue with hopes that it would facilitate the repatriation
of Japanese citizens.[69] An appendix to the plan made it clear that "only those facing
economic hardships" should be selected for expatriation to North Korea and that
"a definite date must be set after which this deportation should be terminated
immediately."[70] Anticipating opposition from South Korea, the Japanese

government introduced these restrictions to keep expatriation to North Korea to a minimum.

This policy, however, was completely revoked immediately before the Japanese delegation left Tokyo for Pyongyang. On December 23, the South Korean government issued a *note verbale* to the Japanese representative in Seoul, expressing "profound concern over the Japanese government's attitude toward the puppet government of the North." What worried the South Korean side, according to the message, was that the Japanese government "has consented to the Japan–Korea Association members' visit to North Korea." That such a delegation had been drawn up, with Miyakoshi included in it, was judged to be "an extremely political act." The *note verbale* also strongly condemned the "state of affairs under which many Japanese politicians and businessmen are visiting North Korea with an aim to discuss with the Northern Puppet government or organizations under their umbrella various issues relating to trade, culture, and fisheries." The note further added that "negotiations or cooperation in any form between Japan and the North Korean puppets constitutes an extremely unfriendly act toward South Korea," and the Seoul government warned that such activities "would entail very negative consequences in the relations between our countries."[71] Having received this statement, the Japanese government was forced to narrow down the agenda of the Pyongyang meeting to the issue of repatriating Japanese citizens from North Korea.[72]

In the end, on February 26, 1956, Japan and North Korea adopted a nine-article Joint Communiqué (the so-called Pyongyang Communiqué), eight months before Japan also finalized an end-of-war treaty with the USSR.[73] More than a month had passed since the Japanese delegation's arrival in Pyongyang. Following heated discussions, both sides decided in the Communiqué to set aside the issue of repatriating the *Zainichi* Koreans "as a matter to be resolved by the Red Cross societies of the two countries." This was an achievement for North Korea: it meant that negotiations with the Red Cross, which mediated the issue of the inmates of the Ōmura Internment Camp, would continue. For North Korea, the issue of repatriating *Zainichi* Koreans was nothing more than a means to keep open a channel for negotiations with Japan. The Japanese Red Cross also achieved its primary goal of limiting the Pyongyang talks to the issue of repatriating the Japanese citizens from North Korea. From the moment it became clear that the Japanese delegation was set for Pyongyang, the Japanese Red Cross attempted to resolve the repatriation issue with the ICRC's mediation.[74] Paradoxically, South Korea's opposition brought about more concrete results in the repatriation issue than the efforts of the Japanese Red Cross, which had long been exploring ways to find resolutions.

The Pyongyang Communiqué was put into practice for the first time on April 22, 1956, when the repatriation ship *Kojima* carrying thirty-six Japanese residents entered the Maizuru Port on its journey from North Korea.[75] On the same day, forty-seven (the number would later rise to forty-eight) *Zainichi* Koreans who had hoped to return to North Korea on board the same ship staged a sit-down strike in front of the Japanese Red Cross headquarters. An investigative delegation dispatched from Geneva in response to the Japanese Red Cross Society's efforts witnessed the sit-in. With this, the repatriation of the *Zainichi* Koreans progressed to the next stage; however, after the signing of the Pyongyang Communiqué, the Japanese Red Cross did not follow up its investigations into the issue of Japanese residents in North Korea. Although the number of Japanese residents willing to return to Japan increased by twenty-one people following the departure of the Japanese delegation from Pyongyang, there was no further repatriation.[76]

## Conclusion

The story of the Japanese engineers who stayed behind in North Korea offers another perspective on the as yet poorly understood processes of decolonization and nation building in the north of the Korean Peninsula. In the time between the establishment of people's committees and the organization of the North Korean People's Temporary Committee, the Japanese lost their colonizer status. The Soviet Army occupation policies hastened this decolonization: they isolated the Japanese residents in detainment camps and deported Japanese residents to the Soviet Union. The Japanese engineers and their families were the only groups that received exceptional treatment from the North Korean government because they were needed to manage the large-scale industrial infrastructure left in the region as a legacy of the Japanese empire. The construction of a united national front was the North Korean government's foremost policy goal, and so it had no option but to extend special treatment to these Japanese engineers who would ensure the smooth transition to post-imperial reconstruction.

However, these Japanese residents "left behind" in North Korea soon turned into internees. As the new nation channeled its energies toward unifying the country through military force, the processes of decolonization and nation building took a turn. National politics tilted further to the left, and emphasis was put on class war and anti-Japanese sentiment. During the Korean War, many Japanese engineers lost their lives for suspected "counter-revolutionary activities." However, the North Korean government's attitude toward and treatment of the Japanese technicians until this time created a significant legacy for the country's socialist system and its relationship with Japan. The policy of promoting Japanese technicians to important posts was crucial in cultivating and educating a new generation of North Korean engineers and technicians, who later made their presence felt in state politics.[77] The nationalization of the colonial industrial complex in North Korea advanced under this new cadre of specialists, as a new relationship with Japan developed.

North Korea decided to repatriate the Japanese technicians along with other Japanese residents because it had seen the value of using them as a diplomatic tool. After the Korean War, North Korea's strategic interest in Japan was not confined to economics; it also had an important security dimension. North Korea had put in place a twofold plan to achieve, by fostering rapprochement with Japan, estrangement between Japan and South Korea on one hand, and a counterbalance to the threat posed by the United States on the other. Moreover, furthering relations with Japan would mean for North Korea an opportunity to outgrow its dependency in foreign relations exclusively on the Soviet Union and China. The proclamation of the national ideology of *juche* and the promotion of a development policy based on prioritizing heavy industry coincided with the timing of the Nam Il Declaration, which initiated rapprochement with Japan. This Declaration overturned the previous anti-Japanese line in foreign policy and aimed for the first time to construct friendly relations between the two nations. The use of repatriating Japanese technicians then came to the forefront as the means to achieve a breakthrough in these relations. The resulting Pyongyang Communiqué was thus the first bilateral agreement achieved through people's diplomacy.

In the end, however, the impact the Pyongyang Communiqué had on the repatriation of Japanese technicians is difficult to judge. True, the government in Tokyo was first to grapple with the issue of repatriating the Japanese residents from North Korea. At the same time, the Japanese government also turned away from some of its citizens in North Korea even after the signing of the Communiqué. In fact, Tokyo responded to North Korea's advances – even in the face of strong opposition from South Korea – only when Pyongyang sounded out the possibility of repatriating the *Zainichi* Koreans to its territory. The number of *Zainichi* Koreans who staged a sit-in asking to be repatriated to North Korea did not exceed 50 people. However, the Japanese Red Cross Society did not miss this opportunity to present the sit-in as a sign of the *Zainichi* Koreans' collective desire to "return" to North Korea, and lobbied extensively to gain the mediation of the ICRC. In the end, the fact that Japan agreed to the terms of the Pyongyang Communiqué was a clear sign that it had succeeded in shifting the responsibility for the legacy of its own colonialism onto the shoulders of its former colony.

The repatriation of the *Zainichi* Koreans to North Korea started in late 1959, three years after the signing of the Pyongyang Communiqué. The reasons why natives of South Korea wished to "return" to the North were numerous, but two fundamental motifs stood out. The first was the Japanese government stance that viewed Korean residents as a financial burden and a threat to Japan's domestic peace and order. The second was that such Japanese attitudes made it difficult for *Zainichi* Koreans to make a living in Japan. The actual problem also concerned the returnees' numbers. When repatriation began in earnest, the Japanese wives of thousands of these ethnic Korean men accompanied them to North Korea. This was a development that the Japanese government had not anticipated and was due in no small part to North Korea's zeal in its policy of people's diplomacy toward Japan with the idea of somehow obstructing Japan–South Korea negotiations. Years later in 1965, when Japan signed a normalization treaty with South Korea, Japan–North Korea relations deteriorated sharply. This was also the time when the abductions of Japanese citizens by North Korea began.

After a long fallow period, normalization talks between Japan and North Korea began once again. Following a pattern established during the lengthy Japan–South Korea talks of 1952–1965, these discussions continued until the signing of the

2002 Pyongyang Declaration.[78] In this declaration, Japan and North Korea agreed to establish diplomatic relations, and they also reached consensus in principle on claims related to the legacy of Japanese colonialism. However, the negotiations unraveled when the issue of the abduction of Japanese citizens by North Korea (13 of whom were acknowledged by North Korea) surfaced again. In 2014, relations between the two nations began to thaw once more, and with the signing of the Stockholm Agreement, discussions between the two countries were resumed.[79] At this point, issues related to Japanese citizens who had migrated to North Korea with their spouses resurfaced, along with, yet again, the abduction issue.

The history of North Korea's decolonization and establishment as a nation unfolds within the stories and struggles of Japanese citizens, particularly the Japanese technicians, who for various reasons and with various hopes participated in and contributed to North Korean nation building, including many who made the new North Korea their final resting place. In a way, this story is different from what occurred in relations between Japan and South Korea. The history of relations between Japan and North Korea consists of a complicated mix of deportation, internment, abduction, and repatriation. The legacies of these painful historical issues are sure to make their presence felt again in subsequent stages of bilateral relations and will certainly continue to be used as diplomatic trump cards in the future.

## Notes

1 Official repatriation from North Korea came last following repatriations from China (November 1945), Taiwan (March 1946), and Manchuria (May 1946).

2 For a review of scholarly research on the repatriation issue, see Tessa Morris-Suzuki, *Exodus to North Korea Revisited: The Repatriation of Ethnic Koreans from Japan* (Seoul: J&C, 2011), pp. 13–23.

3 See Robert S. Boynton, *The Invitation-Only Zone: The True Story of North Korea's Abduction Project* (New York: Farrar, Straus and Giroux, 2016); "Japan-DPRK Pyongyang Declaration," http://www.mofa.go.jp/region/asia-paci/n_korea/pmv0209/pyong yang.html. See also the NHK Special Documentary, *Nicchō kōshō*, which aired on November 8, 2009.

4 See Charles K. Armstrong, *The North Korean Revolution, 1945–1950* (Ithaca, NY: Cornell University Press, 2003); Suh Dong-Man, *Bukchoson shaejui cheje songripsa 1945–1961* (Seoul: Son in, 2005); Lee Yon-sik, "Hebaghu hnabandokoju ilbonin kihan e kanhan yonngu – Chonryon-gun, chosonin, ilbonin ui samjakann ui sannghozakyong ul junnsimuro," PhD dissertation in the Department of National History, University of Seoul, August 2009; Park Jung-Jin, *Reisen ki nicchō kankei no keisei, 1945–1965* (Heibonsha, 2011). (Unless otherwise noted, all Japanese books are published in Tokyo.)

5 Ministry of Finance of Japan, Financial Policy Section, *Shōwa zaisei shi*, vol. 20 (Tōyō keizai shimpōsha, 1982), pp. 431–433.

6 On the industrialization of North Korea before the end of World War II, see Kimura Mitsuhiko and Abe Keiji, *Kita chōsen no gunji kōgyōka – teikoku sensō kara Kimu Iru Son sensō e* (Chisen shokan, 2003), Vol. 1, pp. 5–128. In English, see Aaron Stephen Moore, *Constructing East Asia: Technology, Ideology, and Empire in Japan's Wartime Era, 1931–1945* (Palo Alto, CA: Stanford University Press, 2013).

7 Park Yong-gun, *Urinaraeso ui gongupkwarijojik hyongtae ui keson ganwha* (Pyongyang: Kwahakwon chulpansa, 1961), pp. 12–13. For a more detailed analysis of the

relationship between people's committees and factory boards, see Suh Dong-man, *Buk-choson*, pp. 111–114.

8   *Rodongza shinmun*, September 22, 1945. Quoted in Lee Chong-sik, *Materials on Korean Communism: 1945–1947* (Honolulu: University of Hawai'i Press, 1977), p. 144.

9   Lee Yon-sik, "Hebaghu," p. 109.

10  *Choson zonsa*, vol. 35 (Pyongyang: Kawhak bekkasazon chulpansa, 1980), pp. 183–184.

11  Morita Yoshio, *Chōsen senshū no kiroku – beiso ryōgun no shinchū to nihonjin no hikiage* (Gannandō shoten, 1964), p. 349.

12  Lee Yon-sik, "Hebaghu," p. 12.

13  Sahekahakwonyoksayonguso, *Joson zonnsa*, vol. 23 (Pyongyang: Kahakbekasazon chulpansa), pp. 178–183.

14  To offer one example, of the forty-two technicians who had worked at the Hungnam Chemical Industry Complex at the time, only one was Korean. Kim Sang-chol, "Uri do ui jarang un zeji gongup kwa pulpu gongjang – pyonganbuk dō pyon, August 1949," in *Bukan kwanke saryojip* (Gwacheon: Kuksa pyonchan wewonhye, 1998), p. 131.

15  *Rodongza shinmun*, September 22, 1945. Quoted in Lee, *Materials*, p. 144.

16  The number of deaths prior to that point stood at 25,000, excluding military deaths. As a rule, the share of refugee deaths was around 20 percent of the total. Morita, *Chōsen*, p. 766.

17  "Decision of the Soviet Army Headquarters in North Korea on the transfer of Japanese-owned factories, industrial plants, hydroelectric power stations, banks and other facilities to the North Korean Temporary People's Committees," 30 October 1946, in *Soryon kwa bukan kwa ui kwanke, 1945–1980: Documents and Materials* (Seoul: Kukto tongil yonkuwom, 1987), pp. 55–56; translation of S.L.Tikhvinskiy et al., *Otnosheniia Sovetskogo Soiuza s Narodami Korei: 1945–1980* (Moscow: Nauka, 1981).

18  "Bukchoson imshi inminwewonwhe ui kusong e kanhan kyochong," in *Bukan kwanke saryojip*, vol. 5, p. 149.

19  Kim Il-sung, "Kumhu choson ui jonchijongse wa bukchosoninminiwonwhe ui jojik-munje e kwanhan bogo," *Chongro*, February 10, 1946.

20  On ideas about the "people's nation" and people's democracy in North Korea, see Kim Kwang-un, *Bukan jongchisi yongu 1* (Seoul: Son in, 2003). In South Korean scholarship on North Korea, government in pre–Korean War North Korea is known as "the dictatorship of the people's democracy" and not as the dictatorship of the proletariat.

21  Chon Hyon-su, "Hebangjiku bukan uk kakochonsan, 1945–1948," *Tegusahak*, vol. 69, pp. 47–49.

22  After resigning as North Korea's first minister of energy, Lee Mun-han became a professor at the Pyongyang Institute of Technology.

23  "Bukchosoninminiwonwhe gyulchong 62 ho – gishulja whakpo e kwanhan gyulchongso, August 7, 1946," *Bukan kwanke saryojip*, vol. 5, p. 176.

24  "Gishulja whakpo e kwanhan gyulchongso silheng e kwanhan kon," *Bukan kwanke saryojip*, vol. 5, pp. 178–179.

25  Morita, *Chōsen*, pp. 770–780.

26  Ibid, pp. 748, 767–779.

27  Ibid, p. 794.

28  Ministry of Health, Labor and Welfare of Japan (MHLW), Welfare Support Bureau, *Hikiage to engo sanjūnen no ayumi* (Kōseishō, 1978), pp. 533–534.

29  Morita, *Chōsen*, p. 794.

30  *Bukan kwanke saryojip*, vol. 28, p. 18.

31  The following day, the Japanese technicians established the arrangements committee aiming to set up their self-government organization, Union of Japanese Technicians in North Korea. However, in reality the Union was never established. Morita, *Chōsen*, pp. 792–793.

32 Kim Song-bo analyses both the revision of the "people's nation" as a political course and the introduction of the later, more radical version of the "people's democracy" to North Korea. See Kim Song-bo, *Nambukan kyongjekujo ui kiwon kwa jongye* (Seoul: Yoksabipyongsa, 2000).

33 See Park, *Reisen ki*, pp. 97–98.

34 Information for the section on industry of the "Intelligence Summary North Korea" report was supplied by the Japanese technicians who had successfully repatriated from North Korea: Institute of Asian Culture Studies, *HQ, USAFIK Intelligence Summary, Northern Korea* (1948.7.17–1948.11.26) (Chunchon: Institute of Culture Studies, Hallym University, 1989).

35 Telegram of Mr. Shimazu, President, Japanese Red Cross Society, January 6, 1954, Diplomatic Archives of the Ministry of Foreign Affairs of Japan, 2004–00637, Document No. 6, "Zainichi chōsenjin no hokusen kikan ni kansuru nisseki to sekijūji kokusai iinkai to no ōfuku bunsho."

36 Ibid.

37 "Zaigai hōjin hikiage tōkeihyō (Nenjibetsu, shukkōchibetsu, shōwa 20–36)," in *Zokuzoku: hikiage engo no kiroku* (MHLW, Welfare Support Bureau, 1963), p. 417.

38 On the movement to hasten the repatriation of the Japanese from North Korea, see "Kita chōsen yokuryūsha hikiage undō shi – machiwabiru kokoro no kai no ayumi," in "Machiwabiru kokoro wa kiezu," published by the Association of the Impatiently Waiting Hearts, p. 146; Morita, *Chōsen*, pp. 904–905.

39 *Dai 16 kai Kokkai shūgiin kōsei/kaigai dōhō hikiage oyobi ikazoku engo ni kansuru chōsa tokubetsu iinkai rengō shinsa kaigi jiroku*, vol. 1, July 20, 1953. This number includes military servicemen and in September 1953 was corrected to 2,061 people.

40 Telegram of Mr. Shimazu.

41 Tsuboi Toyokichi, *Zainichi chōsenjin undō no gaikyō*, Ministry of Justice Research Paper (Confidential) vol. 46, issue 3 (1959), p. 14.

42 MHLW, "Hikiage to engo," p. 154. According to the MHLW, the number of *Zainichi* Koreans who could not repatriate because of the Korean War despite their wishes stood at 489 people (see MHLW, *Zokuzoku*, pp. 25–26).

43 Park, *Reisen ki*, pp. 51–55.

44 *Dai 17 kai kokkai sangiin gaimu iinkai kaigiroku*, vol. 5, November 6, 1953.

45 Morita Yoshio, *Sūji ga kataru zainichi kankoku/chōsenjin no rekishi* (Akashi shoten, 1996), pp. 31–32.

46 The North Korean Red Cross sent a positive reply in February 1954, but this was not followed up by further agreements. Moreover, the February 1954 reply did not contain any references to the issue of repatriating *Zainichi* Koreans to North Korea. "Telegram of the Chairman of the North Korean Red Cross Lee Dong-yong to the Japanese Red Cross Society, 6 February 1954," in *Nihon sekijūji shikō – shōwa 21 nen ~ shōwa 30 nen*, vol. 6, p. 263; Naoko Shimazu, "Diplomacy as Theatre: Staging the Bandung Conference of 1955," *Modern Asian Studies* vol. 48, issue 1 (January 2014): pp. 225–252.

47 The Association of the Impatiently Waiting Hearts expected Kuruma, chairman of the Japan–Korea Association, to petition the North Korean representative at the Japan–Korea Association on their behalf by passing on to him the list of Japanese residents in North Korea, as well as information on their living conditions. See Morita, *Chōsen*, pp. 914–915.

48 "Ajia shokoku kaigi nihon daihyō chōsen hōmondan raichō," *Rōdō shimbun*, May 19, 1955.

49 Morita, *Chōsen*, pp. 914–915.

50 "Tainichi kankei ni kanshite – chōsen minshushugi jinmin kyōwakoku gaishō no seimei," *Rōdō shimbun*, February 26, 1955.

51 Park, *Reisen ki*, pp. 111–112.

52  MHLW, *Zokuzoku*, pp. 17–18; Ōsawa Takeshi, "Zaika hōjin hikiage kōshō o meguru sengo nichchū kankei, nichchū minkan kōshō ni okeru '3 dantai hōshiki' o chūshin toshite," *Ajia kenkyū* vol. 49, issue 3 (July 2003): pp. 56–57.

53  MHLW, *Zokuzoku*, pp. 63; Morita, *Chōsen*, p. 916.

54  Because the Japan Peace Committee was already participating in Sino-Japanese talks, it was not part of the Japan–North Korean negotiations.

55  "Zainichi chōsen kōmin to kanren shite – chōsen minshushugi jinmin kyōwakoku gaishō no seimei," *Rōdō shimbun*, December 30, 1955.

56  *Sokoku wa matte iru! – zainichi dōhō no kikoku mondai ni kansuru bunketsu* (Pyongyang: Foreign Language Publishers, 1959), p. 5.

57  For a more in-detail analysis of the establishment of Chongryon, see Park, *Reisen ki*, pp. 151–166.

58  "Chōsen sekijūjikai chūō iinkai iinchō Ri Hei Nan ga nihon sekijūjisha shachō Shimazu Tadatsugu ni okutta denbun," *Rōdō shimbun*, January 1, 1956.

59  *Nihon gaikōshi, Vol. 28: kōwago no gaikō 1, tai rekkoku kankei* (Kajima Institute of International Peace, 1973), pp. 54–56.

60  "Ōmura shūyōjo ni yokuryū sarete iru dōhō o seien suru shūkai, kakuchi de hikitsuzuki shinkō," *Rōdō shimbun*, January 14, 15, 19, 1956.

61  "Nihon sekijūjisha daihyōdan raichō," *Rōdō shimbun*, January 29, 1956.

62  "Chōsen heiwa yōgo zenkoku minzoku iinkai daihyō to nichchō kyōkai daihyō no aida de kyōdō komyunike o happyō," *Rōdō shimbun*, February 29, 1956; "Chōsen bōeki kaisha daihyō to nihon sho kaisha no daihyō no aida de shōhin kyōyaku ni kansuru keiyaku o teiketsu," *Rōdō shimbun*, February 29, 1956.

63  "Chōsen kokusai bōeki sokushin iinkai jōmu to nisso bōekikai senmu riji no aida de okonawareta bōeki sokushin ni kansuru danwaroku," *Rōdō shimbun*, October 22, 1955.

64  "Chōsen minshushugi jinmin kyōwakoku saikō jinmin kaigi jōnin iinkai Kin Ō Ki fuku iinchō to chōsen minshushugi jinmin kyōwakoku hōmon nihon kokkai giindan Furuya Sadao danchō to aida no kyōdō komyunike," *Rōdō shimbun*, October 21, 1955.

65  "(Gokuhi) Hokusen to bōeki sono hoka no sho kankei o juritsu suru koto no kahi ni kansuru ken, 24 October 1955," in *Nichchō kankei 0120–2001–00988 A' – 393, October 1955 ~ July 1968*, Ministry of Foreign Affairs of Japan.

66  MHLW, *Zokuzoku*, p. 63.

67  Telegram from the Chairman of the Japanese Red Cross Society to Deputy Chairman of the North Korean Red Cross Society, December 17, 1955, in *Nihon sekijūji shikō – shōwa 21 nen ~ shōwa 30 nen*, vol. 6, p. 266.

68  Morris-Suzuki, *Exodus*, p. 42.

69  "Hokusen e no kikan kibōsha no sōkan mondai shori hōshin, December 15, 1955," *General Records of State Normalization Negotiations between Japan and South Korea 6 (On the issue of the repatriation of Zainichi Koreans to North Korea and the signing of the repatriation agreement)*, Document No. 126, Ministry of Foreign Affairs of Japan, Documents on Negotiations with South Korea.

70  Ibid.

71  Note Verbale, from the Korean Mission to the Japanese Ministry of Foreign Affairs, December 23, 1955, Ministry of Foreign Affairs of the Republic of Korea, Film # D-0001, Classification No. 725. 1JA, Registration No. 134.

72  Note Verbale, from the Ministry of Foreign Affairs of Japan, January 6, 1956, Ministry of Foreign Affairs of the Republic of Korea, Film # D-0001, Classification No. 725. 1JA, Registration No. 134.

73  "Kyōdō komyunike (pyongyang), February 27, 1956," in *Nihon sekijūji shikō – shōwa 21 nen ~ shōwa 30 nen*, vol. 6, pp. 267–269.

74  Letter from Shimazu to Boissier, December 13, 1955; "Request for Repatriation of those Koreans in Japan who want to go home," attached to the letter from Shimazu to Boissier, December 13, 1955, ICRC Archives, File no. B AG 232 105–002.

75 Of the forty-eight [Japanese] gathered in Pyongyang to be repatriated, twelve later withdrew their requests for repatriation of their own volition.
76 *Asahi shimbun*, March 23, 1956.
77 For more detail, see Suh Dong-man, *Kita chōsen shakaishugi taisei seiritsu shi, 1945–1961* (Seoul: Son in, 2005).
78 http://www.mofa.go.jp/mofaj/kaidan/s_koi/n_korea_02/sengen.html.
79 Full text of the Stockholm Agreement can be found at http://www.mofa.go.jp/mofaj/files/000040352.pdf.

# 12 Humanitarian hero or communist stooge?

## The ambivalent Japanese reception of Li Dequan in 1954

*Erik Esselstrom*

In a scene associated most often in today's Japan with the arrival of sports superstars, cinema action heroes, or global pop music icons, a throng of photographers, journalists, and excited onlookers packed tightly into the cramped area around the arrivals gate of Tokyo International Airport (commonly known as Tokyo Haneda Airport), waiting feverishly for a glimpse of a high-profile celebrity. The arrival of newlyweds Marilyn Monroe and Joe DiMaggio in Tokyo earlier that year had provoked a similar scene, but the eagerly anticipated passenger on this day in late October 1954 was not a trendsetting actress, chart-topping musician, or home run–crushing ball player. It was a middle-aged Chinese woman named Li Dequan, the first state official from the People's Republic of China (PRC) to set foot on Japanese soil since the "new" China was born five years previously in October 1949.

Members of the Japanese media had turned out in such numbers at Haneda on that October evening, at least in part simply because the arrival of any foreign dignitary in Japan was a newsworthy event. The impending arrival of Li Dequan, however, had been the subject of public debate in Japan for many weeks, and the conversation surrounding her visit was often highly contentious. Li's formal position in the PRC government, as Minister of Public Health, was somewhat unique in that, while she was one of the highest-placed women in Beijing, she was not a member of the Chinese Communist Party. Li's high public profile was rooted instead in her own rich personal experiences as a social activist on issues related to women and family, the international recognition she had cultivated since the end of the war by campaigning for those matters overseas, and her humanitarian work as president of the Chinese Red Cross. While Japanese supporters had lauded Li's visit to Tokyo as an epochal harbinger of peace and reconciliation between China and Japan during the weeks prior to her trip, her opponents had launched venomous rhetorical attacks in which Li was dismissed as nothing more than a communist wolf in humanitarian sheep's clothing. These passionate reactions from the Japanese public to the prospect of Li Dequan's arrival reveal significant insights concerning the lingering legacies of Japan's defeat in the Second World War as well as simmering tensions in East Asian international relations during the early 1950s.

The United States looms large in the history of Japanese foreign relations during the first decade of the Cold War in East Asia. Rightly so, since the U.S.–Japan security agreement forged at the occupation's end in 1952 proved an inescapable force in shaping Japan's international interactions in the region and beyond, then and for many decades to come. But for Japanese of that time, relations with the People's Republic of China after 1949 were arguably just as significant as Japanese connections to the United States (if not more so) for reasons related both to lucrative commercial opportunity and to national security anxiety. Indeed, as had been true for the past 2,000 years of East Asian history, China was still Japan's largest continental neighbor and events on the mainland resonated as loudly as ever throughout the archipelago during the early 1950s. American support for Chiang Kai-shek's Nationalist regime on Taiwan, however, strictly circumscribed official Japanese diplomacy with the PRC after 1952, since no Japanese cabinet was free to recognize the Chinese Communist regime when the United States would not do so. With state-to-state engagement between Tokyo and Beijing thereby nearly impossible, laying the foundations during the 1950s for a path toward the eventual normalization in China–Japan relations became a task left to an array of Japanese civilian activists and non-governmental organizations.

Li Dequan's visit to Japan in 1954 was one of the earliest and most visible manifestations of this brand of popular diplomacy that shaped Japan–China relations during the early Cold War era. In fact, a special issue of *Graphic Asahi* (*Asahi gurafu*) in late 1972, produced to commemorate the visit of then Prime Minister Tanaka Kakuei to Beijing, included a 1954 photo of Li and her Japanese Red Cross hosts in Tokyo as an important example of the early postwar "trailblazers" that ultimately made possible the revival of "2,000 years of China–Japan friendship."[1] This chapter will explore the purpose, content, and meaning of Li Dequan's 1954 visit to Japan, with a focus on three specific categories of popular reactions to the Li delegation, as a lens through which the social and cultural dynamics of Japan–China relations during the early Cold War era can be better understood.[2] First, left-leaning social organizations, intellectuals, and activists saw the Li visit as a valuable step forward in the restoration of China–Japan friendship and East Asian peace – goals threatened in their view by the U.S.–Japan security agreement. For politically conservative academics and Japanese rightists, however, Li and her companions were little more than a cynical front for anti-American agitation and the ideological infiltration of Japanese society by the PRC and the USSR. Finally, for women's rights advocates in postwar Japan, the most important part of Li's visit was her high-profile position as a woman in the Chinese political arena. While some surely also aspired toward Sino-Japanese unity to counter U.S. geopolitical hegemony in the region, Li's feminist friends in Japan primarily promoted her as powerful evidence that women could lead the postwar world to a more peaceful era of international cooperation.

The complex ways in which Li Dequan's visit to Japan touched these competing social constituencies remind us that the postwar Japanese state was still in the process of consolidating its own legitimacy in 1954, and the political and social fissures in Japanese life that made such consolidation challenging were abundant. Put differently, the breakdown of the Japanese empire in 1945 had necessitated the re-imagination of sovereignty and national identity not only within those societies brutalized by Japanese occupation during the colonial and wartime eras but within Japan itself. The arrival of Li Dequan in Japan during the late autumn of 1954 serves as a valuable historical moment through which we can explore the social dynamics of that domestic struggle as it unfolded within the context of the early Cold War in East Asia.

## The Li Dequan delegation

Before we turn to an analysis of the varied responses to Li's arrival in Tokyo, it is necessary first to explore briefly who Li Dequan was, how she found her way to this pivotal moment in early postwar China–Japan relations, and what her delegation saw and did during their brief tour of Japan. Although born in the poor rural province of Hebei, Li was the daughter of reasonably well-to-do third-generation Chinese Christian parents. At age sixteen she entered the American missionary–founded Beiman Girls' High School in Beijing (Bridgman School) and next moved on to study at the Christian-affiliated (and later Rockefeller Foundation–funded) Union College for Women. Disillusioned by racist treatment from an American professor there, Li turned increasingly to nationalist and revolutionary ideologies. After graduation, she returned to her former middle school as an instructor and later became involved in numerous social welfare organizations before marrying Feng Yuxiang, the so-called Christian General of China's warlord era, in 1925 at age twenty-nine. How the two met is unclear, but one suggestion is that when Feng took over Hebei province, the Li family offered their daughter to him to cement a valuable political alliance. But it also seems likely that their shared Christian faith worked to cultivate a genuine emotional bond between them. Li turned more intently toward matters of social assistance for women during the wartime years. Working first in Shanghai, she later fled to Chongqing after the Yangzi delta came under Japanese control during the late 1930s, and there she organized and chaired the China Women's Federation. At that time, Song Meiling, wife of Kuomintang (KMT) leader Chiang Kai-shek, was working on similar causes, but Li and Song did not coordinate their efforts, apparently reflecting the impact of Feng's fallout with Chiang years earlier. Critical of Chiang but not ardent supporters of Mao and the Chinese Communist Party (CCP) throughout the wartime years, Feng and Li were closest to left-wing, Soviet-friendly elements of the KMT.[3]

During the Chinese Civil War, they traveled together to the United States, where Feng continued to criticize Chiang from afar and Li became involved more deeply in the international women's movement, bringing her into contact with prominent activists from around the world. The CCP reached out to Feng and Li in 1948, asking them to return to China and to take part in the creation of a new regime. They made the decision to go back to China, but Feng died en route in a shipboard fire on the Black Sea. Li made it home, however, and was appointed Minister of Public Health in the PRC government in 1949, later assuming the position of Chinese Red Cross chief as well in 1950. In those positions, Li went on to represent China at international conferences on women's issues and world peace in locales such as Toronto and Copenhagen throughout the early 1950s. This wealth of experience made Li one of the most cosmopolitan faces of the new communist Chinese state.[4]

While surely Li would not have made the trip to Japan without approval from CCP leadership, the government in Beijing was not directly responsible for sending her. Rather Li's journey was the end result of a process that had been unfolding over several years in which three non-governmental Japanese organizations had played the greatest role: the Japan Red Cross, the Japan Peace Liaison Group (*Nihon heiwa renrakukai*), and the Japan–China Friendship Society (*Nihon chūgoku yūkō kyōkai*). These three groups had worked together in previous years to facilitate a variety of China–Japan cultural exchanges, as well as a series of campaigns to make possible the return to the mainland of the physical remains of Chinese laborers who had died in Japan during the war. Intended as reciprocation for such efforts by the Japanese side, the primary purpose of Li's visit to Japan was the delivery of a detailed list of names identifying Japanese soldiers still held as prisoners in the PRC in 1954.[5]

At the reception held in her honor on the evening of October 30, Li delivered a set of remarks that expressed what she hoped her trip to Japan might achieve. Emphasizing ideals of humanitarianism and peace, Li stressed that both the Chinese and Japanese people knew well the horrors of war and only by working together could genuine peace in Asia be attained. To those ends, she promised that the Chinese government would continue to do all that was possible in facilitating the return of Japanese civilians still on the mainland. Moreover, she assured her audience that Japanese war criminals would be shown humanitarian consideration and sent back swiftly, before ending with a toast to peace in Asia and throughout the world made possible through China–Japan cooperation and friendship.[6]

After initiating her tour on that magnanimous note, the Li delegation (roughly a dozen people) traveled extensively until the group's departure on November 12, making visits to multiple cities including Yokohama, Hakone, Nagoya, Kyoto, and Osaka. At each stop, the three Japanese organizations responsible for bringing her set up welcome events, tours, and discussions with local citizen groups. On the day after her arrival, for example, Li made a visit to the Japan Red Cross headquarters in Tokyo and attended a reception with the eastern Japan Associations of the Families of the Missing (*Nihon rusu kazoku kai*). On November 1, Li moved on to Yokohama, made a brief stop in Fujisawa, and then spent one night in Hakone. The Fujisawa side trip was especially notable, as there she visited the grave of Nie Er, composer of the PRC's national anthem, who drowned in a tragic accident near the seaside town at the age of twenty-three in 1935 while visiting his brother in the Tokyo area. Li headed back to Tokyo the following day to attend a ceremony in Asakusa for wartime Chinese laborers and to participate in meetings with representatives from the association of overseas Japanese left behind in China. November 3–4 were also spent in Tokyo for more meetings concerning problems of Japanese returnees, at a dinner with an area association of Chinese merchants, at a formal reception hosted by the Japanese Red Cross, in a tour of Red Cross facilities in the city, and at an evening *kabuki* performance.[7]

On November 5, the delegation arrived in Nagoya, toured an electronics factory there, attended yet another evening reception, and traveled on to Kyoto the next morning where they had a meeting with staff members of the *Asahi shimbun*. November 7 was spent sightseeing in the ancient capital before joining an evening reception hosted by the Japanese Red Cross. The group traveled on to Osaka on November 8, where they toured more Red Cross facilities, met with representatives from the western Associations of the Families of the Missing (*Nihon rusu kazoku kai*), attended a party hosted by international trade promotion association, and enjoyed a *bunraku* performance. November 10 saw the delegation return to Tokyo for a meetings with both Japanese Minister of Health Kusaba Ryūen and several lower house Diet members, followed by an evening reception hosted by the Federation of Japan Women's Organizations (*Fujin dantai rengōkai*). After more meetings with Health Ministry officials and Diet members on November 11, Li and her delegation departed from Haneda airport on November 12, sent off by a section chief from the Health Ministry.[8]

Missing from Li Dequan's itinerary, of course, was any formal interaction with high-level members of Japanese Prime Minister Yoshida Shigeru's cabinet (with the exception of Health Minister Kusaba) or the Japanese Ministry of Foreign Affairs. Although she was the first official from the PRC ever to visit Japan, Cold War prerogatives demanded that Li's presence on the archipelago could not be recognized with any official Japanese government fanfare or ceremony. In fact, it had proved quite a challenging task throughout the summer and early autumn of 1954 simply to have her travel visa approved. Thus, to understand the deeper meanings of her trip, it is to the lively public response and political debate within Japanese society at large concerning Li's arrival that we must turn instead. Many of the most significant social and political divisions that animated the early postwar Japanese world are revealed through the voices of those who welcomed Li with enthusiastic open arms and those who angrily bemoaned her presence.

## Peace dove? Li's advocates

Support for Li's visit came from a wide variety of political organizations, social elements, and individuals. Most natural, perhaps, was the warm welcome offered by the families of Japanese soldiers still missing on the continent. Nine years had passed since Japan's surrender, but painful uncertainty remained concerning the fate of thousands of husbands, brothers, and sons. As evidenced by the mountains of letters received by the Japanese Red Cross from families across the country inquiring about the status of their missing men, the potential information Li brought with her offered hope and emotional relief to thousands of Japanese families, and the profound gratitude they expressed in return for that long-awaited (and hopefully good) news was both deep and genuine. For these families of the missing, the geopolitics of the Li mission were largely irrelevant; her visit was a blessing because it offered a means of recovery from the trauma of wartime separation.

Many of Japan's leading daily newspapers frequently ran stories on the emotional dramas experienced by these families upon learning from the Li delegation of the whereabouts of their loved ones. The tale of Itō Kōichi's family, for example, no doubt tugged painfully on the heartstrings of others across the home islands. As told by wife and mother Kimi, the family had been together residing in Inner Mongolia until the spring of 1942 when worsening security conditions compelled everyone but Kōichi to return to Japan. His intelligence work with the Kantō Army kept him so busy, she explained, contact was infrequent at best, and after the surrender they lost touch with him completely. While they had once heard from someone repatriated in 1949 that Kōichi was then doing intelligence work for the Kuomintang in north China, the appearance of his name on the Li mission's list gave them more hope than ever that they might see their father and husband again. "They have been apart for so long since the children were very young," Kimi explained, "they hardly know him at all. I can't wait to get them together again."[9]

The story of Saitō Yoshio, who had belonged to a military police (*kempeitai*) unit in Manchukuo, struck a similar chord. His wife Natsuko explained that since hearing from him in late September 1945 that he had been captured by the Chinese Nationalists, they had received no further news of his whereabouts or circumstances. With popular interest in returning soldiers at the time of Li's visit running high, the *Mainichi shimbun* ran a story about the Fushun POW detention center in southern Manchuria with a photograph of some of its prisoners. The daughter Kuniko, who had only been six when she last saw her father, quite remarkably recognized him in the photo, and she and her mother later heard his name read on the radio during a recitation of men on Li's list from their hometown.[10] For every story like these two that appeared in the press there were surely hundreds of other unpublished tales across the home islands that followed a similar plot. The enthusiastic embrace of Li by so many families of the missing is thus not difficult to understand.

Not surprisingly, because it was one of the three groups that facilitated her visit, some of the most enthusiastic press support for Li's tour appeared in the China–Japan Friendship Society's newsletter *Nihon to chūgoku* (Japan and China). Several issues of the magazine covered the lead-up to her arrival as well as each major event on her itinerary, and many also featured editorial essays by well recognized doyens of China–Japan relations, including society chief Uchiyama Kanzō, the onetime Shanghai bookstore owner and active postwar promoter of Chinese studies in Japan. One especially illustrative example of the organization's enthusiasm was a welcome song published on the front page of the paper with lyrics that embodied all they hoped Li's visit would inspire.[11] The final two verses of the song are especially revealing, as they asked Li to look beyond the legacies of Japanese imperial violence to see the eyes of genuine gratitude and joy in all Japanese people upon her arrival. In appreciation of her efforts, the Japanese people promise, the lyrics concluded, to plant seeds of peace as white and pure as Li's smile and to cultivate flowers of peace and love throughout the country.

Many public intellectuals and writers across Japan also held unequivocally positive views on the tour of the Li delegation, but often for overtly political reasons.

In the pages of *Shūkan asahi*, for example, Hitotsubashi University Professor of Chinese studies Kumano Shōhei, who served as a translator for the delegation at their November 4 dinner at the Tokyo Imperial Hotel, offered a purely anecdotal but nonetheless rosy depiction of Li. "She gave the perfect impression of a brave and powerful woman," he wrote. "Even her walk, with back straight and head held high, was stately and dignified."[12] He also then fondly recalled Li's down-to-earth sense of humor at the event in the manner by which she first teased Japan Red Cross chairman Shimazu Tadatsugu for being a lightweight drinker and then chided him over his two- or three-pack-per-day smoking habit. (Shimazu also figures in Park Jung Jin's Chapter 11 on North Korea.) Suetsugu Ichirō, chair of the Japan Youth Health and Welfare Association (*Nihon zenken seinen kai*), an organization involved in providing assistance to repatriated soldiers, tackled more overtly political questions in his evaluation of Li's personal character. Li was not an ideological communist, Suetsugu contended, but a deeply committed humanist. Citing her strong personal convictions and independent spirit, Suetsugu assured his readers that Li was no mere "decoration" (*kazarimono*) put forth by the CCP as a smoke screen for some more sinister agenda.[13]

Well known journalist Hatanaka Masaharu in particular voiced strong support for Li's visit. First, Hatanaka took issue with those critics who argued that Li and the CCP deserved no special thanks for their efforts to repatriate Japanese soldiers. Such critics contended that doing so was only to be expected – it conformed to international norms. But such a position, Hatanaka countered, was one that took no account of the meaning of the history of Japan's brutal imperialist conquest of the mainland. Moreover, Hatanaka was equally critical of those who argued that Japan's efforts to return to China the bones of laborers who died under extreme duress in Japan should be met by equal efforts on the Chinese side to send back to Japan the remains of settlers and colonists. The road to genuine China–Japan reconciliation, he claimed, must start from true self-reflection on the disaster of Japanese militarism and the unconditional acceptance of responsibility for it. Hatanaka went on to explain that the Japanese government's refusal to acknowledge Li in deference to the Nationalist regime on Taiwan was also little more than toadying to the hegemonic prerogatives of U.S. policy in East Asia. Disregarding popular sentiment for the sake of appeasing American benefactors, he argued, was a betrayal of Japanese democracy.[14]

As these examples make clear, Japanese public support for the Li Dequan delegation was both wide sweeping and multidimensional. In the autumn of 1954, however, it seemed that for each voice in Japan that sought to open the doors to Li and her compatriots, there was another that hoped to slam them shut.

## Red menace? Li's detractors

As Japan's militarist regime of the late 1930s had cloaked its aggressive encroachment on Chinese sovereignty under the ideological banner of anti-communism, the ultimate victory of the CCP in the Chinese Civil War in 1949 provoked considerable anxiety and fear within postwar right-wing circles in Japan. Not surprisingly, then, grassroots ultranationalist associations proved one of the earliest and most vocal sources of criticism for the Li Dequan delegation. The Great Japan Patriotic Party (*Dai nihon aikokutō*) led by Akao Bin, for example, along with a handful of lesser known rightist groups, pasted the streets of Tokyo with slanderous flyers during the weeks leading up to Li's arrival. Peddling politically driven hate with phrases such as "Expel the communist stooge Li!" and "Absolutely oppose the invasion of Soviet and Communist Chinese thought!" One rightist flyer even attempted to draw a connection between Li and an infamous episode of wartime violence against Japanese civilians in China by claiming, "Li was a perpetrator of the Tongzhou Incident – Remember Tongzhou!"[15] Beyond the fact that Li's late husband, Feng Yuxiang, had once commanded Song Zheyuan during the late 1910s, and decades later, as a Nationalist general in 1937, Song had collaborated with Yin Rugeng in carrying out the violence at Tongzhou, how exactly Li's opponents in 1954 thought it logical to blame her for the notorious Tongzhou Incident (*Tsūshū jiken*) of July 1937 is unclear.

In their unmitigated loathing of Chinese communists, Japanese rightists found company in the Nationalists on Taiwan. Chiang's regime in Taipei lodged strong formal protests with the Japanese government concerning the Li visit, but those high-level diplomatic protests played out far more violently on the ground when physical clashes erupted between Nationalist Chinese students and left-wing Chinese youth at Haneda airport as Li's flight touched down.[16] The investigative magazine *Shinsō* (Truth) also alleged the existence of a failed scheme by Kuomintang political intelligence agents to kidnap Li by forcefully diverting her aircraft while en route to Japan and also suggested that Chinese Nationalist agents in Japan had sought to assassinate Li during her tour.[17] As Japan Red Cross Section Chief Takagi Takesaburō remembered in a behind-the-scenes glimpse of Li's visit published months after she had returned to China, the fear that Li might be attacked either by Kuomintang assassins or Japanese rightists was very real. In fact, concerns over her safety were so great that the Red Cross organized private security forces with the cooperation of local police that were present at all of Li's public events and followed along at every stage of her travels.[18]

It seems clear as well that local Taiwanese business owners in Japan were another group that voiced strong opposition to Li's visit. *The Japan Times* reported, for example, that a group of pro–Nationalist Chinese merchants chartered a plane to drop 60,000 anti-communist leaflets on several downtown districts of Tokyo on the eve of Li's arrival.[19] The magazine *Shūkan asahi* described a similar incident that took place in the posh Ginza neighborhood of Tokyo. A carefree shopper walking those fashionable streets on October 30 (the day of Li's arrival) could hardly have failed to notice a large advertisement balloon floating overhead from which dangled an enormous banner reading, "Don't be fooled by Li Dequan – The Great Alliance of Overseas Chinese Merchants [*Ri Tokuzen ni damasareruna – Kakyō ōdōmei*]."[20] Such cases of both Nationalist state and resident Taiwanese opposition to the Li visit are fascinating examples of how the struggle for legitimacy between competing factions of the Chinese revolution was still being carried on within Japan long after the end of the Chinese Civil War. A feature story in the *Shūkan yomiuri* published several months after Li's departure claimed as much by arguing that the real backstory to the entire Li affair was the struggle between resident Chinese in Japan. According to this report, resident Kuomintang sympathizers readily allied themselves with Japanese right-wingers in multiple anti-Li activities, while "Red-friendly" Chinese sought out the support of the Japan Communist Party in organizing pro-Li rallies.[21]

By far the most extensive critique of the Li visit appeared shortly after her departure when a conservative Japanese think tank called the Global Democracy Research Institute (*Sekai minshu kenkyūjo*) published a lengthy, multi-authored study of the Li mission and the dangers it posed.[22] Institute co-founder and well known former leftist Nabeyama Sadachika opened the volume by warning that Li was just the bait being used to draw in hungry Japanese on an emotional level. The real aim of the CCP in sending her, he suggested, was to draw popular Japanese sentiment away from the United States and toward the PRC and USSR. Nabeyama claimed further that the Li Dequan matter was an important "test case" of how Japan would respond to these sly tactics of Cold War diplomacy. In his view, it would be foolish to lose sight of Japan's national interests, and alienating the United States by warming up to the CCP would be dangerous step in the wrong direction.[23] In his paper Tateyama Toshitada, head of the Japan Life Safety Research Center (*Nihon seikatsu mondai kenkyūjo*), made similar points about the Li mission using emotional pleas to pursue political goals, but he also went so far as to suggest that the Li mission members and their security team were in fact an intelligence-gathering crew. He pointed out wartime ties between Japanese leftists and certain mission members as evidence of this subversive plot brewing among them.[24]

Expressing precisely the sort of opinions that Li supporter Hatanaka Masaharu had critiqued, Waseda University political scientist Yabe Teiji made two main points in his essay about the highly contentious issue of returnee war criminals: first, Communist China had violated a variety of agreements by holding Japanese prisoners for such an extended period of time; second, the legal process by which these soldiers were condemned as "war criminals" was little more than victor's justice applied after the war according to new rules. So, rather than praising the compassionate humanity of the PRC in returning these men, Yabe argued, Japan should be looking closely at the legal violations of their captivity, as future peace between the two nations depended upon a just settlement of the past war in which both sides received proper judicial treatment.[25] (Issues concerning how Japanese prisoners and war criminals were dealt with are treated in Section Two of this volume and Barak Kushner's Chapter 3 as well.)

Other contributors emphasized in various ways that at its core Li's visit was nothing more than a Chinese Communist Party propaganda tool aimed at destabilizing U.S.–Japan relations. China scholar Kamibeppu Chikashi, for example, suggested that recent developments in PRC–USSR relations revealed clearly their joint strategy for eliminating U.S. influence in Asia and fomenting internal dissent between leftist elements and conservative elites within Japan. The Li visit, he pressed, had to be understood in this context in order to recognize its potentially dangerous consequences.[26] Turning to economic matters, since Li's visit had been promoted by numerous China–Japan trade organizations, Meiji University economist Ōno Shinzō claimed that it was a mistake to believe that only U.S.-imposed limitations on Japanese trade with PRC were to blame for holding back economic links between Japan and China. Thinking so was to fall right into the PRC trap of intensifying anti-U.S. feeling in Japan. In Ōno's view, the PRC was to blame because of its own Soviet-style development programs that did not favor export development. While he agreed that increased trade was a good idea, he urged the Japanese people to remember that "business is business" and not to allow Cold War politics to cloud rational economic judgement and planning.[27] In his contribution, former Ministry of Foreign Affairs China specialist Kusano Fumio turned back to matters of diplomacy in providing a lengthy analysis of a recent speech by Zhou Enlai concerning Japan and its future relations with the United States and Taiwan. The Japanese people, Zhou claimed, could pursue true freedom only if they broke loose from U.S. domination. China and Japan were like brothers, Zhou said, and it was the United States that aimed to damage China–Japan friendship, not the PRC. In Kusano's view, Zhou's speech was indisputable evidence that the PRC aimed to make Japan a "stage for the Cold War" (*reisen no butai*).[28]

The opposition to Li Dequan and her delegation voiced by so many in Japan was just as passionate as the support she received from many others. The historical significance of the Li Dequan visit as a flashpoint of political division in postwar Japanese society should thus be clear from even this admittedly cursory look at the contemporary media of that time. Beyond the explicit and antagonistic political agendas shaping that moment, however, the less obvious but equally significant gendered dimensions of the event also require and deserve closer inspection.

## Li Dequan and the women's movement in Japan

As ironic as it sounds, both U.S. Occupation authorities in Japan and the Chinese Communist Party on the continental mainland laid proud claim to the advancement of female liberation in the postwar East Asian world. To be sure, the Allied occupation had done much to elevate the social standing and political influence of women in Japanese society by mandating female suffrage through the new constitution of 1947, but the Chinese revolution after 1949 promoted even bolder ideals of gender equality that also resonated powerfully with women in Japan.

Perhaps, then, because no woman held a similarly high-profile position in the Japanese government at that time, Li Dequan's tour garnered enthusiastic attention from a wide variety of women's magazines and journals, some feature stories being more overtly political in tone than others. The title page of a late November issue of *Household Yomiuri*, for example, ran a large photo of Li holding a young Japanese girl up with one arm (with a bouquet of flowers in the other) at the reception held for her by the Eastern Japan Families of the Missing Association. The caption praised the Li delegation for warming the hearts not only of those families but of all Japanese people by providing treasured information about missing soldiers and civilians.[29] Likewise, *New Woman* published an enthusiastic welcome to the Li delegation in its November issue expressing deep gratitude for facilitating the return of Japanese soldiers from the continent. In fact, the piece explicitly criticized the Japanese government for its lack of sincere effort on that matter. Japan's leaders had never truly aimed to bring home those citizens left behind, it asserted, because they feared the notion of popular friendship between China and Japan. Cowed by U.S. pressure, the Japanese government instead was hopelessly flustered by China's more sincere attempts to improve relations.[30]

An especially poignant feature story on the Li mission appeared in *Housewife Club* in December. Entitled "The Husband Who Could Not Return, back in My Arms," the article painted Li's visit in a highly melodramatic light. Li wept as she listened to the families of the missing speak about their long-lost husbands and sons, the piece asserted, and the families in turn shed tears of gratitude when Li's delegation promised to bring them home. "For the cause of Sino-Japanese friendship," Li is quoted, "there is nothing between China and Japan that cannot be resolved." The article then concluded on the hopeful note that with Li's visit, the day had finally come when the footfalls of a brighter age of "co-existence and co-prosperity" (*kyōzon kyōei*) for China and Japan could be heard.[31]

Beyond the glowing general coverage in numerous women's magazines, Li's visit also caught the attention of many high-profile Japanese feminist intellectuals. The prominent peace activist Ishigaki Ayako, for example, published a warm welcome to Li several days before her arrival in Tokyo. Ishigaki fondly recalled meeting Li at the International Women's Conference in Philadelphia in 1953. According to Ishigaki, they talked late into the night about Li's life in China, her marriage to Feng, and her Christian values. She was also deeply impressed by Li's down-to-earth humility, strength of personal character, and fundamental human kindness. There could be no one better, Ishigaki asserted, to work on behalf of mothers and children in the new China as Minister of Public Health. In fact, Ishigaki claimed, Li could even rightly be called a "mother of China" and her visit to Japan was sure to be an invaluable bridge to Sino-Japanese friendship.[32]

Ishigaki was not Li's only admirer within the circle of the most widely known female Japanese activists of that day. Of the many photographs that appeared in the Japanese press during the period of Li's arrival and cross-country tour, one in particular stands out. Taken at a reception held for Li soon after her arrival in Tokyo and published in both the *Mainichi shimbun* and the *Yomiuri shimbun*, Li is seen shaking hands with none other than writer and activist Hiratsuka Raichō, founding editor of the influential 1910s feminist journal *Blue Stocking* (*Seitō*) and a widely recognized leader of the postwar women's movement in Japan. The photo appeared in the English-language *The Japan Times* as well, but with the relatively mundane caption of "Women Leaders Meet: Mme. Li Te-chuan, President of the Communist Chinese Red Cross Society who arrived here on Saturday night, was met by Mrs. Hiratsuka Raichō, President of the Japan Federation of

Women's Associations, at the Imperial Hotel yesterday."[33] A discussion between Li and Hiratsuka published in the pages of *Kaizō* (Reconstruction) in early 1955, however, sheds more significant light on the meaning of this intriguing encounter between one of Japan's leading feminist public intellectuals and the prominent stateswoman from the mainland.

Provocatively titled "Asia's Peace through the Hands of Women," the conversation began as Hiratsuka expressed her deep appreciation for Chinese willingness to extend the hand of friendship even after the pain caused by so many years of war inflicted on China by Japan. Li responded magnanimously with the suggestion that many Japanese had also suffered terribly during the war and that the time had now come to forget the past and to forge a new future of peace. The conversation then turned to more practical matters as Hiratsuka asked Li about the most pressing issues facing Chinese women at that time. Li replied that women and men were now working side by side to build up China's industrial capacity. Was that because of state demands for labor from the people, Hiratsuka queried? Not at all, Li returned. The Chinese people were united in their support of state goals, and they gladly gave their labor to achieve the bright future desired by all.[34]

Two short essays by Li and Hiratsuka then followed this transcribed dialogue between them. In a piece entitled "The Current State of Chinese Women," Li described the PRC as a veritable feminist paradise. While women in the new China no longer faced social, cultural, or institutional limits on their personal aspirations, Li explained (with a rosy optimism that likely exceeded the reality faced by many Chinese women in daily life), this was no time simply for satisfaction. "Feudal thought" and customs, Li continued, still possessed a strong hold on Chinese women in some regions, and so the road ahead to complete liberation was still a long one. Li was convinced, nonetheless, that Chinese and Japanese women could join hands and overcome any obstacle as they pursued peace in Asia and around the world.[35] Hiratsuka's essay, "Welcoming Mrs. Li Dequan," elaborated on the numerous reasons behind her enthusiasm for Li's trip to Japan. She first recalled their meeting at the Imperial Hotel in Tokyo just after Li's arrival in the capital. Not only was Hiratsuka surprised that Li could attend the event so soon after her long flight, she also noted how as they first shook hands and spoke for a few minutes, Li looked directly into Hiratsuka's eyes as they talked, never once breaking her line of sight. Very few if any Japanese could look that long directly into the eyes of another, Hiratsuka noted, and in Li's dark and sparkling eyes she saw kindness, vitality, and great confidence. She went on to claim that women of Li's personal power and presence were exceedingly rare in Japan, before then likening Li to a beautifully weathered stone, both worn smooth and strengthened by many years of battling waves. With women such as Li leading the way, Hiratsuka suggested, women from every part of Asia could make great gains in their pursuit of peace and equality around the globe.[36]

Thus, while leftist intellectuals and politicians, humanitarian organizations, China–Japan trade association members, families of missing soldiers, and feminist activists all fundamentally supported Li's mission to Japan, for women's rights advocates there was a deeper meaning to Li's journey. To them, Li's gender was the most inspiring dimension of her sojourn in Japan because, as a woman pursuing the broader aim of China–Japan reconciliation and global public health, she represented not only a brighter future of regional peace and cooperation, but also a future in which women would have greater personal freedom and political influence than ever before, both within East Asian society and beyond.

## Conclusions

After returning to China, Li discussed the meaning of her visit to Japan through an editorial in the pages of *People's China* (Jinmin chūgoku), a Beijing-based Japanese language publication aimed at readers in Japan, which was later reprinted in the widely circulated domestic periodical *Central Review* (Chūō kōron). More than just a review of her whirlwind tour of the archipelago, Li reflected in this essay on her hopes for a new chapter in China–Japan relations. She assured her Japanese readers that, for the Chinese people, their many years of war with Japan were a thing of the past. It was the responsibility of both peoples now to endeavor for the restoration of their 2000-year relationship of peaceful exchange and interaction. She also tried to assuage any fears of China's rising power in the postwar world with a reference to the so-called golden rule of her Christian faith. Japan need not fear aggression from China because so many years of hardship under foreign invasion had taught the Chinese people the value of the notion that one should "do unto others as you would have done to you." Finally, she reminded the Japanese public that they and the Chinese people had the same goal – to prevent the resurgence of Japanese militarism so desired by the United States in order to facilitate American control in Asia.[37]

By Li's own admission then, at least one aim of her delegation was indeed the de-legitimation of the U.S.–Japan security agreement, just as many of her critics in the Global Democracy Research Institute had claimed. It seems likely, too, that the CCP's approval of Li Dequan's mission to Japan reflected yet another dimension of the party's strategy to cultivate a positive image of the PRC in Japanese popular imagination by representing mainland China as a society progressive enough to have women play meaningful roles in statecraft and diplomacy. Viewing the Li delegation visit as little more than a cynical exercise in self-serving diplomatic posturing, however, is to focus solely on why it was sent. When we turn to the matter of how it was received, many additional meanings become clear.

Li's visit brought to a boil simmering internal divisions within Japanese society concerning the legitimacy of a Japanese state so closely linked to the United States. For many of those who supported the Li delegation, the Yoshida government was opposing the will of the people by refusing to formally recognize Li and by extension the PRC as a whole. In doing so, conservative political elites were abrogating their obligation to Japanese democracy and sacrificing their legitimacy in the process. Li's detractors in Japan, however, denied the legitimacy of her proclaimed political independence from the CCP. For them, as for most Cold

Warriors in the United States, red was red, and anyone representing a communist regime was nothing more than a mouthpiece of Moscow or Beijing. If the CCP had indeed hoped that the Li visit would make Japan a stage for the Cold War between the United States and the PRC, it was then certainly also a stage upon which an important early act in the drama of domestic political strife within Japan, a drama that would unfold with even greater passion by the 1960s, was performed.

The evolving conflict within Japanese society over war memory is also evident in the popular reaction to Li's visit. Her critics often focused on the illegal detainment and mistreatment of "innocent" Japanese soldiers, while her promoters focused on the benevolent humanitarianism needed to return Japanese "war criminals" to their families. In other words, on one side of the Li dispute, there was a defense of those who fought and died for a just war while on the other there was recognition of Japan's terribly mistaken militarism and aggression. As such, the shape of popular consciousness concerning the legitimacy of the wartime experience itself was at stake in the debate over the meaning of Li Dequan's arrival in Japan.

A humorous reflection on the frenzied public reaction to Li Dequan's visit shortly after her departure in early November by the prolific political cartoonist Yokoyama Taizō reminds us, too, of the noteworthy gender dimensions of the event. In the comic, a visibly angry Japanese woman in kimono and traditional wooden geta clogs marches boldly with a flag in hand reading "Oppose Li Dequan!" At first glance the meaning seems obvious, but the caption spoken by two other women standing just to the rear of the protester reveals the true reason for her hostility to Comrade Li's visit. It reads: "Yeah . . . her husband's name was on the list of still living prisoners."[38] In other words, the sign bearer was voicing her opposition to Li not out of virulent anti-Communism but because she was so disappointed because her long-lost husband might not be coming home after all! In this sarcastic twist on the grief shared by thousands of families of the missing, Yokoyama emphasized a level of meaning in Li's visit that was important to Japanese women as individuals, not wives and mothers. The "good news" that Li brought to this soldier's wife was met with rage rather than gratitude because it threatened to spoil all of the freedom she had come to enjoy since her beloved husband disappeared.

In sum, the multiple layers of meaning within Li Dequan's 1954 visit to Japan explored here should remind us, if nothing else, that cataclysmic defeat and American occupation did not bring a swift end to Japanese engagement with continental politics. In fact, the domestic social divisions in Japan that had found expression in either support for or opposition to continental expansion twenty years prior were still at work two decades later. During the 1930s, however, it was the Japanese left that had wanted to stay out of China, while the right had aimed to move deeper in. By the 1950s, it was the right that wanted out and the left that sought deeper involvement. While the breakdown of empire had dramatically altered the landscape of social struggle within Japan, it had not resolved the political contradictions that fueled the fight.

## Notes

1  "Senkushatachi no doryoku no ato," *Asahi gurafu*, October 13, 1972, p. 22.
2  Almost no secondary scholarship concerning the Li visit exists in English, and only a handful of Japanese historians have looked closely at her Japan tour. See Hatano Masaru and Iimori Akiko, "Ri Tokuzen hō-nichi o megutte nitchū kankei," *Tokiwa kokusai kiyō* (March 2000): pp. 1–18. Another relevant study is Ōsawa Takeshi, "Zaika hōjin hikiage kōshō o meguru sengo nitchū kankei – nitchū minkan kōshō ni okeru 'san dantai hōshiki' o chūshin toshite," *Ajia kenkyū* vol. 49, issue 3 (July 2003): pp. 54–70. The Li mission is only briefly mentioned in Baba Kimihiko, *Sengo nihonjin no chūgokuzō: nihon haisen kara bunka kakumei – nitchū fukkō made* (Shinyōsha, 2010), pp. 147–148. (Unless otherwise noted, all Japanese books are published in Tokyo.)
3  This short description of Li's life course is based on accounts provided in Nanba Hideo, "Yōkoso kōjūjikai daihyō – chūgoku jinmin kyūenkai to chūgoku sekijūjisha ni tsuite," *Sekai ōrai* vol. 20, issue 12 (December 1954): pp. 100–107, and Takamura Kōichi, "Ri Tokuzen to iu onna – akai chūgoku no kurisuchan," *Jinbutsu ōrai* vol. 3, issue 10 (October 1954): pp. 36–39.
4  Takamura, "Ri Tokuzen."
5  Osawa, "Zaika hōjin," pp. 58–59. A valuable discussion of Japanese efforts to return the physical remains of Chinese laborers is Wang Hongyan, "Chūgokujin ikotsu sōkan undō to sengo chūnichi kankei," *Hitotsubashi ronsō* vol. 119, issue 2 (February 1998): pp. 267–283.
6  Li's remarks entitled "Jindō to *heiwa* no tame ni" are included in Nanba, "Yōkoso kōjūjikai daihyō," pp. 106–107.
7  This rendering of the itinerary is based upon Hatano and Iimori, "Ri Tokuzen hōnichi," pp. 8–9.
8  Ibid.
9  "Yume ka to yorokobu rusu kazoku," *Mainichi shimbun*, November 1, 1954.
10  "Yahari chichi wa ikite ita," *Mainichi shimbun*, November 1, 1954.
11  "Ri Tokuzen obasan o mukaeru uta," *Nihon to chūgoku*, October 21, 1954.
12  Kumano Shōhei, "Mono wakari no ii obasan – tokyo no Ri Tokuzen joshi," *Shūkan asahi*, November 14, 1954, pp. 12–13.
13  Suetsugu Ichirō, "Watashi no atta Ri Tokuzen no inshō," *Tairiku mondai* (March 1954): pp. 30–32.
14  *Hatanaka* Masaharu, "Chūgoku kōjūjikai daihyō no rainichi o megutte," *Sekai* vol. 107 (November 1954): pp. 92–97.
15  "Uō saō no Ri Tokuzen joshi kangei," *Shūkan sankei*, November 14, 1954, pp. 18–19.
16  Hatano and Iimori, "Ri Tokuzen hōnichi," p. 11.
17  "Ri Tokuzen rachi keikaku no shippai," *Shinsō* vol. 75 (December 1954): pp. 20–27.
18  Takagi Takesaburō, "Ri Tokuzen joshi ikkō hōnichi rakuya banashi," *Rōsai* vol. 6, issue 1 (January 1955): pp. 22–25.
19  "Drop Leaflets Protesting Visit," *The Japan Times*, October 30, 1954.
20  "Yōkoso! Ri Tokuzen da ga, ichibu no myō na ugoki," *Shūkan asahi*, November 7, 1954, pp. 12–13.
21  "Ri Tokuzen no akai shita – 'heiwateki sonzai no kage ni tōru nikkyō," *Shūkan yomiuri*, February 13, 1955, pp. 64–67.
22  Sekai minshu kenkyūjo, ed., *Chūso sengen to Ri Tokuzen no hōnichi* (Self-published, 1954). Baba Kimihiko notes that the institute was, in fact, co-founded by a group of 'converted' Japanese socialists who had become ardent anti-communists. Baba, *Sengo nihonjin no chūgokuzō*, p. 458.
23  Nabeyama Sadachika, "Tsuide ni kaete," in *Chūso sengen*, pp. 1–7.
24  Tateyama Toshitada, "Ri Tokuzen hōnichi no haigo ni aru bōryakushō," in *Chūso sengen*, pp. 47–53.
25  Yabe Teiji, "Kokusai dōgi to senpan yokuryū mondai," in *Chūso sengen*, pp. 8–11.

26 Kamibeppu Chikashi, "Chūso kyōdō seimei no igi to yakuwari," in *Chūso sengen*, pp. 21–32.
27 Ōno Shinzō, "Bijinesu wa bijinesu ni todome yo," in *Chūso sengen*, pp. 12–20.
28 Kusano Fumio, "Shū Onrai genmei no nerau mono," in *Chūso sengen*, pp. 33–46.
29 "Ri Tokuzen joshi," *Katei yomiuri*, November 21, 1954, p. 3.
30 "Yōkoso, Ri Tokuzen joshi," *Shin josei* vol. 46 (November 1954): pp. 24–25. This editorial was followed in the January 1955 issue with a collection of photos from the Li visit, all of which depicted adoring crowds of smiling Japanese citizens warmly embracing Li and her colleagues. See "Heiwa to yūjō no okurimono – Ri Tokuzen no hōnichi arubamu," *Shin josei* vol. 48 (January 1955): pp. 9–12.
31 Yanagikawa Reiko, "Kaeranu otto o watashi no te ni," *Fujin kurabu* vol. 35 (December 1954): pp. 146–152.
32 Ishigaki Ayako, "Ai to jindō o tsuranuku," *Asahi shimbun*, October 27, 1954.
33 "Mme. Li Group Presents List of Red-Held Japanese," *The Japan Times*, November 1, 1954.
34 Li Dequan and Hiratsuka Raichō, "Ajia no heiwa wa fujin no te de," *Kaizō* vol. 36, issue 1 (January 1955): pp. 65–67.
35 Li Dequan, "Chūgoku fujin no genjō," *Kaizō* vol. 36, issue 1 (January 1955): pp. 67–70.
36 Hiratsuka Raichō, "Ri Tokuzen joshi wo mukae shite," *Kaizō* vol. 36, issue 1 (January 1955): pp. 70–73.
37 Li Dequan, "Nihon hōmon no tabi kara kaette," *Jinmin chūgoku* (January 1955): pp. 11–14. Published under the same title in *Chūō kōron* vol. 70, issue 3 (March 1955): pp. 208–212.
38 Editorial cartoon in *Shūkan sankei*, November 21, 1954.

# Section four

# Media and the imperial aftermath

# 13 The "pacifist" magazine *Sekai*

## A barometer of postwar thought

*Satō Takumi (translated
by M. A. Mujeeb Khan)*

The Iwanami Publishing Company began publication of the magazine *Sekai* (The World) in January 1946, soon after the end of World War Two, and, since its inception, the magazine has been known for providing critical forums on profound social and political issues. The existence of groups of professional journalists and critics who engage one another in the pages of magazines, *rondan* in Japanese, is not a phenomenon that is unique to Japan: high-quality magazines, journals, and reviews in which intellectuals discuss the pertinent issues of the day can be found in countries all over the world. Neither is it unusual for such debates to have an influence on public opinion. Nevertheless, the activities of Iwanami, a publishing house founded in Japan in the early twentieth century, primarily for academic books and other highbrow publications, lent intellectuals and critics in Japan an overwhelming intellectual authority in the years immediately after the war. And it could be argued that certain aspects of this phenomenon were distinctively Japanese.[1]

*Sekai* is now one of the leading intellectual reviews in Japan. In histories of Japanese publishing, publishers are quite commonly identified with particular imperial reigns: Hakubunkan Publishing is identified with the Meiji era (1868–1912), Jitsugyō no nihonsha with the Taisho era (1912–1926), and Kōdansha with the Showa period (1926–1989), and so on. Iwanami is seldom mentioned in histories of such major publishing houses because popularity (or "lowbrow" appeal) was never its main objective. Where Iwanami is mentioned, however, is in discussions of the development of prewar fascist culture, specifically in a context of Kōdansha versus Iwanami "culture," with Kōdansha representing lowbrow, or popular, culture and Iwanami standing for its highbrow counterpart.[2] This duality cropped up in the 1955 Iwanami publication, *A History of the Showa Era*, which famously criticized the separation between popular and high culture as "a Japanese cultural flaw."[3] As this history explains:

> Kōdansha culture was exemplified by entertainment-focused publications, which were read and enjoyed by an overwhelmingly large portion of the Japanese populace. Iwanami culture, on the other hand, showcased more intellectual leaning works, which were only read by a minority, the nation's intelligentsia. Kōdansha appealed to conventional thoughts and attitudes,

combining vulgar entertainment and practical learning, loyalty and patriotism, along with the emotions of duty and sentiment. Iwanami introduced the latest trends in intellectual thought from overseas but lacked a connection to people's everyday lives. . . . Moreover, there was no bridge that connected these two quite separate publishing cultures.[4]

This lack of a common foundation between low and high cultures has been identified by certain critics and journalists as the reason for the absence of any popular resistance to "fascism" in Japan. Japan did not possess a newspaper comparable to *The New York Times* in the United States or *The Times* in the United Kingdom, media that provided a platform for dialogue between high and low cultures and engagement of the public in contemporary political issues. Before the war, Kōdansha's nine major magazines, which included *King* (*Kingu*), *Women's Club* (*Fujin kurabu*), and *Boys' Club* (*Shōnen kurabu*), accounted for roughly 80 percent of the magazines and journals produced in Japan. Iwanami, on the other hand, published academic journals of limited circulation that targeted intellectuals – *Science* (*Kagaku*), *Thought* (*Shisō*), and *Literature* (*Bungaku*), to name a few. The Kōdansha–Iwanami binary is reflected in the antonyms that were often used to describe this division – rural and patriotic versus urban and Americanized, appealing to the masses and commonsensical versus elite and esoteric, for example – in a paradigm that placed Iwanami in the inferior position. Criticism was leveled against Iwanami's "cult of academism" and "elitist ideology" in the prewar years by journalists like Ōya Sōichi and novelist Tosaka Jun, among others.[5]

## A quality magazine for "postwar democracy"

*Sekai* is among the best known in the category of publications called *sōgō zasshi*, which may be loosely translated as "general-interest magazine," but it is one specifically oriented toward educated and intellectually minded readers. It was born out of a perceived need for a "cultural revolution" and deep social reflection on "the shortcomings of Japanese culture" that had arisen after the collapse of the Japanese empire in August 1945. This premise that postwar Japanese society had broken from prewar culture is also questioned by Matthias Zachmann in Chapter 9 of this volume, in which he stresses ideological continuity in the legal realm between the pre- and postwar. Though not a mainstream nor widely circulated magazine, *Sekai* became a critical forum for postwar journalists and political commentators up until the 1970s, by which time phrases like "postwar democracy" and "progressive intellectuals" had lost some of their luster. Even so, the magazine's stance as a forum where new ideas of state and society are interrogated continues to this day.

As these descriptions suggest, in contrast to mainstream prewar intellectual magazines such as *Central Review* (*Chūō kōron*), founded in 1887, and *Literary Chronicle* (*Bungei shunjū*), founded in 1923, *Sekai* is very much a journal of Japan's "postwar" era.[6] Although it appeared along with an enormous number of other general-interest magazines from the "ashes of defeat," only *Sekai* survived and was still going strong ten years later in 1956.[7] The magazine came to serve as a marker for measuring how far Japanese political thought and public discourse had progressed after the war. Takeuchi Yō, emeritus professor of Kyoto University, has identified this golden age of the 1950s as "the age of *Sekai*," which illustrates the important role that the magazine played in helping to shape postwar Japan's intellectual discourse. Of course, it is difficult for readers today, when they hold a copy of *Sekai* in their hands, to appreciate the brilliance that emerged from its pages during the period when the magazine was at its zenith. In this chapter, I will consider the rise and decline of this "brilliance" in the context of Japan's postwar media.

*Sekai* is often mentioned along with the *Asahi Journal*, which was established in 1959, as one of the two magazines of the era that symbolize "postwar democracy." A popular image of the early postwar was of readers clutching *Boy's Magazine* (*Shōnen magajin*) in one hand and the *Asahi Journal* in the other. However, the magazines are quite different. For one thing, *Sekai* was a monthly magazine, while *Asahi Journal* was a weekly publication.[8] The size and character of their respective readerships also differed. Shimizu Ikutarō, editorial consultant for the inaugural issue of *Sekai*, described the limited demographic of monthly general-interest magazines as follows:

> Intellectual magazines were produced on the tacit assumption that their readership would have completed higher education, which meant that they were without the more inclusive mass appeal of the daily newspapers, and were quite highbrow. Accordingly, these magazines came to be seen as offering topics of general interest for a certain portion of the intellectual classes. [Another way of putting it] might be to say that these journals, while covering a variety of topics, were for a chosen few.[9]

Kido Mataichi, a University of Tokyo Institute of Journalism professor, provided the following characterization of *Sekai* in a tenth-anniversary special issue published in 1956: "The unanimous criticism everyone leveled against *Sekai* was that its articles were textbook-like, didactic, academic, and prim and proper. This reputation remains unchanged today. Basically, it was not a kind of lighthearted magazine that you might read lying around."[10] This educationally principled and politically rigorous character of the magazine remains the same today, fifty years after Kido's original comments.

In 1958, when handing over the baton of editor-in-chief to Ebihara Mitsuyoshi, the first editor-in-chief Yoshino Genzaburō mentioned in his retirement article that *Sekai* shared the memory of "wartime suppression of free speech" with its rival magazine *Central Review*. *Central Review*, a liberal magazine from the prewar period, was forced to completely cease publication in 1944, as was the magazine *Reconstruction* (*Kaizō*), in a series of police raids now collectively known as the Yokohama Incident.[11] Yoshino held Ebihara in high regard as someone who had personally experienced wartime suppression of free speech. He said that Ebihara was a veteran of the field and extremely capable of the job of editor-in-chief.[12]

The importance of the memory of wartime suppression of free speech for Yoshino continued to make itself felt in *Sekai*'s editorial policy, as can be seen in later statements by Yasue Ryōsuke, an editor-in-chief of *Sekai*, who would later become Iwanami Publishing Company's third president. In a roundtable discussion that Yasue participated in decades later with former *Central Review* editor-in-chief Kasuya Kazuki and former *Literary Chronicle* editor-in-chief Tanaka Kengo, Yasue reflected:

> The foundation of our mindset at *Sekai*, that continues to the present day, was a deep reflection on World War Two. Accordingly, we maintain an interest in Asia, and we place weight on Japan's reconciliation with the various peoples of Asia. We also focus on the issue of peace. On the other hand, the editor-in-chief Yoshino Genzaburō wanted the magazine to be a journal of record for important intellectual statements of each era. These things, unchanged even now, are our fundamental principles.[13]

At the same time, part of the inspiration for this new magazine may have resulted from the deep personal reflection on the prewar period by Iwanami's founder Iwanami Shigeo, a regret that he expressed a number of times.[14] Editor-in-chief Yoshino described Iwanami's feelings in a summary he wrote about the history of *Sekai*, printed in a 1966 issue of the magazine.

> Even though Japan possessed highbrow culture, Iwanami told us, that alone had done nothing to help us prevent our country from being destroyed. This was because our culture was utterly divorced from ordinary people – ordinary people had been powerless, which was what had allowed the military and the extreme right wing to completely take over. It was Iwanami Shigeo's view that we should never allow this mistake to be repeated, that we should use it as a lesson: that we had to do something to connect culture to the masses. Iwanami Publishing Company had to descend from its ivory tower, to produce writing more closely connected to ordinary people. We should *not simply leave it to Kōdansha to be producing culture for the masses:* we [at Sekai] must publish more, be it general-interest magazines or popular magazines. This was what Iwanami told us – we had to publish as much as we could. He did not forget to add that one of the reasons why so many Japanese youths were sent to their deaths during the war was that the older generation had been cowardly, not speaking up in an appropriate manner, at the appropriate time.[15]

According to Kuno Osamu, one of the "brains" of Iwanami publishing during the war, the resolve to break the monopoly that Kōdansha had over popular culture in the postwar years stemmed from Iwanami Shigeo's bitter disappointment that "despite their best efforts, Iwanami had been unable to win over readers from the extreme popular ultranationalism offered by [Kōdansha's magazine] *King*."[16] Kōdansha had established *King* in 1925 as a magazine whose strapline was "one copy in every household [in the nation]," and it was the first "national popular magazine" (*kokumin taishū zasshi*) to reach a circulation of 1 million. The magazine that Iwanami Shigeo, with the Iwanami–Kōdansha binary in mind, was looking to create in the postwar period in *Sekai* was like an enlightened version of *King*.

Iwanami's determination to establish this new magazine derived from a sense of regret at having been, as he described it, a mere "courier of culture," someone who "due to cowardice, [did not speak] up in the appropriate manner, at the appropriate time." In *Sekai's* inaugural issue Iwanami wrote, "When I look back and remember that I was unable to do what I knew was right, it is a source of unbearable, deep shame." The renowned Japanese political scientist Maruyama Masao later referred to such feelings, widespread among intellectuals in the years after the war, as "a state of collective remorse."[17]

## A magazine for "collective remorse"

In September 1945, Abe Yoshishige, who had been a classmate of Iwanami's at the First Higher School and later at Tokyo Imperial University, helped a group called the Dōshinkai (literally the "Group of One Mind") present their plans for a general-interest publication to Iwanami, who was already contemplating setting up a new magazine. Dōshinkai comprised a number of men who toward the end of war had started meeting at the invitation of diplomat Kase Toshikazu, a close advisor to Foreign Minister Shigemitsu Mamoru (later convicted of Class A war crimes), and writer Yamamoto Yūzō. The Dōshinkai group included Taisho-era liberalists and luminaries such as the writer Shiga Naoya and the writer and philosopher Mushanokōji Saneatsu, among others, all of whom met for secret discussions about what would happen at the war's end. These men were joined after Japan's defeat by writer and philosopher Nagayo Yoshirō, a member of the Shirakaba literary coterie, philosopher Yanagi Muneyoshi, founder of the *mingei* (popular craft) movement, and others. Various suggestions were made for the new magazine's title, including *Shinsei* (*New Voice*), *Gyōfū* (*Dawn Wind*), *Chikyū* (*Earth*), and *Sekai* (*World*). The final choice came down to *Chikyū* and *Sekai*. Nobutoki Kiyoshi, composer of a well known patriotic wartime song "If We Go to Sea" ("*Umi yukaba*," first released in 1937), apparently stated that "*Chikyū* sounds rather daft," and they opted for the title *Sekai*. Only later was it made known that the suggestion for this had in fact been made by the philosopher Tanikawa Tetsuzō, a promoter of "world government" for the purposes of peace.[18] It was decided that Abe Yoshishige would be the lead editor for the Dōshinkai group and Yoshino Genzaburō placed in charge of editorial responsibilities at Iwanami publishing house.

The inaugural January 1946 issue of *Sekai*, with a print run of 80,000 copies, quickly sold out in mid-December 1945. However, from its inception, differences in opinion arose regarding the "gentleman's agreement" that had been made between the Dōshinkai group and Iwanami publishing company. The two groups clashed over their interpretation of their roles and responsibilities. Dōshinkai assumed that Iwanami was producing Dōshinkai's own coterie magazine, whereas

Iwanami thought that it had appointed Dōshinkai's Abe Yoshishige as head of a general-interest magazine set up under Iwanami's auspices. However, very soon after *Sekai*'s establishment, Abe was appointed as minister of education in the Shidehara Kijūrō Cabinet. As a result, the inaugural edition began with a "Publication Note" from Tanaka Kotarō, who represented the Dōshinkai, and ended with an essay entitled "On the Publication of *Sekai*" by Iwanami Shigeo. Tanaka, who six months later replaced Abe as minister of education for the first Yoshida Shigeru Cabinet, declared in his note that "[we] have no wish to pander to the masses or follow fads, as if laying out products like a department store," a policy that clearly diverged from that of an "enlightened popular magazine" that Iwanami Shigeo had originally envisaged. As Yoshino later reflected, "professional journalists saw us as a group of talented schoolboys while the political left made sarcastic comments that we were a magazine for leftist factions amongst the conservatives."[19]

From the second issue onward, editorial responsibilities were assumed by the socialist Ōuchi Hyōe, while practical responsibilities were undertaken by Yoshino Genzaburō. By Yoshino's own account, it was during a conversation with Ōuchi at the wake of the Marxist philosopher Miki Kiyoshi, on September 28, 1945, that Yoshino hit upon a specific vision for the magazine.[20] Miki had been arrested on March 28, 1945, as an editor for the Iwanami Publishing Company, for violating the Peace Preservation Law, and on September 26, 1945, he died in prison. Ōuchi had himself been arrested during the Popular Front Incident in 1938 and, not wedded to any particular ideology, was able to transcend political factionalism. Though he was a member of the Dōshinkai group, he later helped establish the Socialist Party (*Shakaishugi kyōkai*), founded in 1951, and he took up an editorial position in the Society's journal *Socialism* (*Shakaishugi*).

One event that is often described as epoch-making in the history of *Sekai* is Maruyama Masao's enormously significant article, "Theory and Psychology of Ultranationalism," which ran in the May 1946 issue.[21] A few months later, Shimizu Ikutarō's review in the *Asahi Shimbun* under the name of "Atom," lauded Maruyama's article in the following way:

> Finally, someone has managed to blow open the walls that surround the world of journalists and commentators, in all their empty gesturing. Those who doubt me should take a look at Maruyama Masao's "Theory and Psychology of Ultranationalism" in the May issue of *Sekai*. Words like "feudal" and so on are utterly incapable of capturing all that is covered by the Japanese word *kokutai*, or "national polity," that strange amalgamation of [political] authority and power, but here [the author] subjects [the *kokutai*] to an extremely logical and sound analysis. In his argumentation, and in his utilization of sources, the author creates a new style that makes us really appreciate the value of youth. Above all else, this article demonstrates the clear power of scholarship.[22]

The original reason for the publication of Maruyama's article in the opening pages of the May 1946 issue of *Sekai* was to counter the influence of an article by Tsuda Sōkichi, which had called for the preservation of the imperial system in the preceding April issue. Maruyama's intent to repudiate Tsuda's thrust is clear from the supplementary sections he added when he included this article in his 1956 book, *Gendai seiji no shisō to kōdō*, later translated and edited into English as *Thought and Behavior in Modern Japanese Politics.* "I certainly cannot accept," Maruyama wrote, "the view (expressed in typical form by Professor Tsuda Sōkichi) that the pathology I have outlined in discussing the spiritual structure of the emperor system is merely an 'exceptional phenomenon' produced by the frenzy of an 'emergency period'."[23] Nevertheless, Tsuda's article clearly resonated with those *Sekai* readers who had been born during the Meiji era (1868–1912), as is demonstrated by an article "Mission and Reflections of the Japanese People," written by Yanaihara Tadao in *Sekai*'s August 1946 issue. Yanaihara was a Christian, an economist, and a pacifist, who like Tsuda had been forced to leave his university post during the war. When he wrote the article, Yanaihara was a professor in the Economics Department of Tokyo Imperial University, and he was later appointed president of the university (later renamed the University of Tokyo), as successor to Nanbara Shigeru. He was not a member of the Dōshinkai group, but as someone born in the Meiji era, he shared an ordinary person's view of the imperial family. "I consider Japan's role in the world to consist of the following three things," Yanaihara declared in his article. "First, to present an unbroken line of emperors; second, to provide a fusion of Eastern and Western culture; and, third, to exist as a peaceful nation." He noted that "we discover facts about the lives of the ancients, their feelings about life, and their ideals in our myths and fables," indicating a sympathy for Tsuda's sentiments.[24] Such widely divergent views on the emperor system suggest that the only thing shared by the younger and older generations was the idea of a "peaceful nation." Yanaihara also argued in favor of one further role for Japan, demilitarization, which he described as an "honorable experiment":

> It is Japan's destiny now, whether we like it or not, to try to live in a manner befitting a peaceful nation. But it is by bringing about a change in our idea of this destiny from something that is forced on us and to which we have to resign ourselves into something that we ourselves grasp, making it the historic mission of the Japanese people, that we must find the fundamental spiritual energy for Japan's regeneration. Destiny is something one awaits passively. A mission is something that one actively embraces. Destiny involves resignation. A mission involves hope.[25]

Following the publication of Tsuda's article, more and more younger writers began to appear in the pages of *Sekai*. Up until the issue that had featured Tsuda's article, Dōshinkai members, mostly men in their sixties, comprised the majority of writers published in the magazine. From the May issue onward, however, the average age of the staff and writers of *Sekai* began to get markedly younger, with those in their forties and fifties at the core. Spirited, energetic writers in their thirties, like Maruyama, started making an appearance in front-piece articles. They included the European historian Hayashi Kentarō in the September 1946 issue, the economist Tsuru Shigeto in November 1946, and the economic historian Ōtsuka Hisao in December 1946. Tsuda's article had in fact provided an opportunity for *Sekai* to put some distance between itself and the older liberalists of the Dōshinkai group. Despite this, according to the results of a survey of magazine readers' interests published in *Japan Readers' News* on August 21, 1946, the April issue of *Sekai* with Tsuda's article and the inaugural issue were both more popular than the May issue that had featured Maruyama's article.[26] No doubt many readers felt secure with the sense of continuity with the prewar years provided by the writings of the older Dōshinkai group members. For this reason, even after the infusion of younger writers, *Sekai*'s relationship with Dōshinkai continued.

## An organ of the pacifist movement

We should note that the concept of pacifism in *Sekai* developed under strict American occupation censorship. For example, in the inaugural issue, two passages were deleted from Abe Yoshishige's front-piece article "Fortitude, Truth, and Wisdom" (*Gōki to shinjitsu to chie to o*); and the column "World Currents" (*Sekai no ushio*), underwent particularly strict censorship.[27] According to research by media historian Fuji Haruhide, half of the injunctions, suspensions, and deletions in 1946 were mostly made on the grounds of "nationalistic discourse," "criticism of the Allies," and other similar rationales. However, with the intensification of the Cold War, the reasons given for censorship changed and started to include "left-wing propaganda" and "criticism of capitalism."[28] Yoshino went in person to lodge a protest with the CIE (Civil Information and Education section of the American Occupation Headquarters [GHQ]), which handled occupation censorship matters. As he later recalled, he told the officials: "It baffles me how things that were permitted even under Japanese censorship before the war are not permitted under the Occupation. Does it not affect your sense of honor?" When he pointed out the contradiction between the strict censorship of Iwanami leftist tendencies and the permissiveness shown toward left-wing presses, the American official in charge apparently responded that it was because "we do not wish you to lend the left wing any of your credibility."[29] This episode demonstrates the high value GHQ accorded to the power of the Iwanami Publishing brand. Well known writer, critic, academic, and journalist Katō Shūichi stated in a 1958 discussion that no quality newspaper existed for thinking people in Japan comparable with *The Times* or *The Manchester Guardian* in Britain, and this fact made *Sekai*, and in particular its "World Currents" column, very significant.[30]

The news featured in the "World Currents" column was a digest of the latest discussions from a number of leading overseas magazines, and differed from the usual fragmentary items available in regular Japanese newspapers (which, it could be argued, contributed to the strong sense of ideology conveyed). The demand for such articles was especially high during the period of the Occupation when strict limitations were in place on the import of foreign publications. It is perhaps difficult to imagine in today's world of globalized telecommunications the influence that this magazine column had at the time. Its principal writers were Wakimura

Yoshitarō, a professor of economics at the University of Tokyo, Ministry of Foreign Affairs official Tsuru Shigeto, the historian Kondō Shin'ichi, and the historian Iida Tōji, as well as Tanaka Shinjirō and others at the *Asahi shimbun.* According to Wakimura, the column was created with a conscious awareness of the "World News" (*Sekai jōhō*) column in the prewar magazine *Reconstruction.*[31] Wakimura and his colleagues would go regularly to the CIE public reading room located in NHK's old headquarters near the Ministry of Foreign Affairs, where they would peruse the foreign newspapers and journals. The drafts of the articles that were written on the basis of their reading would be submitted by members of *Sekai*'s editorial department to the American military's Civil Censorship Detachment (CCD), which was located in the same building, for prepublication censorship.

In September 1948, on one of these visits to the CCD, editor-in-chief Yoshino Genzaburō got hold of the July 18, 1948 joint statement made by eight UNESCO social scientists on the causes of world conflict. This document would become the genesis of a new group that would gather to discuss peace, demilitarization, and social justice under the name of the Peace Problems Symposium (*Heiwa mondai danwakai*). Having read the UNESCO declaration, Yoshino consulted Shimizu Ikutarō, a professor of sociology in the midst of writing his book *Journalism*, and the philosopher and critic Kuno Osamu. The plan was to issue a joint announcement by Japanese and foreign academics.[32] Immediately, a Peace Problems Symposium was organized, with one chapter in Tokyo and another in Kyoto, and these chapters were further divided into separate subgroups on education, politics, economics, and natural sciences, all of them discussing and debating the contents of the UNESCO statement. Once the groups of the Peace Problems Symposium had compiled their conclusions, on December 12, 1948, a general meeting was convened at the Meiji Kinenkan (Meiji Memorial Hall). Abe Yoshishige, now president of Gakushūin University, was nominated as chair, and Nishina Yoshio, director of the Science Research Institute, and Ōuchi Hyōe, professor of economics at the University of Tokyo, as vice-chairs. In the end, they adopted a statement drawn up by Shimizu Ikutarō, the "Japanese Scientists' Statement Concerning War and Peace" (*Sensō to heiwa ni kan suru nihon no kagakusha no seimei*). This was the first so-called Peace Problems statement. A few lines from Abe Yoshishige's opening remarks "Peace Problems and Japan" suggest something of the motivations behind the statement, as well as the mindset of people such as Watsuji Tetsurō and Tsuda Sōkichi, men from the older generation, who had also participated:

> If the Allied Nations are going to pass judgment on us in the name of peace and civilization, they have to provide us with a guarantee of that peace and civilization. That is their moral obligation. What we are saying is that the problem of peace is an especially pressing problem for the Japanese people, but at the same time the guarantee of that peace is an important moral obligation that must be duly shouldered by the Allied Nations.[33]

When it was announced on November 1, 1949 that the U.S. State Department was drafting a peace treaty with Japan, the discussions taking place in Japan on

peace and issues surrounding a peace treaty, known as the peace debates, intensified. There were essentially two positions: those who argued for "a single peace
treaty" (*tandokuron*), or an exclusive alliance with a particular bloc, the West as it
was defining itself under the Cold War, centering on the United States; and those
who argued for a "comprehensive peace treaty" (*zenmen kōwaron*), which would
be across-the-board security arrangements with all of Japan's former enemies,
including the Soviet Union and the Eastern Bloc. In the end, this came down to a
choice between U.S.–Japan security arrangements and unarmed neutrality. On
December 21, 1949, the Symposium held a general meeting, and on January 15,
1950 it released a "Statement on the Peace Problem" (which later came to be
known as the Peace Problems Symposium's second statement). The text of this
statement, which outlined four principles of peace (a comprehensive peace [*zenmen
kōwa*], neutrality, opposition to military bases, and opposition to rearmament), was
published in the May 1950 issue of *Sekai*. The list of signatories shows fewer
names than appeared in the first statement, the "Japanese Scientists' Statement
Concerning War and Peace." A note in this second statement explained, "There are
some of our members who, guided by the same zeal for peace and by the same
love of Japan as ourselves, nevertheless recognize the not insignificant value of a
single peace treaty."[34] This second statement appeared in the March issue of many
other magazines.

It was at this point that the magazine *Sekai* started to be seen as the main organ
of the "anti-establishment" factions, which stood against the national security policies being put together by the government. Indeed, it might be said that this was
also the moment when *Sekai* started being viewed as a vehicle of the left wing.
Prime Minister Yoshida Shigeru accused Nanbara Shigeru, who was arguing in the
pages of *Sekai* for a "comprehensive peace," of "twisting the truth and truckling
to the times" (*kyokugaku asei no to*) and brewing merely empty rhetoric.[35] Following this, the left-wing *New Japanese Literature* (*Shin nihon bungaku*) journal
published the results of a questionnaire in response to the prime minister's comments in August 1950. Amidst readers' overwhelming support for Nanbara and
criticism of Yoshida, the writer and literary critic Kawamori Yoshizō, someone
who had played a consulting role during *Sekai*'s creation, added his own laconic
yet stinging remarks: "I have my own reasons to not trust Nanbara Shigeru," he
wrote. "In my view, he is little better than a bureaucrat. But obviously, the statements made by Prime Minister Yoshida are highly offensive."[36]

The next time *Sekai* found itself under pressure to formulate a consistent stance
was after the outbreak of war on the Korean Peninsula on June 25, 1950, when
Japan faced the possibility of being drawn into the crisis. Almost immediately, on
June 26, the Communist newspaper *Red Flag* (*Akahata*) was ordered to cease
publication. On July 24, GHQ initiated a "red purge," which included the mass
media. As if in lockstep with political developments, which form part of what is
now referred to as the Reverse Course (when Allied Occupation policy shifted
from emphasizing Japan's demilitarization to actively propping up Japan to serve
as a bulwark for U.S. plans in the Far East), the economy began to grow rapidly,
helped by the American demand for military provisions. The Peace Problems

Symposium responded by publishing its statement, "On Peace, for the Third Time," in the December 1950 issue of *Sekai*, declaring its political position as a rejection of rearmament and a rejection of a "single peace treaty" – that is to say, of alignment with the United States. By this time, a chasm had opened between general public opinion, which desired an early, or timely, peace (*sōki kowa*), which would suggest a timely end to the occupation (*sōki dokuritsu*). Circulation of *Sekai* then plummeted to around 30,000 copies.[37]

On September 8, 1951, forty-eight nations signed the San Francisco Peace Treaty with Japan, and at the same time the U.S.–Japan Security Treaty was concluded (these both went into effect in April 1952). This effectively marked the re-emergence of postwar Japan as a fully fledged member of the Free World and an ally of the West. The October 1951 issue of *Sekai*, a special issue on the Problems of Peace, was published so that it could go on sale one week before the signing of the Treaty. Unusually for a magazine, the issue had five printings, and it sold all 150,000 copies. Even so, this was not a sign of mass readership. As Midorikawa Tōru, who at the time worked in the editorial department (and later was second president of the magazine), revealed decades later, "We took the magazine ourselves, at their request, to the [offices of] the Japanese National Railways, to the General Council of Japanese Trade Unions, to the Japan Postal Workers' Union."[38] Midorikawa then negotiated bulk purchases with officials at these unions. The networks that *Sekai* continued to build up with these labor unions eventually culminated in January 1952 at a general meeting of the Socialist Party, with the adoption of the Three Principles of Peace (Japan's permanent neutrality, a comprehensive peace treaty with all nations, and opposition to U.S. military bases in Japan), which was what *Sekai* was advocating. Labor union and Socialist Party institutional purchases helped *Sekai*'s circulation to rise to 100,000 copies in 1954.

In a 1952 *Yomiuri shimbun* survey, titled "Best Three Magazines," *Sekai*, *Literary Chronicle*, and *Central Review* came out on top in the category of general-interest magazine.[39] Nevertheless, the number of liberal- and realistically minded intellectuals who were now withdrawing interest from *Sekai* was growing rapidly. Koizumi Shinzō, for example, a Dōshinkai member and contributor to *Sekai*, lambasted the October 1951 special issue on the peace accord problems, claiming that it [*Sekai*] "resembled nothing so much as a coterie magazine for proponents of comprehensive peace and proponents of neutrality."[40] *Sekai* published a refutation written by Tsuru Shigeto and Sugi Toshio in March 1952, and Koizumi hit back in an article titled "My Theory for Peace," which *Sekai* published in May 1952:

> Naturally, it has to be acknowledged that my views and the views of Tsuru and others differ with regard to the Soviet plan for peace. Compared to me, Tsuru is significantly Soviet-friendly, or, one might say, Soviet-trusting. Compared to Tsuru, I am extremely Soviet-critical, or, one might say, Soviet-cautious.[41]

*Sekai*'s editor-in-chief, Yoshino, though not necessarily bothered by the conformity of the views expressed in the pages of the magazine, did replace some members of the Peace Problems Symposium, and in June 1958 he established a Constitutional Issues Research Group with the aim of blocking a revision of Japan's constitution. He also established the International Issues Symposium in 1959 to deliberate on security treaty revision issues. A rise in anti-nuclear weapon activism, spurred in part by the March 1, 1954 Lucky Dragon Incident, when a Japanese fishing boat crew was contaminated by nuclear fallout from a U.S. nuclear test in the Bikini Atoll, lent a certain tailwind to *Sekai*.

## A psychological salve for intellectuals

Who were *Sekai*'s readers – what kind of demographic did they occupy? Internal statistics suggest that company employees (including factory workers) comprised 24 percent, educators 20 percent, and government employees 19.7 percent. Salaried workers thus made up a total of 63.7 percent of the readership. Students came next at 23.2 percent, and traders and farmers at 12.2 percent. Almost 40 percent were either educators or government officials, and the number of white-collar workers affiliated with the Japan Teachers' Union (*Nikkyōso*) and the All-Japan Prefectural and Municipal Workers' Union (*Jichirō*) was overwhelming. The "Letters from Readers" column in the February 1953 issue of *Sekai* carried a letter from a certain "ordinary laborer in Kagawa Prefecture," who wrote that he had taken a look at the magazine for the first time at the encouragement of a friend in his labor union. The writer roundly criticized the magazine for its patently "patrician attitude," the way it "talked down" to "the uneducated masses," as if the matters treated on its pages would be "completely above their heads." The laborer then went on to describe the specific case of "someone who had to borrow a dictionary just to read one of the articles," noting that "it had taken that person a whole month to read it."[42] In his editorial postscript, Yoshino acknowledged "the dissatisfaction of ordinary people with the [over-]intellectualizing tendency [in the content of the magazine] that makes it difficult for them to grasp."[43] He recognized that this had been a problem with *Sekai* since its founding and an issue with which the editors had continually wrestled. But the real root of the problem, he said, and the one that had to be overcome, lay in Japan's deeper social and historical conditions rather than in *Sekai*'s editorial policy, and he asked for readers' understanding. In response to this letter to the editor, the subsequent March 1953 issue published two letters together: one was a letter of opposition to the original complaint from another "laborer in Kagawa Prefecture," and the other was a letter in support of the original complaint from "a bookseller in Wakayama Prefecture." The letter from the laborer claimed that *Sekai* was not especially more difficult to understand than the politics and economics sections of Japan's newspapers. The letter from the bookseller pointed out that it was the magazine's "well-intentioned vanity" that had aroused the anger of the common people. If this was so, it meant the complete breakdown of Iwanami Shigeo's original intention in establishing *Sekai*, which was to produce a magazine that would try to have a positive impact on mass public opinion. Kuwabara Takeo, in the April 1953 issue of *Sekai*, wrote a piece entitled "What Should a General-Interest Magazine Be? What Do *Sekai*'s Readers Want?"[44]

Responding to the readers' complaints, he argued that "people from the uneducated masses, and laborers, would never write anything so snide." He suspected that the identity of "a certain laborer" was in fact "an activist" who felt like "causing a bit of trouble." Kuwabara wrote that in cities of non-metropolitan regions, local government officials generally read the *Literary Chronicle*: the readers of *Sekai* were people in education.[45] *Literary Chronicle*, he said, had the goal of achieving a readership of 1 million, and it tended if anything to go along with rather than lead public opinion. In contrast, Kuwabara argued, *Sekai* was important in being even-handed and in the way it maintained a consistency that was unaffected by political vicissitudes, dispassionately expounding on the meaning of peace.

Years later, however, the critic Nakajima Makoto wrote on the attitudes of "teachers and middle-class educated people and salarymen" who read articles in *Sekai* that dispassionately expounded on the meaning of peace:

> *Sekai* published copious opinions and "statements" on the U.S.–Japan Peace Treaty, on the Security Agreement, on nuclear weapons, and on Japanese–Korean issues. By contributing to *Sekai*, authors were provided with an emotional outlet for their passionate consciences and by reading *Sekai* their consciences were comforted.[46]

If it was true that for readers, that is to say educated white-collar workers, *Sekai* offered a kind of salve for their consciences, for writers *Sekai* offered the chance for a platinum ticket to membership in a critical forum. The fact that people who wrote for *Sekai* dominated journalist circles in the 1950s is clear from the overwhelming frequency of references to statements they made or positions they took in review columns covering contemporary events in national newspapers. A great many of the writers of these columns, for example in the *Asahi shimbun*, were in fact at the same time writers for *Sekai*.

Tsujimura Akira, a media studies researcher, has remarked on the self-propagating effect achieved by the overlapping relationship between the writers of these review columns and the writers who wrote most of the opinion pieces in *Sekai*.

> People who wrote numerous articles that received a lot of attention would gain a reputation, which would then lead to them being selected to write review columns. They would then treat articles that had been written by their own colleagues – all of which created a snowball effect that just fed itself.[47]

A typical example of this "snowball effect" was *Sekai*'s January 1956 ten-year anniversary issue. An article by Kido Mataichi, "Newspapers, Magazines, and Public Opinion," featured a piece by Ōkuma Nobuyuki titled "Ten Years of an Intellectual Magazine – Focusing on *Sekai*."[48] Kido, a professor at the University of Tokyo's Newspaper Research Institute, was the commentator for a column in the 1954 *Asahi shimbun* and would be so again in 1957. Ōkuma had been driven from public office after the war as an Executive Director of the National Diet and Speech Association, but he wrote the "Forum Outlook" (*Rondan tenbō*) at *Jiji Press*. The trend continued in *Sekai*'s June 1958 150th commemorative issue, which featured Nakajima Kenzō (the number two contributor to *Sekai*) and Katō Shūichi (the number three contributor to *Sekai*). These men were respectively in charge of *Asahi shimbun*'s and *Mainichi shimbun*'s intellectual magazine reviews, and in this issue they held a three-way, roundtable discussion, entitled "Requirements for *Sekai* (a Roundtable)," with *Sekai* editor-in-chief Yoshino Genzaburō. The article by Ōkuma Nobuyuki that followed this discussion, titled "The Salability of the Intellectual Magazine and the Critical Spirit – on the Occasion of the 150th Issue of *Sekai*," is highly revealing.[49] The one reason, Ōkuma argued, that *Sekai* was the only magazine that was still going strong, in spite of the demise of the many other intellectual magazines that had sprung up after the war, was the consistency of the magazine's editorial policy. In the end, *Sekai*'s editorial stance was also seen, as Shimizu Ikutarō wrote, "largely as a result of the honesty and wisdom of the editor-in-chief which allowed us to liberate the issue of peace from the worn out framework of the experience of war and place it above narrow ideological interests."[50]

## August 15 as a media memory

One way in which Yoshino attempted to separate theories of peace from the "tired framework of wartime experiences" was an effort to institutionalize the experiences of August 15, 1945. In today's Japan, everyone thinks of August 15 as the official day on which to commemorate the war's end, but for a period immediately after the war, August 14, the day that Japan accepted the Potsdam Declaration, and September 2, the day that Japan signed the Instrument of Surrender aboard the USS *Missouri*, were more important.[51] The institution of the tradition of August 15 as the anniversary of the end of the war was due in no small part to *Sekai*'s annual special issues on the subject.

August 15, 1945 was the day of the Imperial Rescript on Surrender, the speech delivered by Emperor Hirohito, announcing that Japan would surrender, effectively ending the war: it was broadcast to the entire empire via the radio. A formal announcement of the cessation of hostilities was made from the Imperial Headquarters on August 16. Internationally, September 2, the day when the surrender document was signed, is the day that nations around the world commemorate the end of war with Japan, with America calling it V-J Day and Russia Victory Day. China's day for commemorating victory in its War of Resistance is September 3. The only nations that commemorate August 15 as the official anniversary of the war's end are Japan and a few others, including North and South Korea, as well as Great Britain, which like the United States celebrates it as V-J Day.

As Yoshino himself recalled at the start of a talk that he gave in August 1965, entitled "The Meaning of the End of the War, and the Vietnam War," before *Sekai* began its special issues on the theme of August 15, he felt that the memories of this date in Japan had been buried and forgotten:

> After the war, other journalists and I formed something called the [Japan] Congress of Journalists, and every year we would have a gathering on August 15 to mark the anniversary of the end of the war. I remember about ten years ago a newspaper reporter came to our gathering and told me that he had been interested in finding out if any events were being held in Tokyo to commemorate the end of the war. He had apparently done a bit of investigation, and had discovered that not a single event was being held besides ours, and one other, a small gathering of ultra-right-wing groups. I began to feel that with every year that passed, the meaning of this day, August 15, and that of Constitution Memorial Day, May 3, was receding from our consciousness.[52]

While August 14 and September 2 were dates that signified the termination of something, the *end* of the war and of the imperial state, August 15, which was the day that the emperor's speech was broadcast to the entire empire, was a date that made every citizen aware that a new era was about to *start*. The first mention in *Sekai* of the importance of the date of August 15 occurred in its second issue, in February 1946, in a piece by Takahashi Masao titled "The Economics of a Defeated Japan – Before August 15." This was followed by an editorial postscript by Yoshino, in March 1947, in which he referred to Tatsumi Ineo's *Notes on the War's End*.[53] However, the clearest delineation in *Sekai*'s pages of the significance of August 15 came in its May 1946 issue, in the closing paragraph of an article by Maruyama Masao titled "The Theory and Psychology of Ultra-Nationalism":

> August 15 1945, the day that put an end to Japanese imperialism, was also the day when the "national polity," which had been the foundation of the entire ultra-nationalist structure, lost its absolute quality. Now for the first time the Japanese people, who until then had been mere objects, *became free subjects* and the destiny of this "national polity" was committed to their own hands.[54]

Nonetheless, *Sekai* did not then immediately produce a special issue on the theme of August 15. The first sign of general-interest magazines starting to commemorate August 15 was a roundtable discussion published in the August 1949 issue of the *Japan Review* (*Nihon hyōron*) titled "The Days around the Defeat – Commemorating August 15." The next year, other magazines followed suit, compiling special issues on the subject, the most celebrated perhaps being *Sekai*'s August 1950 issue on "Memories of the Day of Defeat" (*Haisen no hi no omoide*). Thereafter it became established practice for *Sekai*'s August issue always to be a special issue focusing on intellectuals' memories and reflections of August 15. While these accounts were published as recollections, they also seem to have been put together with the idea of helping readers to cope with the "new, uncharted path" of peace. The public solicitation of people's memories of the experience of defeat continued: in 1956, the theme was "My 'Postwar' Experience"; in 1957

"Have the Wounds Healed?"; and in 1959 "Daily Life and the Constitution." In 1960, the August 15 issue became an extra special issue with the theme of "Sovereignty lies with the people – Citizens movements against the Security Treaty and future issues." This issue featured articles opposing the New U.S.–Japan Security Treaty (signed in January that year). In a break with tradition, the issue on readers' experiences of August 15 was published in September of that year.

These commemorative essay solicitations in the August issues continued for almost two decades, finally coming to an end in August 1975 with a new collection that included some previously published essays. No other magazine had managed to run August memorial issues for such a long period of time. Even in 1965, Kobayashi Isamu, chairman of the Iwanami Publishing Company, had written proudly about *Sekai*'s commitment to this special end-of-war commemorative issue:

> In a similar manner to our May 3 Constitution Memorial Day, over the past ten-plus years it seems that August 15 is being progressively forgotten. This year a full two decades have passed [since the end of the war], and various [commemorative] events have been planned by several magazines, but right through last year any magazine or newspaper that managed to mark the day every year without fail has been the rare exception. We [at *Sekai*], however, take pride in having managed to do this, in our own modest way. The special issue on war's end that *Sekai* has been putting out has been appearing now for over ten years.[55]

However, it would be a mistake to assume that the future-oriented nature of these memories of August 15 was shared by the general mass of readers. On the basis of an analysis of a large number of such "records of August 15 experiences," Okazaki Mitsuyoshi, editor-in-chief of *Literary Chronicle* after the war, drew attention to the inherent problematic in seeing such "written" experiences as influencing the future:

> No matter how terrible an experience may have been, there is a strange comfort to be gained by fixing [that experience] in writing: it takes on the conclusive quality of a written record. [This means that it] has no effect on the future. By writing it down, the possibility of any further developments arising in the story of the experience is closed off. And sometimes, this is where these experiences "die." A completely fixed, absolute world comes into being, in which no one else is allowed to have a say.[56]

Okazaki had submitted a story of his own to *Sekai*'s records of readers' experiences of August 15 while still a student at the University of Kyoto. His entry, which was selected for the 1958 August issue, was titled "Metamorphosis," and it was an indictment of the postwar "about-face" of Japanese primary school teachers.[57] In fact, rather than being the jottings of ordinary people, most of the pieces selected for publication in the August special issues were polished works written by people who were either potential or emerging writers. This meant that the recollections were not written or selected on the basis of what the recounted experience meant at the time – that is, *in the past* – but rather what the remembered experience might mean for the writer or reader *now*. In other words, they were "memories of the present" rather than the past – literary or imaginative creations by writers who were writing with their readers' responses in mind.

*Sekai* was, up until a certain period, a kind of barometer that allowed one to judge how close or far one's own position was from "mainstream" postwar thought about pacifism; hence the reason for this chapter's title. However, no measuring instrument, not even the very finest one, can escape the changes brought by the passage of time. The question of how long *Sekai* was in fact able to fully gauge a true measure of independence from the mainstream is a topic of interest in the study of postwar media. It is probably accurate to say that the editors' treatment of the economist Ōkuma Nobuyuki, following the article that he published in *Sekai* in January 1964 titled "The Japanese People," constitutes a particularly problematic moment. In his article, Ōkuma wrote that it was simply false to think that any form of democracy could exist in a political system in Japan while it was still under American occupation.[58]

Ōkuma pointed out that Maruyama Masao had misconceived the facts in his reaffirmation of the student demonstrations against the Security Treaty in the 1960s. Ōkuma wanted some sort of recognition of the utter "lack of independence" that characterized postwar democracy in Japan. He saw this emerging out of the refusal to come to terms with the utter devastation that had been suffered on August 15, when the Japanese people had "lost all sense of themselves as a people." Notably, even though *Sekai* published three articles after this issue that were critical of this piece by Ōkuma, the editors never gave Ōkuma any opportunity to refute or even address the criticisms that had been made of his views. As the political scholar Karube Tadashi notes in his history of the Iwanami Publishing Company, "I think we can see the period that follows this as one in which the magazine *Sekai* closed off any criticism of postwar democracy, making such criticism a taboo."[59] *Sekai* might have started out with the objective of becoming a platform for critical discussion and analysis of Japan's past, as well as the path Japan had followed that led it to war, empire, defeat, and the brink of destruction. While the magazine succeeded to a certain extent in encouraging discussion in the years following the war, eventually this ceded to a commitment to uphold a new vision of history, one that was designed to feed Japan's new postwar image of itself.

## Notes

1  This chapter is an expanded and revised version of my Japanese article "'Sekai' – sengo heiwa shugi no mētoru genki," in *Nihon no rondan zasshi: kyōyō media no seisui*, ed. Takeuchi Yō, Satō Takumi, and Inagaki Kyōko (Osaka: Sōgensha, 2014). (Unless otherwise noted, all Japanese books are published in Tokyo.)

2  See Watanuki Jōji, *Politics in Postwar Japanese Society* (University of Tokyo Press, 1977), p. 104. See also the short discussion in Yoshimi Takeuchi, *What Is Modernity? Writings of Takeuchi Yoshimi*, trans. and ed. Richard Calichman (New York: Columbia University Press, 2005), pp. 51–52.

3  Tōyama Shigeki, Fujiwara Akira, and Imai Seiichi, *Shōwa-shi* (Iwanami shoten, 1955): p. 89.

4  Ibid., p. 89. This paragraph was removed in the updated version published in 1959.

5  Ōya Sōichi was an influential leftwing social critic. Tosaka Jun was a novelist and originally a member of the Kyoto School (a school of thought associated with the philosopher Nishida Kitarō founded on Zen Buddhism and engagement with Western philosophy; its left-wing members were Marxist). Ōya gradually became more rightwing while Tosaka, eventually ousted from his academic position for his left-wing views, remained staunchly anti-militarist until his death in 1945. See Harry D. Harootunian, "Time, Everydayness and the Specter of Fascism: Tosaka Jun and Philosophy's New Vocation," in *Re-Politicising the Kyoto School as Philosophy*, ed. Christopher Goto-Jones (London: Routledge, 2008), pp. 98–100. See also Peter Duus "Empire and War," in *Sources of Japanese Tradition, Volume Two: 1600 to 2000*, ed. William Theodore De Bary, Carol Gluck, and Arthur E. Tiedemann (New York: Columbia University Press, 2005), p. 932. Robert Carter, *The Kyoto School: An Introduction* (Albany: SUNY Press, 2013), pp. 9–10.

6  Oku Takenori, *Rondan no sengoshi, 1945–70* (Heibonsha, 2007), p. 59.

7  Ōkuma Nobuyuki, "Shūgō zasshi jūnen no ayumi: '*sekai*' o chūshin," *Sekai*, January 1956, p. 159.

8  *Sekai* and *Asahi journal* came up together in the roundtable discussion by Nishi Yoshiyuki, Kamiya Fuji, Noda Nobuo, and Takahashi Shirō, in *Shokun!* in February 1991, published as "Iwanami bunka no hanzai," *Shokun!*, February 1991, pp. 78–97.

9  Shimizu Ikutarō, *Jānarizumu* (Iwanami shinsho, 1949), p. 41.

10  Kido Mataichi, "Shimbun – zasshi – seron," *Sekai*, January 1956, pp. 156–158.

11  For a brief introduction to this incident, see Ben-Ami Shillony, *Politics and Culture in Wartime Japan* (Oxford: Oxford University Press, 1981), p. 126.

12  Yoshino Genzaburō, "Henshū kōki" in *Sekai*, June 1958, p. 359.

13  Yasue Ryōsuke, Kasuya Kazuki, and Tanaka Kengo, "Sōgō zasshi no 'sekai'," *Ryūdō*, July 1979, p. 106. For details, see Ōe Kenzaburō and Yasue Ryōsuke, *"Sekai" no yonjūnen: sengo o minaosu, soshite, ima* (Iwanami bukkuretto, 1984); Mainichi shimbun henshūhen, *Iwanami shinsho to bungei shunka: "sekai" "bungei shunka" ni miru sengo shichō* (Mainichi shimbunsha, 1996).

14  These expressions of remorse are noted in several biographies. For example, Abe Yoshishige, *Iwanami Shigeo den* (Iwanami shoten, 1957); Kobayashi Isamu, *Sekirekiso shujin – hitotsu no Iwanami Shigeo den* (Iwanami shoten, 1963).

15  Yoshino Genzaburō, "Sōkan made: *sekai* henshū nijūnen," *Sekai*, January 1966. Reprinted in Yoshino Genzaburō, *Shokugyō toshite no henshūsha* (Iwanami, 1989), pp. 62–63.

16  Kuno Osamu, "Shichū ni katsu o motomete: hitotsu no kaisō, Iwanami Shigeo to iwanami shinsho 6," *Tosho*, January 1994, p. 35.

17  Maruyama Masao, "Kindai nihon no chishikijin," in *Kōei no ichi kara: 'gendai seiji no shisō to kōdō' tsuiho*, ed. Maruyama Masao (Miraisha, 1982), p. 117.

18  Ōuchi Hyōe, "*Sekai* no tame ni kanpai," *Tosho*, July 1962, pp. 2–3.

19  Yoshino, *Shokugyō toshite no henshūsha*, p. 84.

20  Ibid, pp. 80–82.

21  Masao Maruyama, *Thought and Behavior in Modern Japanese Politics*, ed. and trans. Ivan Morris (London: Oxford University Press, 1969), p. 1–24.

22  "Kobore banashi," *Tosho*, January 1995, p. 64.

23  Maruyama Masao, "Theory and Psychology of Ultra-Nationalism," in *Thought and Behavior in Modern Japanese Politics*, Expanded Edition, ed. and trans. Ivan Morris (Oxford: Oxford University Press, 1969), p. 23.

24  Yanaihara Tadao, "Nihon kokumin no shimei to hansei," *Sekai*, August 1946, p. 26.

25  Ibid., p. 32.

26 *Nihon dokusho shimbun, 1946 August 21* (Nippon shuppan kyōkai). Fukushima Jūrō, *Sengo zasshi hakkutsu: shōdo jidai no seishin* (Yōsensha, 1985), p. 594.
27 Hanawa Sakura, *Iwanami monogatari: watakushi no sengoshi* (Shinbisha, 1990), p. 27.
28 Fuji Haruhide, "Yoshino Genzaburō to *sekai*," *Rekishi hyōron*, May 1996, pp. 49.
29 Yoshino Genzaburō, "Iwanami bunka no saishuppatsu – GHQ no ken'etsu nado," in *Shōwa keizaishi e no shōgen*, vol. 2, ed. Andō Yoshio (Mainichi shimbunsha, 1966), p. 89.
30 Nakajima Kenzō, Katō Shūichi, and Yoshino Genzaburō, "Sekai e no chūmon (zadankai)," *Sekai*, June 1958, p. 302.
31 Wakimura Yoshitarō, "'Sekai no shio' shuppatsu no koro," *Sekai*, January 1996, pp. 121–122.
32 Shimizu Ikutarō, *Waga jinsei no dampen*, vol. 2 (Bunshun bunko, 1985), p. 83; Kuno Osamu, Maruyama Masao, Yoshino Genzaburō, Ishida Takeshi, Sakamoto Yoshikazu, and Hidaka Rokurō, "Heiwa mondai danwakai ni tsuite," *Sekai Special Extra Issue*, July 1985, p. 9.
33 Abe Yoshishige, "Heiwa mondai to nihon," *Sekai*, March 1950, p. 20.
34 "Kōwa mondai ni tsuite heiwa mondai konwakai seimei," *Sekai*, March 1950, p. 64.
35 Nanbara Shigeru argued this in "Sekai no hakyokuteki kiki to nihon no shimei," *Sekai*, May 1950. Yoshida Shigeru's response was in the *Mainichi shimbun*, May 4, 1950, morning edition.
36 "Ankēto: sensō, heiwa, kyokugaku asei," *Shin nihon bungaku*, August 1950, pp. 83, 88.
37 Hanawa Sakura, *Chihō bunkaron e no kokoromi* (Tomobe-machi: Henkyōsha, 1976), p. 30.
38 Midorikawa Tōru, "Heiwa mondai shindankai to sono go," *Sekai Special Extra Issue*, July 1985, p. 63.
39 Unsigned (Kobayashi Isamu), "Katasumi kara," *Tosho*, July 1952, p. 25. Satō, *Monogatari*, p. 276.
40 Koizumi Shinzō, "Heiwa-ron: setsu ni heiwa o negau mono to shite," *Bungei shunjū*, January 1952, pp. 64–79.
41 "Watashi no heiwaron ni tsuite," *Sekai*, May 1952, p. 247.
42 Ishikawaken ichi rōdoōsha, "Dokusha kara no tegami," *Sekai*, February 1953, p. 230.
43 Yoshino Genzaburō, "Henshū kōki," *Sekai*, February 1953, p. 256.
44 The original Japanese title was "Sōgō zasshi no arikata: sekai no dokushatachi no yōbō o megutte."
45 *Shūkan bunshun*, published by *Literary Chronicle* (*Bungei shunjū*).
46 Nakajima Makoto, "*Sekai, asahi jānaru* ni miru sengo minshushugi," *Ryūdō*, July 1979, p. 82.
47 Tsujimura Akira, "Asahi shimbun no kamen: 'rondan jihyō' no henkō to giman o tsuku," *Shokun!*, January 1982, pp. 141–142. Tsujimura analyzes frequency of citation according to author and magazine in the *Asahi shimbun* reviews columns from October 1951 to December 1980, showing that *Sekai* was mentioned 1,390 times, *Chūō kōron* 1,072 times, *Asahi jānaru* 556 times, and *Bungei shunjū* 467 times.
48 The original Japanese article was "*Sōgō zasshi jūnen no ayumi: sekai o chūshin toshite*."
49 The original Japanese article was "*Sōgō zasshi = sono shōhinsei to hihanteki seishin: Sekai hyakugojū gō ni yosete*."
50 Shimizu Ikutarō, "Sugao: Yoshino Genzaburō-shi," *Asahi jānaru*, December 24, 1961, p. 27.
51 See Satō Takumi, *Hachigatsu jūgonichi no shinwa: shūsen kinenbi no media-gaku* (Chikuma shobō, 2005).
52 Yoshino Genzaburō, "Shūsen no igi to betonamu sensō (1965 nen 8 gatsu)," in Yoshino Genzaburō, *Dōjidai no koto: betonamu sensō no koto o wasureru na* (Iwanami shinsho, 1974), p. 51.

53  Takahashi's article in the original Japanese article was: "Haisen nihon no keizai katei: hachi jūgo izen." *Notes on War's End* (*Shūsen oboegaki*) – Takagi Sōkichi (Kōbundō, 1948). Takagi had been a high-ranking Navy officer in the war and used the pen name Tatsumi Ineo.

54  Masao, "Theory and Psychology of Ultra-Nationalism," in *Thought and Behavior in Modern Japanese Politics*, ed. and trans. Morris, p. 21. (Emphasis added.)

55  "Kobore-banashi," *Tosho*, August 1965, p. 48.

56  Okazaki Mitsuyoshi, "'Hachigatsu jūgonichi taiken'-ki no shūhen," *Kikan gendaishi*, vol. 3, November 1973, p. 112.

57  Reprinted in Usui Yoshimi ed., *Gendai kyōyō zenshu dai 18 – haisen no kiroku* (Chikuma shobō, 1960).

58  The original Japanese article was "*Nihon minzoku ni tsuite.*"

59  Karube Tadashi, *Monogatari iwanami shoten hyakunen-shi 3: 'sengo' kara hanarete* (Iwanami shoten, 2013), p. 56.

# 14 Post-imperial broadcasting networks in China and Manchuria

*Shirato Ken'ichirō*

## Introduction

The telecommunications industry – including telegraph, telephone, and radio broadcasting – formed the core of what served as the imperial nervous system of the Japanese empire and its occupied areas. These information and censorship agencies performed the most crucial roles in controlling the hearts and minds of both Japanese and local populations in Japanese-controlled territories up until the end of World War Two. In Japan, Taiwan, and Korea, telegraph and telephone enterprises were run by the Ministry of Communications and related colonial government offices. Radio broadcasting was managed separately by the *Hōsō kyōkai* (Nippon Broadcasting Corporation, known as NHK). Only in Manchukuo, Japan's puppet state in north China, were telegraph, telephone, and radio run by one single vast company, the Manchurian Telegraph and Telephone Company (hereafter the MTTC). There was thus a significant difference between the MTTC, which was a vast and powerful organization, and other telecommunications agencies within the Japanese empire.

This chapter delves into the establishment of the MTTC, which has been recognized by historians as a unique and remarkable institution with a fascinating role in the history of Japan's empire and the war in East Asia. The planners, who were fundamentally the Japanese government, the Kwantung Army based in Manchuria, and the South Manchuria Railway Company, understood very early on that Manchuria was a massive region in a strategic position with borders contiguous with the Soviet Union and the Republic of China. As such, they saw the need for a highly effective broadcasting network to compete with information and propaganda from Manchukuo's geographic neighbors. To implement such a dream, the Japanese authorities adopted a unique organizational structure, as well as varied broadcasting policies that, among other things, made use of entertainment programming and advertising. This chapter will also touch upon the relevance of the MTTC in the postwar development of private Japanese broadcasting companies to demonstrate the linkages and continuities, as well as its profound influence.

The MTTC was founded in September 1, 1933 and within four years produced dramatic results in all fields of telecommunications, promoting a centralized management of the telegraph and telephone systems within Manchuria. Before the establishment of the MTTC, only six telegraph offices in Manchuria connected Japanese-controlled territories and the rest of China.[1] Each office was independent and not integrated into any larger regional network within the Chinese mainland, and even the government of Manchurian warlord Zhang Zuolin and his son who succeeded him, Zhang Xueliang, had struggled to absorb these communication agencies into their own administrative structures.[2] Furthermore, only ten telephone bureaus connected Japan with China in 1928, even though more than 120 telephone offices existed in Manchuria.[3] Three radio stations existed in the cities of Dalian, Mukden, and Harbin. The Dalian station started in 1925, the third broadcasting station in the Japanese empire; the Mukden station began broadcasting in 1927; and the Harbin station opened in 1926. Although radio broadcasting had started early, the number of listeners remained small, and the broadcasting networks did not expand. After the 1931 Manchurian Incident and the Kwantung Army's occupation of northern Manchuria, Japanese people were able to send telegrams in the Japanese language from southern to northern Manchuria.

After its establishment, the MTTC built infrastructure for telecommunications, implementing a unified tariff and procedures to connect other areas of Manchukuo. The number of telegrams that the MTTC handled increased from roughly 4.6 million in 1933 to 17.5 million by 1942, and the number of its telephone subscribers grew from roughly 30,000 in 1933 to 120,000 in 1942. The number of radio listeners also increased, from roughly 8,000 in 1933 to nearly 80,000 in 1937 and to 340,000 in 1940. Perhaps most remarkably, the number of Chinese radio listeners increased from a mere 409 in 1933 to 16,550 in 1937 and to 96,488 in 1939.[4]

The MTTC ran advertisements and multilingual broadcasts in Chinese, Russian, Mongolian, Korean, and the Japanese languages initially on one radio channel. The MTTC then added transmitters to its station and was able to broadcast Japanese, as well as Korean and Russian programs. This was on what was called the First Channel (*Dai ichi hōsō*). When the second transmitter was added, this enabled the broadcast of programs in Chinese and the inclusion of Mongolian programs. This was the Second Channel. The MTTC used the dual broadcast system energetically, where it could broadcast on both transmitters simultaneously but with different programs, and in 1942 eighteen broadcasting stations in Manchukuo implemented this system of dual broadcasts.

Advertisement-based broadcasting was a method permitted only in Taiwan and Manchukuo, which were two of Japan's most important colonial possessions. Advertisement-based broadcasts provided a means of obtaining financing by selling broadcasting time to companies, or sponsors, who would make announcements about their products on air. These broadcasts were not permitted on the Japanese mainland, and in fact this remained the case until 1952. The Taiwanese advertisement-based broadcasts started in July 1932, continued for only six months, and then they were brought to a halt due to the opposition of newspaper companies who were afraid of the deleterious effect on their own advertisement revenue. In Manchukuo, however, advertising-based broadcasts continued for nearly four years, from 1936 to 1940. Previous studies have situated Manchukuo advertisement broadcasts as the precursor of commercial broadcasting in Japan as it developed after the war, and certainly the experience of advertisement broadcasting in the MTTC proved to be of great benefit to those who later worked in private Japanese broadcasting companies.[5] In short, the imperial experiences for many within Manchukuo radio history became an important precursor and format for how Japanese civilian broadcasting evolved after 1952, following the end of the American occupation.[6]

## The distinctive character of the MTTC

The MTTC was a state-run company that had dual nationality in that it was registered in both Japan and Manchukuo and it combined management from the telegraph, telephone, and radio broadcasting enterprises. The president of the MTTC was a lieutenant general from the Imperial Japanese Army, and Japanese staff occupied almost all executive positions. The Japanese government funded 33 percent of the MTTC's operating costs, while the Manchukuo government covered 12 percent, the South Manchuria Railway Company 7 percent, the Nippon Broadcasting Corporation (NHK) 3 percent, and other private companies the remainder. However, the idea that one organization would comprehensively manage telecommunications enterprises was not an easily reached consensus among imperial strategists. At the outset there were, in fact, several different plans. One plan had proposed that a Manchukuo government department manage the postal, telegraph, and telephone enterprises, and another broadcasting agency, such as NHK, operate the radio broadcasting sections. The idea that the NHK or a similar organization might run the enterprise was particularly strongly supported because before the MTTC had been founded, NHK had managed radio broadcasting in Shinkyō (Xinjing in Chinese, present-day Changchun) and Mukden (present-day Shenyang).

The Kwantung Army, the Ministry of Communications, and the South Manchuria Railway Company held their first meeting in February 1932 to decide communication policies in Manchukuo. Each agency submitted opinion papers and reports, and in the end the Kwantung Army headquarters put forward a proposal titled "A Communication Policy for Manchuria" to the Japanese government in July 1932. Within this package, a Ministry of Communications bureaucrat, Kajii Takeshi, submitted a personal memo, "A Report on Telegraph and Telephone Equipment in Manchuria." His memo argued for the need to create a national conglomerate that combined telegraph, telephone, and radio broadcasting. Kajii would later take up office as president of the Japan Telegraph and Telephone Public Corporation (*Nippon denshin denwa kōsha*, which later became the company NTT) after World War Two.[7] Kajii pointed out that in his opinion, in particular with regard to radio broadcasting, the plans were "too small-scale" to "guide the thought of the entire population [of Manchukuo] in an appropriate manner." In the final draft "The Communication Policy for Manchuria," submitted by the Kwantung Army headquarters to the Japanese government, the scale of the project grew much larger.[8] This final draft proposed establishing a 2-kilowatt transmitter in Dalian and Mukden, a 2- or 5-kilowatt transmitter in Shinkyō, and a 1-kilowatt transmitter in

Harbin. In addition, each broadcasting station would engage in multilingual broadcasts in Japanese and other languages.

However, as it transpired, the actual broadcasting network established for the MTTC transcended even this final proposal. In 1938, two 1-kilowatt transmitters in Dalian, two 1-kilowatt transmitters in Mukden, a 10-kilowatt and a 100-kilowatt transmitter in Shinkyō, and fourteen other small broadcasting transmitters were installed. Another significant outcome was that a 100-kilowatt long-wave transmitter was constructed in Shinkyō in 1934. This transmitter was the largest in East Asia, and a massive broadcasting network with a strong 100-kilowatt capacity was erected to assist in pushing international recognition of Japan's imperial infrastructure projects in Manchuria.[9]

This was a time when radio broadcasts from neighboring countries were being received from across the sea in Japan, and these were considered to have a negative impact on Japanese society. When a Nanjing station started to broadcast from a 75-kilowatt station in November 1932, the Japanese living in Kyushu (Japan's westernmost island) could easily tune into it because the frequency of the Nanjing station was close to that of the Fukuoka city station. Japanese listeners who heard such radio broadcasts in the Chinese language were so surprised and fearful that they made a fuss to their own government, which in turn appealed to the Nanjing authorities to alter their radio channel. However, given the geographic proximity and the powerful transmitters, even during the war Japanese in some sectors of the home islands were still able to pick up Japanese language wartime broadcasts diffused by the Kuomintang from China.[10]

On the other hand, government and military authorities knew that radio broadcasts would be powerful weapons for Japan's "thought war." Masaki Jinzaburō, vice-chief of the staff headquarters, sent a personal memo, "On Establishing High-Power Broadcasting Stations," to Yanagawa Heisuke, vice-chief of the Ministry of the Army, in 1933. The memo advocated the establishment of such broadcasting stations in "significant cities" to combat radio propaganda broadcasts from the Soviet Union and China and to establish a Japanese base in Shinkyō. Masaki pointed out that broadcasting stations in the Soviet Union put out radio propaganda in the Russian, Chinese, Korean, and Mongolian languages, and the Nanjing station diffused propaganda in Chinese and Japanese.[11] To cope with these potential opponents, who would only grow increasingly vocal and more powerful, a large broadcasting network was required in Manchukuo, Masaki opined.

Kajii Takeshi had suggested that it would be much easier if a sole organization in Manchukuo controlled the broadcasting segment of the empire's telecommunications. Because the NHK had already started to manage broadcasting enterprises in Mukden and Shinkyō before the MTTC was founded, it seemed "the obvious thing to do" was to use NHK.[12] After the Manchurian Incident in September 1931, which saw the Japanese Kwantung Army dispatch more troops on the pretext of needing to fend off Chinese attacks, Japanese interest in Manchuria grew rapidly. This led to dramatic increases in the number of radio listeners in Japan: from approximately 770,000 in 1930 to nearly 1,050,000 in 1931, and to almost 1,420,000 in 1932. In other words, the number of radio listeners increased twofold from 1930 to 1932.[13] The increase in 1932 was the largest in NHK's broadcasting history.[14] The possibilities for NHK broadcasting from Manchuria to Japan were clear to see. However, Kajii considered that the costs of heavy investment that would be necessary for stabilizing rule in Manchukuo would be too great for NHK to bear in the long term. Kajii also judged that the Japanese government and people would find it impossible to accept the costs of such a massive investment overseas. He was clearly all too aware of Japan's weak financial basis.

Consequently, even though they knew that telecommunications were an essential element of national policy and empire building, the planners – the Kwantung Army, Ministry of Communications and the South Manchuria Railway Company – judged that management by the NHK or a similar organization specializing in domestic broadcasting would harbor potential weaknesses. This understanding led to a plan to integrate telegraph and telephone enterprises in Manchuria, from which large profits could be expected, with a suitably financially sound broadcasting agency. Kajii also recommended that Manchukuo broadcasts make use of advertising and use a direct-sales system of radio receivers. (In Japan, one could buy a radio in any electronics store, while in Manchuria the geographic expanse was so great that the Japanese believed it necessary to open special stores where radio sets could be purchased.) This was indeed how stability was eventually achieved for the revenue base of the broadcasting system when it combined with the telegraph and telephone enterprises in Manchuria. The MTTC was thereafter able to expand and improve its broadcasting network and facilities.

## Advertising and broadcasting

In its implementation of advertisement-based broadcasting, which it started in November 1936, the MTTC was able to refer to the experience of the Taiwan Broadcasting Corporation, even though this company had been in existence only a mere six months.[15] Two types of advertising broadcasts were used – direct and indirect. For the direct approach, an announcer read out the text of an advertisement that had been submitted by the sponsor live on air. For example, a cleaning shop might advertise itself with a script that encouraged people to use its services to keep their national flags perfectly clean, so that when they waved them in celebration of some victory in war they could contribute appropriately to the atmosphere of the occasion.[16] Many sponsors were happy to use aspects of daily life in wartime to promote their establishments, services, and goods.

With indirect advertising, a sponsor financed the entire production of a broadcast or show. It was a method favored by some quite famous Japanese companies, for example the Kōdansha Publishing Company and the Wakamoto Pharmaceutical Company. (These were both live and taped.) At the end of the program, an announcer would simply state that the show had been financed by a particular sponsor. Programs created with the help of indirect advertisement included classical music, Chinese opera, and popular music, often featuring the well known singer/movie actress Li Xianglan (also known as Ri Kōran or Shirley Yamaguchi).[17] The MTTC preferred indirect advertising to the direct approach because it avoided overt commercialism, but most sponsors chose the direct form, which they thought more effective.

In the first month of advertisement-based broadcasts, November 1936, MTTC broadcast forty-two indirect and direct advertisement-sponsored programs. The number increased as the number of broadcasting stations rose. There were 348 programs in the month of October 1937, and approximately ten advertisement-based programs broadcast per day, with a total of 2,591 for the whole year. In 1939, this figure reached 7,518, and the total sales figures topped 120,000 yen (about 400 million yen or $US3.5 million in today's money). Although small in terms of the total revenue that made up MTTC's budgets, it was still an important benchmark for the company. July 1937 saw the outbreak of a skirmish between Japanese and Chinese troops at the Marco Polo Bridge, on the far outskirts of Beijing. In response, the Japanese Army doubled the number of its troops and used the incident to launch an unofficial war against China. When the conflict then turned into a prolonged war, campaigns to encourage Japanese to save more for the sake of the nation gathered momentum, particularly after 1939. Endeavors that stimulated the general populace to spend money were now viewed with much less enthusiasm, which affected the authorities' attitude to advertisement broadcasts.[18]

On April 1, 1940, the Manchukuo government's Department of Communication issued an order that advertisement-based broadcasts were to be abolished, and this order was mostly followed.[19] However, information concerning the know-how and best practices of these broadcasts was retained in internal reference manuals, such as the *Gyōmu shiryō* (Administration Information) and the *Manshū hōsō nenkan* (Manchurian Broadcast Yearbook). In this way, when the broadcasting industry returned to normal in Japan after the war, Kanazawa Kakutarō, who had been an executive in MTTC and had returned to Japan postwar, was able to put that knowledge and experience to good use and establish a base for commercial radio.

### Policies to emphasize entertainment programs on the second radio channel

The MTTC differed from other telecommunications organizations in the Japanese empire in terms of its broadcasting policy. Since broadcasting began, news, entertainment, culture/education programming all over the Japanese empire had consistently focused on educational and cultural content.[20] In April 1931, the Tokyo broadcasting station established a second radio channel. While the proportion of programs on the Tokyo station's first channel was 37.7 percent news, 26.7 percent educational and cultural, and 23.4 percent entertainment, the proportion on the new, second channel was 41.2 percent news, 52.1 percent educational and cultural, and only 0.8 percent entertainment.[21] Clearly the focus was on educational and cultural programming, not entertainment. The same tendency to give priority to news and educational and cultural programs was discernible in Korea and Taiwan. The broadcast hour of original programs of Channel Two in Korea (in Korean), broadcast out of Keijō (Seoul) in 1940, was comprised of 29 percent news, 24 percent lectures and cultural content, 14 percent music, and 8 percent dramas. Entertainment programs (music and drama) occupied 22 percent of the Seoul broadcasting station's second channel. The Taipei broadcasting station on Channel Two, from April 1939 to March 1940, was formed from 47.6 percent news, 31.8 percent educational and cultural, and 20.5 percent entertainment content. In Taiwan, the focus was also on news, educational, and cultural content. Korea and Taiwan were formal colonies of Japan, so there was a particular emphasis in those two sectors to push material more in Japanese or broadcasts in the local languages to "educate" colonial subjects. On the other hand, the proportion of programs broadcast on Channel Two out of the Shinkyō broadcasting station in Manchuria was made up of 21.7 percent news, 15.1 percent cultural, and 30.8 percent entertainment content, while the proportion on Channel One was 32.7 percent news, 15.1 cultural, and 19.5 percent entertainment content.[22] Only the second channel of Manchukuo broadcasting gave a considerable slice of time to entertainment programs. This was because non-Japanese residents of Manchukuo were listening to Soviet and Chinese Nationalist radio broadcasts, and the MTTC believed that it needed to compete for their support but also as a form of "counter-intelligence."[23] Moreover, the head of the Hailar radio station, Aoki Tarō, commented in his report on the deleterious effects brought about by ignoring listener tastes, that this would "invite the loss" of listeners feeling close to Japan and would actually encourage the "tendency of listeners to tune into other countries' conspiratorial broadcasts."[24]

What is quite clear is that the MTTC staff consciously created and shaped entertainment programs that would appeal to the Chinese people, broadcasting Beijing opera and drama shows based on the Chinese classics. This situation in Manchukuo was different from Korea and Taiwan: there, even though the local broadcasting organizations instituted a second channel to make broadcasts in their own vernacular language, and not in Japanese, to offer broadcasts in languages other than Japanese was controversial because it essentially ran counter to assimilation policies.

In the beginning of the broadcasting era in Manchukuo, the purpose of Manchukuo radio broadcasts was to foster a sense of love and loyalty to Manchukuo, or "Manchukuo nationalism." This was not going to be easy given that the Japanese government consistently stressed in its propaganda that Manchukuo was a utopian kingdom where the five races lived in harmony. The ideal situation, as envisaged by the MTTC, was that Manchukuo residents would simultaneously listen to and enjoy the same programs as Japanese.[25] In the end, the MTTC utilized far more entertainment programs, which were more enticing than any other programs, to help form a sense of being a Manchukuo national. This policy grew more ingrained after the Manchukuo government's Department of Publicity drafted guidelines in January 1941 to shape broadcasting policy. The policy emphasized the importance of entertainment programs on all Channel Twos throughout the kingdom. As a result, the number and overall time of educational and cultural programs decreased, and the number and amount of night-time entertainment programs increased. In particular, there was an emphasis on mass culture, for example comic dialogues and Beijing opera. In addition, the guidelines suggested that programs with a more popular and even erotic character should be selected. To be sure, NHK also used entertainment in its propaganda material during the war; nonetheless, news, education, and culture programs at the time were still higher in proportion than entertainment programs. The MTTC's stress on entertainment programs remained distinctive within the empire.

There were a number of reasons for the focus on entertainment programs on all of the MTTC's Channel Twos, but two reasons are particularly salient. First, increasing radio broadcasting coverage in general was a consistently important policy for the MTTC, and it succeeded in raising the number of listeners, particularly Chinese listeners, dramatically. However, when war started in 1937, the diffusion of radio receivers developed into an urgent issue as the government wished to convey information about its policies and propaganda to as many listeners as possible and to offer selected news items about the war situation and enemy air strikes. The focus on entertainment programs was a useful way to encourage the purchase of radio receivers, which were instrumental as tools to funnel propaganda directly into homes. By increasing entertainment programs, the MTTC was able to present itself as a more appealing and familiar radio company to the Chinese people and encourage them also to listen to the news programs that were invariably broadcast in the course of a day.

Second, Manchukuo had to cope with the so-called thought war. The radio space of Manchukuo, often called the front line of this thought war, was in fact a battlefield of ideas among competing interests. The Manchukuo government could not rule this space stably. The Shinkyō 100-kilowatt radio transmitter erected in 1934 was the core radio broadcast transmitter for Japan's propaganda efforts. However, the transmitters' radio waves had also been interrupted by the Soviet Union ever since the MTTC had begun to manage the transmitter. In addition, Russian and Chinese people who lived in Manchukuo would often listen to programs broadcast from the Soviet Union and the Republic of China because the programs broadcast by the MTTC were not initially considered interesting or worthwhile. Radio does not exist in a vacuum, and neither did listeners in Manchukuo.

## Conflicts between Japan's NHK and Manchukuo's MTTC

The difference in broadcasting ideology between Japan's domestic broadcasting agency, NHK, and the main broadcasting body for Manchukuo, the MTTC, came to a head when Japan invaded China in 1937 and Southeast Asia in 1941, and officials began to consider the kind of broadcasting policy Japan should adopt in occupied areas. After 1937, the Japanese government established numerous telecommunications organizations, for example the North China Telegraph and Telephone Company (1938), the North-China Broadcasting Corporation (1938), and the Central-China Telegraph and Telephone Company (1938), and so on. These telecommunications organizations were authorized to liaise with one another, and they played a central role in the construction of Japan's new order in East Asia. Without such telecommunication infrastructure, the Japanese government could not convey and receive information from distant shores throughout its empire. For instance, the Ministry of Communications in Japan and the MTTC laid telephone cables between Mukden and Osaka in 1938 and between Beijing and Tokyo in 1942. In addition, the Japanese government expressed its support for the people living in the colonies and occupied areas of the empire by creating exchange broadcasts, where political leaders offered each other congratulatory messages on anniversary days from local broadcasting stations. In addition, the East Asia Broadcast Committee was formed in April 1939, and the East Asia Electronic Communication Committee was established in November 1939. The purpose of the Communication Committee was to draw all the many telecommunications organizations closer together and to provide technical and business support. The participants of the first conference came from the Ministry of Communications, the International Electronic Communications Company, NHK, the MTTC, the Taiwan Broadcasting Corporation, the Department of Communication in the office of the Governor-General of Taiwan, the Department of Communication in the office of the Governor-General of Korea, the Korea Broadcasting Corporation, the Mongolia Electronic Communication Equipment Company, the North-China Telegraph and Telephone Company, the Central-China Telegraph and Telephone Company, the Department of Communication in Sakhalin (Karafuto) Prefecture, and the Department of Colonization in the Nanyōchō (the South Seas Islands Mandate, or Prefecture). The representatives of each organization were Japanese.

The purpose of the East Asia Broadcast Committee was to smooth over the transmission of radio relay broadcasts within the Japanese empire and other areas. The previous broadcasting organizations of Korea, Taiwan, and the precursor to Manchukuo (called the Kwantung State, *Kantōshū*) had received programs from Japan and broadcast to Japanese residents in those areas. The broadcasting organization of the colonies also sometimes transmitted programs for Japan. In particular, these programs, such as those from Manchukuo to Japan, increased after the 1931 Manchurian Incident because Japanese interest in Manchuria grew. Similarly, the number of broadcasting programs from China to Japan increased after the outbreak of the Sino-Japanese War in 1937.

On the other hand, broadcasts from Japan to East Asia became an important issue for the East Asia Broadcasting Committee. Radio stations in the colonies broadcast the same programs as were broadcast in Japan to Japanese living in overseas territories before the Sino-Japanese War. However, when Japan expanded its empire and began to rule over many occupied areas, it had to adjust to being home to a variety of ethnicities, mainly Chinese. The MTTC and other overseas broadcasters grew harsher in their critique of the format of simply reusing NHK broadcasts as these were fundamentally aimed only at Japanese listeners. During the first conference of the East Asia Broadcasting Committee in 1939, the MTTC proposed "enforcing the East Asian character of East Asia broadcasts" and a "plan of the general idea to enforce East Asia broadcasts and channels."[26] At the fourth conference, the Taiwan Broadcasting Corporation proposed "the matter to separate

East Asian broadcasts from Japanese national broadcasts," during which the MTTC insisted that the "East Asia broadcasts" (those that were created in Tokyo specifically with the aim of being broadcast across Japan's imperial holdings throughout Asia) should have been made independent and diffused over a third channel.[27] The MTTC and other overseas broadcasters demanded the independence and expansion of the East Asian broadcasts, as well as the creation of this new, third channel for Asian people, mainly for Chinese in the Chinese language.

However, NHK rejected this demand. The reason for this was that the NHK prioritized Japanese audiences and was unable to create programs that had the power to appeal to various audiences across the empire. NHK calmly and realistically recognized its ability to create its own programs. On the other hand, Kanazawa Kakutarō, the vice-chief of the Shinkyō central broadcasting station, criticized the NHK's negligent attitude toward East Asian broadcasts as "provincial expansionism" (*naichi enchōshugi*). Regarding this gap between the NHK, which aimed to broadcast only in Japanese, and the MTTC and other overseas broadcasters, which demanded the establishment of multilingual and independent East Asian broadcasts, Kanazawa pronounced:

> In the home islands, there is only Japanese language broadcasting. Therefore, the NHK staff always think that East Asian broadcasts should be in Japanese, because domestic broadcasts are only in that language. On the other hand, Japanese living overseas, in China and the South Sea islands, are surrounded by native languages. Therefore, they believe that East Asian broadcasts should be conducted in the native languages of East Asia.[28]

In addition, Kanazawa pointed out that the population of Japanese was "only one-tenth of the Greater East Asia Co-Prosperity Sphere."[29] Local broadcasters had recognized that the status of Japanese people in the local area was, in fact, very weak. They therefore demanded the establishment of East Asian broadcasting channels, which would become the nexus of the Greater East Asia Co-Prosperity Sphere, in order to create an East Asian community through radio propaganda and to maintain the status of Japanese outside of the home islands. For this reason, Japanese in Manchukuo and living outside of Japan in the empire more strongly demanded new programs to be crafted in Japan touting the East Asian character of Japan's empire that were supposed to be the focus of Channel Three.

As the war expanded, Japanese broadcasting policy progressed to the establishment of these East Asian broadcasts. In May 1942, an exclusive time for the East Asia relay broadcast was created. In September 1942, the international section of the NHK was upgraded to an international department. The name "East Asia relay broadcast" was changed to "East Asia Broadcast." In November 1944, a segment for "news commentary in the Chinese language" aimed at the occupied zones of Southern China was made over into a news program. The East Asia Broadcast added two frequencies to its diffusion so that it could be heard more clearly in the South Sea Islands and the Philippines. However, the East Asia Broadcast, which

NHK could continue for only a brief period, was probably rather ineffective as a tool in Japan's thought war.

## The MTTC after World War Two

On August 18, 1945, the puppet kingdom of Manchukuo was dissolved following the emperor's announcement of "the end of the war" several days earlier. The MTTC's first and second sections were divided up and continued to broadcast as different organizations, and on August 19 the Soviet Union took over the MTTC at the same time that it seized numerous industrial sites and technological Japanese agencies.[30] The MTTC staff engaged in restoration work of telephone lines and other equipment under the direction of the Soviet Union. The Soviet Army interned some executives of the MTTC, including Kanazawa, who remained a prisoner for three years. The Soviets amassed a great deal of Manchukuo broadcasting equipment, and the total losses due to withdrawal from Manchukuo by the Soviet Union were estimated at US$25 million, according to reports from the Pauley Reparations Missions. In addition, according to the same report, 20 percent of the telephone lines, 50 percent of telephone and telegraph equipment, 50 percent of long-distance telephone equipment, and 90 percent of broadcast equipment were either taken or destroyed by the Soviet Union.[31] The Shinkyō 100-kilowatt broadcast transmitter was used as the radio beacon, and the 10-kilowatt broadcast transmitter was used to relay new Chinese language broadcasts from Moscow. The prolonged presence of the Soviet Union in Manchuria grew into an international issue in December 1945. In January 1946, the Republic of China dispatched a committee to oversee the takeover of communications.[32]

Facing international pressure, the Soviet Union finally withdrew from Shinkyō on April 14, 1946, and afterward the situation in Manchuria proceeded in a somewhat complex manner. The Soviet Union supported the Chinese Communist Party (CCP) implicitly but signed a formal treaty with Chiang Kai-shek's Chinese Nationalist Party (Kuomintang, KMT), which ruled over Manchuria. The civil war between the KMT and the CCP intensified, and the superiority of the latter became decisive by November 1948.[33] Ultimately, the CCP was able to proceed to Manchuria sooner than the KMT and take over the broadcasting stations. The CCP actively used the leftovers of the MTTC. In March 1948, there were already seven broadcasting stations in Manchuria among ten in total operated by the CCP. By July 1949, there were fifteen broadcasting stations in Manchuria among a total of thirty-four.[34] Although it could not completely acquire the MTTC broadcasting equipment because the Soviets had arrived first, the CCP was nonetheless able to employ the equipment that was far more modern and plentiful than anything they had previously used.

The Harbin broadcasting station later proved very important for the CCP. Although the Communist Party took over the Harbin station in 1945, the CCP moved to Jiamusi in Heilongjiang Province temporarily and established the Northeast China Xinhua broadcasting station in May 1946. When the CCP retook Harbin, it set the Northeast China Xinhua broadcasting station in the city and decided that the station should guide and supervise all other stations in the liberated areas of northeast China. A directive the Party sent out in November 1948 stipulated that the new stations in occupied areas resume broadcasting as soon as possible and relay programs from the Northeast China Xinhua broadcasting station to the Shanbei Xinhua station.[35]

The collaboration of Japanese technicians was also necessary to smoothly manage the takeover of broadcasting stations when the CCP gained power. When the CCP started its broadcasts in Dalian in January 1946, approximately fifty staff were engaged in broadcasting, of whom three-fifths were Japanese specialists.[36] Hirose Noboru, who had been the chief of the Dalian central broadcasting station during the Manchukuo period, delivered to the CCP in December 1945 the documents concerning the equipment and real estate that the Dalian central broadcasting station had owned.[37]

In Harbin, both Chinese and Japanese broadcasters were employed continuously after the war. Zhao Jiqiao, who had worked as an announcer in Manchukuo, took office as the vice-chief of the Harbin broadcasting station. After the CCP arrived in Tonghua, they sought out Japanese technicians and employed them continuously because they had the required skills to manage the broadcasting enterprises that the Chinese had not yet mastered. Broadcasting capability, which allowed the authorities to surmount massive geographical obstacles, was key for both the Chinese Nationalist and Communist parties, especially to disseminate their propaganda in the civil war. For example, Sakai Jūsaku was kept on after the war and was actively involved in Chinese broadcasting in Jinzhou, Liaoning Province. Sakai wrote *The Textbook of Wireless Communication* in Chinese and contributed to the more advanced training of Chinese technicians.[38] Japanese technicians, who were highly skilled and knowledgeable, were considered valuable assets to the CCP, who maintained very few such technicians of their own.

Radio broadcasts transcended geographical isolation and were very important tools for the CCP to convey and share information because northeastern China was so far removed from their home base in Yan'an. In addition, about 300,000 radio receivers remained in private hands in Manchuria, so radio broadcasts were an effective means to convey information to citizens. Moreover, Chinese Communist radio propaganda directed toward the Chinese Nationalist government is believed to have been effective during the Civil War. The CCP utilized captured or surrendering former KMT soldiers to go on the air and appeal to their fellow soldiers to lay down their arms. Chinese nationalist soldiers in Yunnan and Sichuan who heard appeals in their local dialect were particularly moved by this tactic.[39]

## The MTTC's human networks

At the same time in the Japanese homeland, Yoshida Hideo, who was an executive at Dentsū (the Japan Telegraph Communication Company), an advertisement company, anticipated that radio broadcasting would be a potential market for advertising. Just after the end of the war, the push to liberate radio for private corporate use grew stronger with the realization that NHK was monopolizing radio broadcasts. On September 25, 1945, the Japanese government decided to establish private radio broadcasting companies, which would be managed on the revenue of advertisement broadcasts. Under this policy, the head of the Ministry of Communication, Matsumae Shigeyoshi, recommended Funada Ataru, chairperson of the Tokyo Chamber of Commerce and Industry, to create a new private broadcasting company.[40] Funada then consulted with Yoshida Hideo concerning the issue of advertising broadcasts. This turned into a prime opportunity for Dentsū to collaborate with a private broadcasting company. On December 1 of the same year, the company submitted an application to the government for "the broadcasting private limited company for the people." However, the American occupation authorities were negatively disposed toward establishing private broadcasting companies because they estimated that the birth of many media organizations would make the information control less effective. In January 1947, the Allied Council for Japan also concluded that establishing private broadcasting companies was unsuitable, and the Ministry of Communications officially established a policy to not permit the establishment of new broadcasting organizations for the time being.

In October 1946, Clinton Feissner, the chief of the Supreme Commander for the Allied Powers (SCAP) Civil Communication Section, sent a memo to the Japanese government pointing out the need to usher in a "freedom to broadcast" to help democratize Japan. Feissner proposed that one autonomous broadcasting organization should not monopolize Japanese broadcasting and that private broadcasting organizations should be allowed to broadcast. He expected that free competition would arise by having multiple broadcasting organizations compete and that this would spur on the promotion of free speech. After receiving the notice, the Japanese government promulgated a Broadcast Act Draft in October 1947, which stipulated the establishment of a "general broadcasting station" in June 1948, and the push to establish private broadcasting grew. This "broadcasting private limited company for the people" was renamed Tokyo Hōsō (Tokyo Broadcasting Company), and an application was submitted once more in January 1949 to restart full-scale preparations.[41] This was exactly what Dentsū had been pushing for over the last several years.

Meanwhile, Kanazawa Kakutarō, who had been interned in Siberia after the war, was released in July 1948 and returned to Japan. Immediately after his repatriation, his knowledge and experience of advertising broadcasting were sought out by Yoshida Hideo at Dentsū, and Kanazawa began to work in the headquarters of the Tokyo Broadcasting Company, located in the Dentsū office building. In July 1949, the first summer advertisement course was held at Dentsū headquarters. Kanazawa gave the course entitled "The Enterprise Character of Commercial Broadcasting." In addition, the summer program included a course on the "Management of a Newspaper Company and Advertisement," given by Nitta Uichirō of the *Asahi* newspaper company and another on "The Science of Advertisement," offered by Yoshida Hideo, and so on. In August 1949, the association for research on radio advertising was launched and Kanazawa joined. This association collected and classified information and materials related to radio advertising and managing a private broadcasting company. In addition, the association made sample recordings of radio advertisements and offered them to sponsors. Furthermore, the association toured major cities throughout Japan and informed people on the importance of radio advertising. Kanazawa wrote many articles about radio advertising in the magazine *Shimbun to kōkoku* (Newspaper and Advertisement), which Dentsū published, and also cooperated in spreading theoretical aspects of radio advertising. In some of these articles, Kanazawa introduced not only the methods of radio advertisement that the MTTC had practiced but also those used in America. In time, these articles were collected and published as *Shōgyō hōsō no kenkyū* (The Study of Commercial Broadcasting) in an issue of *Dentsū kōkoku sensho* (Selected Dentsū Advertisements) in 1951.[42] In addition, Dentsū helped to establish a private broadcasting company in many prefectural centers (Sapporo, Niigata, Sendai, Fukuoka, etc.) under Yoshida's initiative, with help from Kanazawa. Kanazawa gradually became the opinion leader on the subject of advertisement broadcasts in Japan by means of using the knowledge and experience of working for the MTTC. He was fundamental in the actual establishment of the Tokyo Broadcasting Company in 1951 when it was formally named Radio Tokyo.

Although Kanazawa had built up the most brilliant career among the people formerly involved in imperial broadcasting, many other people also played key roles in the new arena of private broadcasting. At least sixty of those who had gained experience in the MTTC engaged in broadcasting enterprises after World War Two, and twenty of them worked for Radio Tokyo.[43] Ten of them worked for the NHK, and the rest worked in other private broadcasting companies. The MTTC people at Radio Tokyo mainly took important posts engaging directly in the broadcasting business. Kanazawa was the chief of the Department of Programming. Takemoto Masayoshi, who had been the chief of broadcasting in the MTTC, took office as both the chief of the program arrangement section and the broadcast announcement section chief. Takaya Masakuni, who had been the chief of program arrangement in the Second Channel in the MTTC, took office as the vice-section leader of the program arrangement section.[44] Private broadcasting earnestly required people with experience in the broadcasting business. In particular, those from the MTTC with knowledge and experience of advertisement broadcasting were in great demand. In addition, private broadcasting companies were better suited to the staff of the MTTC, which had operated under a different broadcasting policy from that of the NHK.

## Merging entertainment and middle-class consciousness

Before the emergence of private broadcasting companies, many intellectuals and ordinary citizens warned that the advent of private broadcasting companies would lower the tone of programs. At the start, therefore, private broadcasters took care to avoid programs of a more popular tenor. In 1955, when the economy revived to its peak level as before the war, investment in advertising increased, private broadcasting companies finally started showing some business growth, and the situation changed dramatically. The competition for audience ratings intensified. A private broadcasting station might air an entertainment program in the same time slots as educational and cultural programs, for which audience ratings tended to be low. This, in turn, led to a decrease in commercials during educational and cultural programming slots.[45] This was a time when TV broadcasting, which had started in 1953, was rising dramatically. While the percentage of people who owned TVs in their homes was 54 percent in 1954, it rose to over 90 percent by 1960. TVs had quickly become one of the middle-class "three treasures," the other two being a washing machine and a refrigerator. The striking diffusion of TV gave rise to much debate criticizing the unrefined tendencies and popular appeal of shows. As journalist and public commentator Ōya Sōichi and others have noted, one phrase that had particular currency in 1957 was the "idiotization of a hundred-million" (*ichioku-sō-hakuchika*), referring to the effect of puerile TV content on the Japanese people.[46] Nevertheless, the airtime given to entertainment programs by the broadcast media, including radio, and the ensuing criticism only confirmed the need for educational and cultural programs, which in a paradoxical move led to the establishment of private TV broadcasting stations that were more educational.

Private educational broadcasters were required to devote more than 50 percent of their airtime to educational content and more than 30 percent to cultural programs. From the outset, there were doubts that these broadcasters would be able to hold to this, since they depended on income from commercials. According to Kanazawa, the distinction between cultural and entertainment programs was so obtuse and permeable that at the time he considered it impossible that the TV stations would manage to carry the stipulated number of educational programs. He insisted that all educational broadcasting stations should aim at "a synthesis of entertainment and education."[47] In his book on TV and society, Kanazawa pointed out the tendency for less developed countries, which had fewer TV channels, to have a higher preponderance of news, cultural, and educational programs and a lower preponderance of entertainment programs and for highly developed countries with more channels to have a higher preponderance of entertainment programs.[48] Kanazawa indicated that the mainly school programs and educational programs in NET (Japan Education Television) could not lose their entertaining side or they would lose audience share as well. NET, which was a special educational broadcasting station, aimed at the synthesis of entertainment and education. In fact, to cover the deficits from educational programs, NET ended up broadcasting American shows, such as the Western drama *Rawhide* (1957–1965) and the legal drama *The Untouchables* (1961–1962), which raised audience ratings and increased advertising income. Although the Parent–Teacher Association strongly criticized the late 1950s American show, *The Untouchables*, as a "detrimental program" (*yūgai bangumi*), it became extremely popular and important for the educational network, and it was often dubbed the "NET of foreign drama." In addition, NET broadcast many classic animations shows. Furthermore, in the morning time, which was called "the blank time zone" because NHK monopolized the lion's share of the TV viewing audience, NET began to broadcast one news program –*The Morning Show with Kijima Norio*. This program aimed to focus on contemporary topics, to present problems, and to combine them with ordinary materials. It was highly rated as it showed "contemporary knowledge and culture" that was beyond the "perspective of classical knowledge and culture of the NHK."[49] This debate about the relationship of media to society parallels the same one that occurred in the print industry in postwar Japan, as Satō Takumi investigates in Chapter 13 of this volume. As one of the first civilian broadcasts, NET had garnered high expectations from teachers and scholars who wanted an emphasis on educational shows. On the one hand, NET Vice-President Kanazawa, who had the experience of creating programming aimed at non-Japanese, also knew that educational broadcasts were not very popular and that this would limit their impact. In addition, Japan already had a well established radio culture, but if they did not continue producing entertainment programs, then the educational broadcasts would become unsustainable in the future. NET thus chose to pursue the path laid out by Kanazawa's prewar experience and reasoning.

The programming policy, which was an attempt to achieve this "synthesis of entertainment and education," contributed to the consciousness that all Japanese were middle-class and that everyone shared a distinctive mindset that ran across the cultural divide. The cultural differences in watching and listening to broadcasts were identified through repeated audience rating surveys. In October 1968, a public opinion poll on educational and cultural programs by the Cabinet Secretariat Public Office showed that the viewer ratings for educational and cultural programs were higher than 60 percent in Tokyo and 45 percent in towns and villages, while the rate of those who viewed no educational television programming was approximately 48 percent. There was a certain difference depending on the viewers' educational level: while the average rating overall for "watch frequently" was 8.5 percent, the rating for the university graduate group was 20 percent. However, more than 50 percent of the viewers with a high school or lower-level education answered that they "rarely watch" such programs.[50] The policy of combining entertainment with education was designed to bridge such differences between regions and education levels and to provide a common cultural foundation for the Japanese nation that crossed various divides.

## Conclusion

The MTTC adopted different broadcasting policies to those of the main islands of Japan and the other Japanese colonies from 1933 to 1945. Manchukuo, in competition with the Chinese and the Soviets, required a massive broadcasting network in order to play a part in the thought war that was an essential part of Japan's project of creating an empire. Radio broadcasts were particularly important in that they could easily cross borders. The MTTC continually had to consider consumer taste when broadcasting programs in order to gain listeners. In addition, the MTTC adopted a multilingual broadcasting policy and considered the profiles of non-Japanese ethnic groups because Manchukuo was, at least in the ideal, the home of "the harmony of five races," even though the reality was far removed from that utopian slogan. The Manchukuo radio broadcasts evolved within a competitive environment, and consequently the MTTC adopted different policies from those in Korea and Taiwan. Developing advertising-based broadcasting was one of the specific broadcasting achievements of the MTTC that later became invaluable for Japanese staff when looking for employment in postwar Japan. Previous research on economic policy, architecture, and city planning has noted that Manchukuo was a laboratory for the Japanese empire, a place where bureaucrats and architects experimented with new ideas.[51] This was certainly the case with advertisement-based broadcasts, and the impact on postwar Japanese media structures was immense. Many former staff of the MTTC took up important positions in private broadcasting companies after the war, and one of them, Kanazawa Kakutarō, became an opinion leader for private broadcasting due to his imperial expertise and experience gained during the war.

In the history of postwar Japanese television, NET, which was established as an outgrowth of the criticism of lowbrow programs and was an attempt to combine education with entertainment, occupies an important place in examining continuities between imperial and postwar Japan.[52] While education specialists joined Kanazawa in wanting a blend of education and entertainment, the programming that they advocated differed very little from what might be found in an ordinary school curriculum. Kanazawa considered, on the strength of his experience in broadcasting in Manchuria, that television programming should place its main focus on appealing to and entertaining audiences, drawing them in and making them feel part of a whole. NET followed Kanazawa's line and created a form of popular culture that would transcend differences of class and locale and that at the same time would incorporate some of the content of educational programs. NET programming appealed not only to the working classes but also to the intellectual class, enhancing the consciousness that all postwar Japanese belonged to the middle class.

## Notes

1 Oka Tadao, *Taiheiyō ni okeru denki tsūshin no kokusaiteki bekken* (Teishinchōshakai, 1941). (Unless otherwise noted, all Japanese books are published in Tokyo.)
2 Matsushige Mitsuhiro, "Hokyō anminki ni okeru Chō Sakurin chiiki kenryoku no chiiki tōgōsaku," *Shigaku kenkyū* vol. 186, issue 3 (1990) pp. 21–40.
3 Kantonchō teishinkyōku, *Mantetsu fūzokuchi gai denshin denwa gyōmu gaiyō*, 1930, FCA173, Yūsei hakubutsukan shiryō sentā, Chiba, Japan.
4 The Manchuria Telegraph and Telephone Company (hereafter MTTC), *Tōkei nenpō: shōwa 17 nendo* (Shinkyō: MTTC, 1943).
5 Ishikawa Ken, "Manshūkoku no hōsōjigyō no tenkai," *Rekishi to keizai* vol. 185 (2004): pp. 1–16; Nippon hōsō kyōkai (NHK), ed., *20 seiki hōsōshi* (NHK, 2001).
6 Hikita Yasuyuki, "Nihon no tai chūgoku denki tsūshin jigyō tōshi ni tsuite," *Rikkyō keizaigaku kenkyū* vol. 41, issue 4 (1987): pp. 1–55; Kawashima Shin, "Teikoku to rajio," in *Teikoku nihon no gakuchi: media no naka no teikoku*, vol.4, ed. Yamamoto Taketoshi (Iwanami shoten, 2006), pp. 207–242; Shimizu Ryōtarō, "Taseisei no kūkan," *Waseda seiji kōhō kenkyū* vol. 96 (2011). See also Daqing Yang, *Technology of Empire: Telecommunications and Japanese Expansion in Asia, 1883–1945* (Cambridge, MA: Harvard University Asia Center, 2011).

7   Kajii Takeshi, "Manshū ni okeru musen denshindenwa ni kansuru ken," March 29, 1932, in *Manshū denshindenwa kabushiki kaisha setsuritsu junbi kankei*, vol. 1, 1932, ed. Denmu kyoku, FCA 177, Yūsei hakubutsukan shiryō sentā, Chiba, Japan.
8   Keizai Chōsakai, "Manshū tsūshin jigyō hōshaku," *Ritsuan chōsa shorui 19–1–1* (1937).
9   In 1934, there was a 75-kilowatt transmitter in Nanjing, a 10-kilowatt one in Tokyo, a 10-kilowatt one in Seoul, and a 10-kilowatt one in Taipei. NHK, ed. *Rajio nenkan shōwa 9 nenban* (Nihon hōsō shuppan kyōkai, 1934). NHK started the establishment of high-power broadcasting transmitter after 1934. In 1937, the Tokyo broadcasting station was upgraded to a 150-kilowatt long-wave transmitter.
10  Fukuoka hōsōkyoku, ed., *NHK fukuoka hōsō kyokushi* (Fukuoka: NHK fukuoka hōsō kyoku, 1962), pp. 126–129.
11  "Kyōryoku naru musen hōsō kyoku kensetsu no ken," The National Institute for Defence Studies (NIDS), Japan Center for Asian Historical Records, *Mitsu dai nikki*, vol. 4, *1933*, Ref.C01003986800.
12  Kajii, "Manshū ni okeru musen."
13  NHK, ed., *Nihon hōsō shi* (Nihon hōsō syuppan kyōkai, 1965).
14  Louise Young documents this idea of Manchuria as a "lifeline" for Japan in her book *Japan's Total Empire: Manchuria and the Culture of Wartime Imperialism* (Berkeley: University of California Press, 1988).
15  Uchikawa Yoshimi, *Nihon kōkoku hattatsushi* (Dentsū, 1976).
16  Aoki Tarō, "Kōkoku hōsō no kōka no mondai 3," *Gyōmu shiryō* vol. 52, issue 4 (1938).
17  Ri Kōran and Fujiwara Sakuya, *Ri Kōran: Watashi no hansei* (Shinchōsha, 1987); Yomoda Inuhiko, ed., *Ri Kōran to higashi ajia* (Tokyo daigaku shuppankai, 2001).
18  Nanba Kōji, *Uchiteshi yamamu* (Kōdansha, 1998).
19  Tanaka Kazuhiro, "Shōwa 15 nendo ni okeru hōsōjigyō," *Gyōmu shiryō*, January 1941.
20  Satō Takumi, *Terebi teki kyōyō* (NTT shuppan, 2008). Broadcasting research in Japan classifies three types of broadcasting programs: news, education, and culture and entertainment programs. This chapter also follows this classification.
21  NHK, *Nihon hōsōshi*, pp. 188–191.
22  MTTC, *Manshū hōsō nenkan shōwa 15 nen kōtoku 7 nen* (Shinkyō: MTTC, 1941), pp. 255–257; MTTC, *Tōkei nenpō shōwa 17 nendo* (Shinkyō: MTTC, 1943).
23  Chūman kaigunbu sanbōhatsu kaigunshō gunmukyokuchō ate, "Manshūkokunai hōsō ni kansuru ken," Shōwa 11 nen tsū kōtsū kishōji, kan 1 no 2, NIDS, JACAR, Ref. C05035341600.
24  Aoki Tarō, "Hōsō jisshi naiyō kōjō no gutaisaku," *Gyōmu shiryō*, April 1939.
25  Takemoto Masayoshi, "Manshū ni okeru hōsōjigyō no genzai oyobi shōrai," *Gyōmu shiryō*, January 1935, pp. 2–13; Kanazawa Kakutarō, *Rajio no seikaku* (NHK, 1941).
26  Kanazawa Kakutarō, "Dai tōa hōsō kyōeiken no keisei to sono kakuritsu," *Gyōmu shiryō*, December 1943, pp. 3–32.
27  Ibid.
28  Ibid.
29  Ibid.
30  Nihon denshindenwa kōsha, ed. *Gaichi kaigai dennki tsūshin shishiryo*, vol. 8 (Nihon denshindenwa kōsha, 1956).
31  Imura Tetsuō, "Bunken kaidai: Pauley chōsadan hōkokusho manshū hen," in *1940 nendai no higashi ajia*, ed. Imura Tetsuō (Ajia keizai kenkyūjo, 1997) pp. 223–240.
32  Nihon denshindenwa kōsha, *Gaichi kaigai*, p. 470.
33  Matsumoto Toshirō, "Chūgoku tōhōku no shengo jōsei," *Okayama daigaku keizai gakkai zasshi* vol. 31, issue 1 (1999): pp. 19–60.
34  Umemura Shuguru, *Chūgoku kyōsantō no mejia to puropaganda* (Ochanomizu shobō, 2015), Chapter 3.
35  Ibid.

36 Ibid. See also, Daqing Yang, "Resurrecting Empire? Japanese Technicians in Postwar China, 1945–1949," in *The Japanese Empire in East Asia and its Postwar Legacy*, ed. Harald Fuess (Munich: Iudicium Verlag GmbH, 1998).
37 Umemura, *Chūgoku kyōsantō*.
38 Chūgoku chūnichi kankeishi gakkai, ed., *Shin chūgoku ni kōken shita nihonjin tachi* (Nihon kyōhōsha, 2005).
39 Umemura, *Chūgoku kyōsantō*, pp. 230–256.
40 This became the Tokyo Hōsō Company.
41 Dentsū, *Niji o kakeru mono yo* (Dentsū, 1991), pp. 154–155.
42 Dentsū, *Dentsū 66 nen* (Dentsū, 1968), pp. 162–163, 204–205.
43 Ishikawa, "Manshūkoku no hōsōjigyō," pp. 13–14.
44 "Minkan hōsōjin hairaito," *Shimbun, radio, kōkoku* (September 1952).
45 Chūbu nihon hōsō, ed. *Minkan hōsōshi* (Shiki shuppan, 1959), pp. 265–266.
46 Ōya Sōichi, "Ichioku sō hakuchika meimei shimatsu ki," *Ōya Sōichi zenshu*, vol. 3 (Chikuma shobō, 1980), pp. 339–348. See also Jayson Makoto Chun, *A Nation of a 100 Million Idiots? A Social History of Japanese Television, 1953–1973* (New York: Routledge, 2008).
47 Kanazawa Kakutarō, *Terebijon: sono shakai teki seikaku to ichi* (Tokyodō 1959), pp. 260–267.
48 Kanazawa Kakutarō, *Terebi hōsō dokuhon* (Jitsugyō no nihonsha, 1966), pp. 13–14.
49 Yomiuri terebi hōsō kabushiki kaisha, "Kyōyō bangumi no imi," in *Terebi bangumi ron* (Yomiuri terebi hōsō kabushiki kaisha, 1972), p. 254.
50 Kanazawa Kakutarō, *Terebi no ryōshin* (Tokyodō, 1970), pp. 225–229.
51 Koshizawa Akira, *Manshūkoku no shuto keikaku* (Chikuma shobō, 2002); Kobayashi Hideo, *Teikoku nihon to sōryokusen taisei* (Yūshisha, 2004).
52 Satō, *Terebi teki kyōyō*.

# 15 Parting the Bamboo Curtain

## Japanese Cold War film exchange with China

*Michael Baskett*

*The total lack of coverage of Chinese films in the Japanese film press would naturally lead anyone to question whether China has produced any films at all!*[1]

*Frankly, Chinese film is something of a problem in Japan. On the one hand there are the zealous fans but they are few in number ... On the other are the vast majority who claim that the artistic value of Chinese films is poor and, poisoned by Hollywood, they fail to see beauty in simple, pure films.*[2]

Separated by nearly two decades, the preceding quotes suggest a curious division among mainstream Japanese film critics over the prevailing image of Chinese films after the end of the Japanese empire and into the Cold War. Under the control of the Japanese film industry, film production in China during the 1930s and 1940s had been a colonial project whose value was measured less in terms of the box office than of its usefulness as an ideological tool for Japanese imperialism. Since the early 1920s, Japanese critics had held mixed feelings toward film-making on the Chinese continent. Shanghai's proximity to Western film studios and exhibitors was especially vexing to Japanese ideologues trying to purge Hollywood-style entertainment films from their newly acquired colonial markets and replace them with Japanese production methods.

After the defeat of Japan and the dismantling of the Japanese empire in 1945 and especially after the Communist victory in mainland China in 1949, Japanese studio heads, together with U.S. Occupation officials, regarded the mainland Chinese film industry as a potential threat that needed to be contained. To the extent that Japanese film journals mentioned them at all, critics typically belittled Chinese (and Soviet) films for having low production values and simplistic, ideology-heavy narratives. In this sense, one may find continuities linking colonial-era Japanese stereotypes of China as a backward and ultimately inassimilable nation with similar Cold War notions of China as economically weak and technologically latent. Cold War Japanese film discourse on Chinese films, however, is noteworthy for its fragmentary and at times politically polarized tone. Within this context, the cinema of the People's Republic of China (PRC), along with other Communist bloc cinemas, would appear to have held little meaningful value to the Japanese film industry.[3] Yet writing on Chinese film and exchanges between Japanese and Chinese film personnel did in fact exist and, as this chapter will argue, intriguingly did link the end of the Japanese empire with the Cold War. The fact that many Japanese film expatriates remained in China after 1945 working on the production of many of what would become the classics produced in new China suggests an astonishingly rich and complex series of relationships. Both Araragi Shinzō in Chapter 4 and Park Jung Jin in Chapter 11 of this volume also discuss these reformed relationships and "sharing" of technical expertise. Continuities between pre- and post-1945 Japanese–Chinese film exchange illustrate the need to more fully examine the Cold War culture within the context of the dismantled Japanese empire.[4]

Although limited in degree, Japanese film journalism did indeed report on a broad range of unofficial and semi-official exchanges among film critics, filmmakers, intellectuals, actors, literati, and politicians. By the mid-1950s, Japanese film critics, some of whom had lived and worked in the Japanese film industry in China during the imperial era, lamented that discourse on Chinese (and Soviet cinema, which was referenced more than twice as often as the PRC) was virtually non-existent within Japanese film discourse. For film workers, film critics, and everyday citizens in Cold War Japan, mainland China remained a double taboo. First, as a symbol of Japanese imperialism, it reminded postwar Japanese of decades of colonial expansionism, war and bitter defeat. Then, during the U.S. Occupation of Japan, China loomed large in Cold War rhetoric as a forbidden nation behind the Bamboo Curtain. This chapter attempts to account for what was a widely perceived lack of interest in Chinese film as the result of something more than American suppression or Japanese colonial guilt. Rather, I seek to analyze how Cold War Japanese attitudes toward the Chinese film industry coexisted with earlier colonial attitudes toward China.

Despite Japan being widely recognized as a geopolitical bulwark against communism within the U.S. Cold War order, remarkably little scholarship exists theorizing Japanese Cold War culture outside of the U.S.–Japan context. As recently as 2005, Marukawa Tetsushi wrote that even pairing the terms "culture" together with "Cold War" seemed unnatural in a Japanese context.[5] He claimed that the absence of the Cold War in academic discourse was the result of a failure by intellectuals to adequately confront Japan's culpability in sustaining the Cold War. Japanese media representations of the Cold War present the conflict as external to Japan but with the potential to victimize the nation in an unprovoked nuclear war. Ann Sherif writes that three ideas in particular have displaced discussions of Japanese culture from the Cold War: the idea that Hiroshima and Nagasaki were centers of peace; Article 9 of Japan's "Peace Constitution" renouncing Japan's right to wage war in perpetuity; and the era of high economic growth based on U.S. military procurements during the Korean War (1950–1953) and continuing through the Vietnam War in the 1960s.[6] Film scholars have followed a similar trajectory of not linking Japanese culture to the international Cold War order except in piecemeal fashion – studies of U.S. Occupation film policy, the Tōhō Labor Strikes, and certain analyses of postwar monster (*kaijū*) films – relegated to a subset of Japan's postwar national culture.[7]

The "postwar" paradigm continues to dominate analyses of Japanese culture by alternately emphasizing Japanese self-determinism in the form of domestic responses to defeat and recovery or Japanese resistance to compulsory membership in the American Alliance. This emphasis on U.S.–Japan relations, which began during the U.S. Occupation and continued throughout the 1952 U.S.–Japan Security Treaty, has diminished attention to Japan's relations with Asia and further bolstered the notion that Japan was an "oasis away from the Cold War."[8] Marukawa struggled to reconcile the disparity between Japanese intellectuals' disconnect with the Cold War and his colleagues in China, Korea, and Taiwan whose engagement with the Cold War was central. They repeatedly questioned Marukawa about the Japanese protest movement against the U.S.–Japan Security Treaty. Whereas Japanese intellectuals framed this movement within a postwar paradigm that is mostly contained by U.S.–Japan relations, Marukawa's Asian colleagues saw the movement within the context of other (ongoing) Cold War struggles in Asia. The centrality of the Cold War in Korean, Taiwan, and Chinese cultural and national identities stands in stark contrast to what Ann Sherif has called the willful silencing of this framework in the analysis of Japan's post-1945 culture.[9]

Yet, as Michael Davidson points out, "One of the truest indications [of] a cold-war narrative is its lack of reference to the cold war," which seems to suggest that some of the ambiguity surrounding the lacunae of studies on the cultural aspects of the Cold War may not necessarily be only a Japanese problem.[10] Here, rather than merely exchange a postwar paradigm with a Cold War one, I propose to examine the ways in which notions of the Cold War as expressed in Japanese film journalism on Japan-China film exchange have been invested with various meanings over time. Of particular concern to my analysis is how such conflicting meanings continue to shape the idea of the Cold War as an object of historical inquiry. Specifically, film exchange between two nations without formal diplomatic ties that share a history of colonialism is a productive site from which to examine shadow discourses of colonialism and the Cold War. It is precisely in the unofficial exchanges where one finds unguarded discourses that can reveal and critique prevailing political and ideological orthodoxies.

Japanese film discourse is especially well suited to examine the illusionary nature of "Cold War" and "culture" in that cinema's materiality and symbolic representation can render abstract concepts "real." In this sense, we might understand that the Cold War is less *reflected* by cinema than it serves as a space within which it *happens*.[11] This chapter examines three key sites of debate over Chinese film in order to examine the ways in which the two major film-making nations in Cold War Asia negotiated a new relationship in lieu of formal diplomatic relations and in the shadow of Japanese colonialism. Each site attempts to define the ways in which Japan's Cold War culture was informed as much by its colonial legacy as it was by the Cold War order. The first site investigates the intersection of communist ideology and Chinese film, the second contrasts Japanese assumptions of China's technological backwardness with Chinese notions of technological exchange as goodwill, and the third analyzes film festivals as transnational sites of ideological competition and conflict dividing not only enemies but also allies. Readers should also take note of how this interaction at the cultural level was, in part, reflected in Erik Esselstrom's Chapter 12 in this volume on one of mainland China's first unofficial cultural visits to Japan.

## Japanese film discourse: Chinese film and ideology

*As the train passed through the long tunnel at the border . . . there was China.*[12]

*Please do not push yourselves on our behalf. No matter what, do not work for us. If you do, you will only put yourselves in a bad position in Japan. Should you find any faults in our films, please do not hesitate to return them to us. But do not attempt to compensate for them under the misconception that it might benefit China, as you will only hurt yourselves. Time will eventually settle everything so please do nothing for us.*

Zhou Enlai (1957)[13]

In 1966, veteran leftist film critic and producer Iwasaki Akira began a six-part series of articles in the film journal *Eiga hyōron* on his trip to the PRC by invitation of the People's Overseas Cultural Association and the Federation of Chinese Filmmakers. Iwasaki, who was head of the seven-person delegation of Japanese film professionals, had traveled to China three times before the war. He was a lifelong advocate of Marxism and founding member of the Proletarian Film League of Japan (*Purokino*). After the League was dissolved due to police pressure, Iwasaki was arrested in 1940 for violating the Peace Preservation Law – one of only two film professionals to ever be arrested for activities critical of the government. Upon his release, Iwasaki worked in the Tokyo offices of the Manchukuo Film Association and was an advocate of Chinese films.[14] After 1945, Iwasaki represented an extreme position in debates over Chinese ideology. His stance on China can be divided into two discernable traits: first, he anticipated stereotypical criticisms of China as being socially and technologically backward or as being anti-Japanese, and he refuted them by explaining how the conditions in new China had completely transformed the nation from the period under Japanese colonialism. Second, he focused on how improved social conditions and progressive government policies in China legitimized it as a potential model for Japan. Although ostensibly writing on China's film industry, Iwasaki's writing focused on ideology to such a degree that discussion of China's films was relegated to a secondary position.[15]

It is no coincidence that Iwasaki should quote the widely acclaimed opening line from Nobel Prize–winning author Kawabata Yasunari's *Snow Country* to set the tone for his series of articles on China. Like Kawabata, Iwasaki sought to induce his readers to take on his (the narrator's) perspective by using language that placed them on the train with him as they traveled into a new land. Iwasaki writes of the pleasures of "New China" in direct contrast to the problems of modern Japan, Hong Kong, and the United States. What made China "new" was more than just a regime change but what Iwasaki called "purity." He linked this purity to well established associations of the purity of Japan's snow country in Kawabata's novel. For Iwasaki and other Japanese expatriates living in China, New China represented the idyllic spirit of Japan that was sullied in the wake of the defeat and U.S. Occupation and irretrievably lost due to the exigencies of the Cold War. Iwasaki noted, however, that, in contrast to Kawabata's novel, which opened with a train passing through a tunnel, Iwasaki's delegation passed over a bridge. More than a mere literary allusion, Iwasaki drew his reader's attention to the fact that this was the bridge that separated colonial Hong Kong from the People's Republic of China (PRC) and that their entry into New China was both a metaphysical and literal journey of liberation.[16]

Iwasaki's lengthy descriptions of his impressions of the places, people, and especially the atmosphere that he encountered directly in new China challenged long-held Japanese stereotypes of China as being brutal, unhygienic, and backward. If previous film critics criticized China's infrastructure as backward, Iwasaki celebrated its lack of "unnecessary artifice" (*muda ga nai*) and claimed that excess accumulation of goods was precisely what was dragging down Japan. Chinese film art, he contended, was also superior for its "plain," "sincere," and "artless" production values. That these delicate features were inaccessible to average Japanese citizens was the unmistakable failure of a restrictive Japanese government focused on maintaining order within the American Alliance. Iwasaki believed the source of Japanese prejudicial attitudes toward China was a direct result of Cold War legislation that blocked the importation of Chinese (and Socialist) films. In rhetoric approaching that of the Chinese ideologues he so admired, Iwasaki proclaimed that only after "all the Kishi's, Ikeda's, and Sato's" (three prominent postwar Japanese prime ministers) disappeared could true cultural exchange take place. That such exchanges were already happening in the world of table tennis, ballet, and sports – but not in film – concerned Iwasaki because, for him, film offered the hope of genuine and meaningful cultural interaction.[17]

The Japanese film delegation's visit happened to coincide with the start of China's Cultural Revolution, a wide-reaching social-political movement that was initiated by Mao Zedong from 1966 to 1976 to preserve "true" Communist ideology in China by purging capitalist and traditional elements from society, but Iwasaki's reportage offers no recognition of it. Such a utopian view of China and its film industry became increasingly untenable by the mid-1960s in the wake of the Sino-Soviet split, a period of deteriorating ideological and political relations between the PRC and the USSR between 1960 and 1989 and the Japanese Communist Party's break with both Beijing and Moscow. When viewed in this context, Iwasaki's impressions of China appear outdated and anachronistic – more in step with those of a decade before.

A decade earlier, in 1956, Kinoshita Keisuke, one of the most respected and successful film directors in Japan whose popularity rivaled that of Kurosawa Akira, led a delegation of film artists to the Soviet Union and the PRC to attend a Japanese film festival sponsored by the Chinese government. Initially, Kinoshita's praise of the USSR and the PRC and criticism of Japan resembles that of Iwasaki, but there were crucial differences. Although both men viewed ideology as the key element separating Chinese and Japanese society, Kinoshita was far more interested in the influence that governments had on the daily lives of its citizens. During his stay in China, Kinoshita found the population and its films to be brimming with energy, self-respect, and good cheer (*akarusa*). This last quality in particular resonated with Kinoshita as it was an ongoing topic of debate in the Japanese film press at that time. Film journals devoted special issues on the topic of good cheer and how it should be added to Japan's somber films. Kinoshita reported that while Japanese films were well received by Chinese and Soviet audiences, many found their topics too "teary" and suggested that directors make lighter films.[18] Such observations about the melodramatic nature and slow pacing of Japanese films were widespread both in Japan and internationally. In a 1956 roundtable discussion, Kinoshita questioned whether it was even possible for Japanese to produce a film that could be recognized as cheerful abroad given what he saw were dismal economic and social conditions in Japan at that time.

> No one in Japan today could make a cheerful film, unless they faked it . . . [but] if you want to make an honest film, it isn't possible . . . the fact is there just aren't any cheerful people. Darkness, cheerfulness, all this talk only draws attention to the pall of unhappiness hanging over Japan. Everyone that feels it wants to break out of it. Showing them what to break through is our job.[19]

By contrast, Kinoshita observed that the Communist government proactively led its citizens by "seeking to love those things that their people love" and that they did so not to pander but rather out of a sense of responsible stewardship. In return, citizens could live meaningful, fulfilling lives that repaid the government's efforts with their support. To Kinoshita, this symbiotic relationship was the root of China's good cheer and was eminently apparent in all of the films he saw, even such Chinese war films as *Dong Cunrui* (1950, Guo Wei). The sheer joy that Kinoshita found in Chinese film only served to further underscore their difference from Japanese films. The difference, he concluded, lay in a government's commitment to represent the will of its people. That Kinoshita and other directors felt the responsibility to show people how to break through despair was further evidence of a failure on the part of the Japanese government. Such a negative assessment of the Japanese government is particularly intriguing when one considers that 1956 was the same year the Japanese government released its White Paper on the Economy with the now famous proclamation "the postwar is over" (*mohaya sengo dewa nai*).[20]

Ultimately for both Kinoshita and Iwasaki, ideology became the decisive element that preceded all artistic creativity and would determine the direction and improve the quality of all national life, not just for Socialists and intellectuals. Kinoshita saw Japan's "darkness" as not merely a by-product of defeat and occupation but also as the natural result of an ineffective, disengaged administration and unchecked consumerism. While neither man stated so directly, the postwar darkness stood in stark contrast to the comparatively productive days of the Japanese empire. The fact that neither linked the woes of contemporary Japan to its imperial past suggests the extent to which even leftist film workers failed to sustain a critique of Japan's colonial legacy. Changing Japan's film industry meant first changing the Japanese government, the result of which would be a more cheerful national life and exponentially better films. Despite the fact that this was precisely when Japanese films began winning international recognition in Europe and America, many critics of the industry like Kinoshita and Iwasaki believed that few domestic films were of the quality of a *Rashōmon* or *Ugetsu*. By the mid-1950s, Japanese studio heads also doubted the commercial sustainability of the early successes of Japanese films in the West and turned their attention to East and especially Southeast Asia as more viable potential markets.

Kinoshita was never overtly critical of China's policies, overwhelmed as he was by the sheer scale of the nation. For instance, he marveled at the Chinese government's decision to distribute 2,000 film prints per title in order to successfully implement Japan Film Week throughout China. Kinoshita compared this massive and expensive effort to Japan where average print runs of 60 prints per title were the norm. Kinoshita recognized, however, that such exhibition methods were unsustainable and correctly surmised that foreign "film weeks" consisting of imported films mostly from the USSR and other Soviet bloc cinemas served a purpose other than economic profit or ideological goodwill alone. Film weeks also supplemented the low output by the Chinese film industry and established a reserve of films to be redistributed as needed.[21]

In 1956, less than one year after Kinoshita's return to Japan, veteran leftist film critic Kitagawa Fuyuhiko documented his vastly different experience as a member of a yet another Japanese cultural delegation to the PRC and North Korea in a four-part series of articles in Japan's leading film journal, *Kinema junpō*.[22] As the sole film professional in the delegation, Kitagawa openly lamented his lack of access to Chinese films, facilities, and personnel. What little interaction he did achieve came about mostly as the result of his own effort and luck. As a result, to a far greater degree than any of his predecessors, Kitagawa provides a more skeptical view of the role of film in New China. Lavish banquets and tours were held for the Japanese literati and theater delegates, but film, Kitagawa concluded, was conspicuously absent from any programming, a fact that he believed underscored film's comparatively trivial status in the PRC.[23] In this regard, New China appeared to share far more in common with contemporary Japan than any of his colleagues might be willing to concede. Kitagawa's series of articles plainly demonstrates that Japanese leftist film discourse was not monolithic but rather multilayered and sufficiently diverse to accommodate opposing voices.

Kitagawa alone criticized the same government institutions that had so inspired Iwasaki and Kinoshita. For Kitagawa, China's vast bureaucracy was little more than a distasteful barrier blocking the natural development of film art. The administration was responsible for Kitagawa's lack of access to the Chinese film industry, and its oppressive traces could be found everywhere: in the haphazard architecture of the Beijing Film Studios, in their shabby projection booths, and especially in the officious (*kanryō kusai*) attitudes of film administrators who were too busy maintaining face to be concerned with bothersome foreign guests and too unimaginative to properly mentor their own artists.[24] For Kitagawa, it was precisely the *unresponsiveness* of the system to any needs other than its own that formed an impression of the industry that was the complete opposite of Kinoshita's. Although not entirely critical of everything, Kitagawa described a film industry in a profound state of disarray, led by arrogant bureaucrats, and consisting of a patchwork of hand-me-down technology cobbled together from Japan, the United States, and USSR. This environment inevitably and negatively impacted the aesthetics of China's films. If Iwasaki glorified the artistry of Chinese films as a victory over material limitations, Kitagawa contended that inferior technology produced inferior technique (craft). What Kinoshita lauded as the revolutionary spirit of optimism in Chinese films, Kitagawa saw as sheer arrogance, which in no way compensated for the myriad deficiencies facing the industry. It is important to remember that each man visited China at different moments in history and under vastly different conditions. As a relatively minor figure in the Japanese film world participating in a delegation consisting mainly of literati, Kitagawa appears to have seen a side of the Chinese film industry that would likely have not been shown to an internationally renowned director such as Kinoshita.

Kitagawa believed that responsibility for this industry-wide disorder rested squarely on the shoulders of the Chinese film industry's leaders. He observed that as long as the Chinese studios were content to use Soviet equipment and uncritically adopt Soviet production methods, the result would be rank formalism and would render China's films obviously and unnecessarily derivative.

> [In *Butterfly Lovers*] the Chinese and Soviets overuse the hackneyed method of employing famous locations in the background of scenes to complement the narrative – it's not impressive. . . . The Chinese seem to have indiscriminately followed the Soviet production model but at least in terms of production and the use of color, I thought they would do better to learn from Japan.[25]

*Dong Cunrui*, the war film that Kinoshita had praised, represented all that Kitagawa found wrong with the Chinese films he saw.[26] Part of the problem concerned his expectations of Chinese films. Both he and Iwasaki were ardent fans of veteran Chinese film-maker Cai Chusheng, a key figure in the 1930s Chinese Leftwing Cinema movement in Shanghai.[27] Kitagawa greatly anticipated seeing Cai's films and meeting with him and was bitterly disappointed when informed that Cai was in France attending the Cannes Film Festival. When Kitagawa managed to screen a copy of Cai's classic *The Spring River Flows East* (1946), he praised it as being "without a doubt the best produced film that I've seen during my entire stay in China. The three-and-a-half-hour running time never lags due to the film's flawless structure and carefully measured pacing. The direction was orthodox in the best sense of the word." Kitagawa was shocked to later learn that the film that he thought was new was in fact ten years old and due to "problems" with it, the director had not been allowed to produce another film since. Director Guo Wei (*Dong Cunrui*), one of the few film people whom

Kitagawa met during his stay, explained that Cai's film was "incorrect" for adding too many scenes depicting physical love and for focusing too much on dark subject matter. As a result, Guo explained, Cai had been ordered to undergo "self-reflection," and the sort of films he made must be "destroyed."[28] Incredulous, while touring the Shanghai Film Academy, Kitagawa asked the secretary to the vice-head about Cai's status and was told that he required "progressive re-education." Coming to Cai's defense, Kitagawa asked, "Isn't the ability to produce excellent films of profound meaning sufficient evidence that one has obtained a progressive education?"[29]

## Chinese film and technology exchange

Japanese debates over China's technology may seem less polemical than the preceding debates over ideology, but they were also politically charged. If the latter tended to reveal a division of opinions within the left, the former displayed a fairly consistent set of opinions across the political spectrum. Most Japanese critics took a fairly dim view of the level of New China's technology, writing in a manner that was reminiscent of the colonial era. Japanese colonial film discourse before 1945 was similarly structured around the acquisition of technology, which produced two main views of China. The first understood *contemporary* China as being chronically backward politically, militarily, and economically. The second recognized *historical* China as a wholly separate entity, one that was artistically and culturally distinguished but hopelessly out of step with the modern era. Japan's cultural colonization of China during 1937–1945 was naturalized in the name of "modernization," and Japanese critics made the case that China's inability to modernize to the same degree as imperial Japan provided justification for using Japan as the model for assimilation.[30]

Gabrielle Hecht reminds us of the decisive role that technology played in the transition from decolonization to the Cold War, producing what she calls "tangled geographies," in which the dismantling of empire proceeded in an uneasy tension with the establishment of the Cold War order.[31] This shift from empire to state is related to what Kawashima Shin discusses in Chapter 2 of this book. One finds similar tensions in Japanese film discourse after 1945, where camps extolling the technological exceptionalism of the Japanese film industry simultaneously deride China's industry as backward. The gap was exacerbated after 1945 by the Japanese film industry's relatively smooth recovery, which appeared to be the fulfillment of the claims of Modernization Theory, achieved as it was by the conscious acquisition of technology to rebuild the industry for the greater national good. Japan's status within the American Alliance enabled its major studios unique access to state-of-the-art technology and production methods. As a result, by 1950 the Japanese film industry once again became held up as a model for emerging cinema industries in Asia.

The bifurcated nature of this Japanese discourse is apparent in articles on China's adaptation of color film technology. On the one hand, China supporters such as Satō Kunio praised the use of color in *Sports China* (1952, Wang Weiyi) as an important first step but questioned the viability of having to send the East German Agfacolor film stock to the Soviet Union for processing and then return to China.[32] Satō noted a vast gap between the relative crudeness of *Sports China* and the technical accomplishment of two Chinese–Soviet co-productions, *Victory of the Chinese People* (*Zhongguo renmin de shengli*, 1955) and *Liberated China* (*Kaifang zhongguo*, 1954). That said, he and other critics praised China's *Butterfly Lovers* – one of the few films to be widely reviewed in the Japanese film press – as approaching the technical excellence of Laurence Olivier's *Henry V* (1944).[33] Although never officially released in theaters in Japan, *Butterfly Lovers* was screened in many independent theaters and community centers under the sponsorship of various pro-Chinese organizations such as the China–Japan Friendship Society. Veteran critic and China hand Shimizu Akira considered the film to have limited appeal: though its topic was more contemporary than Beijing opera, Shimizu questioned whether the narrative style, which was so representative of the Southern Chinese province of its origin, could effectively appeal to a wider audience.[34]

Japanese tours of China were often the result of invitations by the Chinese government and the Chinese film industry. Many occurred just after times of crisis in China – notably after the Great Leap Forward (1958–1961), during the Sino-Soviet split, and the start of the Cultural Revolution (1966–1976). The Chinese tours of Japan received support from private organizations, such as the China–Japan Friendship Society, and funds from individual donors. Collectively, these exchanges functioned in a similar fashion to film festivals, which as Marsha Siefert has argued in the context of Eastern Europe provided one way for individuals to negotiate government regulations restricting the flow of people and goods across national borders.[35]

Japanese reports on these tours of the Chinese film industry during the 1950s and 1960s resulted mostly in descriptive lists cataloging the type, origin, and condition of the film equipment held in China's studios.[36] However, Japanese film journalists also covered visits to Japan by Chinese film delegations, and this provides a productive counterperspective that balances the largely negative assessments of the level of Chinese film technology by Japanese critics. Chinese film personnel shared their frank appraisals of Japanese films in the spirit of "honest exchange," often to the disgust of the latter. Films with socially conscious themes such as Urayama Kiriro's *Foundry Town* (*Kyūpora no aru machi*, 1962) were politely received by the group, but the film that elicited the most agitated critique was Ōshima Nagisa's *Cruel Story of Youth* (*Seishun zankoku monogatari*, 1960). Delegation leader and renowned actor Yuan Wenshu flatly stated:

> I doubt this film would do well with Chinese youth. If I hadn't seen it in Japan, I probably would have misunderstood its intention . . . I think the film overemphasized only the dark aspects of Japanese youth and would have been more effective overall had it focused on the cheerful aspects as well.[37]

Director Ōshima, a participant in this roundtable discussion, was uncharacter-istically silent. However, the fact that seven years after director Kinoshita Keisuke's remarks, the topic of dark themes in Japanese films would remain an issue for international audiences is intriguing. The Chinese delegates displayed a keen inter-est in film narrative and particularly screenwriting. They were awed by how pro-lific Japanese screenwriters were, out-producing their Chinese counterparts by a ratio of five to one. Conversely, Japanese writers and journalists were envious of China's favorable working conditions; two- to three-month paid vacations (exclud-ing food), which enabled writers to experience different lifestyles and thus hone their skills; higher salaries than their Japanese counterparts; and the lack of studio and government censorship (barring "extraordinary circumstances" that might affect the national good).[38]

The discourse on these unofficial exchanges reveals two entirely different expectations on the part of each film industry. Whereas the Japanese expected these visits to be a mostly one-way exchange of technological know-how, for the Chi-nese the exchange and promotion of bilateral "goodwill" was more significant. The fact that these tours were not exclusively conducted between Chinese and Japanese leftists but also included the participation of many of the Japanese major studios was another point that subverted expectations.[39]

## Chinese film and international film festivals

Ideological battles over the role that Chinese film should play within the region led to direct and indirect confrontations waged at international film festivals throughout the 1950s and 1960s. It should come as no surprise that these prolifer-ated during the Cold War, as film festivals were uniquely suited to staging "war by other means."[40] Throughout the 1960s, Japanese film discourse questioned the received logic that film festivals were the modern equivalent to world fairs or the Olympics; they were generally perceived as egalitarian international venues in which films from every nation supposedly competed solely on their artistic (versus commercial) merits.

Following the unexpected success of Kurosawa Akira's *Rashōmon* (1950), win-ning the Grand Prix at the Venice International Film Festival in 1951, the major Japanese studios began to understand film festivals as a way to control and con-solidate the flow of film across the blocs. The Japanese major studios' demon-strated a collectively anti-communist stance from at least the 1920s, which gained significant momentum after the Japanese defeat in 1945 when it received the full and enthusiastic support of the U.S. Occupation forces. A series of studio labor strikes occurred in the late 1940s, disrupting production and ultimately ending only through the intervention of the U.S. military and the Japanese police. Subsequently, an industry-wide "purge" of Communist and/or Socialist film personnel by 1950 solidified the Japanese major studios' anti-communist attitude, which continued and even strengthened after the U.S. Occupation ended in 1952. Elsewhere, I have written extensively on the efforts of Nagata Masaichi, the politically ultraconservative head of Daiei Studios, who in 1954 established the Southeast Asian Federation of Motion Picture Producers – a seven-nation anti-communist film coalition in order to isolate the influence of Red China (USSR, North Korea) throughout Asia.[41] Nagata successfully established the Southeast Asian Film Festival as a regional market in which film-makers could produce and circulate their films without intervention from Communists or even Hollywood. Southeast Asia was an important potential market not only for the Japanese film industry but also for the Japanese economy, as evidenced by Prime Minister Kishi's two tours of the region in May and December of 1957.[42] Some have argued that this coalition was wholly the result of U.S.-sponsored propaganda efforts, but Japanese film discourse clearly demonstrates that the situation was far more complex and that Japan's actions were informed as much by its colonial experience as the demands of the American Alliance.[43]

Chief editor and owner of the *Far East Film News*, Glenn Ireton, claimed that the idea for the Southeast Asian Film Festival (later the Asian Film Festival) was suggested to Nagata in the spring of 1953 by Miles Goldrick, an American working as the Far East supervisor for the Westrex Corporation.[44] However, I have revealed Nagata's plans for a nearly identical pan-Asian film festival/film market that were published almost a decade earlier in 1944. Nagata promoted the festival, The Greater East Asian Filmmakers' Conference, in order to establish a "Pan-Asian" film collective under Japanese supervision. Despite the rhetoric of Pan-Asianism, Nagata's original plan specifically warned of a need to contain the Communist elements in the Chinese film industry due to their success in mobilizing support within China as well as abroad. Nagata wrote, "[M]y only fear is that . . . [a unified] Chinese film industry might one day progress so rapidly that within a few years it would overtake us" and ultimately displace Japan as the "leading film industry in Asia."[45] While the colonial rhetoric is notably absent from the 1954 version, the structure remained virtually identical. As the festival expanded its organization to include South Korea and South Vietnam, the anti-communist tenor of the festival increased. Special awards were presented, such as the Protection of Free Asia Prize or the Asian Progress Prize, indicating the extent to which the festival functioned as an institution of containment against the socialist/communist cinemas.[46]

From the first meeting, Nagata had limited the number of festival delegates to correspond exactly to the number of major studios and thereby block any possibility of participation by Japan's independent (and politically radical) producers. Thus excluded from this international venue, the independent producers actively promoted politically progressive films at film festivals in Moscow and Beijing, as well as Venice and Cannes.[47] Despite winning prestigious awards abroad, these independent international activities received only scant attention in the mainstream Japanese film press. Film festivals warrant our attention because, like the Cold War itself, they became sites where battles between the mainstream conservative film industry and the progressive independent were fought by proxy. Anecdotal reports by Japanese film delegates in China, for instance, parenthetically noted that most of the Japanese films that Chinese audiences viewed were those produced by the Japanese independents that carried socially conscious themes.[48]

In the wake of the Bandung Conference, the first large-scale meeting of newly independent African and Asian states held in Jakarta, Indonesia, in April 1955, support proliferated for the promotion of socialist and non-aligned cultural industries, of which film festivals were a key component.[49] The Soviet-backed Afro-Asian Film Festival (AAFF) was established in 1959 with the intention of bringing together all of the film-producing nations in East and Southeast Asia and in many ways was a response to Japan's Asian Film Festival (AFF). As with the latter, the AAFF also garnered the support of prominent heads of state, such as Indonesian President Sukarno (who had also initially supported the Asian Film Festival).[50] The AAFF learned from the mistakes made by the Asian Film Festival, such as the exclusion of specific nations (China, USSR, North Korea, North Vietnam, etc.) and independent producers. Further, the AAFF anticipated and thus avoided potential criticisms of its membership not adequately representing all of Asia (a common criticism made by the AFF) by taking care to invite all nations. By the third AAFF, which was held in Jakarta, Indonesia, in 1964, the Japanese delegation was overwhelmingly represented by Japanese independent producers.

Beyond its institutional structure, the AAFF also resembled the AFF in its ideological platform. Typical speeches delivered at the podium by delegates bore such titles as "Film Is a Weapon with Which to Break the Imperialist Political Bloc" and "Create a New World with New Films."[51] Japanese leftist critic Yamada Kazuo diligently reported on the festivals, praising them as a much-needed corrective to the AFF, and touted their ideological solidarity. The tone of the reportage, however, changed as the frequency of the festivals declined by the mid-1960s due to the erosion of socialist solidarity following the Sino-Soviet split and the Cultural Revolution.

Articles in the film journal *Eiga geijutsu* noted with uncharacteristic detachment the rift between China and the USSR and particularly the ways in which each strategically used film festivals in Japan.[52] The Soviet Film Festival, which was to be held from October 21 to 23, 1966, appeared to be conspicuously programmed to compete with the Chinese Film Festival that started on October 22. The latter was organized by the China–Japan Friendship Society, with films supplied by the Chinese government, while the former was co-sponsored by the combined Ministries of Foreign Affairs of Japan and the USSR. The Japanese critics dubbed the two sides the "Sino-Soviet Film Split" and carefully observed the various promotion strategies of both festivals. They noted, for example, that the better funded Soviet festival provided free programs, while the Chinese festival overcharged for theirs. Despite the higher production values and better scripts of the Soviet films, Japanese critics were suspicious of the Soviet's conspicuous, almost theatrical sophistication. They noted positively that the less accomplished Chinese films appealed to students and couples and established a welcoming atmosphere, which resonated with Iwasaki's high appraisal of Chinese film's aesthetic of plainness, mentioned at the start of this chapter.[53]

By the mid-1960s, the Cold War had progressed to a new phase. Known in the mainstream Japanese media as the "new" or "second" Cold War, what had been a U.S./USSR split was now clearly a three-way division. The new phase fragmented the Japanese film left into pro- and anti-Mao camps, pushing even politically engaged Japanese critics to adopt an increasingly distant perspective. Further, the Japanese independent producers who only a decade earlier represented the only sustained, organized attempt to create a viable alternative Japanese cinema in opposition to the major studios, by the mid-1960s found that even they became targets of criticism. Independent director Imai Tadashi's *This Is China!* (*Kore ga chūgoku da!*, 1967) opened at approximately the same time as *The East Is Red* (*Dong fang hong*, 1965). Both were criticized for representing a naively positive picture of the Cultural Revolution and glossing over the excesses of Maoism.[54]

## Conclusion

In a very direct way, the discourses analyzed in this chapter highlight the inability of the Cold War structure to resolve the lingering problems of empire. People, resources, and facilities that had served Japan's colonial enterprise of film figuratively and literally formed the basis of the cinema that would come after it.[55] While it is true that the Cold War brought clear breaks with the past, it is important to recognize as well the disturbing continuities, as seen in the colonialist roots of the Southeast Asian Film Festival.

Japan's Cold War culture might be compared to looking at a shadow cast by an object that remains just out of sight: it is, after all, nearly impossible to perceive the exact contours of something whose existence even its contemporary critics themselves denied. In this sense, examining Japanese discourse on Chinese films reveals a glimpse of Japan's elusive experience of the Cold War in Asia as if through a side glance. Ideological divisions, technology exchange, and the use of film festivals as political battlegrounds provide practical examples of direct cultural exchange where Japanese film workers on the right and the left revealed an inability to recognize the extent to which they carried the former Japanese empire within them. This study has built on recent trends in Cold War scholarship that emphasize the roles of culture in the conflict and call for a re-evaluation of its implications beyond the United States and the Soviet Union, extending to the so-called secondary and tertiary powers.[56]

Ultimately, what was most striking about the nature of film exchange between Japan and China during the Cold War was not the degree of influence each actually had on the other's film industries but rather how little. Despite the various official and unofficial attempts to enhance cultural exchanges via Film Weeks, Equipment Fairs, and other events, when actually faced with the chance of mutually engaging with the "other side," both camps frequently found that they were speaking at cross purposes. Long-held assumptions toward each other's culture remained remarkably resilient throughout the dismantling of Japan's empire, the birth of New China, and throughout the Cold War. Chinese film workers resented the Japanese obsession with modernizing China. Stubborn Japanese perceptions that Chinese film workers were less interested in technique and craft than they were in ideology have a specific history that cannot be accounted for by the tensions resulting from the U.S.–Soviet conflict. And yet anti-colonial alliances found momentum as a result of Cold War alliances, as illustrated in the political uses of such film festivals as the Asian Film Festival and the Afro-Asian Film Festival. These troublesome film exchanges offer no clean resolutions but serve to highlight the extent of the frictions and contradictions brought about by empire and its aftermath.

## Notes

1 Nozu Ura, "Chūgoku: atarashii jōsei ni yoru eiga seisaku," *Kinema junpō* vol. 1 (1950): p. 33.
2 Iwasaki Akira, "Chūgoku eiga no tabi – jō," *Eiga hyōron* vol. 2 (1966): p. 19.
3 Here I am adapting a concept by Irina Sandomirskaia, "Cinema Thinking the Unthinkable: Cold War Film and the Non-Reality of Russia," in *Russia and Its Other(s) on Film: Screening Intercultural Dialogue*, ed. Stephen Hutchings (New York: Palgrave Macmillan, 2008), pp. 130–131.
4 Baba Kimihiko, *Sengo nihonjin no chūgokuzō: nihon haisen kara bunka daikakumei nitchū fukkō made* (Shinyōsha, 2010). (Unless otherwise noted, all Japanese books are published in Tokyo.)
5 Marukawa Tetsushi, *Reisen bunkaron: wasurerareta aimai na sensō no genzaisei* (Sōfūsha, 2005).
6 Ann Sherif, *Japan's Cold War* (New York: Columbia University Press, 2009).
7 See Hirano Kyōko, *Mr. Smith Goes to Tokyo: The Japanese Cinema under the American Occupation* (Washington, DC: Smithsonian Press, 1994); Satō Hiroshi, "Tōhō sogi: reddo pāji towa nan datta no ka," in *Senryōka no eiga: kaihō to ken'etsu*, ed. Iwamoto Kenji (Shinwasha, 2009), pp. 269–291, or Naoko Shibusawa's *America's Geisha Ally: Reimagining the Japanese Enemy* (Cambridge, MA: Harvard University Press, 2006).
8 Sherif, *Japan's Cold War*, p. 7.
9 Ibid., p. 204.
10 Michael Davison, "A Cold War Correspondence," *Contemporary Literature* vol. 45, issue 3 (Autumn 2004): p. 545, cited in Sandomirskaia, "Cinema Thinking the Unthinkable."
11 I am indebted to Irina Sandomirskaia for making this connection. See Gilles Deleuze, *Cinema 2: The Time-Image* (Minneapolis: University of Minnesota Press, 1986), cited in Sandomirskaia, "Cinema Thinking the Unthinkable," p. 132.
12 Iwasaki, *Chūgoku eiga no tabi*, p. 12.
13 Sawamura Sadako and Itō Yūnosuke, "Shū Onrai to no nijikan: chūgoku ryokō no inshō," *Eiga geijutsu* vol. 6 (1957): pp. 62–65.
14 For a record of his first trip to China, see Iwasaki Akira, *Eiga no geijutsu* (Kyōwa shoin, 1936).
15 Film critic Sekine Hiroshi noted that this trait is noticeable in writing by other leftist critics and considered it a major fault in their journalism. Sekine Hiroshi, "Eiga ni okeru chūso ronsō," *Eiga geijutsu* vol. 1 (1965): pp. 86–88.
16 Iwasaki, *Chūgoku eiga no tabi*, pp. 12–13.
17 Ibid., p. 15.

18 Kinoshita Keisuke and Kinoshita Junji, "Nihon eiga no kadai – taidan," *Eiga geijutsu* vol. 10 (1956): p. 34.
19 Ibid., pp. 34, 37.
20 Keizai Kikakucho ed., *Keizai hakusho,* Shōwa 31 nenban (Ōkurashō insatsukyoku, 1956).
21 Kinoshita Keisuke, "Watashi no mite kita chūgoku to soren," *Kinema junpō*, December 1, 1956, pp. 35–37.
22 Kitagawa Fuyuhiko, "Chūgoku, chōsen no eigakai bekken ki," Article series, Part 1, *Kinema junpō*, January 1, 1957, pp. 45–47; Part 2, *Kinema junpō*, January 15, 1957, pp. 58–59; Part 3, *Kinema junpō*, February 15, 1957, pp. 60–61; and Part 4, *Kinema junpō*, March 15, 1957, pp. 64–65.
23 Kitagawa, "Chūgoku," Part 1, p. 45.
24 Ibid., pp. 46–47.
25 *Butterfly Lovers* (*Liangshan bo zhu ying tai*) was the first Chinese musical opera to be filmed in color. The film was directed by Sang hu and Huang sha and starred Yuan xuefen, Fan ruijuan, Zhang guifeng: Kitagawa, "Chūgoku," Part 2, pp. 58–59.
26 Kitagawa, "Chūgoku," Part 3, p. 60.
27 In Chinese, Cai Chusheng. *Cai Chusheng wenji*, vol. 4 (Beijing: Zhongguo guangbo dianshi chuban shè, 2006); Wang Renyin ed., *Cai Chusheng yanjiū wenji* (Beijing: Zhongguo dianying chuban she, 2006); Chen Peizhan, *Zhongguo dianying yishu dashi: Cai Chusheng* (Guangdong: Guangdong renmin chubanshe, 2008).
28 Kitagawa, "Chūgoku," Part 3, p. 61. In another article on Chinese Film Policy, an unidentified representative of the Japan–China Friendship Association explained the process of "self-reflection" in a similar attack on the 1930s director Sun Yu. The euphemistic term "self-reflection" was "far more than what any of us in Japan could imagine; for film-makers it is literally a life and death struggle." See Nitchū yūkō kyōkai, "Chūkyō no eiga seisaku," *Kinema junpō*, July 15, 1955, p. 38.
29 Kitagawa, "Chūgoku," Part 3, p. 61. For a complete Japanese translation of Cai's "self-reflection," see Cai Chusheng, "Watashi no ayamachi," *Sobieto eiga* vol. 2 (1953): pp. 22–23.
30 Michael Baskett, "Eigajin tachi no 'teikoku': daitōa eigaken no shosō," in *Eiga to daitōa kyōeiken*, ed. Iwamoto Kenji (Shinwasha, 2004), pp. 157–179.
31 Gabrielle Hecht, ed., *Entangled Geographies: Empire and Technopolitics in the Global Cold War* (Cambridge, MA: MIT Press, 2011), pp. 1–12.
32 Satō Kunio, "Chūgoku no karā eiga," *Shinario*, vol. 1 (1955), pp. 37–38.
33 "Chūgoku eiga ga ōatari," *Yomiuri Shimbun*, April 2, 1956, evening edition; Sono Shinsuke, "Chūgoku eiga 'ryō zanpaku to shuku eidai' o miru," *Teatoro*, vol. 3 (1955), pp. 30–32.
34 Shimizu Akira, "Chūgoku eiga mango," *Kinema junpō*, July 1, 1955, pp. 32–33.
35 Marsha Siefert, "East European Cold War Culture(s)?" in *Cold War Cultures: Perspectives on Eastern and Western European Societies*, ed. Annette Vowinckel, Marcus M. Payk, and Thomas Lindenberger (New York: Berghahn Books, 2012), pp. 23–54.
36 Machida Hiroshi, "Atarashii chūgoku: eiga no tabi," *Eiga geijutsu* vol. 5 (1957): pp. 18–19; *Eiga geijutsu* vol. 6 (1957): pp. 36–38.
37 "Zadankai: 'Chūgoku daihyōdan o kakonde'," *Shinario* vol. 7 (1962): p. 84; "Zadankai: 'chūgoku daihyōdan o koete'," *Eiga geijutsu* vol. 7 (1962): p. 62.
38 Ibid., pp. 86–87.
39 See Iwasaki Akira, "Chūgoku eiga shisetsudan no rainichi," *Eiga geijutsu* vol. 7 (1962): pp. 4–5, 8; Ushihara Kiyohiko, "Chūgoku daihyōdan o koete," *Kinema junpō*, June 1, 1962, pp. 72–73.
40 Edgar Snow, "Red China's Gentleman Hatchet Man," *Saturday Evening Post*, March 27, 1957, p. 119.
41 Michael Baskett, "Japan's Film Festival Diplomacy in Cold War Asia," *Velvet Light Trap* vol. 74 (Spring 2014): pp. 4–18.

42  Kon Yonsoku, "Kishi no tōnan ajia rekihō to taibei jishu gaikō," *Hitotsubashi ronsen* vol. 123, issue. 1 (January 2000): pp. 170–189.

43  Lee Sangjoon, "It's Oscar Time in Asia: The Rise and Demise of the Asia-Pacific Film Festival 1954–1972," in *Coming Soon to a Festival Near You*, ed. Jeffrey Ruoff (St Andrews, UK: St. Andrews Film Studies, 2012), pp. 173–187.

44  Glenn F. Ireton, "8-Year Historical Highlights of Film Federation and Festival," *Far East Film News*, Special Supplement (1960–1961): p. 9. For background on the establishment of the *Far East Film News* see, Glenn F. Ireton, "Brief History of Far East Film News," *Far East Film News*, Special Supplement (1960–1961): p. 8.

45  Nagata Masaichi, "Daitōa eigajin taikai o teishō su," *Eiga hyōron* vol. 1 (1944): p. 45.

46  Yamada Kazuo, "Ajia eigasai ga nerau mono," *Bunka hyōron* vol. 10 (1965): p. 39.

47  "1956 nen benisu eigasai de 'biruma no tategoto' ga jushō," *Eiga geijutsu* vol. 8 (1956): p. 10; Yamada Kazuo, "Mosukuwa eigasai de no zadankai," *Eiga geijutsu* vol. 11 (1961): pp. 52–55; Shindō Kaneto, "Mosukuwa eigasai to 'ningen' seisaku e," *Eiga geijutsu* vol. 2 (1964): pp. 90–93.

48  See for example, Sawamura and Itō, "Shū Onrai," pp. 63–64. Curiously, Itō sees this as a problem and demonstrates concern that Chinese were receiving a mistaken impression of Japanese cinema and that until "regular" Japanese films could be exported freely to China and that until "regular" Japanese films could be exported freely to China, conditions would not improve.

49  Christopher J. Lee, ed., *Making a World after Empire: The Bandung Moment and Its Political Afterlives* (Athens: Ohio University Press, 2010); Okakura Koshirō, "Ajia-afurika eigasai," *Ajia-afurika kōza 4: ajia-afurika kenkyū no tameni* (Keisō shobō, 1966), p. 85.

50  Mochizuki Yūko, "Ajia-afurika eigajin to no kōryū," *Bunka hyōron* vol. 6 (1965): p. 71.

51  Sukarno, "Eiga wa teikokushugi o funsai suru seijiteki rentai no buki de aru," *Bunka hyōron* vol. 11 (1964): p. 91; Utami Suryadarma, "Atarashii eiga de atarashii sekai o kizukō," *Bunka hyōron* vol. 11 (1964): pp. 96–101; Yamada Kazuo, "Daisan kai ajia-afurika eigasai," *Bunka hyōron* vol. 11 (1964): pp. 90, 101–104.

52  Saitō Ryūhō, "Eigasai chūso ronsō," *Eiga geijutsu* vol. 1 (1964): pp. 7–10; Sekine, "Eiga ni okeru"; Senba Teruyuki, "Shin chūgoku eiga no nanameyomi," *Eiga hyōron* vol. 3 (1967): pp. 82–86.

53  Saitō, "Eigasai chūso ronsō," pp. 8–9.

54  Takeuchi Minoru, "Kore ga chūgoku da: kakumei wa bika shite iika," *Eiga geijutsu* vol. 5 (1967): pp. 80–81; Satō Tadao, "Imai Tadashi no kiroki eiga 'Kore ga chūgoku da,'" *Eiga hyōron* vol. 5 (1967): p. 60; Saitō Ryūhō, "Chūgoku '26-'66 no kono danmen wa tadashii ka," *Eiga geijutsu* vol. 5 (1967): pp. 76–77; Obata Mannosuke, "Chūgoku no nama no sugao," *Shinario* vol. 6 (1967): p. 73.

55  For a useful history of the transition of the film industry in China from imperial Japan to Communist China, see Ni Yan, *Senji nitchū eiga kōshōshi* (Iwanami shoten, 2010), especially the last chapter; also see the preface and afterword to the Japanese edition of Cheng Jihua, *Chūgoku eigashi*, trans. Morikawa Kazuyo (Heibonsha, 1987); Morikawa Shinobu, *Morikawa Kazuyo ga ikita kyū 'manshū', sono jidai: kakumei to senka o kakenuketa seishunki* (Shinpūsha, 2007); Chang Hu and Quan Gu, *Man'ei: kokusaku eiga no shosō*, trans. Yokochi Takeshi and Aida Fusako (Pandora, 1999).

56  For cultural surveys of the Cold War, see Christina Klein, *Cold War Orientalism: Asia in the Middlebrow Imagination, 1945–1961* (Berkeley: University of California Press, 2003); Thomas Doherty, *Cold War, Cool Medium: Television, McCarthyism, and American Culture* (New York: Columbia University Press, 2005); Nicholas Cull, *The Cold War and the United States Information Agency: American Propaganda and Public Diplomacy* (New York: Cambridge University Press, 2009); Tony Shaw and Denise

Youngblood, *Cinematic Cold War: The American and Soviet Struggle for Hearts and Minds* (Lawrence: University of Kansas Press, 2010). Representative works on the Cold War in Asia include Tuong Vu and Wasana Wongsurawat, eds., *Dynamics of the Cold War in Asia: Ideology, Identity, and Culture* (New York: Palgrave Macmillan, 2009); Zheng Yangwen, Hong Liu, and Michael Szonyi, eds., *The Cold War in Asia: The Battle for Hearts and Minds* (Leiden: Brill, 2010); Tony Day and Maya H.T. Liem, *Cultures at War: The Cold War and Cultural Expression in Southeast Asia* (Ithaca, NY: Cornell University Press, 2010); Kitamura Hiroshi, *Screening Enlightenment*: *Hollywood and the Cultural Reconstruction of Defeated Japan* (Ithaca, NY: Cornell University Press, 2010).

# Comparative epilogue

# 16 Germany as a role model? Coming to terms with Nazi war deeds, 1945–2015

*Kerstin von Lingen*

In a speech during a ceremony held on May 3, 2015, to mark the seventieth anniversary of liberation of the former Nazi concentration camp at Dachau at the end of the Second World War, the German Chancellor Angela Merkel stated:

> It is the voices and the reports of the survivors that allow us all, including the younger generations, to find answers to the questions, and to fully appreciate why the memory of the horror of National Socialism is so important and indispensable for us today. It is a memory that is not limited to memorial speeches, but a living memory that is committed to endure into the future.

Then she continued:

> That is our governmental and also our civil obligation, to realize over and over again that we bear the guilt for all of the victims of National Socialism. We owe this to the survivors, and to ourselves, to all of us.[1]

This speech, which was the only one that Chancellor Merkel gave in all of the many commemorations to mark the occasion of the seventieth anniversary, reflects the current official German version of how the country's Nazi past is to be remembered. The significance of the message of the commemoration is two-fold. We have a duty to remember the evil, and we have an obligation to give the victims a voice – their voices will provide the frame for official German narratives. Nevertheless, such efforts of German officialdom to present this awareness of a duty to remember the evil and the horror, as well as this obligation to give a voice to the victims, are the product of a long and tortuous process, marked by many errors and failures, in which the nation has gradually worked out how to come to terms with its past.

Over the seventy years since the end of the war, German acknowledgement of the facts of the Nazi regime has changed, from a desire to conceal to a willingness painful to acknowledge, and then to an albeit belated interest in attempting to settle the moral debt owed to the victims with official state apologies and memorialization. Notwithstanding the massive political efforts that were made toward reappraisal and toward the criminalization and punishment of Nazi crimes, which was accompanied by a huge social learning curve, this process took three generations to achieve, and if we speak of a success it was only finally belatedly achieved.[2]

The issue of guilt and acknowledgement has been the underlying theme within the history of postwar Germany for the last seventy years: it was a continual attempt to manage, in various forms, the issue of punishment and purification, or self-purification, through criminal proceedings.[3] However, the process had its flaws: many perpetrators were left unpunished due to inadequacies in the legal system and a general disinterest of the German judiciary to prosecute, especially in the 1950s and 1960s. This gave rise to a specifically German phenomenon, the issue of "belated trials," as shown in the 2015 trial in Lüneburg against former Auschwitz bookkeeper Oskar Groening, then in his early nineties, in the district court of the northern German town of Lüneburg. Groening was employed at the Auschwitz concentration camp with the task of registering the monetary possessions of all arriving detainees, many of whom were murdered within hours of their arrival. While not denying having worked at Auschwitz, Groening continued to emphasize that he bore no personal guilt since he was only seventeen years old at the time and a mere "desk person." This belated trial, which brought to the stand one of the lowliest of Auschwitz guards, speaks to the larger issue of the terribly slow pursuit of justice in German courts when it comes to Nazi and Holocaust crimes. Most politicians, journalists, and academics agree that Germany has a moral duty to bring to trial all those who might be guilty of such crimes, regardless of age, as the trials are often seen by former victims as a sign of recognition of their suffering and as a form of apology from the nation. However, others, especially people positioned at the conservative end of the political spectrum but also including general members of the public, argue that the courts should have addressed the question of responsibility for these lowly officials much earlier, with the trials of higher-ranking officials who were keeping the extermination process running and that now such trials were not helpful.

The judge in Groening's trial gave a verdict sentencing the defendant to four years in prison. The judge ruled that even though Groening was not directly responsible for the deaths of prisoners, he had witnessed enough violence to know what the extermination camps entailed and that to join the SS and take a "safe desk job" at Auschwitz to avoid being sent to the front had been his own decision.[4] The lawyers and the surviving plaintiffs were satisfied with the verdict, which they called "historic," and emphasized the previous decades of lax prosecution of Nazis in German courts. Indeed, of the roughly 6,500 guards at the concentration camp at Auschwitz alone, only 43 were brought to trial before German courts.[5] Where did the other 6,457 go? What are the implications of a society after a war integrating a huge number of criminals of the merely-following-orders kind, such as Oskar Groening?

This chapter describes the legal measures adopted after Germany's surrender and discusses the impact of these measures in terms of memory politics in order to analyze possible lessons learned and also to offer material for comparison with the situation in Japan after the surrender and the fall of its empire. If we want to speak about Germany as a role model for positive transition after the Second World

War, an analysis of the legal measures taken to come to terms with war deeds is crucial. The trials held by the Allied Nations played an important role in coming to terms with the Nazi past, as is evident in the following figures: in West Germany, there were 4,400 convictions by 1949 and 11,000 in the Soviet-occupied Eastern Zone.[6] In 1949, the Federal Republic of Germany (FRG) was formed out of the Western occupation zones of the United States, Britain, and France, and the Soviet occupation zone became the Democratic Republic of Germany (GDR). Here, I intend to focus largely on the FRG, that is to say West Germany, since the FRG is what most researchers refer to in discussions of whether Germany can serve as a role model for the adjudication of war crimes.

Regime change is usually followed by a period that is characterized by something researchers call transitional justice.[7] The new regime has several tools at its disposal to legitimize power and to rebuild society: war crimes trials to ascertain responsibility; population displacement to restore order or to accommodate exiled or evacuated people; and administrative purges of political elites to restore internal stability.[8] In my analysis of the German example, we can chart a "memory model" that has three stages: first, concealment and amnesty; second, integration of old elites; and finally, a sharp delineation from the Nazi past through all strata of society.

Dealing with the old elites was a particular challenge in Germany. German society had to recognize responsibility for war atrocities all over Europe, at the same time rebuilding its own devastated nation and integrating destitute German refugees who flowed back to the bombed-out cities of Germany in their thousands, a visible symbol of defeat. The Allied decision at Potsdam meant that the eastern territories formerly belonging to Germany of East Prussia, Silesia, and Sudetenland were lost to accommodate reparations to the Soviet Union, Poland, and Czechoslovakia for war deeds. One crucial element of German society in the first decade – albeit the perpetrator's past – was thus a sense of victimhood, which left little space to acknowledge war guilt and redress the suffering of survivors.

When assessing the legal record of German war guilt, one caveat has to be made. Even if elements of the German experience, especially with regard to occupation crimes and forced labor, are adaptable to other countries and contexts, one element of the German case is unique, namely genocide. The racial and ideological dimension of the crime of murdering European Jews, a crime now referred to as the Holocaust, is not comparable to any other crime, and it had no parallel in Asia. Incorporating these unspeakable atrocities into a national memory was a huge challenge for postwar German society.

## Allied measures

Democracy came to Germany not as a joint effort made by German society but from the outside, meaning that the Allies set the pace. Under the rubric of "re-education," they had to prove the criminal character of the Nazi regime in court, and they focused their administrative purges on the old elites who had backed

Hitler.[9] However, after the German surrender in May 1945, the occupying forces became aware of other extremely pressing needs such as keeping the population supplied with food and necessities, restoring the industrial and transportation sectors, not to mention organizing a basic administration to facilitate the occupation. At first the Allies were simply pragmatic and undiscriminating in their overall approach to force Germany to come to terms with the past. All elites over a specific rank were automatically arrested, and thousands of German citizens spent the summer of 1945 in internment camps awaiting clearance. Legal measures were given high priority: after the failure of First World War German war crimes trials, which had taken place before the Reich's Imperial Court of Justice in Leipzig, the Allies decided to set up an international court.[10] The decision to create the first International Military Tribunal (IMT) in Nuremberg in 1945 later became a beacon for international commitment to legal norms, and this culminated fifty years later in the long cherished dream of an International Criminal Court (ICC), which opened in 2002.[11] The IMT was important because it was the first international prosecution of state-legitimized crimes. Thus Nazi elites could not avoid responsibility by hiding behind their different jurisdictions. The American prosecution at the IMT focused on outlawing aggressive war, but unlike in later proceedings, the Holocaust did not stand clearly at the center of proceedings. Instead focus was placed on war crimes in a narrow sense – crimes of occupation policies, forced labor, and mistreatment of prisoners of war.

The international Nuremberg proceedings had an impact on national war crimes tribunals that subsequently took place all over Europe. Between 1945 and 1949, following the pattern set at Nuremberg, coming to terms with the past meant focusing on a small number of groups of perpetrators in court, with a strong focus on special Nazi units and the SS.[12] A considerable number of war crimes trials were held Europe-wide, the ones by U.S. and UK courts focusing on crimes where their nationals had fallen victim to German atrocities; on the other hand, national courts all over Europe opened proceedings against German war criminals and local Nazi collaborators. The inclusion of the latter shifted the focus of war crimes trials to the problem of wartime collaboration and served as a tool to sort postwar societies into "good" or "bad" wartime behavior, which in turn had consequences for the possibilities to restart a postwar career.[13]

In an extensive trial program in all four occupied zones of Germany, the Allies attempted in military courts to establish legal responsibility for different professional groups and thus emphasized the widespread acceptance of the Nazi regime among all professional and social classes. In the subsequent U.S.-led Nuremberg Military Trials (NMT) 1945–1949, there were lawsuits against doctors, economists, journalists, diplomats, and officials of Nazi ministries.[14] The entire elite administration of the Nazi state was affected but to varying degrees. While politicians and heads of public agencies belonged to the ostracized elements of the population and were denied a return to power, elites from the administration, as well as justice, health, and education departments experienced this to a much lesser degree, while business professionals and journalists were almost ignored. After all, in a way that is comparable to the case of Japan after 1947 and the "reversal" of

American policy in East Asia, the Allies now wanted to prioritize Germany's speedy recovery.[15]

The second element of the Allied measures was a social purge, called *denazification*, which sought to identify Nazi Party members of various ranks who had held positions in the regional administration, from *Gau* leaders (party leader of a region's administration), Nazi women's corps, to "*Blockwart*" (Nazi neighborhood surveillance). Information was gathered through a questionnaire distributed among all adults in German society, a precondition to receiving food stamps, to elicit information concerning engagement with the Nazi state. Whoever had held a party position in Hitler's empire then had to undergo proceedings in so-called denazification courts (*Spruchkammer* trials). These courts sorted German society into five categories, ranging from "major offenders," "offenders," "lesser offenders," "followers" to "persons exonerated." Once cleared in court, there was nothing to be feared; the citizen could start afresh. Former elites were very creative in inventing exculpating strategies, and party members who were cleared gave affidavits for old comrades still under review. Using the name of a renowned German washing detergent of the time, these affidavits were soon nicknamed "Persil" tickets (*Persil Schein*), as their purpose was to whiten even the blackest of records.

With the emergence of a practice to label most defendants under category IV ("follower" of Nazi politics), seen as a minor failure, the whole process of denazification was soon given the nickname "follower-factory" by critics, to indicate that apparently no high-ranking Nazi had ever existed, and all were just following orders. It became apparent that the courts did select a few scapegoats, however, in order to prove the non-liability of the majority.[16] Denazification thus became, paradoxically to its intent, a vehicle for reintegrating a large portion of the old party warriors into postwar German society.

In sum, the politics of the Allied Nations' handling of war crimes in the four occupied zones, on the one hand, played a significant role in singling out high-ranking Nazis; on the other hand, it facilitated the continuity in status of the lesser incriminated ranks between the Third Reich and the Federal Republic. To a lesser extent, this continuity of elites in power also occurred in the GDR, where commitment to the new communist cause saved people from overly tenacious inquiries into their ideological stands. Through the denazification clearance, many groups did, as if with official blessing, gain the chance to have a second career after the war.

In spite of their lenience, Allied transitional justice measures were rejected as an attack on German national sovereignty, and the emotion behind such rejection resonated with very similar reactions in Japan at the same time, as Barak Kushner explains in Chapter 3 of this volume and Sandra Wilson details in Chapter 5. However, and most importantly, the administrative purge constituted an important mental turning point in Germany. As Norbert Frei notes, the coming to terms with the past represented a "political and judicial boundary" drawn with an eye toward old values and ideologies, a "demarcation line," the crossing of which became publicly impossible.[17] Nevertheless, most of the German people rejected the *Spruchkammer* trials as unjust. Although simple cases were processed relatively quickly and punishments meted out, more complicated proceedings of "major offenders" usually took many years. High-ranking Nazis benefited from a change in Allied policy after 1948 and the adjustment to end the Allied war crimes program, which often brought them impunity. Thus, for procedural reasons, the small fry often received more severe sentences than the bigger fish, the high-ranking Nazi functionaries, which made for an imbalance in the program, and as a result denazification lost its overall moral credibility. Measures that had been intended to determine the degree of social infection of National Socialism and the level of partnership in repression and crime in effect turned into a farce, in which most of the German public thought of themselves as victims of "victors' justice."

With the rise of the Cold War, the Western Allies shifted their focus from punishment of war criminals to amnesty and, for many, to reintegration in society. The Allies decided to form a semi-sovereign western German state by uniting their three occupation zones in June 1948 and introducing a new currency, the Deutsch Mark. Then in the same year, the divide between the United States and the Soviet Union grew wider during the Berlin Blockade, when Stalin cut off all rail and road links to Berlin (which resulted in an airlift by the Western Allies to supply the city for nearly a year). The foundation of two separate German states in 1949 was the consequence of this new bipolar world order.

## West German ways of coming to terms with the past after 1945

The processing of German Nazi criminals in German courts went through three phases: a comprehensive prosecution program held under the auspices of the Allies that lasted from 1945 to 1949; a pause in prosecution in the 1950s; and finally a renewed prosecution at the end of the 1950s that lasted till the 1980s. A final burst of prosecutions began in the mid-1990s. Allegations have frequently been made that German courts remained inactive for decades, and the journalist Ralph Giordano even referred to a "Second Guilt."[18] But such a term is inaccurate. German courts in the western occupation zones were commissioned by as early as the end of 1945 by the Allies to carry out legal action against Nazi defendants autonomously. Pursuit was made on the basis of Control Council Law No. 4, which designated the responsibility for criminal proceedings, and Control Council Law No. 10, which codified the handling of war crimes and crimes against humanity. These early criminal proceedings, despite certain deficiencies, contributed significantly to the re-establishment of the rule of law, especially since at this time lawyers of the Nazi regime were banned from office (they were allowed to return in 1951).[19]

However, the first wave of these trials all dealt with crimes against communities in Germany. They addressed crimes committed during the Nazi seizure of power in 1933; the incineration and destruction of synagogues in November 1938; the crime of *Aryanization* (a term referring to the economic persecution and seizure of Jewish property, the expulsion of "non-Aryan" citizens, mainly Jews, from all areas of public life [e.g. doctors, lawyers, academics] and entailing the transfer of German Jewish property into "Aryan" hands); the systematic murder and euthanasia of the disabled; cases of denunciation; and crimes committed in the final days of the war, mainly against German deserters or civilians who had hoisted white flags.[20]

But after the end of the denazification phase, the criminalization of the Nazi past was no longer of great interest to the German state. Scholars have coined a term "communicative silence" to describe this disinterest.[21] In the climate of the early 1950s, a clean slate mentality dominated. This mentality demanded an end to the Allied war crimes trials and debates about amnesty for prominent generals and generated the struggle for the reinstatement and pension entitlement for the old elites.[22] The awarding of pensions was also of great social importance in that it influenced memory culture: service to the old state was recognized and in a sense awarded with money and thus re-evaluated. Something of this trend was also seen in Japan at the end of the occupation in 1952 when former veterans and war criminal support groups pushed for a redrafting of the pension law. The rearmament movement that followed the Korean War – a high moment for the nascent Cold War – allowed former army officers in Japan to regain some of their prestige, and the war also led to the re-installation of a German Army that had the blessing of the Allies. With the resumption of German sovereignty in 1952, the formal decision for rearmament in 1956 for most Germans signaled not just the end of the Allied occupation but also the end of an era in which they were *obliged* to come to terms with the past.[23]

The pension debate benefited Army officers and also bureaucrats. Law No. 131, issued by the Adenauer administration in 1951 to facilitate the inclusion into the FRG of German refugees from Eastern Europe who had lost all their official papers during expulsion from the East in the summer of 1945, following the Potsdam agreements to resettle Germans in central Europe from the Eastern provinces, also helped to camouflage people's employment history under Nazi rule. Many former functionaries (even if they were never refugees) claimed merely that they had lost their paperwork and were subsequently reinstalled into new positions, even though the Allies had banned some of them in 1945 due to their position in the Nazi bureaucracy. The result was particularly devastating in the judiciary: numerous former Nazi judges regained their seats, completely stalling the pursuit of justice against the Nazis.[24]

Numerous perpetrators found shelter under the guise of ordinary police officers. No one inquired too closely, for example, into what being a police inspector in Lithuania during the war had entailed, though it had been common knowledge that the Nazis often required killings to be carried out by ordinary policemen – this was part of the Nazi extermination policy. The Allies' lack of awareness of these "special tasks" made it possible for people such as Karl Schulz, an officer from Bremen – who featured prominently in a 2015 Berlin exhibition on remembering the end of the Second World War in Europe – to return to police service and even to be promoted to chief of a department.[25] Schulz's colleagues all shielded him, and his involvement in Holocaust mass murder was not investigated right up to his retirement in 1968. A social pact of silence is one of the features of the postwar period, the era of Chancellor Konrad Adenauer (the "Adenauer era"), and this reticence, or "tact," ensured a remarkable social peace in the so-called wonder period, the era of the German economic resurrection.

The late 1950s saw a shift in social attitudes regarding the treatment of Nazi criminals and the start of a second phase with a new wave of trials. This was the result of massive and aggressive propaganda from the GDR (East Germany), which started exposing on a near monthly basis the former Nazi careers of high-ranking officials in Chancellor Adenauer's government. It was also triggered by controversial court decisions and justice scandals following the reinstatement of various elites who had allowed military and SS judges back into civil service.[26] When swastika graffiti was found at the newly built Synagogue of Cologne in December 1959, frightened German politicians grew anxious about the reaction of the international community. It suddenly became clear to the political and intellectual leadership how ineffectual the postwar purges had been, as well as the great risk posed to the political achievements of the last decade if old Nazis regained positions of authority.

The final wake-up call was the scandal leading to the so-called *Einsatzgruppen* trial in Ulm in 1958, when a former perpetrator from an SS killing squad, who had targeted Jews and Soviet civilians, was exposed as a result of having sued the German state for a police officer's pension. The exposure of perpetrators who had regained their postwar civil careers and simply returned to their former positions and roles, claiming what they saw as justified reward for services rendered to the German state, at last helped shift the legal focus to non-German victim groups and thus to the complexity of the Holocaust. Finally, the issue of achieving justice for victims started to occupy people's attention. In the 1958 Ulm trial, an increasingly critical public asked, together with philosopher/intellectual Hannah Arendt, how many were still to be discovered as having been involved in this state-organized mass murder? A commentator in the *Stuttgarter Zeitung* shrewdly observed that the worst was still to come; the entire nation, indeed "a whole epoch [could] stand on trial."[27] With the creation of a central Office of the State Judiciary at Ludwigsburg, near Stuttgart, a coordinating legal body was established to systematically investigate perpetrators who had committed deeds in the former Nazi empire that stretched far beyond the postwar borders of the Federal Republic.[28] The bulk of these crimes had taken place behind the front lines and were thus not real "war crimes"; they needed to be prosecuted under the category of concentration camp or Holocaust crimes, or *Einsatzgruppen* crimes.[29]

One of the most significant events of the second phase was the Frankfurt Auschwitz Trial in the 1960s. The first Frankfurt trial against former members of the Auschwitz camp staff, held from 1963 to 1965, received more publicity than the Nuremberg International Trial in 1945.[30] The second and third Frankfurt Trials followed soon thereafter. Frankfurt State Attorney General Fritz Bauer formulated as a new creed at the start of the trial that the whole society stood in judgement.[31] The trial changed the collective memory of West Germany decisively and permanently, for the fact that it made absolutely clear what life had been like in the death camps. The circuitous testimony of eyewitnesses clearly evoked "the atmosphere of *Lager strasse*," as a journalist called it, referring to the main "street" of the camps, and was broadcast by newspapers and television, albeit in snippets, into the living rooms of German society.[32] It was impossible now to turn a blind eye toward the Holocaust. It became suddenly very clear that only legal proceedings could initiate an authentic process of reevaluation and reflection in society, and trials were an essential tool in coming to terms with past deeds.

The Vietnam War and student protests triggered discussion and social unrest in 1968 not only in Germany but all around Europe, as well as the United States and Japan. In Germany, the debate covered all sorts of topics, including coming to terms with the past, German complicity, and postwar reparations.[33] It is striking that the student and civil rights movements initially emerged with the purpose of achieving social reforms, and the protests about memory consensus became a focus only after suggestions for reform were rejected and the older generation's indifference became apparent.[34] The generational shift during the 1960s caused a social upheaval that refocused attention on the role of fathers and the work they had put into the Nazi empire. This conscious questioning of one's parents' role in the Nazi regime and in the Holocaust led to attention being paid to the crucial role that silent bystanders had played.[35] As a result, political demands for recompensation were heard for the first time in the early 1970s and were reinforced through Chancellor Willy Brandt's *Ostpolitik*, the idea of normalization of relations between West and East Germany, as well as his famous *Kniefall*, his genuflection in 1970 in front of the Warsaw ghetto memorial. This gesture was perceived as a symbolic recognition of Nazi occupation policy and its particular oppressiveness in Eastern Europe, although the Polish state was unhappy that the gesture emphasized the Jewish victims more than the suffering of the Polish nation as a whole under Nazi occupation.

At the same time, the legal burden of continuity became obvious. In parliament, an important initiative arose in 1965 that addressed the elimination of the statute of limitations for murder by Nazi perpetrators. This eventually won cross-party support, though it also met with fierce resistance from conservative forces who wanted to bring an end to the trials of Nazis. A UN resolution confirmed the non-applicability of statute of limitations to Nazi war crimes persecutions.[36] In 1969, the parliament decided that the murder of the Jews by the Nazis would enjoy no statute of limitations and postponed the debate by ten years. After the broadcast in 1979 of the American TV series *Holocaust*, social sensitivity in Germany regarding the topic increased still further. In the end, in late 1979, a law was passed excluding all Nazi crimes from the statute of limitation for all time.[37]

With the increase in awareness about the continuing influence on society of the old elite, as well as their roles and responsibility in the judiciary in the 1950s for hindering swift punishment after the war, a new wave of trials was held in Germany from the mid-1970s onward. Such tribunals included trials in Düsseldorf on crimes committed at the Majdanek concentration camp and also the trial against Klaus Barbie in Lyon, France, in 1987. Social criticism created a sea change in attitudes, witnessed, for example, in the 1979 resignation of the conservative politician Hans Filbinger, prime minister of Baden-Württemberg, after allegations about his role as a naval lawyer and prosecutor in the Nazi era, who had sentenced German soldiers to death as deserters even after surrender had taken place, showing a remarkable degree of Nazi commitment against "traitors." Filbinger was particularly criticized for the fact that he seemed to show no sense of culpability or professional qualms, and he immortalized his ignominiousness about the regime change with the statement, "What was lawful then cannot be unlawful today."[38] The public furor over this response demonstrated that there was no hope of sympathy for such a stance, and it was politically finished. Thereafter the topic of unpunished Nazi crimes was taken up by film-makers, journalists, and academics and achieved widespread notoriety.

The processes of acknowledging and integrating a "perpetrator's past" – meaning not only the Nazi past but the fact that nearly every member of society could have been a perpetrator to a greater or lesser degree – and of abandoning the narratives of self-victimization were slow and painful. But they were marked by a new determination to unveil survivors' narratives. By digging into daily life in the Nazi era on a local level and looking at the regional and neighborhood dynamics of exclusion and persecution, it was possible to have debates about one's degree of guilt. Even in the smallest of towns in Germany today, one is likely to find a monument to a forced labor camp or a small metal plaque in the old cobblestone streets (*Stolper-Steine*) that mark the houses of murdered (mainly Jewish) neighbors. These initiatives arose in the mid-1980s and have regained considerable momentum in the last decade, as many cities have followed on the project with the official blessing of the city councils and local firms, engaging in installing thousands of these memory stones into the pavements before their former homes. At the same time, a movement of fierce resistance, especially amongst Jewish communities in Germany, has been formed against this "second humiliation," as the stones lie in the pavement and people walk on them.[39]

The year 1987 saw the outbreak of renewed and fierce debates in the wake of the so-called academics' dispute, a quarrel between historians concerning the comparability of Nazi injustice to communist violence. The question was asked: what did our new beginning in 1945 achieve? For the first time, the flaws in the legal proceedings against Nazis that had taken place in the Adenauer era became a topic of discussion.[40] An exhibition about "Perpetrators in the War of Destruction," showing private photos and snapshots of Army soldiers killing people or posing in the company of their victims, launched a discussion in 1995 about the lack of prosecution of perpetrators in Army ranks. The fall of the Berlin Wall on the night of November 9, 1989, was the high point of a process that had encompassed almost the entire previous decade. When the GDR collapsed, what took place was less a merger of two equal states and more a political and legal takeover of the GDR by the FRG. The peace agreements of 1994 guaranteed the withdrawal of all occupying troops from West and East Germany and thus marked the end of the most visible consequences of a lost war. The inclusion of the GDR into the FRG was not only difficult economically: the merger also created much social debate and turmoil. In essence, the question was how to form a new German identity, soldering together the Eastern and Western elements of postwar experiences. The debate about the deeds of the communist secret police (*Stasi*) brought to light appalling parallels in shielding former party members and urged reconsideration of the guilt and personal involvement of "ordinary men." Within a few years, citizens came to realize the need to form new recollections of the past, and yet again a renewed public discussion emerged regarding the success or failure of the various ways in which postwar Germany had come to terms with its Nazi past. Over the course of the 1990s, an attitude developed of supporting the relentless search for perpetrators within the German populace, bringing them to court no matter how much time had passed and compensating and apologizing to the victims.

A new wave of trials started after 1999 but under considerable difficulties: defendants were now in their nineties and often unfit to stand trial or to serve their sentences. Many witnesses were now dead, and written evidence thin. Nevertheless, with the help of historians called in as "expert witnesses," trials took place and verdicts were handed down; those who were found guilty were placed in custody in old people's homes. These trials helped to sharpen the reputation of the Federal Republic as a credible guardian of the law and to separate the current government morally from previous regimes. These moves certainly help to distinguish Germany from Japan, where no equivalent proceedings at the behest of the government have ever taken place.[41]

Today, German memory culture is characterized by what has been called an "institutionalization and nationalization of negative remembrance." This refers to the idea of an enduring preservation of national shame in collective memory, by making memory policies and speech, among other things, a national priority.[42] This process has channeled the idea of "Never again!" coined by the survivors into an agenda of new moral values regarding past deeds. A conference at Stockholm on Holocaust Education, Remembrance and Research in 2000 emphasized the memory of the Holocaust as a legacy for the whole world and a relevant educational tool for world peace.[43] German historiography therefore speaks of a "memory imperative" to characterize the pressure derived from a sense of commitment and obligation, of providing a warning to the future, of educating the next generation, and of a transnationally reasoned reconciliatory political stance.[44] Some might argue, however, that this new idea of the memory imperative is a mere theoretical construct and that it fails to recognize the significant transformations that occurred before 1990, as well as the role of the worldwide economic networks that pressured German companies who made use of forced labor in the war to pay recompensation to long forgotten victims.

## Recompensation

Reparations in the form of monetary payment are often a sign of acknowledgement and of coming to terms with the past; they help settle disputes between states. As the legal successor to the Nazi empire, West Germany had already in the 1950s sought reparations agreements with nearly all western European nations and the state of Israel. However, the topic arose again on a different level at the end of the

Cold war, when several individuals who had worked in Nazi factories sued individual German companies in U.S. courts (since they offered wider legal possibilities). To distinguish their individual claims from state claims, the term "recompensation" has been coined, to describe the debt to pay monetary compensation for slave labor or economic losses during the Nazi era. The press campaigns and threats to boycott German industrial goods in the United States wielded such economic pressure that the companies urged the German state to find a political solution and to take the burden off their shoulders. This led the German state to create a foundation titled Memory, Responsibility, Future (*Erinnerung, Verantwortung, Zukunft*), endowed with €5 million derived from industrial funds and taxpayers' money, to compensate claims from individuals who had worked in wartime factories. This benefitted victims of forced labor mainly from Eastern Europe who had previously been excluded from the state-to-state level reparation payments due to the East–West divide. With this procedure, recompensation was handled by offering a symbolic lump sum payment through specific organizations, in order to keep the matter legally and administratively separate from acknowledging it through governmental channels.[45] Such redress has played an important symbolic role in demonstrating the will for political cooperation, as a hallmark of partnership within the international community.

Through the investigations established in Ludwigsburg, as well as the public discussions in the 1980s about the "forgotten victims," and the reparations in the twenty-first century for forced labor in the Nazi regime, the perception of the Nazi period has changed over the years.[46] Now, memory culture in Germany is victim centered and not preoccupied with shielding perpetrators. By taking into account forgotten victims and their often precarious social circumstances, it became possible to develop an understanding of the history as well as of the symbolic significance of financial reparations for the reconciliation process. As previously shown, the restitution process has moved from the state to semiprivate foundations, and it is now easier for former victims to access redress.[47]

Considering the political efforts that were necessary in order for these changes – the criminalization and punishment of Nazi crimes, as well as the social "learning curve" of this process – to come about, if one can speak of "success," it would have to be "late success."[48] In a political and social sense, it is fair to use the word "success," it having been achieved despite the changing constellations of power and conflicting group interests over the course of three generations. Germany can now turn its gaze to the victims and take notice of their suffering, offering solace not only in material redress but also in the representations of suffering and persecution in film, literature, and exhibits and can also count on public appreciation of these remembrance initiatives. But to speak of recompensation as representing success in the moral or ethical sense would be inappropriate and presumptuous. The discrepancy between the expectations of the victims, their individual and monetary expectations, and their hopes for coming to terms with the past for losses is unresolvable.[49] "Reconciliation" itself is not possible through money, even though the German word "*Wiedergutmachung*" (literally: "making it good again") seems to suggest this possibility.

## Conclusion: the impact on memory

The globalization of Holocaust remembrance, as well as new genocidal conflicts all over the world, have meant that the Germans of today are no longer equated with the Nazis of yesterday. This transformation is evident on days of remembrance: following the global alliance against terrorism after the attacks on the World Trade Center in New York in 2001, Germany's international image has been upgraded and seems to have overcome the war guilt. This is especially visible on anniversaries. For example, since 2005 the German Chancellor has been invited to attend Allied victory celebrations, be it for the landing in Normandy or the victory day in May. Commemorations emphasize less the victory and more the triumph over evil as a task for humankind. The result of this new partnership that Germany has been able to forge with its neighbors concerning its history has helped to shape the political role of the European Union, in which a nation that was a former perpetrator dares to stand in line with people and nations who are victims and show solidarity with them.[50] This is a major obstacle that we have not seen overcome in East Asia, and much responsibility for that must be placed at the feet of the Japanese, the instigators of the war in East Asia.

At the sixtieth anniversary of the liberation of Auschwitz in 2005, Chancellor Gerhard Schroeder drew the connection between memory and democratization, in order to conjure a European future:

> The memory of war and genocide under the Nazis has become a part of our living constitution. For some, this is a difficult burden to bear. Nonetheless this remembrance is part of our national identity. Remembrance of the Nazi era and its crimes is a moral obligation. We owe it not only to the victims, to the survivors and their relatives: No, we owe it also to ourselves.[51]

The German president Horst Koehler came in 2006 to a similar conclusion:

> [W]hat a long way we Germans have come in the decades since 1945 in regards to our past – from the beginning only demanded by a few voices, to the present apparent self-evident readiness, to elucidate and atone for the crimes of the National Socialist period. [. . .] The contention with the past is fundamental to our self-understanding as a nation. We have this contention and consequently also the work on places of memory like this one to thank that Germany today is again a respected member of the family of nations.[52]

The memory of war, defined together with former enemies, serves today no longer as a warning but as a moral justification for a common European action in the fight against new injustices. The memory of the Holocaust as "reminder of the power of evil," as the Vatican termed it, today exists on a transnational European level of reference for its ability to forge transnational partnerships and solidarities.[53]

The German role within this reconstructed Europe in the last decade has been to maintain the memory of past atrocities. This was remarkably visible in a speech that German Foreign Office Secretary for European Questions Michael Roth made in May 2015:

> Not in spite of, but *because of* all of the severity of the guilt, Auschwitz has become a part of the German identity. Since we cannot get around it to acknowledge those years in which Germany had sunk to her deepest point in history. [. . .] We cannot get around it because every one of us, despite all of the reworking of the historians and all of the attempts to explain, still asks in silence: "How could it have happened? How could Germany have been the land of Nazi terror?" A satisfactory answer is still difficult today, perhaps impossible.[54]

He concluded that the German people were now looking back with humility on the long and tortuous path toward recognizing that guilt, as after all it had given Germany the chance ". . . to return, step-by-step, to the center of Europe and the international community. The chance that we Germans, despite all of the awful crimes of the war years, have been awarded the hand of reconciliation."

The German example demonstrates, following the idea of transitional justice, that notwithstanding certain legal flaws and inadequacies, it is only through the admission of guilt in symbolic actions and compensatory gestures of apology, such as through commemorations, reparations, memorial sites and personal encounters, that a stable reconciliation can be reached. It is upon this basis that political partnerships can thrive in the global world of tomorrow.

## Notes

1  Speech of the German Chancellor Angela Merkel, May 3, 2015, at Dachau Concentration Camp Memorial Site. The Chancellor's official website, https://www.bundeskanzlerin. de/Content/DE/Rede/2015/05/2015-05-04-merkel-dachau.html. I would like to express my thanks to Emily Hruban for her translations of the passages from speeches in this chapter.
2  Kerstin von Lingen, "Historische Gerechtigkeit? Deutsche Bemühungen um 'Wiedergutmachung' und Opferausgleich, 1945–2005," *Jahrbuch für Politik und Geschichte* vol. 1 (2010): pp. 45–61.
3  For a comprehensive overview of this issue and for a transnational approach, see Annette Weinke, *Die Verfolgung von NS-Tätern im geteilten Deutschland, Vergangenheitsbewältigungen 1949–1969 oder: Eine deutsch–deutsche Beziehungsgeschichte im Kalten Krieg* (Paderborn: Schoeningh, 2002).
4  Alison Smale, "Oskar Gröning, Ex-Soldier at Auschwitz, Gets Four-Year Sentence," *The New York Times*, July 15, 2015, http://www.nytimes.com/2015/07/16/world/europe/oskar-groning-auschwitz-nazi.html?_r=0.
5  "Auschwitz Prozess: Das letzte Gericht," *Die Zeit*, May 28, 2015, http://www.zeit. de/2015/22/auschwitz-prozess-oskar-groening-ss-gericht.
6  For an overview of West German proceedings, see Annette Weinke, "'Alliierter Angriff auf die nationale Souveränität?' Die Strafverfolgung von Kriegs- und NS-Verbrechern in der Bundesrepublik, der DDR und Österreich," in *Transnationale Vergangenheitspolitik. Der Umgang mit deutschen Kriegsverbrechern in Europa nach dem zweiten Weltkrieg*, ed. Norbert Frei (Göttingen: Wallstein 2006), pp. 37–93. For an overview on

Eastern Germany, see Hermann Wentker, "Die juristische Ahndung von NS-Verbrechen in der sowjetischen Besatzungszone und der DDR," *Kritische Justiz* vol. 35 (2002): pp. 60–78; a former state attorney of the GDR compiled a document edition, see Günther Wieland (ed.), trans. Laurenz Demps, Klaus Marxen, and Ursula Solf, *DDR Justiz und NS-Verbrechen: Sammlung ostdeutscher Strafurteile wegen nationalsozialistischer Tötungsverbrechen* (Amsterdam: Verfahrensregister und Dokumentenband, 2002), p. 97.

7 Neil Kritz, *Transitional Justice: How Emerging Democracies Reckon with Former Regimes: Laws, Rulings and Reports*, vol. 3 (Washington, DC: United States Institute of Peace, 1995); Ruti G. Teitel, *Transitional Justice* (New York: Oxford University Press, 2000); Jon Elster, *Closing the Books: Transitional Justice in Historical Perspective* (Cambridge: Cambridge University Press, 2004); David Cohen, "Transitional Justice in Divided Germany after 1945," in *Retribution and Reparation in the Transition to Democracy*, ed. Jon Elster (Cambridge: Cambridge University Press, 2006), pp. 59–88.

8 Kerstin von Lingen, "Erfahrung und Erinnerung. Gründungsmythos und Selbstverständnis von Gesellschaften in Europa nach 1945," *Archiv für Sozialgeschichte* vol. 49 (2009): p. 149.

9 Arieh J. Kochavi, *Prelude to Nuremberg: Allied War Crimes Policy and the Question of Punishment* (Chapel Hill: University of North Carolina Press,1998); Wolfgang Krieger, "Die amerikanische Deutschlandplanung: Hypotheken und Chancen für einen Neuanfang," in *Ende des Dritten Reichs, Ende des Zweiten Weltkriegs: eine perspektivische Rückschau*, ed. Hans-Erich Volkmann (München: Piper,1995), p. 28; Tom Bower, *Blind Eye to Murder: Britain, America and the Purging of Nazi Germany – A pledge Betrayed* (London: Andre Deutsch, 1997).

10 Gerd Hankel, *Die Leipziger Prozesse. Deutsche Kriegsverbrechen und ihre strafrechtliche Verfolgung nach dem Ersten Weltkrieg* (Hamburg: Hamburger Edition, 2003); James Willis, *Prologue to Nuremberg: The Politics and Diplomacy of Punishing War Criminals in the First World War* (Westport, CT: Greenwood Press, 1978).

11 *Der Prozess gegen die Hauptkriegsverbrecher vor dem Internationalen Militärgerichtshof. 14. November 1945–Oktober 1946*, vol. 42 (Nürnberg, 1947–1949); Gerd R. Ueberschär, ed., *Der Nationalsozialismus vor Gericht: Die alliierten Prozesse gegen Kriegsverbrecher und Soldaten, 1943–1952* (Frankfurt: Fischer Taschenbuch Verlag, 1999); Michael Marrus, *The Nuremberg War Crimes Trial 1945/46: A Documentary History* (Boston, MA: Bedford 1997); Joachim Perels, "Probleme der Ahndung völkerrechtswidriger Staatsverbrechen im 20. Jahrhundert: Einige Grundlinien," in *Kriegsverbrechen im 20. Jahrhundert*, trans. Gerd R Ueberschär and Wolfram Wette, p. 18.

12 The war crimes trials thus unintentionally functioned as a retroactive platform for a revisionist view of history, in that the defense strategy of the accused left the impression of the innocence of the perpetrators and could ground this perspective in the collective memory. See the case study by Kerstin von Lingen, *Kesselring's Last Battle: War Crimes Trials and Cold War Politics, 1945–1960* (Lawrence: University Press of Kansas, 2009).

13 This is true for the Netherlands, Norway, Poland, and France. See Wolfgang Form, "Transitional Justice: Alliierte Kriegsverbrecherprozesse nach dem Zweiten Weltkrieg in Europa," in *Kriegserfahrung und nationale Identität*, ed. Kerstin von Lingen (Paderborn: Schoningh, 2008), pp. 52–73.

14 Kim Priemel and Alexa Stiller, eds., *Reassessing the Nuremberg Military Tribunals. Transitional Justice, Trial Narratives and Historiography* (New York: Berghahn, 2012).

15 Norbert Frei, ed., *Karrieren im Zwielicht. Hitlers Eliten nach 1945* (Frankfurt: Campus, 2001).

16 Lutz Niethammer, *Die Mitläuferfabrik: Die Entnazifizierung am Beispiel Bayerns* (Bonn: Dietz, 1982).

17  Norbert Frei, *Vergangenheitspolitik: Die Anfänge der Bundesrepublik und die NS-Vergangenheit* (Munich: Beck, 1995), p. 14.

18  Ralph Giordano, *Die zweite Schuld oder: von der Last ein Deutscher zu sein* (Hamburg: Kiepenheuer & Witsch, 1987).

19  Martin Broszat, "Siegerjustiz oder strafrechtliche 'Selbstreinigung'? Aspekte der Vergangenheitsbewältigung der deutschen Justiz während der Besatzungszeit 1945–1949," *Vierteljahreshefte für Zeitgeschichte* vol. 29 (1981): pp. 477–544, here p. 544.

20  Weinke, "Alliierter Angriff," p. 50.

21  Wulf Kansteiner, "Losing the War, Winning the Memory Battle. The Legacy of Nazism, World War II, and the Holocaust in the Federal Republic of Germany," in *The Politics of Memory in Postwar Europe*, ed. Richard Ned Lebow, Wulf Kansteiner, and Claudio Fogu (Durham, NC: Duke University Press, 2006), pp. 102–146; see p. 108.

22  Lingen, *Kesselring's Last Battle*, pp. 173–237; Oliver von Wrochem, *Erich von Manstein: Vernichtungskrieg und Geschichtspolitik* (Paderborn: Schöningh, 2006), pp. 128–212.

23  Weinke, "Alliierter Angriff," p. 57.

24  Frei, *Vergangenheitspolitik*, p. 69.

25  The German Historical Museum at Berlin during the summer of 2015 hosted an exhibition entitled "1945 - Defeat. Liberation. New Beginning. Twelve European Countries after the Second World War," which focuses on biographical approaches to the end of the war. Every country was represented by three personal histories, and Karl Schulz was one of the German examples portrayed. Website of the German Historical Museum, https://www.dhm.de/en/ausstellungen/1945.html, last accessed October 2, 2015. For biographical details on Schulz, see https://de.wikipedia.org/wiki/Karl_Schulz_(Kriminalbeamter).

26  Weinke, "Alliierter Angriff," p. 57.

27  *Stuttgarter Zeitung*, June 4, 1958, reprinted in exhibition catalogue edited by Haus der Geschichte Baden-Württemberg, *Die Mörder sind unter uns. Der Ulmer Einsatzgruppenprozess 1958. Katalog zur Ausstellung* (Ulm: Haus der Geschichte, 2008).

28  See Annette Weinke, *Eine Gesellschaft ermittelt gegen sich selbst. Geschichte der Zentralen Stelle Ludwigsburg, 1958–2008* (Darmstadt: Wiss. Buchgesellschaft, 2008); the perspective of the state attorney is reflected in Kurt Schrimm and Joachim Riedel, "50 Jahre Zentrale Stelle in Ludwigsburg. Ein Erfahrungsbericht über die letzten zweieinhalb Jahrzehnte," *Vierteljahreshefte für Zeitgeschichte* vol. 56 (2008): pp. 525–555.

29  Timothy Snyder, *Bloodlands: Europe between Hitler and Stalin* (New York: Basic Books, 2010).

30  Devin Pendas, *The Frankfurt Auschwitz Trial. Genocide, History and the Limits of Law* (New York: Cambridge University Press, 2006).

31  Irmtrud Wojak, ed., *'Gerichtstag halten über uns selbst . . .'. Geschichte und Wirkung des ersten Frankfurter Auschwitzprozesses*, Jahrbuch 2001 des Fritz-Bauer-Instituts zur Geschichte und Wirkung des Holocaust (Frankfurt: Campus, 2001), p. 7.

32  Norbert Frei, "Der Frankfurter Auschwitz-Prozess und die deutsche Zeitgeschichtsforschung," in *Auschwitz. Geschichte, Rezeption und Wirkung*, Jahrbuch 1996 zur Geschichte und Wirkung des Holocaust, ed. Fritz Bauer Institut (Frankfurt: Campus, 1996), p. 124.

33  Norbert Frei, *1968: Jugendrevolte und globaler Protest* (Munich: Deutscher Taschenbuch Verlag, 2008).

34  Richard Ned Lebow, "Future Conditional: The U.S. and Its Past," in Lingen, *Kriegserfahrung*, p. 88.

35  Ulrike Jureit and Michael Wild, eds., *Generationen. Zur Relevanz eines wissenschaftlichen Grundbegriffs* (Hamburg: Hamburger Edition, 2005), p. 21.

36  UN Convention on the Non-Applicability of Statutory Limitations to War Crimes and Crimes against Humanity from November 26, 1968, 754 U.N.T.S. 73.

37 Weinke, "Alliierter Angriff," p. 84.
38 "Affäre Filbinger: was damals rechtens war . . .," *Der Spiegel*, May 15, 1978.
39 For information on the artist's project, see webpage at http://www.stolpersteine.eu/de/.
40 Weinke, "Alliierter Angriff," p. 90.
41 Weinke, "Alliierter Angriff," p. 93.
42 Volkhart Knigge, "Abschied der Erinnerung," in *Verbrechen erinnern: Die Ausein-andersetzung mit Holocaust und Völkermord*, ed. Norbert Frei and Volkhart Knigge (Munich: Beck, 2002), pp. 423–440, here p. 423.
43 The result of the conference was the foundation of the "International Holocaust Remembrance Alliance," IHRA; see website for educational activities and protocol of Stockholm: https://www.holocaustremembrance.com/.
44 Knigge, "Abschied der Erinnerung," p. 433.
45 Jose Brunner, Norbert Frei, and Constantin Goschler, "Komplizierte Lernprozesse. Zur Geschichte und Aktualität der Wiedergutmachung," in *Praxis der Wiedergutmachung*, ed. Jose Brunner and Norbert Frei (Göttingen: Wallstein, 2009), p. 32.
46 Brunner et al., "Komplizierte Lernprozesse," p. 30.
47 Ibid., p. 31.
48 Lingen, "Historische Gerechtigkeit," p. 57.
49 Brunner et al., "Komplizierte Lernprozesse," p. 23.
50 Kansteiner, "Losing the War," p. 129.
51 Cited in Tony Judt, *Postwar: A History of Europe since 1945* (New York: Penguin, 2010), p. 961.
52 German State President Horst Köhler's speech at Dokumentationszentrum Berlin, May 6, 2006, http://www.bundespraesident.de/SharedDocs/Reden/DE/Horst-Koehler/Reden/2010/05/20100506_Rede2.html. Translated by Emily Hruban.
53 Pope Benedikt XVI caused uproar on January 28, 2009, when he rehabilitated the British bishop Richard Williamson, a leading figure of the Pius brotherhood, who denies the Holocaust. His clarifying remarks came some days later. See http://www.welt.de/politik/article3105203/Papst-Benedikt-XVI-verurteilt-Holocaust-Leugnung.html. The scandal is particularly interesting as the Vatican itself has not yet come to terms with its own role during the Holocaust and early support for Nazi politics.
54 State Secretary at the Foreign Office Michael Roth's speech at the former Eastern border museum Schifflersgrund, May 10, 2015, http://www.auswaertiges-amt.de/DE/Infoservice/Presse/Reden/2015/150510-StM_R_Grenzmuseum_Schifflersgrund.html.

# Index

Made in United States
North Haven, CT
21 March 2022

17392657R00191